THE VIKING

saga two

Quest for Faith

Christopher Tebbetts

PUFFIN BOOKS

For Laura

PUFFIN BOOKS
Published by Penguin Group
Penguin Young Readers Group,
345 Hudson Street, New York, New York 10014, U.S.A.
Penguin Books Ltd, 80 Strand, London WC2R ORL, England
Penguin Books Australia Ltd, 250 Camberwell Road, Camberwell, Victoria 3124, Australia
Penguin Books Canada Ltd, 10 Alcorn Avenue, Toronto, Ontario, Canada M4V 3B2
Penguin Books (N.Z.) Ltd, 182-190 Wairau Road, Auckland 10, New Zealand

Penguin Books Ltd, Registered Offices: Harmondsworth, Middlesex, England

Published by Puffin Books, a division of Penguin Young Readers Group, 2003

1 3 5 7 9 10 8 6 4 2

 Text copyright © 17th Street Productions,
an Alloy Inc. company, 2003
All rights reserved
Book design by Jim Hoover
The text of this book is set in Arrus BT

LIBRARY OF CONGRESS CATALOGING-IN-PUBLICATION DATA

The Viking saga two: the quest for faith / by Christopher Tebbetts.
p. cm. – (The Viking)
Sequel to: The Viking saga one: Viking pride.
Summary: Through the power of a magical key, fourteen-year-old Zack is again
transported from twenty-first century Minnesota to a ninth-century land, where he
continued a prophesied quest to find Yggdrasil's treasure with the help of Vikings who
look just like his family and friends back home.
[1] Time travel—Fiction. 2. Vikings—Fiction. 3. Mythology, Norse—Fiction.] I. Title. II. Series.
PZ7.T2235Vk 2003 [Fic]—dc21 2002036874
ISBN 0-14-250030-5

Printed in the United States of America

CHAPTER ONE

Time was running out. Zack grabbed his shield—if he was going to make it out of here alive, he would have to be a lot faster, smarter, and stronger than he had been so far.

He pushed through the first line of defenders, swinging his iron hammer like it was a Louisville Slugger. The hammer bounced off a plate of unyielding armor, sending a shock wave of pain up his arm. But he made it through.

Now run. Don't look back.

Quick feet took him through a blockade of hardware and fallen bodies. He feinted left, sprinted right, ducked around a corner. Fast, short breaths. Steady, rapid heartbeats.

Down there. Duck!

Zack slipped between two gnarled shrubs and hit the frozen ground with a dive. He lay facedown, catching his breath for two seconds. When he raised his head again, the wolf was there. It stared at him with a chilling calm in its eyes. White foam dripped from a mouthful of teeth made for one thing only—ripping through flesh.

Wolves, he knew, were pack animals. Traveling alone was rare. The rest of them couldn't be far behind.

Zack pulled up slowly onto all fours. He kept his eyes down. Eye contact would only aggravate the animal. He crept backward, trying to watch where he was going without losing track of the wolf, who might attack at any moment.

Hurry—get out of here.

Take your time—no sudden moves.

Both impulses were nearly drowned out by the drumbeat in his chest.

Worse, a thumping of heavy footfalls sounded nearby.

Friend? Enemy? Sword-wielding psychotic killer?

From here on the ground, it was impossible to know. And standing up to look around meant risking an arrow right through the neck, or worse.

A chain rattled, followed by quicker steps. A sharp gust of cold wind blew, momentarily masking the sound. Then two feet moved into Zack's sight line, right in front of him, as if out of nowhere. He raised his head and found the eyes of a stranger staring back at him. The man had an ugly jagged scar on his cheek and an even uglier expression on his face. This was no friend. In his hand was a heavy chain, the other end of it looped around the wolf's neck.

So the wolf has a master, huh?

The thought was almost left behind as Zack leapt to his feet and dashed away. He ducked around another corner, and ran into the tallest soldier he had ever seen. The man stood absolutely still, a seven-foot-high, immovable pile of armor.

From behind, Zack heard more footfalls and the rattling of chain. The wolf and its master were closing in.

Given two ways to go, Zack instinctively went for the one-on-one. With the explosive force of a linebacker, he charged.

The only way past the armored soldier was going to be straight through. He'd either make it, or die trying.

Zack slammed into him. Metal went flying. The soldier gave way like a house of steel cards. A shower of heavy parts came down on Zack as he pushed through. He dove, but a crush of iron caught his leg, pinning him to the ground. He was stuck.

Zack strained to reach the fallen soldier's sword, just beyond his grasp. The wolf slunk forward, its teeth bared in a hungry grimace. Its master stepped in to watch the kill.

Zack shielded his face with one hand and pulled helplessly at his stuck leg with the other, in a desperate attempt to break free. But it was too late.

He howled out a defiant good-bye to the world. "Nooo!"

"Uh, Zack? What are you doing?"

Huh?

Zack lowered his arm, opened his eyes. Rusted engine parts lay at either side of him on the cold muddy ground. Two old tires were piled on his leg where they had fallen off a tall stack. Ollie was shaking his head, looking half-concerned and half-embarrassed. In front of him was Mr. Hm-hmph, the owner of the junkyard, whose name they never could understand. He stood looking down at Zack with a curious expression. His German shepherd, Gladys, bounded forward and offered several wet kisses.

"Blech." Zack closed his mouth a second too late.

"This is not a playground," said Mr. Hm-hmph in his thick German accent.

Zack felt like a thermometer, the red spreading up his face as he rolled out from under the pile of rubble he had tackled. He dropped the copper pipe and hubcap he had been carrying like a sword and shield. "Sorry, Mr.—uh . . . sir. I kind of lost track of where I was."

Ever since he had come home from the ninth century, it had been the same. Two nights earlier, he had taken a swing at his sister Valerie in the bathroom when they both got up for a drink of water in the dark. It wasn't until Valerie screamed and turned on the light that Zack had realized he was holding a toilet plunger, not a club, and that Valerie was his sister, not a flesh-eating hobgoblin.

Obviously traveling back in time to the Viking world—where he'd fought in terrifying battles and helped strategize war plans alongside members of a Viking tribe who looked exactly like people in his real life—had really thrown him for a loop now that he was back in the good old twenty-first century.

"You are a big boy," said the junk man. He looked up and down Zack's six-foot-three frame. "Too big for playing soldiers."

Vikings, actually.

Zack stifled the thought. Vikings sounded even more babyish than soldiers, anyway.

"You want to buy something, that is fine," continued the junk man. "Otherwise, you go on your way. Someone could get hurt." Gladys pulled at her leash, tail wagging.

Ollie cleared his throat. "We were just leaving anyway. We'll take all this." He pointed to a pile of spare parts and an old tricycle. Some of it would go in the maybe-we'll-use-

4

it-later pile. The rest would be used to build a prototype for Ollie's latest idea: an arm-mounted miniature catapult.

They paid Mr. Hm-hmph and headed up the street, carrying their new junk. A dry winter wind worked against them, blowing in the opposite direction.

Ollie looked up into Zack's glazed eyes. "Not that I mind," he said, "but you are definitely getting weirder."

"Huh?" Zack gave his head a shake, trying to focus. He hardly even remembered leaving the junkyard. Now they were two blocks closer to home. "Oh, uh . . . sorry, Olaf. What did you say?"

Ollie stopped on the sidewalk, set down his load, and extended his hand. "Hi, I'm Ollie. Remember me? Ollie Grossberg. I'm one of your *nonimaginary* friends."

Zack squinched up his eyes. "Sorry," he said, "again." It was the third time that day he had called Ollie "Olaf" without realizing it.

Zack wasn't going crazy, even if he felt like it sometimes. He knew full well the difference between Jok, the Viking chieftain, and Jock Gilman, his father. He knew that Valdis, who was Jok's daughter, was not the same person as Valerie, his sister. And he knew that while Erik the Horrible made life miserable in the ninth century, and Eric Spangler did the same thing in the twenty-first century, they were two totally separate power-hungry jerks.

And each of those pairs looked exactly alike.

Olaf and Ollie, on the other hand, were far from being identical twins. Olaf was a ninth-century, three-foot-tall, gray, hairless troll, with red dots for eyes. Ollie was a twenty-first century human. But there were reasons Zack kept lumping them together in his brain. Both of them had the same sort of fierce intelligence. Both were much shorter than Zack and had big ears that stuck out like open car doors. They also shared a certain unexplainable confidence, not to mention a tendency to drool. And, in their two different worlds, each of them was Zack's best friend.

"I don't really mind your calling me Olaf," Ollie said, picking his things up from the sidewalk. "Your fantasy life is totally your business. And this little troll guy sounds kind of cool. But I'll just, you know, probably miss you a lot when they lock you up."

Zack grimaced. "I know. I know, I know. It's crazy. But what do you do when the crazy stuff actually happens?" He pushed on in spite of Ollie's skeptical look. "What if your dog started talking to you one day? Crazy, right? Certifiable. But what if it *really* happened? What do you say to people? How do you convince anyone you're not imagining it?"

Ollie's eyes floated upward as he thought about it. "That's actually an interesting question."

Zack went on. "And pretend for just a second that I really did go back there. That I'm part of some kind of Viking prophecy. I'm the Lost Boy, and I'm supposed to lead this tribe on this quest." He took a breath, waiting to see if Ollie would cut him off. "So say that's all true. What now? Is there any reason to try and convince anyone? I mean, you think I'm crazy, and you're my best friend."

"Correction," Ollie said. "I used to be your best friend. Now I'm just nice to you so you won't hurt me. Come on. This stuff is heavy. Let's get something to eat."

Zack smiled and shook his head. He couldn't blame Ollie for doubting him. He'd probably feel the same way if it were the other way around. But not talking about what had happened to him was like trying to stick a cork in a volcano.

They continued up the sidewalk toward Zack's neighborhood. "Now, about this catapult," Ollie said, "I'm thinking we should build the model at your place. You've got the workbench and better tools than me. And besides—"

"Do you think time continues in the past even if it doesn't here?" Zack interrupted. He couldn't stop himself. "I mean, I was gone for almost a week, but when I came back it was like no time had passed here at all."

Ollie let out an exasperated sigh. He opened his mouth to reply when a familiar car horn blasted from behind them. It honked out the first line of the Minnesota Vikings fight song.

"It's the Zack! And the Ollie!" Zack's father pulled up alongside them, behind the wheel of his beloved Winnebago. The Winnie, as Jock and his friends called it, was one part family car and one part Minnesota Vikings football museum. In purple paint on the side, it read VIKINGS RULE!

"Want to ride home in style?" Jock asked.

"No thanks," Zack said. It was a little less embarrassing to be seen outside the Winnie than actually riding in it.

"Yeah, sure," Ollie countered. "Come on, Zack. It's cold out here, and this stuff is heavy."

Zack followed reluctantly on board. At least his father wasn't blowing the horn anymore.

Jock howled like a coyote and stomped on the accelerator. "And we're gone!"

Zack and Ollie both stumbled as the Winnie took off. They dropped their belongings and sat down at the dinette.

Ollie leaned across the table. "Your dad is so—"

"Big?" Zack said. Jock was even taller than Zack and somewhere in the neighborhood of three hundred pounds.

"No," said Ollie.

"Crazy?" Zack guessed.

"I was going to say funny."

"Funny ha-ha, or funny weird?" Zack asked quietly. "You should try living with him."

As if on cue, Jock raised a fist and screamed, "Touchdown!" The sounds of a game were coming over the radio.

"Good game, Mr. Gilman?" Ollie shouted up to the front.

Jock popped a CD out of the stereo and the football commentary cut off. "Just got this. It's a compilation—Minnesota Vikings' Greatest Hits. It's all their best plays from the last ten years."

Zack looked at Ollie with raised eyebrows that said, *See what I mean?* "Just don't ask him how this season is going," he whispered.

"So, Mr. Gilman," Ollie said right away, "how's this season going?"

Zack punched Ollie lightly in the arm. Ollie stifled a laugh, rubbing the place where Zack had hit him.

"Out-STAND-ing!" Jock yelled. "I don't want to jinx it or anything, but I'm thinking"—his voice lowered to a very loud whisper—"Super Bowl." He squirmed excitedly in his seat like he had to go to the bathroom, and flapped his elbows at his sides like chicken wings. Zack recognized it as the Jock Gilman Super Bowl dance. Jock did it every time he thought about his favorite team going all the way.

"So, anyway," Jock continued, "they're looking good. And you know why?"

Zack silently shook his head at Ollie.

Don't encourage him.

"No," Ollie called out, "why?" He scooted away from Zack to avoid another punch.

"Speed and accuracy, that's why." Jock was warming to the topic, Zack could tell. This could go on awhile. "Speed and accuracy. That's what it takes, and that's what they've got this season. You've got to know how to get the job done fast, but not too fast. It's a balance. And it's going to get them right through the playoffs to you-know-where." Jock jiggled around in his seat again. He took a swig from a can of soda in a purple-and-gold foam holder, and went on. "And the only thing that would make it sweeter would be going up against Chicago for the NFC title in the process. String the Bears along and then—wham!—leave them high and dry." Jock pounded the can of soda against the steering wheel and it sloshed onto his lap, but he didn't seem to notice. He was in the zone.

Two weeks ago, Jock's constant football chatter was just

blah-blah-blah to Zack's ears. Now Jock would say "Chicago Bears" and Zack would think *Bears of the North*. He would say "tackle" and Zack would smile with the memory of creaming Erik the Horrible on the battlefield. He could still see Erik's wide eyes and gaping mouth as he went flying.

"Meanwhile," Jock continued, "we're all heading down for the game in Green Bay this weekend. With the playoffs right around the corner, it's going to be a big day. If everything goes right, the Vikings are going to walk right over the Packers, and down in Chicago, the Bears are going to give it up to the Giants. I just wish I could be in both places at once." He stopped and looked over his shoulder, a serious expression darkening his face. "Not that I'm a Giants fan. Don't get me wrong. I just want to see the Bears lose their home-field advantage going into the playoffs. And the Giants are just the ones to do it, you know what I mean?"

Ollie nodded, although Zack knew Ollie had no idea what Jock was talking about. Ollie was even less of a football fan than Zack.

"Ollie, you should come along," Jock said. "Ask your parents. You could keep the Zack company."

Zack's antennae went up. He scooted to the front of the Winnie and sat in the passenger seat next to Jock. "Keep Zack company? I'm not going to Green Bay. I'm staying home with Valerie this weekend."

"Change of plans," Jock said. He steered the Winnie down Robinson Parkway toward the river and Ollie's neighborhood. "Your sister's going up to Lake Hurley with the North twins.

Looks like you'll be stuck with me and the guys."

Zack's face tightened with frustration. He had enough to deal with. This weekend with his father away was going to be a perfect time to try and get his head together. Camping out in the Winnie with Jock and his gang—Swan, Larry, Harlan, and Smitty—sounded about as appealing as a couple of days in the gorilla cage at the zoo.

"Come on," Zack said. "I can stay home by myself. I'm fourteen." He stopped short of saying the rest of what he was thinking. *This time last week, I was knocking off hobgoblins and marching into battle.* A weekend alone in the twenty-first century didn't seem like much of a threat.

"Sorry," Jock said.

"But—"

Jock erupted into a half-growl, half-laugh. He reached back and ruffled Zack's hair. "Where are you from anyway? How can Jock Gilman's son *not* be a Vikings fan?"

Zack heard Ollie snort with laughter behind them. He crossed his arms over his chest and stared out the windshield.

"Besides," Jock said, "you've seemed so out of it all this week. I think you could use a little R and R."

Zack knew that he had been acting like a zombie around the house. Since he couldn't find a way to say everything he was thinking, he hadn't said much at all.

He looked his father in the eye. "Do I have a choice?"

Jock gave him the latest in a series of concerned looks. "Zack, you're a great kid. I trust you, okay? But you are still a kid. You've got to have a little faith in Dad's judgment here."

As usual, there was so much to say and no way to say it. How could Jok and all the other Viking people in Lykill think of him as some kind of hero, and his father still think of him as a baby? Was fourteen years old that different in the ninth century than it was here?

After they dropped Ollie at his house, Jock steered the Winnie through a fried-chicken drive-thru, and they headed home.

"Dinner's ready!" Jock called as they came in the door, an open bucket of chicken in one hand and two drumsticks in the other. He set the bucket on the coffee table.

Valerie, Zack's sixteen-year-old sister, was on the couch watching TV. She spoke without taking her eyes off the screen.

"Zack, don't even think about stopping. Take that stuff into your room. I just cleaned up."

Zack looked around at the piles of magazines and newspapers in the living room. From where he stood, he could see the usual sinkload of dirty dishes in the kitchen.

"Just cleaned?" Zack repeated. "What, your belly button?"

All three Gilmans shared the housecleaning chores, though to Zack it was more like they took turns *not* cleaning the house. If there were a contest for biggest slob, it would be a three-way tie. Height wasn't the only thing that ran in the family.

Valerie ignored Zack's comment. "And change your clothes," she said. "You've been wearing that same sweater all week."

Zack grabbed a piece of chicken. "Thanks, Mom, I'll get right on that." He wished right away he hadn't said it. Winnifred Gilman had died when Zack was five. Her home-

12

cooked meals and the clean house she kept were just ancient history now. But it was an unspoken rule among the Gilmans that no one joked about Winnifred. His father and sister's silence reminded Zack as much, as he headed off to his room.

Sitting at his workbench, Zack looked at the parts he and Ollie had salvaged from the junkyard. He halfheartedly mulled over some ideas for their catapult.

Maybe shoulder-mounted, portable. Use the wrist as part of the whole thing. Some way of increasing arm power for long-distance throwing.

For the umpteenth time that week, his mind veered off track and onto the Prophecy.

Yggdrasil's Chest, Yggdrasil's Key, and Lost Boy will unite as three . . .

He pulled out a sketch pad from the back of a drawer and flipped it open to where he had written down the whole thing. The Prophecy's words were already etched into his brain, but he stared at the page anyway, willing it to offer some answers.

> *Yggdrasil's Chest, Yggdrasil's Key,*
> *And Lost Boy will unite as three,*
> *Beginning then the glory quest*
> *That opens with Yggdrasil's Chest.*
>
> *Glory found is glory earned*
> *And what is Lost must be returned.*
> *Size of a man, this Boy will be,*
> *And with him comes Yggdrasil's Key.*

With the key there comes a price:
Courage, Faith, and Sacrifice.
The way is far, the road will bend
The Boy will lead until the end.

Instead of answers, the words only brought him back to the same questions. What did it mean by "the end"? If he was back home, how could there be any more? Was the quest already over somehow? In some ways, it had to be, since it was hundreds of years ago. But that possibility didn't feel quite right to Zack, either.

His hand went to his chest, touching the key underneath his bulky sweater. Yggdrasil's Key, on a cord around his neck. It was kind of crazy to wear it all the time. But on the other hand, what about all this *wasn't* crazy? Zack took it off and set it down on the workbench in front of him.

The round metal key seemed to age as it moved through time with Zack. It had been burnished silver when he was in the ninth century, but now it was a dark brown rust, and ancient-looking like something out of a museum. He stared at its carved pattern of branches and leaves, and its three stems, which opened the three locks of Yggdrasil's Chest.

Three locks, three empty chambers. Would Jok's tribe be able to look for the three treasures of Yggdrasil's Chest without the key? Without Zack, for that matter?

These were not new questions. Zack had asked them all a million times by now. They just replayed over and over in his head. The ninth century and everything that had happened to him stuck in his mind like a houseguest who wouldn't leave.

A tap at the window grabbed his attention. He automatically flipped the pad closed and set it on top of the key, even though he knew who was there. Ollie was the only person who ever came in this way. He was about the only person who ever came over, period.

Zack pushed up the window. "What's going on?"

"Do you have that refrigerator door handle? I meant to take it." Ollie started to climb inside. His sneaker caught the edge of the windowsill and he fell the rest of the way into the room. He sat up with one of Zack's old T-shirts over his face. "Man, Gilman," he said, whipping it off his head, "my cat's litter box smells better than this."

Zack grunted. "Ha. You should smell—" He stopped short. *You should smell some of those ninth-century guys.* More than once, he had wished for a deodorant stick to pass around Lykill. Ollie wouldn't want to hear it, though.

"Here you go." Zack pulled the part from a pile on the floor.

"Thanks," Ollie said. "Gotta go."

"Wait." Zack said it before he could help himself. He held up his sketch pad. "Will you look at this again? Just one more time, I promise."

Ollie sighed. "All right. But it's got to be fast, Viking Boy."

"Lost Boy," Zack corrected him.

He flipped open the sketch pad again, to a map he had drawn from memory. "This is what was carved inside the chest. Supposedly it shows the three places we can find the three things that go in the chest. The chest has three compartments and three lids. Everything's a three." He pointed to the tri-pronged key on his desk. "See? Three keys in one."

"Well, I'll tell you one thing," Ollie said, reaching for the key. "That key looks real."

"Don't touch it!" Zack yelled, knocking away Ollie's hand. "I already told you. It'll blow your butt clear across the room. I swear."

Zack had seen it happen before. And the god Odin's two ravens, Huginn and Muninn, had confirmed it for him. *It is up to you to know when the key must be surrendered,"* they told him. *"It cannot be taken from you. The key must be given willingly."* Their high-pitched voices came back to him while Ollie stared incredulously.

"Wow, Gilman," Ollie said, "I didn't think you could get any farther around the bend than you already were."

"Believe me," Zack said, putting the key back around his neck. "This thing knows how to protect itself."

Now Ollie laughed. He shrugged and looked back at the map. "Why did you write *yo ton haim*?" He pointed to a phonetic note Zack had written on the page.

"Jotunheim," Zack said. "It's one of the three places where the treasures are."

He stopped short of telling Ollie that Jotunheim was the land of the giants, and that the other treasures were said to be in Niflheim, which was the world of the dead, and Asgard, the home of the gods. He knew he was on the edge with his friend, probably past it.

"Gilman, I gotta go," Ollie said.

"All right, I'm sorry," Zack said. "I'll stop talking about it."

"No really," Ollie said. "I really do have to go. My parents don't even know I'm over here. Are you going to be okay?" Ollie had a genuine look of concern on his face.

Zack nodded. "Sure. I'll see you in school tomorrow."

"Think about something else for a while," Ollie said. "Think about this catapult idea."

"Good advice," Zack said. "I will." But by the time Ollie was out the window, Zack was back at his workbench, staring at the map.

After hours of searching his mind for some new clue, some different way of thinking about all this, Zack had come to only one conclusion, and it wasn't much help. It weighed heavily on him, like a stone trying to drop through the bottom of his stomach.

The only thing he feared more than going back to that cold and dangerous world, he realized, was never going back at all.

CHAPTER TWO

Don't do anything stupid. Be cool. Look now—wait! Okay, now.

Zack watched Ashley Williams twirl the combination on her locker. She lifted the handle and, as usual, found she couldn't open it. Zack had been watching her deal with the stubborn locker since the beginning of the school year.

"Put your foot against the bottom." He blurted it out before he had time to think.

Then she looked at him. "Excuse me?" It wasn't a smile, it wasn't a frown.

"Um, well . . . uh . . ." Zack smiled weakly.

Speak, Gilman. Words.

"To open your thing . . . your locker. Put your foot against the bottom and then pull up and out with the handle."

Go over there and show her, idiot. No! Stay where you are.

His impulses fought it out in the back of his mind while his feet stayed frozen to the tiled hallway. Ashley braced her foot against the locker and pulled. The door popped open.

She looked slightly surprised. "Cool, thanks," she said.

I'm Zack.

Go ahead. Say it. Say it!

"Sure," he said tightly. Suddenly, operating his feet, mouth, brain, and hands all at the same time seemed like a huge challenge. He reached for his backpack in his locker and slammed it shut at the same time. The metal door mashed his fingers, bounced back, and caught him in the mouth. It was pure Cartoon Network. Zack didn't know if Ashley had seen it or not, but if he didn't look he wouldn't have to find out. He turned and walked the other direction up the hall, fighting the urge to rub his sore chin.

Lost Boy, meet Loser Boy.

In the other world, he had not only spoken to Ashley's double, Asleif, but he had actually done it without humiliating himself. Here, he couldn't even manage a five-word conversation. He felt like all Three Stooges rolled into one.

❧

One thing twenty-first-century life would always have over the ninth century was the food. Compared to a week of barley mush, soured goat's milk, and dried meat in Lykill, Zack's high school cafeteria was like a five-star restaurant. He piled his tray with a stack of cheeseburgers and double fries before joining Ollie at their usual spot.

"So I was thinking . . . " Ollie launched right in. "Maybe we could build a prototype by the end of this weekend." He reached over, popped a handful of Zack's fries into his mouth, squirted them with a packet of ketchup, and chewed.

"I can drop off the parts," Zack said, "but I have to go to Green Bay with my dad whether I like it or not."

"Yur dud us so kul," Ollie said through a mouthful.

"Yeah, my dad is cool," said Zack, "if you're not his kid."

Ollie took a swig of milk and a bite of his own sandwich.

Then he pointed to the window. "Thurs bat nu guy."

"What?"

Ollie swallowed. "There's that new guy. An exchange student. More like ex-*strange* student. He's in my calculus class." Ollie was a freshman like Zack but took several senior classes. "He's from Norway. Really smart and really weird. He just sits out there at lunch feeding the birds."

Zack turned to look. A piece of cheeseburger stuck in his throat, and he hacked it back up onto his tray.

"No thanks," Ollie said sarcastically. "I'll just have my sandwich."

Zack barely heard him. Sitting outside was the Free Man— or someone who looked just like him. The hair was the same, as were the pale eyes and the thin frame. Up until now, the Free Man was the only person from the other world who didn't have a double in Zack's life. But this was the first time it had gone in reverse—someone from there, showing up here.

"What's his name?" Zack asked.

Ollie looked up, thoughtfully chewing some more French fries. "Stephan," he said. "Stephan Freeman, I think. . . . Hey, where are you going?"

Zack ducked outside through the nearest door. He stood off to the side, watching Freeman from a distance. The Free Man—or Stephan Freeman, if that's who he was—sprinkled bread crumbs on the ground. A dozen or more birds gathered around his ankles, pecking and tweeting. Zack could see Freeman's lips moving. He wasn't just feeding the birds. He was having a conversation with them. Just like the Free Man.

Zack took a step toward where Stephan Freeman was sitting but stopped. Eric Spangler and Doug Horner, the first and second most obnoxious guys in school, were headed straight toward Freeman as well. They came around the corner from the other direction. Zack's blood ran cold. Just the sight of these two made him feel strange, and unusually angry. It was like he had two enemies in Eric—the modern day Spangler, who was right there in front of him, and Erik the Horrible in the ninth century, who was even worse.

Doug Horner, Eric's main goon of a sidekick, had his arm in a sling. Zack couldn't help smiling at that. Doug's double in the other world was a fur-covered ogre named Orn. The last time Zack had seen Orn, his hairy arm had been sliced clean off. Doug Horner had probably hurt himself imitating some big-time wrestling move, or maybe tackling parked cars.

Freeman seemed not to notice Eric and Horner approach.

"Hey, dude," said Horner. "You're new here, huh?"

"Ya," said Freeman in a thick Scandinavian accent. "I am Stephan Freeman. I come from Norway."

"Yeah, great, whatever," Eric said. He shuffled his feet into the cluster of birds. The birds took off, landing as a flock in a nearby tree. "What's with the bird fixation?" Eric said.

Freeman stayed seated. "I do not know what you mean."

"I mean," Eric said, "why are you so freakin' weird?"

Horner picked up a rock with his good arm and threw it into the tree where the birds were nesting. The birds fluttered up again and landed on a nearby utility wire.

"Don't do that," Freeman said calmly.

"Wow, you're a real animal lover, aren't you?" Eric said sarcastically.

Horner picked up some more rocks and kept throwing. "A little target practice," he said.

Freeman looked up at the birds from where he sat and let out a short series of squeaks and tweeting kind of sounds.

"What the—" Before Eric could finish, the birds launched off the utility wire. Their small flock split into two groups, dive-bombing Eric and Horner separately.

Spangler and Horner swung at the birds but only succeeded at making them angrier. One of the flock grabbed hold of Horner's hair with its claws and started nailing him on the skull with its beak.

"Get it off, man!" Horner yelled, swatting himself in the head with his one good arm. Eric was already running back inside, and Horner followed closely behind.

Zack grinned, watching Eric and Doug flee back into the cafeteria. A line of students stood at the windows, laughing and pointing.

Ollie pounded on the glass from inside. He held up his arms in a what-are-you-doing? kind of shrug. Zack held up a finger—*just a second*—and turned his attention back to Stephan Freeman's bench. But Freeman was gone.

"What's going on, strange one?" Ollie asked, stepping outside.

Zack looked around. "Did you see which way he went?"

"Who? That Freeman guy?" Ollie was maddeningly casual. "No. This isn't my week to watch him."

Zack groaned. This had been the closest thing to new information he had found since leaving Lykill, and it had just slipped through his fingers. He could only hope that Stephan Freeman wasn't as hard to pin down here as the Free Man was in the ninth century.

Zack scanned the halls between classes the rest of the day. Freeman wasn't anywhere to be found. After eighth period, he finally had a chance to stop in the school office. Ms. Berry, the nicest of the office workers, was the only one behind the main counter.

"Hi," Zack tried, friendly as possible.

"Hmm?" Ms. Berry looked up from her computer screen.

"I was curious about the new exchange student, Stephan Freeman?"

Ms. Berry squinted over the top of her glasses. "Tall fellow? From Sweden or somewhere?"

"Norway," Zack said. "I was wondering who his host family was, or where he was staying."

"Why do you need to know, honey?"

Zack hated lying, but this felt like a good enough reason. "My dad wanted to invite him over for dinner. Like a welcome-to-Minnesota kind of thing."

"Aw, that's sweet." Ms. Berry tapped on the keyboard. Zack leaned over the counter, trying to see the computer.

"Hmm, that's strange," she said, frowning at the screen. "We had a file on him, I'm sure. . . ." She trailed off and started riffling through a stack of folders on her desk. "I just had a hard copy, too, right here somewhere." She cocked her head to the side. "But now I don't see it." She looked up at Zack, almost as if she expected him to explain.

Zack shrugged. "Hmm." His mind was spinning, but he kept his face expressionless. The missing files felt like a huge clue, even if it was like hitting a dead end. Something weird was definitely going on. He thanked Ms. Berry and turned to go.

Just then, the door to the principal's office swung open. Out stepped Eric Spangler.

"Come back anytime you need to use the phone," said Mr. Ogmund. "And tell your mother I said hello."

Eric's mother was also Superintendent Spangler, and Ogmund's boss. The principal made an art of kissing up to the whole Spangler family. Worse, he didn't bother to hide it. If it hadn't been so gross, it would have been funny.

Zack stared back at the floor and made a beeline for the exit. The less he had to interact with either of these characters, the better. As he reached for the door, a high pile of plastic letter trays clattered to the ground next to him. A shower of papers landed around Zack's feet. He looked up to see Eric standing there, right next to where the trays had been sitting on the counter.

"Nice move, Gilman," Eric said. "You want some help cleaning that up?" He looked defiantly into Zack's eyes.

"I think Mr. Gilman can handle this on his own," Ogmund said. He hadn't noticed a thing. "You go ahead, Eric."

Zack stood seething under Ogmund's disapproving glare. He wanted to pile-drive Eric right there and take him down, just like he had done to Erik the Horrible once before. It would have been easy, too. The top of Eric's head only came up to Zack's shoulder. But it was a losing proposition with the principal right there. Instead, he knelt down and started cleaning up Eric's mess.

"See you later, Gutless Gilman," Eric muttered just low enough to be heard. As the office door swung closed behind him, he called out in a fake cheerful voice, "See you later, Mr. Ogmund."

Zack froze halfway between the floor and the counter.

The name sounded in his head with new meaning. Something he had completely forgotten, until now.

Ogmund. Ogmunder the Wizard.

Olaf had told him about a wizard by the name of Ogmunder, working for Erik the Horrible. Of course. It made perfect sense that Principal Ogmund would be Eric Spangler's puppet here in this world.

Zack had never seen the wizard, but his principal's pinched face gave him a good idea what Ogmunder looked like. He knew Ogmunder made replacement body parts for Orn, who seemed to lose pieces of himself at every turn. Whatever else the wizard was capable of doing, it couldn't be good news for Jok's tribe.

Zack put both hands to his head as if to silence his thoughts. He hardly noticed the shower of papers falling back to the floor.

One more thing to worry about. One more rope around his neck, pulling him somewhere he didn't know how to get to.

CHAPTER THREE

"Soda?"

"Check."

"Chips."

"Check."

"Pretzels."

"Check."

"Backup chips."

"Check."

"Vikings banner."

"Check."

"CDs."

"Check."

"Body paint—purple."

"Check."

"Body paint—gold."

"Check."

Jock, Swan, Larry, Harlan, and Smitty were passing supplies from the hatch of Swan's station wagon into the
Winnie, fire brigade–style.

Zack had been pressed into service. He was in the back of
the Winnie, plastering Minnesota Vikings team photos into
the rear window. Jock didn't want there to be any chance

someone might mistake them for Packers fans when they arrived at Lambeau Field in Green Bay.

"We need two radios," Jock yelled, his voice reverberating inside the Winnebago. "Anyone got an extra? I figure Green Bay's close enough to Chicago that we should be able to tune in the Vikings–Packers game *and* the Giants–Bears game at the same time."

Zack heard the smack of a high five and then Larry's voice from outside. "I'm all over it. Don't want to miss hearing the Giants bring the Bears down a notch before we finish them in the playoffs."

"That's right!" Swan yelled.

All five men began growling at one another, their voices rising in a uniform crescendo. The Winnie tilted on its shock absorbers as Jock leapt outside for one of their frequent group belly bumps. They all laughed like crazy as if they had just invented the move.

Zack finished his job as quickly as possible and headed for the house. He was going to be spending the whole weekend with this crew. He didn't have to surrender his Friday night as well.

Larry and Harlan blocked the door of the Winnie.

"Hang on there, bud," Larry said. "What makes you think you can just take off like that?"

"Yeah," Harlan joked along. "How do we know you aren't going off to consort with some covert Cheeseheads from Green Bay?"

Zack smiled indulgently.

"Careful, guys," Jock called. "He may not be a player yet, but he's built like a linebacker." Even at fourteen, Zack was already taller than all of them, with the exception of his father.

Larry and Harlan stood their ground. "Go ahead, Little Jock," Larry said. "Show us what you're made of."

"Yeah," said Harlan with a grin. "Earn your way out of there."

Zack looked at their expectant faces, each one a reflection of someone he had met in Lykill. He recalled a similar moment from that place, and smiled. "Here you go," he said. "A little nonviolent coercion." He took a deep breath and let it out as one long, spoken belch.

"V–I–K–I–N–G–S. Go. Vi. Kings. Let's. *Goooo!*"

"Now *that* is a Vikings fan," said Harlan, stepping out of the way while everyone else applauded.

"You guys are easy to please," Zack said. He stuck around while the others put in their entries. Swan stepped up and burped "This Land Is Your Land" in three huge breaths. Harlan tried burping some birdcalls. And even Smitty broke his usual silence to recite the burp-abet.

Before a winner could be declared, a familiar tune broke through the evening air.

"Purple Pride is coming to get you. . . ."

A pale green Range Rover rounded the corner onto Lyman Avenue, sped up the street, and stopped at the foot of the Gilmans' driveway. The Vikings fight song played loudly over the stereo.

"Hi, Mr. Gilman! Hi, Zack," Hilary and Helena North called out in chorus.

"Howdy, ladies." Jock waved back.

One of the twins got out of the car. "Is Valerie ready?"

"I'll go see," Zack offered. As he headed into the house, he heard Hilary and Helena getting in on the action. One of them burp-yodeled, and the guys all cheered.

"We have a winner!" shouted Jock.

In the living room, Valerie was sitting on an overstuffed suitcase, trying to zip it closed.

"They're here," Zack said.

"No duh," Valerie replied. "Help me zip this closed."

Zack went over and tugged on the zipper. "How much stuff do you need for a weekend?" Zack had just planned on bringing an extra pair of underwear and his Discman for the trip to Green Bay.

"Don't start," she said.

"Well, whatever," Zack said. "At least he lets you go off on your own. I may as well have a car seat and stroller as far as he's concerned."

Valerie hopped up and down, squashing the suitcase as much as she could. "At least he shows an interest in you and the stuff you like to do, like football."

Zack shook his head. Typical, but still amazing, that Valerie could think he was even remotely interested in football. Just another day in Valerie Land. She put on her coat and lugged the suitcase out the door.

Back outside, one of the twins was standing on the hood of Swan's car, burping the last of the national anthem.

". . . and—the—home—of—the . . ." She paused, burped

again for emphasis, and then finished with "braaaaave." As she climbed down, her sister held a hand out, collecting bills from the other guys.

"Well, that was worth five bucks for sure," Jock said, still laughing.

"Hey, Zack, she's even better than you," yelled Larry.

Zack wasn't surprised. In the Other Place, the twins' doubles, Hilda and Helga, were the leaders of their own tribe. They could hold their own against Jok and the others, whether they were eating, sailing, or fighting, or anything.

"Now you girls travel carefully," Jock said as they climbed back into the Range Rover. "I think this fog is only going to get thicker." A gray mist had settled over the neighborhood, blending with the light snow cover on the ground. Jock squeezed his huge frame in through the window and gave Valerie a kiss good-bye. Then the Range Rover took off down the street with a roar.

At least it was going to be a Valerie-free weekend.

⁙

By seven o'clock, it was completely dark out. Jock's gang had gone home to get ready for their early-morning start the next day. Zack sat in his room, staring endlessly at Yggdrasil's Key as if it were going to suddenly offer up some new information. Maybe it was time to put the key away and move on.

The phone rang. A moment later, Jock pounded on Zack's door. "Zack, it's Ollie."

Zack opened his door a crack and took the cordless phone. "Hey."

"Hey," said Ollie. "I'm going to come over for a second and get some more stuff. I want to keep working on this catapult over the weekend."

Zack looked at the untouched pile of parts on his floor. "Yeah, okay. Come on over." He hung up and went back to his workbench.

A few minutes later, there was a tap at the window.

What the—?

Unless Ollie had called from a cell phone on his bike halfway to Zack's house, he had gotten there in superhuman time. Zack looked outside. Nothing but night and fog. He walked over and raised the window.

"Ollie?"

No answer. Zack leaned out to get a look. He could almost feel the mist against his cheeks. He could barely even see the ground three feet below.

"Ollie?" he called again.

Like sharks in the ocean, two enormous sets of jaws sprang out of the mist. Zack saw them almost as quickly as they latched onto him. Jaws clamped around his wrists. In one swift movement, they pulled him forward. He fell halfway out of the window, and his chest hit the sill hard. His breath rushed out all at once, and a sudden panic rushed in.

With a flash of fur, something had him at the back of his neck. Zack opened his mouth to yell, but nothing came out. The light of his room seemed to rush away, replaced by a blur of fog. He was outside. His legs hit the ground. Zack twisted with all the force his two hundred pounds could muster, but

31

whatever it was had him virtually immobilized. Even his vocal cords were frozen. His mouth flapped open and closed in a series of shouts that sounded only inside his head.

Help! Somebody help me!

It was a feeling of near insanity to yell on the inside and hear nothing on the outside, except the howl of the wind. And what sounded like wolves. *Wolves.* They had both his arms and legs now, four of them, lifting him off the ground. Carrying him. Their jaws kept an iron grip. The pressure was intense but they didn't seem to be tearing into his flesh. At least not yet.

Gray fur.

Howling wind.

Howling wolves.

Fog, mist.

It all registered with Zack, but nothing came together in the form of logical thought. His brain pulsed, almost painfully, trying to latch onto something that made sense. Or something he could do.

How are they doing this?

Wolves would be too small to carry someone as big as him. The strength of these creatures was beyond normal.

Their pace was swift, too. Zack vaguely saw the ground rushing past beneath him. Images flashed through his mind. His body torn apart into so much raw meat. Dinner for the others in the pack.

Again he twisted his body, trying to break free of their grip. But it was like trying to get out of a straitjacket—the more he moved, the more claustrophobic he felt. It was becoming difficult to breathe.

Dark columns in the fog told him they had moved into the woods behind his house. Trees loomed. Everything passed by in a misty blur. He and Ollie had spent countless hours and days in these woods, but now it felt more like an alien planet than his own backyard.

And then they let go. All at once the movement stopped. He thumped softly to the ground and scrambled onto his feet. He wanted to leap away. Run. Something. But the wolves were all around him now. At least a dozen of them closed in. Zack froze. Several wolves sprang toward him—

This is it.

—then kept going. The entire pack moved low and silently away from him, deeper into the woods. He heard their calls several feet away but couldn't see them anymore through the mist. The howling had turned to strange guttural moans, high at first, then sliding down to a low pitch. Almost like a plea—come with us.

"Zack?"

What? They talk now?

"Zack?" It was Ollie's voice. Zack spun around. Ollie's silhouette stood like a short black cutout in the white fog. The weak finger of a flashlight beam poked through the mist. "Zack, what the heck's going on?"

Again, Zack opened his mouth to speak, and again, something stopped him. Not a physical force this time, but a feeling. Something he couldn't explain told him to stay mute.

Just wait a second. Be still.

He held his tongue and watched Ollie's shadow.

"Are you there?"

Zack could hear the edge of fear in Ollie's voice. He knew he should walk toward his friend, shout out to him. But he didn't. A stronger impulse seemed to take him by the shoulder and turn him toward the moaning of the wolves.

He took a single step forward, away from Ollie. The moment he did it, the key around his neck sparked warmly to life. It sent an unmistakable heat through his chest.

I'm going back.

It was happening again. He was sure of it.

And he wanted to go.

The mist seemed to give way around him, like ripples in the water. Zack looked over his shoulder once more. He squinted as Ollie's flashlight caught him in the eyes. He could hear but not see his friend on the other side of the beam.

"Zack, what are you—"

With another step, everything fell away. The ground seemed to evaporate. Only fog remained. Zack's voice suddenly broke free as he plummeted downward.

"Auuuuughhh!"

Zack could feel the uncontrollable pull of a free fall, while his stomach seemed to fight upward, as if it wanted to push past his lungs, up his throat, and out his mouth. After the yell that escaped him, Zack was sure his dinner would follow.

"Auuuuughhh!"

The key grew steadily warmer as he dropped through endless fog, until it burned like a cattle brand against his chest. He kept going. He wasn't hitting ground.

What now?

It was a bizarre moment, falling through the air long enough to wonder what would happen next.

With a bone-crunching slam, the ground rushed up to meet him. Zack hit it with a shock. He lay facedown, not wanting to move, not even sure if he could.

There was no curiosity about where he was. His mind was just a dull buzz. It was somehow satisfying to lie still and make no decisions at all. Sleep was the only thing that would be better right now. To feel as little as possible. He closed his eyes.

A moment passed, or maybe several minutes. Someone was there.

Zack opened his eyes and saw two feet. Firelight played across the ground. He tentatively turned his head upward to see.

Standing there, holding a torch in his hand and looking down at Zack, was the Free Man. "Welcome back, Lost Boy."

CHAPTER FOUR

Zack's head began to clear. He turned to look around, firing up pain in muscles he didn't even know he had. The mist had continued to thin. Watery light from a quarter moon gave some shape to his surroundings.

I'm back.

He was in Lykill. He was sitting on the ground just outside Jok's gate. Beyond that was the yard and Jok's long-house, a dark but familiar shadow.

"This is where I . . ."

"Yes," the Free Man said simply. This was where Zack had been standing when he shot forward in time and ended up back in Minneapolis a week ago.

He rolled over and sat up. The pain in his body moved to the background as a mountain of questions pushed to the front.

"How did you do this?" he asked.

"I didn't do anything," the Free Man said. "I was following you."

"From . . . Minneapolis?" Zack said. The Free Man nodded.

"So then, are you the . . ." Zack stopped and tried to figure out how to even ask his question. "You're the . . ."

"Yes," the Free Man said. "I'm the same person you saw

at school. Stephan Freeman doesn't exist." Zack could see the Free Man was wearing ninth-century clothing again, a plain cloak and trousers. His own clothes, however, were the same jeans and sweater he had been wearing all day.

"Is anyone else going back and forth like this?" Zack asked. "Besides you and me?"

The Free Man shook his head. "Not any of the people you know."

Zack got slowly to his feet. His mind began to speed up. *Okay. I know where I am. But . . . When am I?*

It had been nighttime in Lykill when he left, as it was now. But that had been in a snowstorm, with a raucous feast going on inside the longhouse. Now it was cold and foggy with no snowfall. And the village was as quiet as a grave.

"How long have I been gone?" he asked, not even sure if it was later in Lykill than when he left. Maybe he had come back to an earlier time.

"Three days," the Free Man answered.

It was strangely disorienting, like waking up in the hospital from a coma. "I've been home for a week," Zack said, almost to himself.

"The travel is not always the same," the Free Man answered. "Particularly in this direction."

Thoughts and information were coming in so fast, Zack could not take it in all at once. Making sense of it would have to come later.

His hand floated up to Yggdrasil's Key, under his sweater. It had gone cold again. He took it out and could feel in the dark that its rusted metal had given way to a smooth burnished surface, just as it had done once before. "Is the key doing all this?"

"The key is your portal," said the Free Man. "What you bring is the ability to use it. It is a rare gift, one that only appears every thousand years or so."

"Every thousand years?"

"Give or take a few hundred."

"I thought you said no one else was doing this," Zack said.

The Free Man spoke slowly. "You are the first in a very long time to use that key. But there are other people, who have nothing to do with you, traveling in their own way. Yggdrasil's Key is your way."

So there was more than one way in and out of here. Zack squinted, trying to read the Free Man's shadowed face. "What's . . . your way? Do you use a key, too?"

"That's difficult to answer," the Free Man said. "I follow you through."

"Through time?"

"Something like that."

Zack opened his mouth to ask another question, but the Free Man cut him off. "Zack, you need to think about what is important right now. This gift is also a responsibility. There is a reason you are here."

Zack let out a big sigh. "What do you mean?"

The Free Man didn't respond. The silence seemed to speak for itself. *You know what I mean.*

"Okay," Zack said, "I'm sure this is all like a trip to the car wash for you, but just give me a second, all right?"

And then all at once, he focused. His heart had barely begun to slow down when it picked right back up again. The most important question of all, and he was just now thinking of it.

"Where is everyone? Where's Jok? Are they . . ." He didn't want to finish the sentence.

Are they alive?

"I don't know," the Free Man answered plainly.

Zack's sense of purpose fired up like a cold engine roaring to life. He pushed through the gate, crossed the yard, and entered Jok's longhouse. Everything was as he remembered it except for the stillness. Normally, Jok's house had been a hub of activity, the center point of every village feast. Now it was deserted.

Empty spaces on the shelves jumped out at Zack. Normally they were filled with jars and cauldrons and bags of herbs, all the things Valdis used as the village healer. Valdis, or someone, had taken a large quantity of her supplies.

Deeper inside the house, the hearth was cold and the sleeping area looked undisturbed. A loom in the corner held a familiar tapestry, half-finished. Jok's wife, Winniferd, had begun it years ago, before she disappeared. Jok had left it where it stood, insisting that he would someday find his wife. And now he was probably looking for Zack, too.

Jok's sword, which he called Lightning, and his axe, Thunder, were both gone. It was normal for Jok to take them with him everywhere, so that was no surprise. The house showed no signs of struggle. Nor did the rest of the village as Zack and the Free Man walked slowly toward the waterfront.

"Why couldn't I come back to the same time? Right after I left?" Zack asked, kicking the ground. He couldn't help feeling as if he had deserted his friends.

"Twenty-first-century people look at time travel as both science and fiction," the Free Man said. "It is neither. There are many factors, but you can't control them all."

They reached the waterfront, as eerily still as the rest of Lykill. Even in the darkness, Zack could see that Jok's ship, the *Winniferd*, was gone. Of course. If they left, it wouldn't have been on foot. Not the entire village.

The sharp sound of cracking wood split the air like a gunshot.

"Ow!" Something caught Zack on the elbow with a jarring pain. Something else whizzed past his ear. Zack heard it ricochet off the fallen tree next to him.

He cradled his elbow and crouched low. "Free Man?" he whispered.

"Right here," the Free Man whispered back, so close it made Zack jump.

Another missile bounced off the tree trunk over Zack's head. A tiny crumble of bark sprinkled down. "Are we on the right side of the tree?" he suddenly wondered aloud. He twisted around and pressed his body up against the trunk, to peek over the top. The waterfront was silent again, not even the soft lapping of water.

Something struck him at the top of his forehead. Like a

skipping stone, it glanced off Zack's head and continued on its way. Zack fell back, his hand pressed to his skull. He could feel the warm blood on his palm.

A rush of anger came with the pain. He jumped back up, not thinking, just ready to throttle someone. The first thing he saw was two red dots. They blinked in the darkness.

"Olaf?" The troll's eyes were unmistakable. The dots blinked again and went out.

"Olaf, it's me!" Zack yelled. He stayed low just in case.

Then he heard the soft steps of small feet running toward them.

"Is Zack!" Olaf cried, jumping up and over the fallen tree all at once. He landed right on top of Zack with a combination wrestling move, hug, and drool bath.

Zack used the sleeve of his sweater to dry his slobbered cheek and bloodied forehead. None of that mattered. Finding Olaf was like finding gold in an abandoned mine.

"What are you doing?" he asked.

"And is Free Man!" Olaf launched himself against the Free Man. "Olaf thought Zack and Free Man were raiders, or Bears of North."

"Yeah, I know," Zack said. His elbow and head were still singing with pain.

"Olaf hiding since Jok and all left. Olaf guarding Lykill."

"By yourself?" Zack asked.

Olaf stopped fidgeting and stood up very straight, reaching to about Zack's waist. "Trolls very dangerous," he reminded them.

It was strange to be back, but even stranger to see this three-foot, pointy-eared troll and feel like he was an old friend.

"Where is everyone?" Zack asked. "Where did they go?"

"Went looking for Zack," Olaf said evenly. There was no blame in his voice. "Took everyone in Lykill to Konur for safe keep."

"Konur?"

"Hilda and Helga's village," the Free Man said. "It's not far from here, but it is walled, and safer."

"Is going to Konur, then go find Zack," Olaf interjected. He jumped from foot to foot. "But Olaf found Zack!"

"Let us go back to the longhouse and build a fire," the Free Man suggested. "We can continue this conversation there."

"Sounds good," Zack said. He had almost, but not quite, forgotten about the freezing temperature.

"Wait," Olaf said. He ran back toward his cave and returned dragging a box of some kind. Zack reached down and helped him lift it up. It was too dark to see, but from the size and the weight of it, Zack's heart leapt.

"Is this Yggdrasil's Chest?"

"No," Olaf said as they carried it toward the village. "Is decoy. Real chest with Jok."

"It's a decoy? Like a duplicate?" Zack asked.

"Like fake chest, yes," Olaf said. "Is built long time ago. Is left now with Olaf in case Bears raid. Can be used to fool. Keep Bears from looking for real chest."

They carried it into Jok's longhouse and soon had a fire

roaring in the hearth. The heat felt good, but it also thawed Zack's hunger. Only a few hours ago, he had been eating chicken at home—that was, unless he counted the twelve hundred years he had traveled to get to Lykill. A quick trip to the storage shed produced a slab of meat, which they put over the hearth. Olaf hungrily watched it cook.

"Has been days since no fire, no hot food." He leaned over the cut of meat and sniffed deeply. "Mmmm." A string of saliva dribbled out and basted one side of the meat.

Zack made a mental note—*eat from the other end.*

Then he put his attention on the duplicate chest.

"Harald is fine woodworker," Olaf said. "Built two years ago."

"This is amazing," Zack said. "Have you ever seen this, Free Man?"

The Free Man was sitting across the fire from him, looking quizzically at the chest. "No. It is a very good copy."

"Free Man has seen real chest before?" Olaf asked. "Olaf thought—"

"It is a very good copy from what I can tell," the Free Man said. "There are certainly drawings and other renderings of the chest. I have seen those before."

Zack put Yggdrasil's Key to the three locks but none of them fit. "Where are the keys for this one?" he asked.

"No key," Olaf said. "Is just fake. No one try to open real chest anymore without Yggdrasil Key."

That made sense. The real Yggdrasil's Chest looked like plain wood, but everyone knew it was impervious to axes, swords, fire, and any human means. The only thing that opened it was the three-pronged key around Zack's neck.

"So when did Jok leave?" Zack asked. He tore off hunks of hot meat and handed one to Olaf.

"Is two days," Olaf said. He took a huge bite, chewing, drooling, and speaking at the same time. "Jok go to Konur now, will leave many of the village behind, and go sail north to find Zack."

"Why did he take everyone to Konur?" Zack asked.

"Is thinking Bears raided Lykill, took Lost Boy. Is thinking Lykill not safe."

"So they're going north from Konur, after the Bears, and looking for me?"

Olaf nodded, grunted, chewed, and nodded some more.

Zack's appetite suddenly left him. He was responsible for all this, and Jok was on a wild-goose chase. A potentially fatal wild-goose chase. The realization left a sunken feeling in the pit of his stomach.

Everyone thought I was here to protect them. And now this.

His dropped his head and stared at the floor. Olaf's small hand came into view and rested on the chunk of meat Zack held.

"Is going to eat this?"

He let go of it and heard Olaf continuing to chew.

Okay. Sitting still isn't going to help. I can do this.

He looked up suddenly. "Can we catch Jok before he leaves Konur?"

"Is possible," Olaf said.

Zack was already on his feet. "Let's go, then."

"Where do you want to go?" the Free Man asked quietly. He looked at the ground, slowly chewing a crust of bread.

"To Konur," Zack said. Wasn't it obvious?

"And what if they've already sailed from there?"

"Then we get Hilda and Helga to go after him. What's the alternative?"

"That's up to you to decide," the Free Man said. "What is the alternative?"

It sounded like a question, but the Free Man's steady tone made it *feel* like he was saying something else. Not *what is the alternative?* but *there is an alternative.*

"What about Huginn and Muninn?" Zack asked, with a flash of inspiration.

Olaf breathed in sharply. "Olaf always want to meet Huginn and Muninn."

"What about them?" asked the Free Man.

"They know everything that goes on, practically everywhere, right?"

"They fly over much of the world, that's true," the Free Man said. "Odin depends on them to bring news to him in Asgard."

Zack had met the two ravens once before and the information they gave him had been invaluable. "How long would it take to find them again?" Zack pressed.

"It's hard to say. We could go back to the woods above my cabin and look there."

Zack remembered his harrowing climb to meet the ravens

the first time. It was not one he cared to repeat. "That took almost a whole day."

The Free Man nodded. "That's true."

A whole day for a *maybe* didn't cut it. "Never mind," Zack said. He closed his eyes.

Think, Gilman, think.

He envisioned a straight line from himself to Jok. The only place he could imagine the line leading was Konur. He looked up again. "We're going to Konur."

He watched the Free Man's face for some sense of approval or disapproval. The Free Man, however, only nodded. He seemed neither pleased nor displeased.

As dangerous and difficult as everything had been here the last time, Zack hadn't imagined things could actually get harder. And they just had. Jok had always called the shots before. Now it was Zack's turn. And the stakes could be the lives of the entire village of Lykill. Not to mention the Prophecy itself.

No pressure. Noooooo . . . Just another day in the ninth century.

His father's face flashed in his mind. Right now, Jock thought Zack was tucked into bed, safe and sound. If only Jock could see all this.

Gee, Dad, letting me stay home for the weekend doesn't seem like such a big deal anymore, does it?

Zack paced the longhouse, his impatience rising. "Can we go tonight?"

"It will be harder going at night," the Free Man said.

"Do you think we'll get there faster if we go now, or if we

wait until morning?" Zack asked. Even without an answer, he was already wrapping himself in one of Jok's wool cloaks.

"It's possible I could find some help," the Free Man said. He led them outside.

"Wait!" Olaf cried. "Olaf not to leave this." He dragged the decoy chest outside with him.

"That's going to slow us way down," Zack said.

"Could help, too," Olaf said. Again, the troll was right. It might be very useful to have a decoy if the Bears found them before they found Jok. Besides, it didn't look as if Olaf was going to leave it behind under any circumstances.

They found a small, flat sled behind Sven's longhouse, next door to Jok's. Its wooden runners were made to go through snow, though certainly not as smoothly as the modern sleds Zack was used to.

"Well, let's try it at least," Zack said. While he and Olaf worked, the Free Man went to the edge of the woods. He stopped and hooted into the air then listened for a response. When it came, he hooted back again with a long series of birdlike sounds. It wasn't a birdcall, Zack noticed, but bird language. The Free Man was having another conversation.

Soft hoofbeats thudded in the night air. The Free Man continued to call out, but his voice changed. He spoke in an unrecognizable language from deep in his throat. A few moments later, two large shadows came forward, out of the trees. Zack looked over and could make out the shape of antlers. Deer—or bucks, he supposed.

The Free Man held up a hand and spoke to them again

briefly. Then he turned to Zack and Olaf. "They've agreed to take you to Konur. When they come back to me, I've promised to show them to the woods above my cabin, where they can eat as much as they like. This is a hungry time of year for them."

"Hang on," Zack said. "What do you mean, they'll come back to you? You'll be with us." He looked at the Free Man searchingly. "Right?"

"No," the Free Man said. "You'll be traveling on your own."

"What?" Zack couldn't believe his ears. How hard did this have to get?

"You must do this without me," the Free Man said.

"Alone," Zack said bitterly.

Olaf cleared his throat.

"Sorry, Olaf," Zack said quickly. "I didn't mean without you." He turned back to the Free Man. "Why can't you come with us?"

"I have many places I need to be," the Free Man said.

"More important than this?" Zack blurted out.

"Zack, I cannot hold your hand through this." The Free Man's voice was clipped and short, almost like a lecture from a parent.

The Free Man didn't owe him anything. But Zack couldn't help feeling angry. He kept his mouth shut and turned to the two bucks. They were the biggest he had ever seen by far. Even so, the idea of riding on one of them seemed dicey at best.

They worked quickly, using walrus-skin cord to secure their cargo to the back of one of the bucks. The buck tried it out, dragging the sled along behind him. Then he knelt down next to Olaf. The Free Man helped lift Olaf onto the buck's back. Now it was Zack's turn.

"Remember," the Free Man said, "act respectfully. These are not beasts of burden. They are doing us a service. I've told them the way, so they should have no trouble."

Zack nodded silently, contemplating the kneeling buck in front of him. He put a hand on its back and lifted himself up and over. With nothing else to hold on to, he leaned forward and wrapped his hands around the antlers.

The buck rose shakily to its legs. It let out a kind of whinny to the other one, who responded. Zack felt oddly self-conscious about his size.

Are they laughing at me?

It didn't matter. Soon they were off.

"Good luck," said the Free Man.

"Thanks," Zack called back.

We're going to need it.

They headed straight into the woods. It was no darker or lighter in the forest, but Zack could feel the closeness of the trees. The night seemed to move in around him. As the buck sped up from a walk to a trot, Zack lurched backward in the darkness. He barely kept hold of the antlers and managed to pull himself forward again. The buck's strong spine pressed into him like a lumpy steel rod. The pointed antlers pulled back and forth with every stride, as if their purpose was to poke his eyes out in one direction and yank his arms off in the other.

Maybe if I sit like this . . . or . . . maybe over here. No. How about . . .

Zack quickly realized that comfort was out of the question. Staying upright was the only thing to shoot for.

"O-o-o-laf-f-f?" he called out as they bumped along. He hadn't heard anything from his friend since they'd started. For all Zack knew, Olaf had fallen off long ago.

"I-i-i-s-s o-ka-ay-ay" came Olaf's thin voice. Neither of them said any more. It was easier not to speak.

And then the animals sped up. They seemed to know exactly where they were going through the forest. But they definitely didn't know what they were doing to Zack's butt.

"How-ow-ow far-ar-ar-ar?" Zack managed to ask finally.

"One-un-un-un day-ay may-ay-ay-be," Olaf squawked back.

A whole day of this?

Given the choice, Zack would have stopped right there and taken his chances on foot. But the bucks galloped along. The winter air whistled past, though the cold was the least of Zack's problems. He tried to focus away from his discomfort and onto what he would do when they got to Konur. That was, assuming he got there in one piece.

CHAPTER FIVE

With the first rays of sun coming over the horizon, Zack found himself in an open field. The snowy ground was orange and pink in the sunrise. Somewhere along the way, he had dropped off to sleep. Or at least dozed. It seemed impossible that he would still be on the back of his buck, but there he was. He saw for the first time just how large the creature was. His boots hung at the buck's sides, at least four feet off the ground. Still, he imagined, the buck was going to be as glad to be done with this trip as he was.

Ahead of Zack, Olaf was sitting straight up. His arms hung loosely; he didn't seem to have the same balance problems as Zack. And the decoy chest was still safely lashed to the sled dragging along behind.

"Do you know where we are?" Zack croaked. They hadn't spoken in hours. His throat was as stiff as his frozen limbs. Only his rear end and the tops of his legs weren't cold, and that was because they were completely numb.

"Not far now," Olaf said. "Soon is river. Village is after."

As they plodded along, all of Zack's worries wormed their way into his tired mind.

What if Jok's gone when we get there? What if we're too late? Why wouldn't the Free Man come with us? What could possibly be more important than this?

As usual, no good answers came. When he tried not to think about it anymore, his wondering gave way to thoughts of food. Twenty-first-century food. He tried to do the alphabet to distract himself.

American cheese. Bacon. Coke. Doughnuts.

His stomach protested with a painful growl before he even got to "E."

"I don't suppose there's a drive-thru around here?" he said, half out loud.

"Is what?" Olaf said.

"Nothing."

Then a much pleasanter thought popped in.

Asleif.

He suddenly remembered that he would be seeing her soon. It was like a rope cast out from Konur, pulling him in. Although, even that situation seemed sticky.

Yeah, I met this girl. She's not from around here. Where's she from? Well, uh, the ninth century.

And meanwhile, Ashley, who went to Zack's school, might as well have lived a million miles away for all the progress he was making. Not exactly your average romantic problems, but easier to think about than everything else he had on his mind.

"Is river," Olaf called out. Zack looked up and saw a strip of white at the far end of the field they were crossing. It was too far to tell how wide it was, or how frozen. But as they drew nearer, the unwelcome sound of rushing water found Zack's ears. He closed his eyes as if to block it out.

Nice little shallow stream. Easy crossing. Please . . .

"Sound like waterfall," Olaf said. Zack opened his eyes again and cocked his head to the side.

"Sounds like Niagara Falls." The water noise was coming from a distance, but it had a low thundering quality to it. Definitely more than a nice little stream.

The bucks drew up and stopped at the riverbank. Zack threw up his arms in disgust. The river was at least fifty feet across and even wider upstream. The surface was mostly frozen but the ice was in pieces like a great jigsaw puzzle. Where the river narrowed, it created a bottleneck. The ice floes all pressed together around several boulders that stuck up through the surface like a miniature mountain range.

Upstream to their right, the huge pieces of ice were much looser, floating freely in the river. Downstream to the left was the waterfall, far enough to be out of sight but close enough to be heard, like an ominous drumming.

"Is this the only way to Konur?" Zack asked.

"Is not far," Olaf said. "Just this way."

The bucks shifted on their feet, either from exhaustion or nervousness.

"All right," Zack said. "I guess we're on our own from here." He patted the buck on its muscular neck, and it knelt down for him. Zack tried to lift one leg up and over but he was so sore, his body just slid off like a sack of potatoes into the snow. Still, it was a great relief to be on the ground again.

Olaf busied himself untying the wooden sled from his buck. Once they were free, the animals turned and left unceremoniously. They ran full tilt across the field. Zack imagined they must have felt amazingly light on their feet after such a night.

"Thanks," he called after them. Not that they could understand or even hear him anymore. They were already out of sight.

"So, how are we going to do this?" Zack said.

Olaf looked at the river and back to Zack. "With careful."

There was nothing to do but get going. The longer they waited, the less chance of catching Jok in time. Zack picked up the chest and carried it to the water's edge. He put a foot out and tested the ice. It was thick and solid but it wavered, like a two-by-four sitting on a water bed.

The chest was definitely going to raise the level of difficulty. "Does this thing really have to come with us?" he asked.

"Olaf promised to keep," said Olaf. He stared up at Zack, not blinking.

"Okay," Zack said reluctantly. He pushed the chest out onto the ice. It slid easily enough across the first floe. Zack stepped out, careful to hit the piece of ice in the center. He stood there a moment to get used to the wobble under his feet before moving on.

Olaf stepped lightly onto the frozen river as well. He tiptoed nimbly around Zack and the chest to help pull it along.

This is crazy.

Zack reminded himself that Jok and the others were risking their lives to go looking for him. He owed it to them to keep going.

He reached down and gave the chest another careful push.

"No!" Olaf cried. Zack had pushed too hard. Olaf stumbled back out of sight behind the chest.

"Olaf!"

No sudden moves.

Zack craned his neck to try and find Olaf without actually moving his feet. The troll was flat on the ice, both arms splayed out to steady himself.

"Zack be more careful," Olaf said sharply. "Zack learn own strength."

"Sorry," Zack said. "Sorry, sorry. Are you okay?"

Olaf stood up. "Trolls—"

"—always okay," Zack finished for him. "That's true, you are."

Pushing softly and working slowly, Zack found a rhythm with Olaf. They made sure never to have more than one of them—Zack, Olaf, or the chest—on any single ice floe. The sound of the waterfall in the distance served as a constant reminder of just how careful they should be.

At the midpoint, Zack stopped to rest against one of the large rocks sticking up through the ice. The work wasn't so strenuous as it was nerve-wracking. Olaf stood on his own piece of ice, gently but nervously standing on one foot and then the other. The chest rested between them.

"Okay," Zack said, "let's get this done once and for—"

As he stood up, the ice shifted. Several chunks slipped around the boulder and flowed downstream in a quick movement as the ice jam began to break up.

It all happened without warning. Zack lost his balance as the ice on which he was standing tilted crazily. His arms swung in a circle. He twisted around and fell onto his front against the boulder. His palms landed on rock as his feet lost their ground. The ice floe under him rotated and slipped away in an uncontrollable slow motion.

"Olaf!" Zack shouted. He was facing the rock and couldn't see where Olaf or the chest was. His feet dangled in the icy water. He strong-armed himself a bit farther up the boulder and turned over onto his back. Olaf was standing on an alarmingly small floe, several feet away from the chest. The jigsaw puzzle of ice was breaking up all around them. If Zack didn't get off this rock now, he was going to have to swim.

"Go!" he said to Olaf.

"Chest!" Olaf cried.

"I'll get it. Go!"

Olaf had no choice. His ice floe tipped, and he leapt from it to the nearest other piece toward the shore.

Zack stepped out onto a passing floe where he could, and fell onto the ice. Several more pieces jammed around him but only for a moment. He had to keep moving. The only way to stay steady was on his hands and knees. He kept his head down and crawled as quickly as he could toward the bank. When he reached the chest, he tried pushing it with one shoulder as he went. The chest slid but then tilted.

"No!"

He reached up and grabbed one of the handles on the side of the chest.

Hang on. Hang on.

The chest pushed through a widening crack in the ice and fell into the water. Zack's arm submerged up to the elbow as he slid farther forward.

Let go! Let go!

No choice. The chest was going to pull him in with it if he didn't release his grip. He let go of the chest's handle and steadied himself.

"Zack, come now! Watch, look!" Olaf was waving wildly and pointing upstream. Zack twisted his head to see. A log the size of a phone pole was headed straight for him, cutting through the ice like a plow.

Go, go, go, go! SLOWLY . . .

He eased himself up into a crawl. If he wasn't out of the way in about five seconds, he was going to be riding that log straight for the waterfall. His wet knees and hands slipped from underneath him like a cartoon character running in place.

The log pushed closer, like a huge arrow with Zack as its target.

He lurched forward again, finding some purchase on the ice and landing shakily on the next floe, just as the log slid through behind him. He lurched again toward shore, onto the next floe, and the next. His hands and feet dipped in and out of the water as he went, stingingly cold each time.

Olaf had broken off a long tree limb and held it out for Zack. When he was within reach, Zack grabbed on. Olaf pulled him in the last ten feet, and Zack fell onto the shore.

"I'm sorry, Olaf," he gasped. "I lost it."

"Zack okay?" Olaf asked. "Zack okay?"

Zack nodded. He looked back at the river. The jam of ice floes they had crossed was gone, and the river now flowed swiftly past them.

"Good thing we didn't come along any later," Zack said. He thought about the decoy chest heading over the waterfall. *That could have been us.*

Still, it was hard to feel lucky. "All that trouble for nothing, just to lose it here. I should have held on."

"Is not Zack's fault," Olaf said. But Zack couldn't help feeling as if he had let his friend down. He wrapped his arms around himself, fighting off the shivers.

"Come, keep going," Olaf urged him. They had both begun to shake uncontrollably from the cold. "Is not far now."

They slogged through a misery of deep snow and back into forest. An incline slowed them down even more as they headed up a steep hill. Zack could see his breath, gushing out in quick bursts of steam.

Eventually, they came out of the trees and found themselves on a high ridge. A sharp slope dropped away in front of them to the valley floor below. To their left, the ridge sloped gently down for what looked like several miles, toward a network of fjords and other waterways. The river they had crossed no doubt spilled into this basin. Beyond all of it, Zack could see open sea stretching to the horizon.

"There!" Olaf pointed straight down into the valley. From

this bird's-eye view, Zack could see the village of Konur. It was contained by something that looked like a giant horseshoe butting up against the shore. Inside the horseshoe were dozens of buildings, with some sort of roads or walkways running between them and down to the waterline, where a ship was harbored. Zack could even make out several tiny figures moving about the village.

Please let one of them be Jok.

The most direct route was straight down. Taking the ridge to their left would be easier but much slower. "What do you think?" Zack asked.

Olaf peered down the slope in front of them. "Is possible," he said. Zack recognized a twinge of doubt in the troll's normally confident tone.

Zack stood looking one way and then the other. As he scanned the valley, something caught his eye. A ship was headed away from Hilda and Helga's village. Its sail showed a yellow-and-white diamond pattern. The *Winniferd*.

"Jok!" Zack yelled it involuntarily. They weren't even close to being close enough. The ship was just a miniature from here. "They're leaving! What do we do?"

Zack stared at the ship, his mind racing. The *Winniferd* was fast. Getting down there would take at least half an hour.

A bright spark of light flashed across the water below. Some kind of fireball. It landed just off to the side of the *Winniferd*.

Zack knew in an instant. "Erik the Horrible." Just saying the name made his stomach churn. He watched transfixed as another fireball flew through the air from somewhere near the shore. It landed directly in the center of Jok's ship. Zack's eyes grew wide as the flames quickly spread. People on board scrambled. Zack's entire body tensed.

Still another shot came. The sail of Jok's ship went up in a bright flash of flame. Zack watched as the oars were put to, and the ship navigated toward shore.

Another ship sailed into view, advancing from an unseen tributary. Its half-red, half-black sail was the unmistakable mark of Erik the Horrible. It advanced on the *Winniferd*, now engulfed in flames.

Not the Winniferd. *Not Jok's ship.*

It was a horrible, helpless feeling to watch the ship burn from such a distance. Zack was rooted where he stood.

This isn't possible. This isn't happening.

This is my fault.

"Must go!" Olaf said. He pulled on Zack's arm. "Not helping here!"

Zack snapped into action. He leapt in the direction of the battle and began running down the ridge.

"Zack!" Olaf's small voice came behind him. Zack stopped short. Olaf pointed down the steep slope into the valley. "Is best this way. Better to get help."

Zack's breath came in quick gasps. His fists clenched at his side. He knew that again, Olaf was right.

"Okay," he said, with a snap decision. "Come on."

Zack attacked the slope, rushing down in huge long leaps. His sense of urgency pushed him on, but gravity did its part as well. He half-ran, half-fell down the valley toward Konur, just hoping he wouldn't lose his footing and become the center of a giant, rolling snowball.

The valley floor slowly grew closer. Trees blocked Zack's view of the *Winniferd* and whatever battle might have been going on. It seemed like forever until they were going to be able to reach Jok with any help. And then it could be too late.

Zack blocked out his doubts. Keeping his footing required every bit of concentration he had anyway. His boots pounded through soft snow onto rocky ground, downward, over and over and over.

His foot hit a hard lump, a rock maybe. His ankle twisted and he went down. Everything spun in a blurry jumble. His body seemed to leave the ground and find it again a dozen times, with a dozen different kinds of pain—in his arm, in his shoulder, in his foot.

Finally, he came to a rest on his side.

Definitely not like in the movies.

Adrenaline cut through his pain, and he was back on his feet. Olaf was quite a ways up the slope from him. Zack gave a thumbs-up and kept going, though slower than before.

Finally, the ground evened out. Zack could no longer see any sign of Konur.

"Which way?" he yelled up to Olaf, who pointed straight on. Zack ran. He passed through a stand of birch trees and up a short slope. His breath seared his lungs. His whole body screamed at him to stop but he couldn't hear anything except—

—*don't stop.*

He looked back again to make sure Olaf was with him. The troll was doing his best to keep up and was still in sight at least. Zack powered down the hill, across a field, and halfway up another short, steep slope.

"Stop!" An unfamiliar voice shocked Zack to stillness.

He turned around and saw two soldiers behind him. They wore leather tunics, chain mail, and finely etched silver helmets. Both had their swords unsheathed. Both were women.

I'm here. I made it.

"We need your help!" Zack gasped between breaths. One of the soldiers advanced on him. She didn't look pleased.

"Wait!" Zack saw the menace in her eyes too late.

The soldier grabbed him by the collar of his borrowed cloak and threw him roughly down the bank. Zack landed at the feet of the other soldier, who drew him up and held her sword to his gut. She was taller than Zack, well over six feet. Her grip was like iron.

"What's your business?"

Zack could hear the Scandinavian language they spoke, and could hear the same language coming out of his own mouth. But it all sounded like English to his ears. Something about the key's magic had always allowed him to communicate in this way. Without the key, he knew, he wouldn't be able to understand a word. He had learned that once the hard way.

"I need to see—"

"Huh?" the soldier pressed. She shook Zack roughly. "Tell me!"

Zack said quickly, "I need to see Hilda and Helga."

"Who are you?" asked the other soldier.

Olaf came running up behind, waving his arms. "Stop! Stop! Is Lost Boy! Is Zack!"

The second soldier whirled around and stopped Olaf in his tracks with her poised sword. "What did you say?"

Olaf held up both hands but spoke calmly. "Is Lost Boy."

Both soldiers looked at Zack.

"The Lost Boy disappeared," said the tall one. Her sneer was gone but not all of the attitude. She stood firm.

"I'm back," Zack said. He didn't know what else to say. He reached into his sweater and took out the key. "See? I've got—"

The soldiers' swords dropped immediately to their sides. Each of them grabbed one of Zack's arms and they whisked him roughly away. Olaf followed along behind.

The soldiers led Zack along the base of the steep slope to a high wooden gate. Zack suddenly realized that the hill where they had caught him was the village wall. The horseshoe he had seen from above, the one that enclosed Konur, was made of earth.

Two other soldiers guarded the gate. The ones holding Zack spoke sharply. "Open it," said one. The soldiers let them pass, and Zack was swept inside. One of the two gate guards came with them.

"Listen," Zack said, "I have to see Hilda and Helga right away. Whatever you think I'm doing, just let me see them first." Their grip on his arms was unshakable. He turned his head to make sure Olaf was still following along behind.

Konur was similar to Lykill in some ways, but there were also noticeable differences. The buildings here were in the same style, but looked more finely crafted. Instead of having turf roofs, these longhouses were topped with slate. Several of them had thatched shingles on the outside walls, where the homes in Lykill were mostly rough planking, sealed with mud and leaves.

They followed a wooden walkway through the village, between several buildings. Eventually, they came to a large house, more elaborate than any Zack had seen in this world. It was a large T-shaped building, with two small wings off the main chamber. Its roof was shingled in a decorative cross-hatched pattern. Outside the front door hung a green-and-gold banner, the mark of Hilda and Helga's tribe.

One of the guards knocked on the door. It was opened by another guard, a man this time. He mutely stepped aside to let them in but then blocked Olaf's way.

"It's all right," said one of the guards, still holding Zack.

The main room was similar to every other longhouse Zack had seen in Lykill. It was a single long room dominated by a stone hearth in the center. A fire was burning, the smoke escaping through triangular holes at the ceiling peak. Several people milled about. One man tended the fire. A man and woman were seated on stools, playing some sort of board game that looked like chess, but with fewer pieces. A woman was weaving on a loom in the corner. They all stopped what they were doing and stared at Zack.

At the end of the room were two doorways, leading to other parts of the house. One of the soldiers disappeared through a door and returned shortly, followed by Hilda and Helga. Their familiar faces were a welcome relief.

"Lost Boy! Olaf!"

Zack felt a spark of hope as he shook the twins' hands. He hoped he would soon figure out which one was which.

"We need your help," he said right away.

"Where's Jok?" asked one of them.

"In trouble," Zack replied.

"Is terrible trouble," Olaf added.

Zack spoke as quickly as he could. "We were up on the ridge, coming here to find him, and we saw the *Winniferd* sailing away. Erik the Horrible attacked them. We saw it all. They burned the ship."

"Are they still there?"

"I don't know," Zack said. "We were too far to do anything. We came here instead."

Hilda and Helga turned away from him and began barking orders immediately.

"Get the ship ready."

"Pull together two dozen soldiers. We leave in fifteen minutes."

The guards set to work right away. Two of them left the house, while the other one remained at the door.

"Hilda, show Zack and Olaf downstairs. I'll be at the waterfront," said Helga. She peeled off and ran out of the longhouse.

Hilda led them into one of the back rooms. She pulled a tapestry away from the wall, revealing a small door. "Come this way," she said. She swung open the door, into what looked like a dark closet. Zack peered inside and saw that it led to a shaft. A ladder extended down into a shadowy cellar of some sort.

"What is this? We need to get going."

Hilda put a hand on his shoulder. "The ship will be ready soon. There's nothing you can do right now. Come. Your friends are here."

"Is Asleif here?" Zack blurted it out without thinking. "And, uh, everyone else?" Now he blushed.

"She—and everyone else—are fine," said Hilda. "Go."

He went first down the ladder. A dull glow from below showed him the way.

His feet had scarcely hit the ground when someone grabbed him from behind. Strong arms twisted him off his feet and body-slammed him back down to the dirt floor.

Zack groaned.

How much more of this am I supposed to . . .

A familiar face hovered over him. "Oh, it's you."

He looked up. "Hi, Valdis. Good to see you, too." Leave it to his sister's look-alike to give him a greeting like that.

Before he was on his feet again, a small crowd had already gathered. Zack heard excited voices and shouts deeper inside the underground rooms.

"The Lost Boy is back!"

"It's him!"

They ushered Zack into a round chamber with several doors. Lykill villagers came in from every direction, smothering him in hugs and pats on the back. For a place he had never been before, it felt amazingly like coming home.

Asleif pushed her way to the front and hugged Zack, then Olaf.

"Where have you been?"

Zack looked at her. Still just as pretty as Ashley Williams. And still easier to talk to, even if his stomach was flip-flopping. The pleasure of seeing her mixed strangely with the danger at hand.

"Long story," Zack said. This wasn't the time or place to go into it. "But we have to go again, right away." He and Olaf quickly filled everyone in on what they had seen.

"Where's my father now?" Valdis asked. Her voice quavered, a kind of nervousness Zack had never before heard from her.

"I don't know," Zack answered honestly. "Hilda and Helga are going to take us as soon as everything's ready to go."

"What about Yggdrasil's Chest?" Hilda asked.

"Did Jok have it with him when he left?" Zack asked.

Several people nodded silently. There was no need to say out loud what had probably happened. Erik had the chest again.

"They should have taken one of the decoys," Hilda said.

Zack reluctantly told them about losing Olaf's duplicate chest.

Valdis breathed heavily. "Just typical of men," she said quietly. "Now we only have one."

"One what?"

"Duplicate chest," said Valdis. "I've got the other one."

"There are two fakes?" Zack asked incredulously. The surprise around here was going to be when there were no more surprises.

"Yes," Olaf said. "Is as easy to make two as one."

"And no," Valdis said, plucking the thought from Zack's head, "you are not taking this one with you."

Hilda, Zack, and Olaf tried to reason with Valdis, but she would have none of it. She had hidden it away and wouldn't say where. Zack stifled a yell of frustration. He couldn't decide who was more hardheaded—his sister or Valdis.

Soon Helga called down from above. "Come! We are ready."

Hilda, Zack, Olaf, and Asleif stood up. Everyone looked at Asleif.

Before anyone could speak, Asleif broke in. "I am coming," she said resolutely. "I intend to see this through, just as I have before."

"Not this time," Zack said. "I have a bad feeling about this."

Asleif put her hands on her hips. "Is that so? Now let me think for a moment." She looked around the room. "No, I can't seem to recall that you were put in charge of me. Maybe I'm wrong?" She looked back to Zack with mock curiosity on her face.

"I think she wants to be near the Lost Boy," said someone in the crowd. Everyone laughed and nodded.

"This is crazy," Zack said, looking to Hilda for support.

Hilda started toward the exit. "She has already proven herself capable. Asleif, if you wish to come, you may, but we are leaving now."

Asleif nodded. "I'll be right there."

Zack followed her deeper into the underground compound. "You know you're going to get yourself killed, right?"

Asleif stopped abruptly. Zack stumbled, almost running into her. "And you?" she said.

"What?"

She looked him in the eye. "Are you going to get yourself killed?"

"Well, uh . . . no. I hope not."

"Good," she said. "We'll watch out for each other."

Asleif smiled just enough to quicken Zack's pulse. "I'm glad you're coming," he said honestly.

"We'd better hurry," Asleif said.

They came into a long bunkroom. Low sleeping platforms ran along each wall, with crates of supplies stacked in the middle of the room. At the far end was a tall rectangular wooden cage. Zack could see half a dozen small gray birds clustered inside.

Asleif went over to the cage and covered it with a cloth. The birds cooed softly.

"Are those yours?" Zack asked.

Asleif nodded. "They inspire me," she said. "The music I play often comes from their song."

Zack had only heard Asleif play her harp and sing once,

at a feast in Lykill. As the village *skald,* she recorded Lykill's history in music and poetry.

"When I escaped Erik the Horrible's slavery," Asleif said, "these were all I brought with me." She absently put a hand to her head. "He took my parents . . . and my entire village. He even cut off my hair. But at least he didn't take my birds."

"Wow," Zack said quietly, not sure what else to say. Asleif was so self-assured, it was easy to forget how hard her life had been.

"Well," Asleif said, snatching up a brown woolen cloak. "Valdis will take good care of them while we're gone."

"Are you going to be okay?" Zack asked.

Asleif regarded him for a moment. Then her face changed. She fluttered her eyelids and spoke in a high-pitched voice. "Oh, help me, Lost Boy. Saaaaave me!"

Zack had to laugh. "All right, all right, let's go."

Asleif shouldered her cloak and strode out the door ahead of him.

CHAPTER SIX

Zack stood at the prow of Hilda and Helga's ship, the *Freya*. He had forgotten how quickly these tribes could load and launch a ship. Now they were rowing up a snaking waterway that wound its way between low snow-covered hills toward the sea. A dozen rowers on either side of the ship pulled in time with Hilda's calls.

"And . . . hoahh . . . And . . . hoahh."

"It shouldn't be long," Helga said. "May Freya guide our journey well, to safety and a quick return."

"Who's Freya?" Zack asked Asleif.

Asleif looked surprised. "Who is Freya? Why, she's Njord's daughter, of course."

"Huh?" Obviously, this was something he should know.

"Njord," Asleif said, pronouncing it like *nyord*. "God of the sea? Certainly you know Njord? Freya is his daughter. She watches over us as well."

"Okay," Zack said slowly, taking it in.

I need to go to Viking school.

With Asleif's wide eyes on him, Zack felt like there was a big "duh" written across his forehead.

Asleif continued, more gently now. "Freya welcomes dead warriors to her home as well. Half go to Odin and half go to her when they fall in battle."

"Which is why we ask her to watch over us now." Helga stepped up next to them. "We want to be welcome in her hall when the time comes."

The gravity of her statement caught Zack off-guard. This was no game. He turned to face forward, craning his neck and trying to see as far ahead as possible.

Let them be there. Let them be alive.

"Is anything you see?" Olaf asked anxiously.

"Nothing," Zack said. The bends in the waterway made it impossible to see very far.

"Look!" Asleif pointed upriver, where a thin column of black smoke trickled over the hills. Zack's stomach tightened. The *Winniferd* could easily be ashes by now.

Without any urging from Hilda, the rowers picked up their pace. A silence fell over the *Freya* as they navigated around one more bend.

The waterway opened up into a long narrow lake. At the far end was a V-shaped pass between two hills, leading to open water. The *Winniferd*—or what remained of it—was straight ahead to the left, lodged in a rocky outcropping near the shore. No signs of life anywhere.

"No!" It was a quiet cry from Zack, but in the silence around him it sounded like a yell.

Several rowers stood up to see better. Asleif grabbed Zack's arm and put a hand to her mouth.

The *Winniferd* was a charred black skeleton of itself. It listed to one side at a sharp angle. Lazy fingers of smoke rose from the prow and stern. The dragon's head that had once loomed majestically over the ship was gone, as if the *Winniferd* itself had been beheaded. The mast floated like a dead tree in the water, just a thin line of blackened wood.

Nothing about the sight of the burned ship was magical or extraordinary. And yet, it was harder to believe than anything else Zack had seen since coming here. Somehow, he had thought of the *Winniferd* as indestructible. Unbeatable. It was the same way he felt about Jok—and about his father, he suddenly realized. Each of them was supposed to always be there. Always.

And now the *Winniferd* was gone.

So if this can happen to the ship, what about . . .

"Jok," Olaf whispered, as if speaking Zack's next thought.

Zack scanned the water and the shore looking for people—or bodies.

Several of the crew stood along the rail while the rest rowed slowly closer to the burned ship. It was impossible to pull alongside, as the *Winniferd* had run amidst several rocks and sunk to the shallow bottom in this part of the lake. From where Zack stood, none of the ship's original details stood out. The entire thing was like a silhouette of flat, ashy blackness, just a suggestion of what it had once been.

"Hello!" Hilda roared. Her voice echoed off the surrounding rock walls.

"Jok?" Helga tried. No answer came.

The silence weighed down on Zack, just as it had when he found Lykill deserted. But the silence meant something else, too, he suddenly realized. Zack spoke out with a rush of adrenaline. "They're alive," he said.

Hilda and Helga seemed to have the same thought. They were already calling the rowers back to their positions.

"If they aren't here, then they must be alive," Zack said excitedly to Asleif. "If Erik was going to kill them, why wouldn't he just do it here? He has to have taken them hostage for some reason."

"Yes, but which way?" Hilda asked.

Zack scanned the lake. It had three possible exits. One way led back toward Konur, from where they had just come. Another way was out toward open sea. And a third opening led fifty feet or so upstream to a high waterfall.

"We would have seen him if he headed back toward Konur," Zack said.

"And Erik couldn't possibly have rowed *up* Baklav's Falls," Helga added, pointing in that direction.

Without further discussion, the *Freya* headed toward open sea. The enclosed landscape fell away and a rocky coastline spread out behind them endlessly in both directions.

The sight of an entire ocean took Zack's breath away. It was as if this world was expanding right in front of him. And if the world was getting bigger, then their chances of finding Jok were fast shrinking. This was worse than a needle in a haystack.

But there, almost dead ahead, was their needle. A flash of red, then black, showed up as a tiny dot toward the horizon. Erik the Horrible's ship was sailing directly away from them.

"Is many miles ahead," Olaf called out. "Should sail fast."

"Straight on!" Hilda called. Zack and Asleif stepped over to the mast and helped the twins raise the *Freya*'s sail. Zack barely felt the rough cord cutting into his hands. "Where could he be going?" he asked between pulls.

"He has Yggdrasil's Chest," Hilda mused.

"Would he have any way of knowing about the map inside?" Helga asked.

Olaf was standing by. He shook his head. "Was closed. Chest shut when Zack disappeared."

"Jok didn't want to take any chances," Asleif added. "He shut it back up that same night."

"And I've had this with me the whole time," Zack said, patting the key against his chest.

The sail billowed out like a giant green-and-gold flag. The wind, unblocked by hills and mountains, picked them up right away with a cold blast. Zack wrapped himself more tightly in his borrowed cloak. His fingers and toes were ice cubes. His sweater and jeans were stiff and frozen.

Helga paced the deck. "The problem," she said, "is that everyone on the *Winniferd* knew about the map. It is possible Erik kept them alive to torture information out of them."

The idea of it was like a punch in the stomach. Zack's hand went from the key to his midsection.

"Wouldn't tell, not Jok. Not anyone," Olaf said.

"Well, Erik knows something," Hilda said. "Because it's obvious he's headed toward Jotunheim."

Zack looked again at the sea. It was nothing more than a

flat expanse of water. "How can you tell where he's headed?"

Helga pointed up the coast to their right. "That's north. If Erik was headed home, he'd be going that way." She pointed to the left, down the coast. "That's the way toward Hedeby and several other towns. He could have gone raiding in that direction. But he didn't." And then she swept her arm in an arc, indicating the entire horizon of green sea and gray sky in front of them. "There's only one thing on the other side of all this."

"Jotunheim," Zack said. The land of the giants. The first stop on the map inside Yggdrasil's Chest. "So it's either a crazy coincidence, or he's going after the first treasure."

"No coincidence," Hilda said. "Somehow, he knows exactly what he is doing. He is headed straight for the vaults of Utgard."

"Hang on—what?"

"Utgard," Hilda said. "The giants' fortress in Jotunheim. Anything they have of value would be there. If I were Erik the Horrible, and I knew enough, that is exactly where I would go."

They sailed on in silence as the *Freya* caught a stiff westward wind toward Jotunheim. The ship's narrow construction was obviously meant for slicing through the water even in heavy chop. But Erik's ship was fast, too. From this distance, it was hard to tell if they were catching up or falling behind. It was like a slow-motion chase scene.

"How far to Jotunheim?" Zack asked.

Helga shrugged. "It could be days."

Zack remained at the *Freya*'s prow for the first few hours, willing the ship to make good time. The land slowly receded behind them. Finally, the only thing to see in any direction was water, and the dot of Erik's ship on the horizon ahead of them.

"Sit down, Lost Boy." Helga put a hand on his shoulder. "There is nothing we can do for them but sail on as fast as we can."

"I'm just going to stay here a little longer," Zack said.

"You'll serve them better by getting some rest. Who knows what we'll be facing next? Go ahead. I'll keep watch."

Helga was right. This wasn't going to be quick. He hunkered down next to Asleif, who sat with her knees drawn up against her chest. Asleif, like everyone else, hadn't uttered a single complaint since they headed out.

"I hope this ship is faster than Erik's," Zack said.

"He sails very fast," Asleif said. "I'm sorry to say that his ship is one of the finest. I sailed on it many times as his slave."

Zack's face flushed just thinking about all the misery Erik caused. For every escaped slave like Asleif, he must have hundreds more in captivity. Asleif spoke about her past matter-of-factly, just something that had happened and was now over. It was impossible not to admire her.

After another long silence, Asleif spoke up again. "What do you think we'll do when we get there?"

"I don't know," Zack said. "Get everyone back."

"What about Yggdrasil's Chest? And the first treasure?"

Zack closed his eyes and leaned his head back. "I don't know. I hope so. But first, we need to find Jok and the tribe."

As the sky grew dark, the crew broke out a barrel of water and a side of cured meat. The rations were divided up between the fifty or so people on board.

Zack chewed on the tough meat, which was like salty shoe leather. He gratefully accepted a drinking horn as it was passed to him, and drank a long gulp of water before reluctantly passing it on. The tiny meal filled only a fraction of the gaping space in his stomach.

Cheese fries. Fried baloney sandwich. Chocolate chip cookies.

Thinking about food didn't help but he couldn't stop himself.

Microwave surprise.

Even his father's favorite—and only—cooking specialty sounded good about now. Jock called it microwave surprise, unless he was feeling fancy. Then he'd put on his best French accent and call it *left eau-vairs*. Whatever it was, it was still warmed-up leftovers. But compared to the unchewable lump of dried meat in his mouth, Zack salivated at the mere thought of it.

As the ship sailed into the darkening night, Zack's thoughts bounced from his father to Jok and back again, their identical faces meshing together in his mind. He could never forget that Jock Gilman was his father. But it was getting harder to remember that Jok of Lykill was not. It was like having two fathers or one two-headed father—Zack couldn't decide which.

Either way, his own mother was long gone. His real father was in another century. And Jok was somewhere out in this vast ocean. Zack was beginning to feel like the orphan everyone in this world seemed to think he was, just like Jok himself, who had been left on a doorstep and raised by the people of Lykill.

The hours crawled by. The gray daylight had given way to a starless night. Zack, Olaf, and Asleif pressed together, trying to share body heat against the chill. Even without the cold, Zack wouldn't have been able to sleep. His thoughts poked him awake over and over.

He wished a fake wish, to be home. He knew that truly, the last thing he wanted was to desert his friends and leave behind this quest. It was part of him now, as much as anything else he had ever known. But the cold gnawed at his resolve and the stress made anywhere-but-here sound good. Everything pointed his thoughts to the warmth of his house on Lyman Avenue. And to his big, embarrassing, overgrown child of a father who, Zack knew, loved him very much.

The *Freya* sailed blindly west. The twins took the tiller in shifts. Zack overheard their conversation somewhere in the middle of the night.

"We'll just have to hope Erik keeps on this course as well."

"And that we can catch him before he reaches the vaults of Utgard."

"And that the giants don't catch us first."

"If we make it to Jotunheim at all."

They laughed coarsely between them, the laugh of warriors who weren't afraid to die. Zack closed his eyes, more wide-awake than ever.

Find Jok first. Worry about getting squashed like a grape later.

❦

Dawn showed them a strip of land on the horizon. The ocean, however, was one dot emptier than it had been.

"Where's Erik's ship?" Zack asked. He had been staring west into the darkness for an hour, willing the sun to rise faster. Somewhere in the night, Erik had slipped away.

"He has likely passed through," Hilda said. She pointed to a tall rectangle of white on land. It seemed to meet the ocean in a cloud of mist.

Several of the crew jostled among themselves, pointing excitedly.

"Something I never thought I'd see," said one.

The waterfall was beautiful, almost magical-looking, even from this distance. It spilled over a cliff in a wide swath, and fell like a sparkling white curtain straight into the ocean.

Zack jolted.

"Hang on a second, did you say 'passed through'?" He looked at Hilda.

"The Falls of Midgard," Hilda continued. "The way to the unknown sea and Jotunheim beyond."

Zack looked over at Olaf and Asleif, both of whom had come to stand next to him at the rail. "Did you know about this?" Both of them nodded their heads.

"Is the way to Jotunheim," Olaf said. "Everyone know."

Zack looked at the huge waterfall and gulped. "How many times have you done this?"

Hilda looked at Helga and then back at Zack again.

"This will be our first journey through."

"Ever?" Zack tried to keep from shouting. "How do you know it can even be done?"

"We don't," Helga said. "But Erik seems to have made it through."

The ship drew closer to the coast. Zack could hear the water now, crashing around the base of the falls in a constant low roar. What had looked like a billowing white curtain now began to look more like a concrete wall.

"So we just . . . sail right through?" Zack asked.

"No," Hilda said. She and Helga went to the mast and began lowering the sail. "We row."

Half of the crew began loading their oars into the oarlocks and took up rowing positions in the back half of the ship. Others began cutting lengths of rope. The rope was passed around and each person tied him or herself to the ship rail.

Those who weren't rowing took up wooden bailing scoops from the cargo hold. Zack, Asleif, and Olaf were directed to the stern, where they tied themselves in.

The great waterfall loomed nearly over their heads now, as the rowers took the ship on a crash course.

"Are you all right?" Zack shouted to Asleif over the growing roar. She nodded, her jaw clenched.

The churning water at the bottom of the falls created a strong current. The ship's progress slowed considerably as they grew nearer.

"Hold fast to the rail!" Hilda shouted. "Watch for each other. This will be . . ."

Zack couldn't hear the rest. He turned to Asleif. "What did she say?"

"Unpleasant!" she shouted back.

Yeah—unpleasant. You could call it that.

A fine mist sprayed out at them now, like an icy taste of what was to come. The ship crawled steadily forward, nosing into the white water. Hilda tried calling to the rowers but quickly gave up. It was impossible now to hear anything.

As water began crashing over the side of the ship, each of the bailers began frantically bending over and scooping water back out. It seemed to Zack like a futile exercise, since they were about to pass under something like Niagara Falls.

I guess every little bit helps.

Those who weren't rowing locked at least one arm over the side of the ship. The rowers, it seemed, were going to have to make it up as they went along.

And then they were in it. One moment the falls towered directly overhead, almost invisible through the thick spray. The next moment, an unearthly deluge of water crashed down on the *Freya*. The ship lurched downward, and Zack's stomach lurched with it. The water came down on his head like a barrel of bricks. In the same instant, his feet were swept out from under him. The ship was thrown to the side, and his body slammed into something hard.

The icy water was no longer a factor. Survival was the only thing that mattered now. Zack's arm tightened instinctively on the edge of the ship as his feet swung free.

All his brain knew was that he had to hold fast to the rail.

His other hand went automatically to his chest. He fought to keep it there, holding the key in place where it hung inside his sweater.

The side of the ship, and everything else, was invisible in the downpour. He could only hope that Olaf and Asleif were still holding on next to him. And that the ship was still moving forward, not stuck under the falls. Too much more of this and the *Freya* would certainly be smashed to pieces—not to mention the people on board.

Then, for a brief moment, they passed through a gap in the downpour. The noise was still deafening, but for a second Zack could see. He whipped his head around to make sure his friends were still there.

No!

Olaf was gone. Asleif was halfway overboard—she dangled precariously over the rail, the rest of her body hidden in the mist.

Zack reached out and wrapped an arm around Asleif's legs, just as another deluge of water hit them. He pulled as hard as he could but the force working against him was stronger. Asleif slipped forward, her legs sliding through his arms. Zack had grabbed her at the knees, but now she was hanging by her ankles, upside down and completely overboard.

Zack summoned all his strength just to hold on. The wall of water pulled at Asleif like liquid gravity. He didn't dare try to make a move for fear of losing his grip altogether. Asleif seemed to understand and stayed still.

Unless she's unconscious. Or worse.

Thoughts were the only thing he could hear, and they were working against him, too.

Again, they passed through a brief gap. The water lessened for a fraction of a second. Zack seized the moment. He grabbed her ankles with one arm and reached overboard with the other to get a better grip. Another wall of water bore down on them. Holding on to her as tight as he could, Zack pulled Asleif and threw himself down to the deck.

WHOOSH!

He felt the weight of Asleif's body fall onto him at the same time as the water itself. In another moment, she had disappeared again. The force of the water tried to wash Zack across the deck. With both his hands off the rail, he slid free. The rope around his waist held tight—too tight, as if it wanted to slice him in half. He scrambled back toward where he hoped the side of the ship was, pushing himself along the ground with the heels of his feet. He vaguely felt Asleif back at his side again, doing the same thing. In the blinding whiteness of the water, they struggled to link arms and crouched down just under the rail.

Olaf.

He had managed to get Asleif back, but Olaf was gone. And who knew how many others had been washed overboard? Once you were off the ship in these falls, you were done.

Zack and Asleif managed to stay pressed against each other for what felt like another eternity of blinding and deafening water.

Olaf.

They had come all this way, only to lose him here, to a waterfall. Just like the decoy chest, only much, much worse. Zack's mind reeled with the pain of it.

Finally, almost suddenly, the water eased. Zack opened his eyes. The ship had passed through the back of the falls and into a cave of some sort. The sound was still enormous, but the water was almost calm here. And the ship was in one piece.

Asleif was pressed up next to Zack, with one arm wrapped like steel around his own. With her other arm, she had Olaf in what looked like a fierce headlock. Her eyes were still shut tight. Olaf's eyes were wide open—bugged out, in fact, as Asleif seemed to be nearly strangling him.

"Olaf!" Zack shouted. Asleif's eyes popped open and she looked almost surprised to find both Zack and Olaf there with her. She released her grip on the troll, and he rolled free, holding his neck and coughing.

"You saved him," Zack said to Asleif.

Asleif blinked several times. She turned to Olaf and helped him sit up. "Are you all right?"

Olaf smiled a drooly, toothy grin and wrapped his thin gray arms around Asleif in a hug.

"Is saved by Asleif!" he said. He peppered her face with slobbery kisses as she laughed gamely.

Zack couldn't help being just a tiny bit jealous.

Lucky troll.

"And by Zack," Asleif said to Olaf. "I had hold of you, but Zack pulled us both back on board."

"Is everyone all right?" Hilda shouted out. She was untying the rope around her waist and counting heads. Somehow, several of the rowers had managed to stay to their oars through the whole ordeal. They sat slumped on their seats now. Others lay flat out on the deck, breathing hard.

Soon all were accounted for. The tribe let up a shout, and it echoed through the long narrow cave. Everyone began bailing all the water they could from the ship. Those who hadn't been rowing in the falls took over and powered the ship the rest of the way through. A circle of daylight, several hundred yards ahead, beckoned them on.

Before long, they emerged from the cave into open air. Where the landscape had been mountainous and rocky on the other side, here it was strangely uniform in color and texture. Zack looked at it with curiosity.

The entire coast was like a single long mound that snaked back and forth in both directions. As Zack stared at it, he noticed that the land itself had an odd, and somehow familiar, appearance. Long ridges ran along it like stripes. And instead of snow and rock, a brown color covered it everywhere. Not like earth, but more like . . . tree bark.

It wasn't a regular coastline at all, Zack realized. They had just passed through one of Yggdrasil's three roots. It might have been the size of Florida, for all he could tell. The tree Yggdrasil itself was said to be bigger than anything else in this world. Zack was beginning to understand what that meant. It was hard to fathom that this stretch of "land" was actually just a single tree root. But it also meant that they were on the right track—toward Jotunheim.

A quick scan of the horizon showed no sign of Erik's ship.

"Do you think he could be in Jotunheim by now?" Zack asked.

Hilda stood looking out at the water. "Hard to say. I don't know how much farther it is."

"We should stop here," Helga said. "It looks like the best place in sight to pull in the boat, and fire is more important than anything right now." The crew stood shivering around them. A fire on board was out of the question.

Zack reluctantly nodded his agreement. "Maybe just a quick stop."

A warm breeze seemed to beckon them on toward the shore. Zack remembered how the winter weather had dropped away the last time he had been near Yggdrasil. By the time they were clamoring off the ship, it felt like a warm spring day.

The ground where they stood sloped and jutted like any other landscape, but with brown ridged bark instead of rock or sand or earth. Trees and bushes seemed able to grow here as well. They looked artificial, jutting up through the strange ground cover.

"It's like we landed on Mars or something," Zack said.

"What's Mars?" Asleif asked.

Oh yeah. Ninth century.

"It's . . . another world," Zack said. "Humans live in Midgard. Giants live in Jotunheim. And, uh . . . Martians live on Mars." It wasn't much of an explanation. Asleif nodded, but Zack could tell she was just being polite.

The crew quickly built several fires. "This shouldn't take long," Hilda said.

Zack took off his wet cloak and sat on the ground.

He looked over and saw Helga standing to one side, looking up a steep slope. "What is it?" he called out.

She pointed up the slope to a landing of some kind. Lush greenery flowed out over the edge in a dense clump.

"Come," Helga said.

Zack looked over at the others, lazing around the fires, laughing and talking. "Where are you going? Shouldn't we tell the—"

"Just come," Helga said. "I'm not sure, but I think . . ." She didn't finish her sentence, and instead began climbing. Zack followed closely behind. In a few minutes, they came to the top, where the ground flattened out. Small trees formed a natural archway, leading to a shadowy glade beyond.

"This may be the Well of Mimir," Helga whispered, her eyes wide.

"The what?" But she had already slipped ahead.

They stole into the glade. The lapping of the ocean fell away, and a new watery sound permeated the air. It was a soft tinkling, like wind chimes. Rough tree bark underfoot gave way to soft mossy earth. A pale green light filled the clearing, but not from the sun. The ring of trees around them seemed to block out all daylight and sounds from outside.

They moved deeper inward, as if into a green cave. The tinkling sound grew louder. The light, which came from some unknown source, grew brighter.

They stepped through a hedge and found themselves in front of a large round pool of water.

Several small waterfalls spilled into the pool from different directions, yet the water was mirror smooth. Within the undisturbed water, Zack saw a reflection of a full moon. He looked up instinctively, though he knew it was day. And besides, the greenery formed a natural dome over them. The sky was completely blocked out. The moon reflection was coming from somewhere inside the pool.

Zack felt as if he had stepped from one strange dream into another completely different one. A much nicer one.

"Ah, hello."

Zack and Helga turned to find the voice. It echoed in the air, and the silvery water rippled. Then the glade was silent.

"What?" Zack said finally.

"Hello." Again the water rippled, and the gentle voice reverberated around them.

Zack looked into the pool. "Are you . . . in there?"

"Yes, of course," said the voice. When it spoke, the reflection of the moon disappeared and was replaced with the image of a face.

"It is Mimir," Helga whispered.

"Yes, Mimir. Yes." The face smiled up at them from the pool. "So good to see you. I don't often have visitors."

The voice and the face were completely unthreatening. Zack stepped forward to get a better look.

"Agh!" He jumped back again.

"Don't be alarmed," Mimir prodded softly.

Zack pointed at the water, his mouth flapping open. The face was that of a smiling older man. His dark hair and eyes gave off an air of gentle wisdom. But where his neck curved to meet with the rest of his body, a jagged line of torn flesh stopped him short. He was just a severed head—or at least, the reflection of one.

"Yes, I understand," Mimir went on. "Not exactly what one hopes for in a host. But please don't go."

Zack stood back from the pool, trying to maintain eye contact with Mimir without actually being able to see all the way down to his bloodied throat.

"Most unpleasant, I know," Mimir said. "I was once a full-bodied ambassador on behalf of the gods. I was sent by Odin to make peace with the Vanir."

"Vanir?" Zack asked. The word sounded like "veneer," and made him think of his father's Winnebago, with its veneered, fake-wood paneling.

"The Vanir are an older family of gods," Mimir told him. "Not quite what they once were. Very defensive about it, actually. I was sent to make a peaceful settlement, and instead—" Mimir raised his eyebrows. If he had a finger, he would no doubt have drawn it across his throat to indicate what had happened.

"All-knowing Mimir," Helga spoke up, "we are honored by your hospitality. We come humbly asking for your aid."

Helga reached behind Zack and pushed him forward. Zack stumbled to the edge of the pool. He waved at Mimir and felt like an idiot before his hand was even back at his side.

I'm waving hello to a reflection of a head. Welcome to the far side.

"Sit, please," Mimir urged. "Stay awhile. I'll tell you a thing or two."

Zack and Helga exchanged looks again. They both reluctantly sat down. "We're in kind of a hurry. . . ." Zack tried.

Mimir ignored him. "Did you ever hear the story of how I ended up here?"

Given that he had just told them, Zack was unsure how to respond. "Well, sort of."

"So there I was . . ." Mimir jumped back in, telling a much, much longer version of what he had already told them.

Zack and Helga made several attempts to break in, with no luck. Zack's thoughts kept flying back to Jok and the tribe. Where were they now? How far ahead might Erik have gotten?

Finally, Mimir reached something that sounded like an ending. "So I have this post instead," he said. "Odin was kind enough to preserve what was left of me. Really, it's not bad. Everlasting life, the well of knowledge, and all that. But not many visitors, as I've said. And you can probably tell I don't get out much."

Zack grabbed the opportunity to speak. "I have to ask you a question," he said quickly.

"Ahh, a question," Mimir answered, his voice picking up something of an edge. "How original." His face grew stern for the first time. "No one ever wants to listen—they just want answers, answers, answers."

"Yes, I know, and I'm very sorry," Zack said, although he didn't know and he was barely sorry. Mostly, he was in a hurry.

"May I have a drink from the Well of Knowledge?" Helga jumped in. "It might help us in our quest."

"Yes, certainly, go right ahead," Mimir said.

Helga looked surprised but stepped forward. She leaned over the edge of the pool. As she reached to take a handful, the water dipped away from her. She reached again, and the pool gave way, making a space where her hand was.

Helga tried several more times, jabbing at the water, and trying to fake it out. Mimir, or his well, was too fast for her. No matter where she reached, the water dodged away.

"Odin himself, king of the gods, gave one of his own eyes to drink from this well," said Mimir. "Did you really think it would be that easy?"

Finally, Helga stood up, disgusted. "We should go. We are wasting our time."

They turned to leave.

"Wait!" Mimir cried out. "You just got here."

"Our friends are in danger," Helga said. "We have no time for this."

"All right," Mimir said. "I will make you an offer. Ask me a question that I cannot answer, and I will answer any other question you please."

"That is impossible, too," Helga said. "You are all-knowing. Come, Zack."

"Please," Mimir said, almost whining. "How often do I get

to have a little fun? Never, that's how often."

Zack felt sorry for Mimir in spite of himself. It was worth a shot anyway. "Okay," he said. "Where is Jok of Lykill right now?"

Mimir chuckled, and the water rippled. "That doesn't count. That is the information you are seeking, yes? Try another question."

"Who is Thor's first son?" Helga said.

"Modi." Mimir yawned. "Surely you can do better than that."

"What's my middle name?" Zack tried.

"Joseph," Mimir shot off without a pause.

"I knew this was impossible," Helga said.

Something obvious suddenly occurred to Zack.

I'm in the ninth century. Of course.

"What's the capital of Minnesota?" he practically shouted.

Mimir opened his mouth to speak, then paused. "The capital . . . "

"Of Minnesota," Zack said. Since Minnesota didn't exist yet here, it seemed worth a shot.

Mimir thought for several more seconds.

"Do you know, or do you not?" Helga pressed him.

Finally, Mimir had to admit it. "Amazing. I am not accustomed to losing this game. Of course, I rarely get to play it."

"Rochester," Zack said.

"Excuse me?"

"The capital of Minnesota," Zack said.

"Ahhh," said Mimir with a broad smile. "*Now* I am all-knowing."

Zack didn't say anything about the other forty-nine state capitals. He didn't want to burst Mimir's bubble.

"All right," said Mimir. "Now you want to know about your friends, yes?"

"Yes," Zack said.

Mimir's eyes closed. The image of his face in the pool grew fuzzy. It blurred entirely and then came back into focus, showing a new picture. Erik's ship, sailing toward a mountainous coast. In the distance, the towers of a tremendous fort stuck up between sharp peaks.

"Jotunheim," Helga said. "It must be. Those towers—that has to be Utgard."

"It is," Mimir said simply from somewhere behind the image.

The pool was too blurred for details, but the red-and-black sail of Erik's ship was unmistakable.

"You said you would tell us about our friends," Zack said. "Does this mean they're alive and on board that ship?"

"It does," Mimir said.

Zack breathed half a sigh of relief. At least they were still alive.

"Where is the first treasure of Yggdrasil?" Helga pressed. "Is it in the vaults?"

The pool wavered again, and Mimir's face returned. "Ah, now that is a separate question. If you want to know, we will have to start the game over."

Zack and Helga turned to go.

"Wait!" Mimir called.

"I'm sorry," Zack said to him. "We can't stay here any-more. We have to go."

"Stop," Mimir persisted. "There is one more thing I will tell you, Lost Boy."

Zack stopped. *Lost Boy?* "How did you know I was the Lost Boy?"

Mimir looked up at him dubiously.

Oh yeah. All-knowing.

"So, what is it?" Zack said tentatively.

Mimir took a long pause. It seemed to last for minutes, though it was only seconds. Zack shifted uncomfortably. Finally, Mimir spoke.

"This quest," he said. "It is in three parts, yes?"

"It looks that way," Zack said. "But we're not even on the quest. We're just trying to get our friends back."

"Perhaps," Mimir said. "And perhaps not. Just know this: The search you are on—the search for the first treasure—will require a great leap of faith from you."

"What do you mean?"

"Remember that, Lost Boy. Remember that." The pool shuddered, and Mimir's face faded from the pool. The re-flection of the full moon was back. "Good-bye." They heard his deep voice as if from a great distance. And then he was gone.

As they ran back toward the *Freya*, Zack cataloged every-thing he had just learned.

A great leap of faith.

Whatever Mimir had been talking about, he would have to worry about that later. More importantly, the tribe was still alive, if not yet safe. Erik's ship would be reaching the shores of Jotunheim soon.

Back at the temporary camp, Zack recounted everything for the others.

Helga then addressed the group, speaking in a grave tone. "Our journey from here grows ever more dangerous. As you all know, giants are treacherous. Stories of humans returning from Jotunheim are rare. If anyone wishes to stay behind, there is no shame in it."

"Of course there is!" called out one soldier. "We are nothing without courage."

"And faith!" shouted another.

"And sacrifice!"

The tribe cheered raucously.

"To Jotunheim!" roared Hilda, and they raced back to the ship.

CHAPTER SEVEN

Within hours, the icy peaks of Jotunheim loomed into view. Just as Zack had seen in Mimir's Well, the red stone towers of Utgard pricked the sky like the mountains themselves. Even from this distance, Utgard made the Metrodome in Minneapolis look like a dollhouse.

The fortress stood on a massive peninsula. To Zack's left, the land came to a tip where the mountains dropped sharply off into the sea. To his right, Jotunheim extended beyond the horizon.

He blew into his hands, watching it all loom slowly closer. "Are you nervous?" he asked.

"Yes," Asleif said simply. "I've never seen a giant. Have you?"

Zack smiled. He wished Ollie could see all this.

"Why are you smiling?" Asleif asked.

"I don't know. It just seemed like a funny question." He wiped the grin off his face. "But I know it wasn't. There's just a lot that I've never seen before."

Asleif stepped farther away from the others and motioned for him to come closer. She looked very serious now, and a little sad. "Zack, I want you to know that I understand there is nothing more important than that key." She pointed to Zack's chest.

"I don't know if that's true," Zack said. "Jok, Olaf, the tribe . . . you, everyone . . ."

Asleif shook her head. "No, not always. Sometimes there is a greater good."

Zack paused, unsure what to say.

Asleif went on. "If Erik the Horrible has taken Yggdrasil's Chest, he is going to want the key more than ever."

"Let him try," Zack said.

"I'm going to stay as close to you as possible," Asleif said. "The key is more important than anything. And you are more important than any one of us."

Zack started to interrupt her. "Now wait—"

But Asleif went on insistently. "If there is anything I can do to help you protect that key . . ." She stopped again and looked him straight in the eye. "*Anything*. I will do it. You only have to ask."

The more Asleif showed of herself, the more complicated she seemed. Zack had always thought of himself as one of her protectors. Now she was offering to protect him.

"Thanks," Zack said. It seemed like a lame answer, but it was all he could think to say.

"Is burned ship again!" Olaf called out. He stood on a trunk, looking over the rail.

Sure enough, Zack could just make out the charred remains of a ship's hull and mast on shore.

"I don't see anyone," Zack said to Helga. The beach showed no signs of life. "Do you think it's Erik's ship?"

"I don't know," Helga answered. "This makes no sense."

"Unless Jok took over somehow," Zack said, "but even then, why would he burn it?"

"Best to be ready," Helga said. She relieved the rowers and ordered them to arm themselves as they sailed the last half mile to Jotunheim. Soon the tribe was gathered at the front of the ship, chain mail rattling and swords at their sides.

Olaf clapped his hands together. "Is time to get back Jok and all." Inch for inch, Zack thought, Olaf was probably the bravest one on board. He seemed to thrive on danger.

As the *Freya* drew near land, the burned ship stood out starkly against the snowy landscape. But other ships came into view now, too. They were wreckages mostly, at least a dozen of them littering the shore, and most of them smashed to pieces.

"Something tells me those ships didn't crash into the rocks," said Zack.

The moment the *Freya* hit land, the tribe leapt ashore and began scouting the beach. Zack and Asleif ran over to the burned ship. As they drew near, they ran down a short slope into a large ditch on the shore. Another ditch was dug into the ground directly next to the ship. It was about the width and length of his father's Winnebago.

"Look." Asleif pointed away from the water. A whole series of similar ditches seemed to be carved into the ground.

"Footprints," Zack said.

Whether or not Erik and Jok had been here when the giants had arrived was impossible to tell. There were no signs of struggle but that didn't mean anything. With something that left Winnebago-sized footprints, it wouldn't exactly have been an even match.

The burned ship was unrecognizable. It was the same size as Erik's, but no one could think of a reason why he or Jok would destroy it.

"We shouldn't stay here," Helga said. "Where there is one giant, there will be more."

"At least we know which way to go," Zack said, pointing toward the trail of craters that led toward Utgard.

A scream filled the air.

"Watch out!" One of the tribe shouted from across the beach.

Everyone scattered. Zack whirled around.

How can a giant sneak up on you?

But the beach was empty. A second later, a thick white goop hit the sand. It missed Zack's head, barely, but a gallon or more of it splashed off the frozen earth and onto his pant leg.

"What . . . is . . . this?" It was like thick paint except that it smelled strongly of ammonia.

Another scream pulled his attention upward. Zack looked and saw the largest seagulls he had ever seen, three of them circling overhead. Their squawking was almost human. Each one was the size of a minivan. Their beaks looked big enough to bite off a person's head in one snap.

Helga and several others whipped arrows from their quivers and shot at the birds. They narrowly missed, but it seemed to get the message across. The enormous gulls banked sharply and continued up the shore.

Zack dashed to the water's edge and tried to wash off the gunk without soaking himself completely.

"Welcome to Jotunheim," Helga called out.

Zack grimaced, trying not to gag from the smell. "More like Poopunheim," he said.

Helga came over and handed him one of their round wooden shields to carry. "Here," she said. "You might need this. On top of your head." Everyone around them laughed.

Zack looked down at his wet and only slightly cleaner leg. "Can we just go?" he asked.

The tribe headed inland. Straight toward Utgard.

Asleif walked with Zack. The shield and helmet she had taken from the *Freya* were both too big for her small frame. "What do we do when we get there?" she asked under her breath.

"Good question," Zack said. "I guess we'll find out."

They followed the giant footprints, skirting each one to avoid the climb down and back out again.

"This is probably just a short walk for them," Asleif said. Utgard's towers were still a good two miles off. The tribe trudged along.

As they grew nearer, Olaf sniffed deeply. "Is smoke," he said. "There." He pointed up a steep hill, where a waft of gray seemed to be leaking out of the ground.

"And over there," Zack said. "And there." Several of the small peaks around them seemed to be burning from the inside.

What the heck?

Then he realized. This wasn't a mountain range. It was a village.

Helga must have realized it, too. "Off!" she whisper-barked, and the tribe moved swiftly to the cover of an enormous shrub.

"I want to go check this out," Zack said. If there was any information to be had about Jok, he wanted to be the first to know.

"I'll go," Asleif added quickly.

"Fine," Hilda said. She took two other volunteers, and the party of five hiked half a mile up the snowy slope toward the nearest smoke hole. They worked their way around to the upwind side of the chimney. Zack set down his shield. He lay close to the ground and peered into the dim chamber below.

Two men, the size of four-story buildings, sat at an equally enormous table in the middle of a sparsely furnished cavern of a room.

Zack had seen the Grand Canyon once a long time ago, before his mother died. But he could still remember the feeling of looking at something so unfathomably large that it had to be seen to be believed, and even then seemed impossible. This was the same feeling. The giants moved and looked like humans, but the similarity was nothing compared to the size difference. Zack's mind boggled at their sheer enormity. For several moments, he couldn't think about anything else.

The two giants hunched over a game of some sort, throwing large blocks that looked like dice with strange symbols on their many sides. Each of the blocks was about the size of an armchair.

At the far end of the single room Zack could see an open door leading to a tunnel.

The tunnel could explain why they hadn't seen any giants walking around. It put Zack in mind of Minneapolis, with its downtown maze of interconnected breezeways and underground passages between buildings. No one ever had to go outside to get from place to place. This giant village was probably the same way. Like a rabbit warren—for really, really big rabbits.

One of the giants, with a crooked nose and greasy, dark hair, rolled the dice and laughed. "Four times!" he shouted. He slid several wooden markers from the center of the table over to his side.

"Your luck can't hold all day," said the other. From up above, his bald head looked like a domed building.

The greasy-haired giant continued to roll. He chortled again. "Five times!"

Suddenly the other stood up. "That's enough. You're cheating."

"What do you mean?" said the greasy-haired one. "You're just unlucky."

"I'll show you unlucky," said Dome Head. He cocked his fist and slammed the other giant on the side of the face. Greasy flew out of his chair and to the ground. When his gigantic body hit the dirt floor, Zack felt a reverberation in his chest, as if he were lying on top of a big drum.

Another moment later, Greasy was back on his feet with a roar. He covered the distance between himself and the other in a few huge strides and sacked Dome Head at the waist. The two of them slammed into the wall directly below Zack. Outside, the ground shook harder, as if from a brief earthquake. Hilda, Asleif, Zack, and the two other soldiers exchanged a silent alarmed look across the chimney hole. Zack pressed himself into the snowy ground and held on.

Don't fall through. Don't fall through.

Dome Head turned again and tackled the other giant, forcing him into a headlock. Then he pulled him to the ground in a full body slam.

The earth shook again, more violently this time. A layer of loose snow and ice rippled down the hill.

"We should go," Zack mouthed to the others, pointing down the mountain. But it was too late. The carpet of snow under them began to move. To the giants, it would just be a bit of snow off their roof. For Zack and the others, it was the start of an avalanche. Zack jumped up and tried to run, but his feet slipped away on the shifting ground. The others were scrambling and falling in the same way. Zack looked uphill again and saw a wall of snow running down the mountain, a white monster poised to swallow them whole.

Zack's mind clicked.

Holding his shield out in front of him, Zack dove downhill. He landed on the shield belly-first and began to slide. Out of the corner of his eye, he saw Hilda and one soldier following his lead. He had lost track of the others. The sliding snow carried him on his makeshift sled, ten times faster than he could have gone on foot.

It was hard to see anything in any direction. Bits of snow and ice pelted him in the face. Zack tried to look over his shoulder as he raced downward.

Let the others be there, too.

When he turned back, a fat pine tree rushed up to meet him.

"No!"

Without thinking, Zack leaned hard to the right. The tree whizzed by but the shield tilted and spun around. He continued down the hill, backward now.

All the others were there, barely hanging on to their own shields but safe, so far. The wind and downhill speed sucked away Zack's sigh of relief.

He leaned hard to the left, trying to turn around again without flipping over. The edge of his shield caught the snow, slowing him down just slightly. Asleif shot past.

Was she smiling?

Zack edged around slowly, wobbling like a jellyfish on a plate.

How long can this hill go on?

Now he was sliding sideways—better than backward, but not much. One of the other soldiers sped past, clipping Zack at the feet and sending him spinning, once again, like a car with bald tires on ice. He made three or four complete rotations as the sloping landscape whirled by in a nauseating blur. On one pass, he caught sight of the rest of the tribe at the bottom of the slope, out from their hiding place and cheering. Apparently, he was the only one *not* having a good time.

WHOMP!

His sled hit a bump, and he was airborne.

"Auuughhh!"

Zack was aloft just long enough to wonder if this could possibly get any worse. He sailed in one direction, his shield in another. When he hit the ground, he kept going, rolling out of control.

He was vaguely aware of the ground flattening out, just before his body came to a stop. It rested gently against a pair of feet. He looked up and saw Helga smiling down at him.

"That was quite good," she said.

Zack's head lolled. He saw three Helga faces, then two, then finally one. "Huh . . . ?"

She chuckled to the others gathering around. "He'll be fine."

Olaf came running over. "Is anything you saw? Is anything you learned of giants?"

"Yeah," Zack said, holding his spinning head in his hands. "They like to fight."

CHAPTER EIGHT

The tribe regrouped and continued up the valley toward Utgard. The fortress loomed higher and higher. Its stone walls, Zack could see, were built right into the mountains, as if they were an extension of the natural rock formation.

More giants began to appear outdoors, coming and going from Utgard. The tribe traveled in small groups now, rushing from one bit of ground cover to the next. Zack kept going because he had to. His brain, though, was stuck in an awestruck loop.

He couldn't decide if it was amazing because the giants were so big, or because, for the first time in his life, he felt so small. At school back home, Zack Gilman *was* the giant.

Helga halted the tribe at the back of a stone outbuilding, out of sight of the fortress's guarded main entrance.

"This is getting too risky," Helga said. "Too many giants around for daylight travel. We should camp until nightfall."

"What about Jok and the others?" Zack knew Helga was right, but this was taking forever.

"Must go carefully," Olaf whispered. "Not to end up under giant shoe."

Zack sighed. Of all the challenges here, patience was definitely one of them.

The tribe took cover underneath an overturned wagon with one of its wheels missing; it seemed unlikely anyone would come to use it. They burrowed through the snow and crawled inside. Daylight leaked through the loose boards of the wagon, filling the space with a dim, smoky light.

The tribe sat down and leaned against the wagon walls, waiting for night. Zack sat with Asleif, Olaf, and the twins.

"We can't travel as a large group," Hilda said. "I think it's best to send a scouting party first."

"I'm going," Zack and Asleif both said at the same time.

"Olaf go, too," Olaf said. "Not to be left behind. Is good at not being seen."

"That's true," Zack said, patting Olaf on the shoulder. Olaf had helped him slip through more than one tricky situation.

"That will be enough," Hilda said. "The five of us will go."

They waited for the last of the daylight to fade before setting out.

Hilda went first, moving slowly, then whispered for the others to follow. Zack was the last one out.

The clouds had moved on, and a clear field of stars was beginning to show overhead. A three-quarter moon hung low in the sky.

The scouting party kept to the shadows as they approached the fortress. They stopped at last and ducked down in a furrow across from its main gates, hunkering under a frozen patch of weeds.

Zack saw that the high wooden gates were bookended by a pair of bored-looking guards. They stood, rocking back and forth on their heels, hands clasped behind their backs.

No wonder. Who's going to be a threat to these guys?

Besides the two guards, pairs of armed sentries ambled back and forth on a dirt road that fronted the fortress. The sentries carried torches, but the road was otherwise in shadow. The human party would have darkness, and their relatively tiny size, working for them. Still, it was going to be dicey. There wasn't much chance of outrunning any of these guards, and less than zero chance of outfighting them.

Yeah, giant, you want a piece of me? SPLAT.

That's what a fight with one of these guys would be like, Zack thought grimly to himself. He remembered a song Asleif had once sung about the god Thor's journey to Jotunheim, and how he had conquered the giants with his famous hammer.

I wouldn't mind having that hammer about now.

He scanned the area for their next hiding place, and for a way in.

It seemed to Zack that the fortress walls were heavier than they were well constructed. The weight of the enormous stones and bricks themselves must have done a good part of the work to keep the walls intact. He could see holes in the mortar and great sections where no mortar was used at all.

And a tiny hole was all they would need.

"Wait for the next sentries to pass," Helga ordered.

They stood still for several minutes. Finally, a pair of

glum-looking guards trudged past. Both had their right hands resting nonchalantly on their swords as they continued up the road.

"Go!" Helga whispered. Zack took Asleif's arm. The two of them scurried across like mice, away from the gate and toward a shadowed section of the fortress wall. Giants would have covered the distance in a few strides, but it was more like a hundred-yard dash for Zack and the others. Hilda and Helga came right behind. Olaf, however, was still hurrying across the path.

One of the guards at the main gate stirred. "Ergh," he grunted. "It's a rat. Get it."

Another guard picked up a stone and pitched it in Olaf's direction. Zack watched helplessly as the rock whipped through the air. It was the size of Olaf himself. The troll's red eyes flared in the dark, wider than Zack had ever seen them. The rock hit the ground and skidded just past Olaf as he dove out of the way.

The giant who had thrown the rock started toward them. In the shadows, Zack could see Olaf lying low to the ground, his body heaving with rapid breaths.

"Leave it," said the other guard. "If you tried to kill every rat in this place, you'd have time for nothing else."

The rock thrower turned back, his voice tinged with malice. "Are you saying I can't manage a little rat?"

"No," said the guard, "but now that you say it . . ."

The thrower picked up a dirt clod off the path and flung it at his companion. It exploded against the guard's face, leaving a brown patch on his forehead.

The one who had been hit let loose with a guttural growl. He charged his opponent, grabbed him around the neck, and hit him in the face with several rapid-fire punches. The other flipped him over his back and stomped on his chest, only to have his own feet knocked out from under him by the first one's sword. He fell with a yowl. Zack felt the earth tremble as the giant's body hit the ground like a redwood.

Several other guards came running. It seemed as if they were going to break up the fight, but instead they jumped right in and began kicking and punching. No one seemed concerned with who was fighting whom, or even why anyone was fighting in the first place. Two of the giants teamed up on a third, beating him from either side with their fists, only to turn on each other when the one in the middle slipped to the ground.

It was just the distraction Olaf needed. He sprang up and ran over to where Zack and the others were waiting. Hilda meanwhile had been searching the wall for a way in. Zack helped her climb up to where she could peek through a gap between two stones.

"This should be big enough," she whispered. Speaking low was hardly necessary. Twelve or more guards were now cursing and fighting and rolling in the snow and dirt, sending a low, continuous vibration through the ground. Dust and mortar sprinkled down onto Zack from somewhere on the wall above.

He helped Asleif up, then Olaf and Helga. Each of them

scrambled through and disappeared to the other side of the wall. Then he pulled himself up.

Uh-oh.

Each of the others had probably slipped through quite easily. This was going to be tight. None of them were even half his size.

Argh.

Zack had spent his life feeling huge around everyone he knew at home. Then they had come here and he felt tiny. Now, contemplating this little hole in the wall, he felt huge again.

Well, you aren't getting any smaller, Gilman. Go. Now.

Every minute of delay could be the minute that Jok and the tribe needed them most.

He crawled in as best he could, keeping his arms at his sides. The little passage was just longer than he was tall—not far to go. He did an awkward commando crawl, rocking his body and pushing himself forward, until he could see out the other side. They were in a dimly lit and thankfully empty corridor.

"Zack," came a soft whisper. He glanced down and saw Helga looking up at him. The others were pressed into a crevice below, waiting. Helga gave him a wide-eyed, impatient look. Zack glared back at her.

I'm going as fast as I can.

He snaked forward a few more inches. The passage narrowed around his shoulders, pinning his arms. It felt like suddenly being mummified in stone.

Don't panic.

"Helga," he whispered down.

Helga poked her head out again. Zack heard Olaf's soft whisper from below. "Why so slow for Zack?"

He tried to take a deep breath to calm himself, but his body was too tightly pressed in even for that. It was as if the rock wall were closing around him.

"I'm stuck," he hissed.

Helga disappeared for another second and then climbed up to where Zack's head was sticking out of the wall.

"How stuck?" she asked.

How stuck? How do I answer that?

"Help me," he said. "Try and pull me through."

A sudden roar of voices filled the passageway. Then a clatter of footsteps. Zack and Helga both looked around. In the echoey stone hallway, it was hard to know which direction the voices were coming from.

"Get back!" Helga whispered, and she dropped to the floor.

Easy for you to say. I can't move.

Zack scrunched himself, trying to squeeze his body back the way he had come. A crowd of giants appeared around the corner.

Think small. Teeny. Tiny.

Adrenaline pumping, he managed to pull in a few inches as the giants drew near. Zack saw a dozen or more jumbo legs pass by, the roar of laughter and voices reverberating in the hallway.

"I'm told there are at least two dozen of them," said one.

"Not enough for a proper feast, to be sure," said a giant female voice. "We'd best hurry."

Zack had to imagine he knew what they were talking about. It gave him a sick feeling in his gut. But at least they were in the right place.

When the voices had faded, he pushed forward once again. Helga reappeared and grabbed onto his collar. After several pulls and lots of painful pushing and scraping, Zack managed to free an arm. From there, he was able to wriggle forward enough to fall out of the hole onto the stone floor.

"Is all right?" Olaf said.

"I'm fine, I'm fine," Zack whispered.

Asleif was watching him with concern. Hilda and Helga stood back waiting for him to get up again.

"Stop looking at me," Zack hissed, standing up. It seemed like every time he turned around here, he was on the ground with people staring at him.

"Is sometimes good to be small," Olaf muttered, just loud enough for Zack to hear.

Zack cut off any more discussion. "Let's just go find Jok."

More giant voices, shouts, and laughter reached their ears from down the hall.

It seemed as good a direction as any. They moved toward the voices, quickly but carefully. Helga stood at the rear, sword poised and walking backward. When anyone came near, they pressed into the corners of the walls, between the bricks or under a doorway if they could find one. The sounds of the celebration grew louder as they went.

Finally, they reached the main hall. Straight ahead through an open archway, Zack could see several long tables lined up, and dozens of giants milling around. They were stuffing themselves from great platters on the tables, with barn-sized slabs of meat, and drinking from horns as big as water towers.

Feeding time in the dinosaur zoo.

For a flash, Zack surveyed the food jealously, his empty stomach begging for attention. One slice of bread would have fed them all.

Smash! A drinking horn sailed through the air, out of the hall, and landed with a clatter near the group. Gallons of yeasty-smelling ale spilled out over the floor. Zack jumped out of the way to keep from getting soaked.

"Better than a seagull, huh?" Hilda said with a jab to his ribs.

"Ha-ha," Zack whispered back dryly.

"Very carefully now," Helga whispered. They stole quietly to the outside edge of the archway.

"How are we going to see anything?" Asleif whispered.

Zack looked around for a vantage point.

How do we even know this is where we want to go?

As if in answer, a familiar voice came from the dining hall. "Fiends! You have no idea what you are doing!"

Jok. His low growl was unmistakable.

CHAPTER NINE

A booming giant's voice sounded right on top of Jok's. "Quiet!" It was followed by a loud crash and laughter.

Zack's insides quickened. His blood seemed to hurry on its way toward his thumping heart. His ears strained, working even harder than before, listening for anything more from Jok.

He's alive.

It was the first piece of good news in a long time.

"We can't just charge in," Hilda reasoned.

"And we can't stay here," Zack said. "Too exposed."

Helga slipped away from the group and looked inside. Her eyes went to something on the inside wall. She motioned for the others to follow, and disappeared around the corner of the archway.

Zack followed next. Staying low, he moved inside. It was a dangerous corner for them, but the giants' attention was well above their heads, on the food.

The hall was lit with wall-mounted torches as well as several elaborate candelabra that hung from the ceiling. Despite the warm glow, the feeling in the room was decidedly dangerous. No one was fighting, but these giants looked ready for anything. Even as they ate, most of them kept one hand on their swords. One giant with a missing eye paced back and forth, gnawing a piece of meat he had impaled on a hunting knife. The knife blade alone was the size of a surf-board.

It was hard to see much through the forest of giant legs. Zack looked around for Jok or any humans at all. The light was dim and the far side of the room, several football fields away, was in shadow. Anything on top of the tables was completely out of sight.

They must be up there somewhere.

"Psst," Helga whispered to him. He looked over and saw her standing behind a wall tapestry. It hung next to the entrance, its bottom edge nearly reaching the floor. Zack was too close to see the image it portrayed, but he could see that it loomed high over their heads. High enough to give them a view of the room, he realized. Helga had stepped in behind it and was climbing up, using the threads on the back like a ladder. Zack and the others soon followed.

The spiderweb of fibers made for difficult climbing. Zack's bulky frame didn't help. He stepped up and his arm slipped through a loop. He swung awkwardly before finding his footing again. Soon Helga, Hilda, Asleif, and Olaf were well ahead of him.

Olaf moved up the easiest, skillfully reaching from one strand of thread to the next with his thin fingers. Zack looked up, gauging their progress.

Just have to get high enough to check out the room.

WOOF!

What was that?

WOOF! WOOF!

Suddenly, an enormous wet nose pushed at the edge of the tapestry, directly across from Zack. It sniffed hungrily.

WOOF!

"Go!" Zack whispered fiercely to the others. They had already picked up their pace. Now there was a mad scramble to get up and out of reach of this dog that seemed to have jumped off an IMAX screen.

The barking turned to growling. Huge teeth clamped onto the edge of the tapestry. Zack pulled his foot free from a loop of thread just in time to avoid having it snapped off. The deep bass of the dog's growling vibrated in his chest. He reached up and pulled himself another rung higher just as the dog jumped. It nosed in behind the tapestry, pulling the fabric away from the stone wall.

Zack held on tight, feet flying loose. He braced himself as the tapestry whooshed back again. He heard a crunch of bodies and several stifled groans, including his own.

WOOF! WOOF!

Again the wet nose poked persistently in and out. One wrong move and they would all be Puppy Chow.

"Helga," he whispered up. "Hand me your sword."

Helga hooked her knees into two loops and hung upside down, handing her weapon over. Zack took it gently and waited for the next sight of the dog's invading snout.

WOOF!

He shut his eyes and thrust the sword. It made contact

with a small, sickening crunch. The dog let out an eardrum-shattering yelp and pulled back. Its whines grew fainter as it ran off to some unknown corner.

Sorry, pooch.

It felt kind of cheap to poke a dog in the nose, even one the size of a T-rex. But at least they were safe to keep climbing now.

Finally, they came to the top. Zack poked his head out and surveyed the room.

It didn't take long to find Jok. He was shouting from where he stood at the end of a long, food-laden table. In front of him was a giantess seated in an elaborately carved chair.

"You have precious little time to waste!" Jok yelled up at the woman. His face was drawn but he stood as strong as a marble statue, shaking his fist in the air. The stature, the red beard, the gut—they were all the same as Jock Gilman. But it was Jok. Zack reached out to him with his thoughts.

We're coming. I don't know how, but we're coming.

"Silence, human!" screamed the giantess. She slapped her short sword on the table next to Jok. Jok didn't flinch.

She was a large woman even for a giant, almost as big across as she was tall. The scowl on her face looked as though it had been there for a long time. Her dark hair was wound in a tight braided arrangement that wrapped around her head like a helmet.

"What do we think?" she said to several others clustered around her, peering at Jok. "Slaves? Or soup?"

"Why not both?" offered one young giant, leaning in for a closer look. "Let them fight among themselves. Those left standing shall be slaves. The rest will make a nice soup."

The giantess reached up in a blur of motion and caught the younger one in the face with the flat of her sword. He reeled back, with a hand to his cheek.

"Your breath offends," she said. "Stay well back."

"Forgive me, Sottar," said the young one through gritted teeth.

Jok growled out his frustration. "Don't you see what time you're wasting?"

Sottar looked down her considerable nose. "This, from a human stupid enough to burn his own ship on the shores of Jotunheim?"

"That wasn't my ship!" Jok growled. "How many times must you hear this? It was already there, a wreckage. We were dropped onshore, and the wreckage was burned by our captors, to pull your attention to the east. As I speak, they are likely raiding your vaults from the west."

Zack's mind spun. So that's what Erik was up to.

Sottar laughed haughtily. "I doubt that. We have no word from my guards. And it amuses me that you think any humans could pose a threat." She turned to the room. "I can't decide if these humans are more stupid, ugly, or funny. Hmm?" Everyone around her laughed nervously. A few reflexively covered their nearest cheek.

"You are too sure of yourself," Jok said threateningly.

Sottar laughed harder and waved him away. One of her

servants picked Jok up between two fingers. She carried him, kicking and swinging, to a bucket at the far end of the table and dropped him in.

Sottar took a deep breath and rubbed her hands together. "I think it shall be soup, then. I don't want to listen to these humans any longer than I have to. Put some water on to boil."

Zack stared at the bucket. A rabble of voices came from inside. His mind leapfrogged from Jok to Sven to Lars, Sigurd, Harald, and all the others. He could only hope the whole tribe was still there.

With another wave of Sottar's hand, the same servant picked up the bucket, carried it to the hearth, and set it on the floor among the cooking supplies. As Zack watched in horror, a cauldron of water was placed over the fire.

He realized suddenly that Hilda, Helga, Asleif, and Olaf were next to him. All of them had been watching. They ducked behind the tapestry again.

"We have to get them out," Zack whispered. "Now."

"If we can get over there and find some rope," Helga whispered. "We might be able to—"

Zack pointed at the loops of thread holding their feet. "Rope." There was miles of it woven into the tapestry. And the crates and sacks of supplies next to the hearth would provide some cover once they got there. What they didn't have was time.

The twins immediately began cutting sections of the thick thread with their swords. Zack looked out again while Asleif and Olaf began tying the pieces together.

The bucket looked to be about twenty feet high, in human terms. And there were probably—hopefully—two dozen or more of the tribe inside. "Make as much as you can," he whispered back down to the others.

A new giant's voice broke above the crowd noise in the dining hall.

"Sottar, Sottar, Sottar. I see you've made yet another in your long history of foolish mistakes."

Zack looked over and saw a giant man standing with several others around him in the entryway. He had a round face and a scrubby beard that hung to his chest. His dark eyes shot daggers of contempt in Sottar's direction.

"Aflun. Humph." Sottar's face was pinched, as if she smelled something foul. "I knew it was only a matter of time before you came crawling back."

"I crawl for no one, Sottar," Aflun said. He hawked something up and spit it on the floor. Several of Sottar's guards growled in response. They drew their swords and tightened their formation around where she remained seated.

Aflun walked casually to the hearth, took an apple from a bowl, and bit into it. He glanced down into the bucket. "I heard you had some humans," he said through a mouthful. "I am here to warn you."

"Warn me?" she said with a snort.

"Yes," Aflun said. "You may hold sway over Utgard for now, but your support is weak. Your first mistake was taking it, like the common thief you are—"

Several of Sottar's people rushed forward. Aflun's did the

same. They faced off in the middle of the room, each side holding its ground, not attacking, but snarling at each other like two packs of dogs.

"My people beg to differ," Sottar said calmly.

"As I was saying," Aflun went on, "you may hold Utgard, but you do not have the right to endanger all of Jotunheim."

Again Sottar snorted. "Endanger? How? By taking on a few humans?"

"Humans are bad luck," Aflun said. "I dislike them as much as you. They are vermin and scavengers." He turned to the room, speaking to everyone like a lawyer in front of a jury. "But they are also friends of the gods. Thor protects Midgard and its people as if they were his own. All of the gods look well upon the humans, and I do not need to remind you that the gods are no friends of ours. No good can come of this."

"Aflun," spoke up one of Sottar's guards, "you always were a coward. Just like your father and his father . . ." A drinking horn flew across the room and hit the guard in the face.

Before a real brawl could start, Sottar halted them with a shout. "Stop! Aflun, take your men and go."

"I am telling you now." Aflun was seething. "Put a stop to this. Put the humans out to sea and send them back to Midgard."

"These clever humans whom you are so fond of burned their own ship," Sottar said. "They are bigger fools than you." A chorus of opposition sounded from Jok and his men. One of Sottar's soldiers kicked the bucket that held them. It teetered precariously, then righted itself.

"You would say anything to bring disfavor upon me," Sottar said.

"I would like nothing more," Aflun said. "But even more than I despise your ways, Sottar, I love Jotunheim. We cannot afford the wrath of Thor, I assure you."

Sottar laughed. "Aflun, thinking like that is exactly why I am sitting here now and you are standing there." She waved him off with her hand and turned away.

Zack watched as Aflun considered Sottar's dismissal. Meanwhile, his own mental gears were spinning wildly. Aflun turned to go.

Don't think about it, Gilman. Just do it.

He leaned over to Hilda and whispered as quickly as he could. "Get over to that bucket. I'll try to be back soon."

"What?" Hilda almost shouted. "Lost Boy, what are you—"

But there was no time to listen. Zack scrambled to the edge of the tapestry as Aflun marched past. The timing was going to have to be just right.

Now!

He jumped. For a sickening second, he was in free fall. Then he landed in a sea of rough cloth. He grabbed on and pulled himself as far into the folds of Aflun's cloak as he could. Aflun paused. Zack felt the forward movement stop, then start up again as Aflun strode out of the dining hall, apparently unaware that he now had a passenger.

CHAPTER TEN

Zack hung on blindly, whipping back and forth like human spaghetti. He had hoped to keep track of where they were going but that proved impossible inside the dark folds of Aflun's cloak. Mostly, he saw wool cloth, as the rough material scraped back and forth across his face.

Soon, he heard a door creak open and then slam shut. The chill of Utgard's vast corridors was replaced with the warmth of a more enclosed space. Zack's stomach lurched as Aflun removed the cloak and threw it across the room. The thick cloth cushioned Zack's fall as he hit the ground. It was like being thrown down a hill inside a pillow.

"Hello, sire." Zack heard the voice of a young boy. Then he heard feet shuffling and other noises he couldn't identify.

"Bring me something to drink and eat," Aflun growled. "Now!"

I guess catching him in a good mood is out of the question.

It was tempting to stay right where he was, but Zack knew he had to make a move. He crept slowly through the mass of cloth.

"How was the feast in Utgard?" asked the boy.

"Sottar is an idiot!" Aflun groused. "She thinks the humans are as dumb as they are small. With any luck, she'll choke to death on that soup."

Zack poked his head out far enough to see into the room. A young giant, only as tall as a house, was ladling stew into a swimming pool–sized bowl. The boy had thick red hair like Zack's, and an eager face. "So it's true?" he said. "Humans have actually come to Jotunheim?"

Aflun growled in response and accepted a drinking horn, which he guzzled.

Zack looked around for somewhere small, somewhere he couldn't be grabbed. The room was roughly round in shape, like the one they had seen earlier that day. Smoke from the hearth floated up through a roughly hewn hole in the ceiling.

"Sire! What's that?" Zack looked back to see the boy pointing straight at him. He froze.

Aflun peered over, squinting. Suddenly, his eyes grew wide. His eyebrows knit together, and his lips pulled back to reveal the biggest, yellowest teeth Zack had ever seen.

Zack unfroze. He scrambled to get free of the cloak just as Aflun snatched it off the ground. "Auuughh! They're everywhere!" shouted the giant.

Zack went tumbling across the dirt floor. He rolled over on his back in time to see the bottom of Aflun's shoe hanging over him.

Just like a cockroach.

"Wait!" Zack yelled as hard he could. He held his hands up, as if they could hold back a size 3,000 shoe. To his surprise, Aflun paused.

"Kill it, sire!" yelled the boy.

"Don't do it!" Zack countered, scrabbling backward out of

the shadow from Aflun's foot. "You said yourself. It's bad luck!"

Aflun cocked his head to the side and thought for a moment. His expression went from fierce, to puzzled—Zack breathed—and then back to fierce again. "Nah!" he said, and brought his foot down.

Zack threw himself to the side. He felt the breeze at his back as Aflun's foot slammed down next to him. He tried to roll farther away but he was stuck. The edge of his own cloak was trapped under the giant's shoe.

Zack shrugged the cloak off his shoulders and sprang to his feet in one motion. Aflun took a step forward and raised his back foot, poised for the mother of all field-goal kicks.

"I'm the Lost Boy!" Zack shouted. It came out of nowhere. He didn't even know if Aflun would understand. Or care.

Again, Aflun paused. He lowered his leg and regarded Zack skeptically. "The Lost Boy? You?"

"Yes," Zack spat out. "I can prove it. Look, here!" He clawed at his sweater and pulled out Yggdrasil's Key. "See?"

Aflun leaned way over and squinted at it. His foul breath blew over Zack like a rotten-egg windstorm. Zack held his ground. He looked Aflun in the eye.

"That's supposed to be Yggdrasil's Key?" Aflun said, wetting Zack's face with spittle. "It's a fake."

"No!" Zack said. "I can prove it."

At least, I hope I can prove it.

"Prove it how?" Aflun asked.

Zack gulped. "Try to take it."

Aflun laughed a wicked laugh. He seemed to almost be having fun now. "All right. But let us at least even the match a bit." He turned to the houseboy. "Take the key."

The boy came forward. "I've never seen a human before." He leaned down and looked at Zack.

Zack willed his hand to stay steady. "Go ahead." He braced himself.

The giant boy reached down. Using two fingers like tweezers, he grasped the key. Zack held as firmly as he could.

A jolt of electricity ran up Zack's arm. The giant boy stood frozen in place. His huge fingers seemed to be fused to the key and his eyes grew wide. When his hand began to shake, Zack flopped around like a rag doll, unable to let go of the key himself. The shaking moved up the boy's arm and into his body. He clenched his teeth as the invisible force surged. With an explosive finish, he launched into the air and sailed across the room. Zack shot back in the other direction, slamming into the far wall and then sliding back to the ground in a heap. The houseboy did the same, leaving a crack in the opposite wall big enough to drive a truck through.

Zack groaned.

Now I know what it's like to be a crash test dummy.

The boy looked dazed, but he was on his feet in a second with a grin on his face. "Can I do it again, sire?"

Aflun ignored him. He stared at Zack. "So the human is telling the truth."

"See?" Zack called, getting back to his feet.

"And are those your people back in Utgard?"

Zack nodded. "I'm here to get them."

Aflun frowned. "So it's worse than I thought."

"What do you mean?" Zack asked.

The giant began pacing. "Sottar is a bigger fool than she will ever know. Keeping humans is one thing. But the Lost Boy's tribe . . . This is bad. This is very bad."

"So will you help us?" Zack asked, running out of the way as Aflun paced by him.

"Help you how?"

"All I'm asking," Zack said, "is for you to throw up a distraction. Just give us a chance to get away. That's all. Go back in there and . . ." Zack threw a few punches at the air, pretty sure that "kick some butt" wouldn't mean anything to Aflun if he said it.

Aflun, however, looked unconvinced. He seemed to be deep in his own thought.

"You said you wanted to get Utgard back," Zack continued. "Maybe now's the time."

Aflun stopped pacing. He stared at the floor for a moment, stroking his wiry beard. Then he jumped back to life and picked up his tremendous sword. "Find my men," he told the houseboy. "Tell them to meet me outside the dining hall."

"All of them, sire?" said the boy.

Aflun nodded. "Now."

The boy was gone in a moment.

"And what about you?" Aflun said, turning his attention

to Zack. "How do you propose to leave this place?"

"We've got a ship back at the shore. We'll be out of Jotunheim before you know it."

Aflun thought some more. "Fair enough. But if we find you here again—"

Zack held up a hand to cut him off. "You won't."

∾⌒

Zack rode Aflun's shoulder back into the halls of Utgard. He held on to a long strand of hair to keep from falling while he spoke into Aflun's ear.

"Just get near that bucket and give me a chance to climb off. That's all I need."

Several dozen of Aflun's men were waiting for them in the corridor. Aflun conferred in hushed tones while Zack climbed down into the giant's cloak once again, where he wouldn't be seen.

He took a deep breath, steeling himself for whatever was about to happen. Jok would have been able to stay calm here. For that matter, Zack realized, so would his father. This would be like a game to Jock Gilman.

Get in. Get them out. And . . . run like crazy.

It wasn't exactly something out of his father's football playbook, but it was going to have to be good enough.

A moment later, he felt Aflun on the move again as they entered the dining hall.

"Sottar!" Aflun's roar echoed, even inside the cloak.

Sottar's voice followed. "Aflun, what are you doing back here? I'm going to lose my patience."

130

"You'll lose more than that, by the time this night is through," Aflun threatened.

Zack watched the stone floor move by below him. He let himself down to the edge of Aflun's cloak, hand over hand, his arm muscles straining.

There it was. The wooden bucket passed through his limited field of vision, too fast to see if anyone was inside. Aflun came to a stop next to a nearby stack of crates.

"I have decided this has gone on long enough," said Aflun.

"And what does that mean?" Sottar asked.

With the tower of Aflun's leg between himself and the rest of the room, Zack hung down and dropped the last several feet to the floor.

"It means," Aflun continued, "that this is your last night in Utgard." He strode away as Zack slipped into the shadow between two crates and the high wall of the bucket. No other humans were in sight. The hearth fire was blazing nearby. Steam wafted from the big iron cauldron.

Zack watched as Aflun stopped at the far end of the long table where Sottar sat. She looked bored. "Take him away," she ordered.

She had barely said it when Aflun reached down and grabbed hold of the table. With a bellow, he flung it aside. Bowls, plates, jugs, and mounds of food went crashing to the floor. "Now!" he shouted, and the battle began.

Zack tore his attention from the action overhead and worked his way around the bucket. To his intense relief, he found Hilda, Helga, Asleif, and Olaf working in the shadow of a large sack next to the hearth.

Olaf jumped up and down when he saw Zack. Asleif grabbed his arm. "Where have you been?" she said. Zack could barely hear anything over the clashing of giant swords, and the cursing and shouting.

Hilda and Helga remained focused, tying knots and finishing off the stack of makeshift rope. They looked up at Zack and nodded eagerly, but kept working.

"We'll need something to weight these ropes, for throwing," Helga said.

Asleif pointed to where several giant onions had spilled from another nearby sack. Hilda rolled one over and began hacking at it with her sword. The fumes wafted up right away. A sharp burning sensation took hold of Zack's eyes.

Onions. It had to be onions.

They squinted at one another, working as quickly as possible. Zack wiped at the uncontrollable tears with his sleeve.

Olaf alone seemed unaffected, his red eyes unchanged. He took Helga's sword and used it to shish-kebab two bowling ball–sized pieces of onion. Then he quickly threaded each with a length of rope and tied them off.

"Throw, now. Go," he shouted above the noise.

Zack held the thread-rope loosely in one hand and threw the weighted end up and over the bucket's edge. Several feet wound out of his hand as someone on the other side grabbed it and pulled. Zack, Hilda, Helga, and Olaf held on to their end of the rope to anchor it. Asleif, meanwhile, picked up a second rope and threw it in.

The cord bit into Zack's hands. He held on tightly, ignoring the pain, and waiting to see who was climbing up the other side.

Jok's face appeared, his expression stony. He was in battle mode. As his eyes met Zack's, a hint of elation crossed his features, but he remained focused. He motioned to the others still inside, making sure they all made it to the floor before he finally flipped over the top of the bucket and let himself down.

In a moment, his huge arms encased Zack in a bear hug. "I knew you'd be back," he said, close at Zack's ear. Zack's heart thumped like it wanted to jump from his own chest into Jok's. He had no words, much less time, to say what he was thinking. It was as if he had just been reunited with his own father.

Immediately Jok, along with Sigurd, Lars, Harald, and Sven, fell right to the task of getting everyone ready to move on. The giant fight continued all around them.

Zack turned to Harald, who was next to him. "Is everyone still with you guys?" he shouted.

Harald nodded grimly. "We are all here."

Zack smiled in relief.

Once the whole group was ready, Hilda pointed them toward the main archway. Gargantuan shifting feet and falling giant bodies had turned the room into a massive sudden-death obstacle course. They were going to have to make a run for it. The tribe spread out and sprinted for the hallway.

The mixture of danger and joy energized Zack in a way he

had never felt before. Freeing the tribe was like medicine for his tired system. His senses ratcheted up. He dodged and weaved across the dining-hall floor, as light on his feet as he had ever been.

"Faster!" Asleif shouted. She was at his side. He grabbed her hand.

"This way," they both shouted at the same time, and pulled in opposite directions. Their grasp broke just as a giant spear crashed to the ground between them. They ran alongside it toward the door, their eyes still on each other. Zack looked back to see the spear's owner clutching his gut and stumbling like a wounded Godzilla in the other direction.

As they neared the arch, a shadow crossed the floor. They both looked up and saw the round frame of a candelabra hurtling downward. Asleif dove. Instinctively, Zack froze with his arms at his sides and the whole thing crashed around him like a huge iron fence.

He opened his eyes, not even realizing he had shut them. *Still alive. Amazing.*

Asleif was standing at the archway, eyes wide. She beckoned Zack on while several tribe members streamed past her out into the hall. Zack climbed over the bent iron frame and sprinted the last twenty yards to where she stood. They ducked out of the dining hall, with the giants' brawl still raging behind them.

Zack leaned onto his knees, catching his breath. He felt hands slapping his back and squeezing his shoulder. When he stood up, he saw Harald and Lars grinning at him, almost calmly.

"What took you so long?" Lars asked sarcastically.

"We're very disappointed in you, Lost Boy," Harald added.

Zack took a gulp of air and burped in their faces. All three of them burst out laughing. For about five seconds, Zack let himself forget that they weren't even halfway out of danger.

Olaf poked a bony finger into Zack's side. "Is good time to go," he muttered.

"Olaf's right," Jok said. "It's only a matter of time before they realize what's happened."

The tribe turned and ran in a long line down the edge of the deserted corridor. Hilda and Jok debriefed each other as they ran. "We can slip out through the wall," Hilda said. "It's filled with holes. Just around the corner here, near the main gate."

"What about the vaults?" Jok shouted back. "How do we get down below this level?"

"We'll regroup with the rest of my tribe, get fresh volunteers, and come back," Hilda answered. Jok gave one sharp nod of his head.

Zack couldn't believe what he was hearing. Even now, they were thinking about Yggdrasil's Treasure.

Here's a different idea. Let's get the heck out of this place and never come back.

A booming sound echoed in the corridor.

"What's that?" Sven said.

"Someone's coming," Helga whispered back

A long shadow emerged from a side passage just ahead. Before the tribe could run past, Sottar loomed out in front of them. She stood with arms folded, the corners of her gigantic mouth turned down.

"Well, what have we here?"

"Go back, Sottar," Jok yelled. "You have more important business to attend to."

"I think not." She advanced slowly, backing them all up against the wall of the passage with feet that may as well have been steamrollers. She leaned down and easily plucked Jok out from the group. "You again," she said bitterly. Her huge fist closed around him as he struggled to get free.

"Go!" Jok grunted down to the others. Sottar, however, put out one foot and pushed the tribe into a tighter cluster. Half a dozen Viking soldiers crashed into the rest of the group as the side of her shoe pounded into them.

"Have you ever seen a human explode?" Sottar said to Jok, holding him up close to her face. Zack could hear Jok wheezing. He said something Zack couldn't understand, and Sottar laughed. "Of course," she said, "you won't see it this time either." She held him out in front of the tribe. "But they will." Jok's face was purple, the rest of his body encased in her grip.

Zack pushed his way to the front.

They weren't going to lose Jok like this. Not now. Not ever.

"Wait!" he shouted. His voice came out as big as his father's after a Minnesota touchdown. The tribe around him grew still. Even Sottar stopped and looked down.

"Sottar," he yelled, "I have an offer for you."

She looked almost amused. "Oh, you do?"

Zack reached for the key around his neck. There was no fear, no reservation, just a clear sense of purpose. "Yggdrasil's Key," he said, holding it up. "Let us go and it's yours."

Even from the floor, Zack could see the greed in Sottar's eyes. Her basketball-sized pupils flared at the sight of the key. "So it's the famous Lost Boy," she said.

"Zack, no!" Jok yelled. His voice was clear now. Sottar had obviously loosened her grip.

Zack barely heard him. Anything he felt for the key, and the quest, dropped away at the harsh possibility of losing Jok.

"Take it," he said.

Sottar's eyes narrowed. "How do I know you are giving it willingly?" she asked.

"I'm telling you now," Zack said. "Take it. It's yours." Again, he held the key up in the air. Sottar reached for it.

"Wait," Zack said. "Put him down first."

Sottar's eyes stayed on the key. She reached down and dropped Jok to the floor like an old toy. He collapsed for a moment, with a hand to his chest, but then leapt back up. "Zack, stop this, right now. Do you hear me?"

Sottar put a big foot in Jok's way. She grinned at Zack. "My good fortune," she said, bending toward him, "is that I can have the key and still do as I will with you. You'll be soup yet."

"What?" A lightning bolt of anger hit Zack as her giant fingers closed around the key.

No. Forget it. No deal.

"No!" he shouted.

His mind changed like a switch, and the key's electricity came alive. Sottar's face froze. Her hand began to shake. Zack braced himself. It was almost worse, knowing what was about to happen.

Panic crossed Sottar's features as the tremor in her arm grew. She was across the corridor before Zack even saw her explode backward. His own body blew the other way, straight through the tribe, taking them down one row after the other until no one was left standing.

The corridor wall didn't have a chance against Sottar. It gave way like a stack of cardboard boxes when she hit it. Dust, mortar, and chunks of stone tumbled everywhere. A great section of the ceiling broke free, slammed to the floor, and kept going. Sottar slid into the newly formed chasm, coming to rest on a great slope of rubble that led down to whatever chamber may have been below.

For a moment the tribe stood still.

Zack stood up slowly, rubbing his arm. "I have got to find another way of doing that," he muttered.

"Is she dead?" Hilda asked. All they could see in the clearing dust were the bottoms of Sottar's feet.

Jok moved closer and peered inside. He shook his head. "Just out like a torch," he whispered. "But I do believe we've found our way down to the vaults."

CHAPTER ELEVEN

Jok came over and took Zack by the shoulders. "You must never sacrifice the key, do you understand? Never."

"What?" Zack said. It definitely wasn't the reaction he had been expecting.

Saved your life, Jok—you're welcome.

Jok spoke firmly but without anger. "Always remember that the prophecy exists above all. No person, not even this entire tribe, is more important than what you have around your neck. Do you understand?"

"But—"

"Do you understand?" Jok repeated.

Zack was surprised to feel a lump rise in his throat. He couldn't imagine ever sacrificing Jok, or anyone, even for this.

"We have to keep moving," Helga interrupted.

Jok nodded in agreement. "If Erik finds the first treasure, we'll be chasing him instead of leading this quest as we should be doing." He grasped Zack at the elbow and wrist, and shook his hand. Zack swallowed hard. "On we go," said Jok.

They quickly climbed down the pile of rubble. The tribe swarmed over Sottar's unconscious body, holding on to her clothing like climbing ropes. At the bottom, one of her braids hung loose to the floor. Zack and Asleif stepped onto her left ear, grabbed onto the braid, and slid down one at a time.

Zack dropped to the dirt floor and looked around. They were in another corridor, similar to the one above, but with natural stone walls. It seemed to be carved right into the mountain. Torches were mounted along the way, illuminating the passage. Not far ahead, it wound to the left and out of sight. The pile of rubble behind them made their choice clear.

"Only one way to go," Jok said, and they set off. Overhead, the sounds of the ongoing battle rumbled on. With Sottar out cold, it was a good bet that Aflun would take back Utgard.

The corridor was blank stone for several hundred yards, winding back and forth somewhere beneath the fortress. "I believe we're heading west," Helga whispered. "Erik may well have come in from the other direction."

As they got to the next bend, Jok pulled up short, stopping their progress.

Zack peered around the corner and saw a huge door standing open. Voices sounded from inside. Human voices.

In the corridor, three giant guards lay on the ground, several enormous keys scattered around them. Zack could also see a tall human with his back to the door, waving his arms. He seemed to be conducting a yellow-gray cloud that hung over the unconscious guards. They were snoring loudly, and the man seemed intent on his work. When he turned to check nervously over his shoulder, his long thin face was exactly that of Zack's principal, Mr. Ogmund.

"Ogmunder!" Zack whispered.

"Yes," said Olaf, peeking through Zack's legs. "Is Ogmunder."

Zack had never seen the wizard before, but his reputation preceded him. Just like Principal Ogmund, Ogmunder the Wizard was said to be self-serving, only so-so at his job, and firmly under Erik's thumb. A well of contempt bubbled up in Zack as he watched Ogmunder working.

Erik the Horrible's voice echoed from the chamber beyond. He was murmuring to himself. "I don't know what is taking them so infernally long." He strode out into the corridor, followed by his right-hand ogre, Orn. "How long can you keep them asleep?" he asked Ogmunder.

Ogmunder stayed focused on his work. "We've got some time. But I would suggest you go as quickly as you can."

"What do you think we're doing?" Erik spat back. "Those keys are enormous. It takes ten men just to unlock one door. And there are dozens of doors to be tried yet. He thumped the ground with his staff, a rod that was taller than himself, topped by a metal torch in the shape of a skull. It looked like a human head, burning from the inside.

At Erik's side, Orn held an axe in one hand and a smaller torch in the other. The hand holding the torch was attached to Orn's new arm. Zack smiled, remembering how the old one had come off. The new arm had a peach fuzz of hair over a layer of pale yellowish skin. The rest of Orn was entirely covered in dark fur. The new arm, it seemed, was not taking too well to its owner.

Nonetheless, Orn held fast to the torch as he hovered

about. Erik murmured something to Orn, who turned and dragged one of the huge keys back inside. Erik followed behind and began shouting orders again.

Jok was already giving instructions of his own. "Leave the wizard. Let him do his work for now." He pointed to two members of his tribe, instructing them, "You keep an eye on him. Make sure he stays put. The rest of you, we go in fast, catch them unaware. Take what weapons you can. We'll need them."

Everyone nodded their assent, and Jok turned to Zack. "You need to stay back here out of sight."

Zack opened his mouth to speak. He wanted to be personally responsible for instructing Erik in the fine art of eating dirt.

"No," Jok interceded firmly. "Has Erik seen you since you returned?"

Zack shook his head.

"We will be better off keeping it that way."

It was hard to argue. Erik probably wanted Zack's key more than anything.

"They can't have found the first treasure yet," Hilda said. "They would be gone if they had."

"Do we wait for them to find it?" Helga asked. "Or go straight in?"

In answer, Jok began a low roar. Several others joined in right away. In a moment, the tribe raced headlong into the vault chamber.

Zack reached out to hold Asleif back with him. She evaded his grasp and rushed with the others into the group of surprised-looking Bear soldiers.

Ogmunder looked back behind him in alarm as they charged. He cowered but the tribe had passed by in a moment. Zack watched him turn nervously back toward the sleeping guards. His arms shook while he worked, and the yellow-gray cloud began to shrink almost immediately.

Zack's determination to hang back lasted less than a minute. Standing there uselessly in the shadows of the corridor was more than he could stand. He watched to make sure Ogmunder's back was to him once again, then stealthily whisked into the vault chamber.

The chamber itself was another great, long, giant-sized hallway, lined with dozens of wooden doors along either side.

These must be the vaults. How many do they need?

Several of the doors nearest Zack were already open. He stepped in behind the closest one. The vault beyond was filled with armor and fighting equipment, all of it size extra-extra-extra-extra large. He quickly turned his attention to the fighting at the far end of the chamber.

Jok and the others clearly had surprise on their side. It looked as if they had taken down an entire pile of soldiers. One of the keys was fitted into an unopened door, with a heavy skirmish directly beneath.

Jok had two Bears by the scruff of the neck. He pulled them together, crashing their heads like cymbals. As they collapsed to the floor, he pulled the swords from their sheaths, one with each hand, and tossed one to Sven nearby. All in one motion.

Jok's fighting was smooth and assured, like a great athlete. Zack pumped his fist at his side in a moment of celebration, just like his father had done after countless plays at countless games.

Farther down, Erik had apparently beaten a hasty retreat. He ducked behind a wall of guards at the far end. The guards stood firm, their swords poised. Next to Erik, behind them, was what looked like Yggdrasil's Chest.

So Erik did have the chest. At least for the moment.

"Ogmunder!" Erik yelled from his spot. "Do something! Put them to sleep."

Ogmunder cast an annoyed glance over his shoulder into the doorway. "I'm a potions man," he called out, "not a magician. Everything I've brought is out here." He stopped and looked back, then yelled out again. "And that won't last much longer."

Zack rocked on the balls of his feet. It was all he could do not to rush into the battle. Before he knew what he was doing, he slipped past the open door where he stood, and ran to hide behind the next one down the line, and then the next. At least he could get a closer look at what was going on.

Bzzzzz. As he moved past one of the open vaults, something vibrated against his chest. He looked down and a soft glow seemed to emanate from underneath his sweater.

It was the key.

Oh no. Don't send me back now.

Zack looked up again. The two tribes were locked in battle, still some distance away.

He squeezed his eyes shut and waited to be hurtled forward to the twenty-first century again. But nothing happened. What was going on? Then he realized—the key had never done this before. It had gotten hot when he traveled through time. But this was different. He stared down at it. The glow and vibration were light, steady, and unchanging. Not sure what else to do, he pushed on.

Zack crept closer to the fighting, slipping over to stand behind the next open door. As he moved, the vibration and light from the key cut off. It went still against his chest.

Huh?

He stepped back, retreating to the previous doorway. And the key sprang once again to life.

Cool.

Zack stepped into the dark chamber. Unlike the other vaults, this one looked to be empty, but it was so dark, he couldn't tell. The torchlight from the hallway outside showed him only a few feet of smooth stone floor.

Another faint light caught his eye. Just a glint, straight ahead.

Zack took several steps toward it. The light grew brighter. He moved backward and the light diminished.

Got it.

He plunged into the vault. Whatever the key was trying to tell him, it seemed worth finding out. He took it off and held it out like a flashlight.

He could see ten yards or more ahead. Farther away, he could see now that whatever was glowing was mounted to the far wall, deep inside. It was vaguely round in shape, and it gave off the same sort of light that was coming from his key.

With every step, the brightness inside the chamber increased. As it did, Zack's pace quickened, along with his heart.

This could be it. This could be it.

Yggdrasil's Treasure. This could be the first of them. He began to make out some details.

It was a helmet. Human size. It wasn't mounted to the wall after all but sat on its own low pedestal. It looked tiny all alone in the middle of this vast chamber.

The helmet was all in gold, carved with the shape of feathered wings on the side. It was much more ornate than a battle helmet. Some kind of ceremonial piece, maybe. And solid gold, almost definitely.

This had to be it.

Zack squinted as the glow from the helmet grew. It was like staring into a truck's headlights. Likewise, the key sent back its own intense beacon, so bright now that it was difficult for Zack to keep his eyes open. The vibration picked up as well, reverberating through his arms and body, with a high singing tone he could feel as much as hear.

He sensed he was almost to the helmet. No doubt there was going to be some trick to lifting it off its pedestal. Bright light or not, this was all too easy.

Then his foot hit air. He stopped short and took a step back. It was impossible to see what kind of drop-off was in front of him. A few inches? A hundred feet?

He got down on all fours and felt along the edge. The

floor definitely dropped away here. The helmet was on the other side of a gap way too big to step over.

But maybe not too big to jump.

He felt around for stones he could throw to gauge the distance, but found nothing on the smooth cave floor. Outside, he could still hear shouts. The battle was on, and none of them knew that what they were fighting for was right here.

Zack took a dozen large strides away from the helmet. The glow diminished, giving him a better sense of the gap.

Too big.

No, it's not. Just do it.

Too big.

Shut up—go.

Go.

He tucked the key back inside his sweater. Without another thought, he rushed forward, sprinting as hard as he could. The light flared up fast, blinding him. His boots skidded to a halt on the floor. Where was the edge? This was going to be even harder than he thought if he didn't know when to leap.

He turned around and took a few practice jumps in the opposite direction. Maybe they were long enough, maybe they weren't.

Jock Gilman had always told Zack he was a football star just waiting to happen. Zack mulled his father's words over. How many times had Jock said it? Zack had the natural strength, the height, the weight. Great for football, wrestling, rugby maybe.

But long jump?

The more he thought, the more impossible it seemed.

The ceiling overhead rumbled. The giants' battle upstairs was still on. And Zack could hear the clashing of swords and shouting between the Bears and his tribe just outside the vault door.

One thing was for sure: waiting around was not going to help.

Now or never, Gilman.

He felt his way to the edge of the gap, toeing the drop-off. Then he turned away from it and ran, counting his strides.

One two three four five six seven eight, nine, ten, eleven, twelve, thirteen . . .

Fourteen strides. His age. It was as good a number as any.

He took a step backward.

Plus one for luck.

He took a breath.

Okay. Ready?

On the count of three.

One, two—

And he was off. If he waited until three, he never would have gone.

His strides measured the floor.

One two three four five six seven eight nine ten eleven twelve thirteen—

fourteenJUMP!

Zack catapulted himself over the gap, into a brightness so hot he could feel himself passing through it. He cranked his legs in the air. He pinwheeled his arms. Reaching. Hoping.

His arms slammed onto a ledge. His legs flopped against a vertical surface. The helmet glowed directly overhead.

The ledge that had him was precipitously narrow, about as deep as a single bookshelf cut into the cave wall. Getting onto it was going to be a good trick. If he could even hold on long enough.

And even before that, an unwelcome realization reared its ugly head. He hadn't thought about how he was going to get back. Bookshelves didn't offer much room for a running start.

The commander in his brain took over.

Save your neck now, Gilman. Worry later. Pull!

He forced the energy in his legs, his gut, his chest, all into his arms. He leaned into the ledge and pulled himself up onto it by a few inches. His feet leveraged against the hard wall below, helping him bring his body just a bit higher.

The brightness in the room grew, if that was possible. All Zack could see of the helmet was a white core of light.

He focused. He pulled himself up another inch. The helmet—the place where the helmet seemed to be—was within reach. The key sang like an opera star in his head, one high, clear note.

It made no sense in the world for Zack to let go of the ledge and reach for the helmet. But he did it anyway. It was almost as if the helmet were reaching out for him, and he gave in to an overwhelming urge to respond.

He reached up and put a hand on it. As soon he did, the light all around him dissipated to a soft glow. The helmet was surprisingly cool to the touch. The key's vibration softened down to nothing, almost like a sigh. And then, most surprisingly of all, the helmet floated up into the air. And Zack floated up along with it.

No way. NO. WAY.

Zack reached up farther and instinctively mashed the helmet onto his head. It stuck there with a strong, almost magnetic force. He rose several more feet.

I'm flying. Check. It. Out. I am totally flying.

He looked down, where he was suspended, unmoving in midair.

Well, okay. I'm floating.

In the soft light, he could just make out the floor of the pit, some fifty feet below. It was littered with what looked like human remains. Several skeletons lay on the ground, most of them at the base of the pit wall closest to the vault entrance. Without the key, Zack realized, he might not have slowed down enough to avoid walking right into the pit, there in the darkness.

Thanks.

Crazy to thank a key, but he did anyway, at least in his mind. That key had saved his life more than once.

Now, could you maybe get me over there?

Zack looked across the pit to solid ground. Next problem—how did he navigate this thing? Keeping one hand on the helmet, just in case, he leaned forward in the direction he wanted to go. His body lurched in the air, and he sped across the gap. Another twenty yards of floor sped by beneath his feet before they caught the ground and he came down with a rolling tumble.

We'll have to work on the driving later.

He was back up and at the vault entrance in a moment. Before he got there, he could hear Ogmunder shouting frantically.

"Time to go!"

The battle between the two tribes had stopped, at least for the moment. Jok and Erik were conferring in the center of the chamber, each of them flanked by his own soldiers, with several yards of space between the two sides.

Zack looked over to where Ogmunder and the sleeping guards were. The yellowish cloud that hung over them was down to the size of a loaf of bread. Ogmunder was waving his arms at it desperately.

Jok spoke to Erik, but loudly enough for everyone to hear. "You have the chest," he said. "Neither of us has the treasure."

Zack wanted to shout out. He kept his tongue.

"We are clearly running out of time." Jok pointed to where the giant guards were beginning to stir. "If we don't leave soon, it won't matter who has what. We'll all be finished."

Erik sneered. "You have a good point. And besides," he said, patting the chest, which was surrounded by six of his men, "I am still one step ahead of you."

Jok continued. "I say we leave now, and settle our differences once we're well clear of Jotunheim."

"Augh!" Ogmunder screamed. One of the giants rolled over, his hand nearly hammering the wizard into the ground like a nail. What was left of the little cloud popped like a bubble, sending a small shower of ash down over the giants. One of them groaned and rubbed lazily at his eyes.

"I agree to your terms," Erik said quickly, and turned to Orn. "Orn, you are the last one out. I want to make sure these people aren't coming back for anything." He looked spitefully at Jok.

Orn nodded nervously, eyeballing the giants, who were now half-awake.

Zack pressed back farther into the shadows while the two tribes moved quickly out of the vaults, peeling off into the corridor in opposite directions. Better to get Erik out of the way before catching up with his own tribe.

It was difficult to watch Yggdrasil's Chest slip away from them like this. But Jok was right. Another few minutes, and none of it would matter. As soon as Orn was out of the way, Zack would make a break for it.

As the last of the soldiers moved out, another of the sleeping giants stretched, yawned and rolled over, pinning Orn. Orn disappeared briefly, then emerged, grunting and struggling from underneath the giant's leg. He shouted for the others to help, but no one stopped. Zack held back, unsure what to do.

Finally, Orn writhed his way out. He jumped to his feet. "Ha!" he said, defiantly kicking at one of the giant's fingers. Then a baleful look came over his face. He looked down at his own shoulder. His new arm was gone.

"Not again!" he screamed. He leaned over, trying to see under the giant, where Orn's arm was no doubt mashed into the dirt. Orn stomped the ground and shook his one fist in the air, shouting curses. Suddenly, he stopped short. He looked in both directions at the empty corridor.

"Wait!" he yelled. "Wait for me!" His voice echoed against the cold stone as he ran off in the direction of his tribe.

So much for Orn being the last one out. Zack stepped out of his hiding place and caught up with the others.

"Jok!"

Jok turned and looked to where Zack stood, holding the helmet. "Is that . . ."

Zack nodded.

"Did you . . ."

He nodded again.

"Then we . . ."

It was the first time Zack had ever seen Jok at a loss for words. The tribe let up a collective shout, filling the void. They crowded in on Zack to get a closer look. Zack held the helmet out for everyone to see.

"Thor is smiling on us today," Jok said, finally coming up with a whole sentence. He went down on one knee and the rest of the tribe did the same, in a circle around Zack.

"Hail the Lost Boy," Jok called.

"Hail the Lost Boy," they all replied.

"Hail Yggdrasil's Key," said Jok.

"Hail Yggdrasil's Key."

Zack was only slightly more accustomed to this treatment than the last time it had happened. Even after everything he had been through, it always felt as if they must have mistaken him for someone else. Luckily, they had little time to spare. The tribe was quickly on its feet and back to business.

When they arrived at the rubble pile, Sottar was gone.

"That could be good news or bad news," Zack said to Olaf as they climbed up toward ground level. Olaf barely responded. His eyes were glued to the treasure under Zack's arm.

When they arrived at the ground level, a long line of giant soldiers ran past, toward the main gates. The level of activity was high, but the feeling in Utgard seemed to have changed. The battle was over. In the ongoing excitement, no one seemed to notice the band of tiny humans slipping through the many holes in the fortress's external wall.

Outside, Aflun presided over what looked like a trial of some sort. A great kettle of water had been set up over a roaring fire. In the middle of a ring of soldiers were Sottar and several of her people. Each of them was bound at the wrists and kneeling in the snow.

"We will discover your innocence or guilt," Aflun was saying. "Reach into the cauldron and remove a stone. The innocent will be unburned, and the guilty will be punished."

Zack whispered to Asleif as they moved in small groups away from the fortress. "That seems kind of harsh."

"It is the way," Asleif whispered back. "Jok has presided over many such ceremonies in Lykill."

Zack looked back at the giants once more. "Good luck,"

he whispered, and then ran to catch up with Jok.

Jok eyed the helmet solemnly as they moved along. "We owe much to you, Zack," he said.

Zack shrugged. "Hilda and Helga were the ones who got us as far as we did."

Jok nodded slowly and looked into Zack's eyes. He obviously wasn't so convinced. "And it was no one but yourself who recovered this." He pointed to the helmet.

Zack didn't respond. But Jok was right. He actually had done that himself.

"I wish we could have gotten back Yggdrasil's Chest, though," Zack said.

Jok looked over at him, eyes wide. "What do you mean?"

"What do I mean?" Now it was Zack who stared. "What do you mean, what do I mean?"

Jok cocked his head. Both walked in silence trying to figure the other out.

"The chest," Zack said finally. "Erik left with Yggdrasil's Chest. We still have to get it back."

Jok breathed in suddenly. "Ah, yes, you don't know, do you?"

"Don't know what?" Confused as Zack was, Jok's manner had good news written all over it.

"That wasn't Yggdrasil's Chest," Jok said. "It was one of our decoys."

"But I thought they took it from the *Winniferd*—" Zack stopped short. It didn't do any good to remind Jok about his lost ship right now. But Jok seemed unperturbed.

"When Erik attacked, we bound up the chest with an anchor and some cord. Thor willing, it still sits at the bottom of the lake where we were captured."

"But then, when did they get that one . . . ?" An image flashed in Zack's mind. The decoy chest he had been carrying, falling into the river, bobbing downstream. Toward the falls. "Where were they hiding when they attacked you?" he asked.

"Off the lake, in an inlet just downstream from Baklav's Falls," Jok said. "He called us fools for losing the chest. Chided us as idiots, said he plucked it from the river like a fish. Of course we kept our mouths shut. He never even looked for the real one because he thought he already had it. So who's the fool, huh?"

Zack was stunned into silence.

Talk about turning bad luck into good.

Jok looked down at him. "I don't suppose you have any idea how it ended up in the river to begin with?"

Zack looked over at Olaf, who looked back. The troll's face turned curious. He didn't seem to understand why Zack was staring at him, grinning like someone who had just pulled a winning lottery ticket out of the trash.

CHAPTER TWELVE

The tribe hurried toward the eastern shore as night turned into gray dawn. Zack managed to find and say hello to everyone he knew. Each of them was almost as happy to see the golden helmet in Zack's hands as they were to see Zack himself.

"You'll have stories to tell, Lost Boy," Sven said happily, with an arm tightly around his neck. Lars and Harald crowded in on him as well. Sigurd, ever the silent one, marched happily along beside them.

"That's only one of three treasures," crowed Lars. He shook his head in mock frustration. "What about the other two, Lost Boy?"

Zack shrugged, playing along. "I'm working on it, okay?" He turned and bellied into Lars, knocking him off his feet and into the snow. Harald grabbed at his arm, and Zack turned expertly, hip-checking him to the ground.

"What was that about?" Jok yelled, coming up to them.

Harald and Lars looked up from where they sat. "It's nothing, Jok," Harald said. "We were just—"

"We are on a mission here," Jok said sternly. "Do I need to remind you of that?"

"Sorry," Zack said. "It's my fault, I—"

Jok threw his arms in the air with a huge laugh. He thrust

out his belly and knocked Zack backward over Lars and Harald. Now everyone was laughing. Jok reached down to help Zack up, with tears running down his cheeks. "We'll have to remember that move, Lost Boy. It may come in handy."

Zack smiled sheepishly. It would have been a proud moment for his father if he could have seen it.

Just as well. He'd never let me hear the end of it.

When they reached the familiar stone outbuilding and the overturned wagon, Hilda and Helga quickly gathered up their own tribe. "We will need your strength on the oars," Hilda told them. "We have twice as many to bring home."

The twins' soldiers joined the hike toward shore, eagerly listening as Sven recapped the events inside Utgard, including some details no one else seemed to remember.

"I had three of the Bears of the North under my arm, and snapped their necks in one pull," Sven said. Lars, Harald, and Sigurd exchanged a look.

"When exactly was that, Sven?" Lars asked, elbowing the others. "I think I missed it."

Sven ran a hand through his silver hair. "Let me think. I believe it was right after the giants started to wake up, and you wet your pants. But I could be mistaken." Before Lars could launch a punch at him, Sven quickly continued, "Anyway, if the guards hadn't woken up, we might still be back there teaching the Bears a thing or two."

"And that other one, Aflun," Zack said. "He kind of helped us out, too."

Harald nodded. "In a strange way, we owe a debt of gratitude to the giants, for helping us best our enemies, even if that wasn't their purpose."

Zack shook his head, somewhere between laughter and disbelief.

Vikings, Bears, Giants.

So the giants had helped out the Vikings in their own way. Exactly what Jok Gilman wanted to happen in the weekend football games. Weird.

"What's that strange look for, Lost Boy?" Lars asked.

Zack opened his mouth to answer, then realized he couldn't begin to explain. "Let's just say . . . someone out there has a sense of humor," he said.

The rest of their hike went quickly. At the shore, the two tribes boarded the *Freya* and had it on open water in a matter of minutes. Hilda held her hand up to feel the wind. Zack automatically went to the mast and helped raise the green-and-gold sail. The routine was familiar, almost comfortable now. Helga grabbed the tiller and headed the ship in a direct line away from Jotunheim.

"We should have a good breeze, at least for a while," Hilda said cautiously.

Most of Jok's tribe sat on the floor of the ship, leaning wearily against one another. They passed dried meat and jugs of water among them.

"Erik kept us chained and awake for the entire crossing, with no food or water," Jok muttered. "He knew he had to work down our strength if he was to have any chance of making it to Jotunheim alive—" his voice grew steadily louder—

"with Jok of Lykill on board." He shouted the last part like a lion roaring its pride into the wind. Even if Erik couldn't hear him, Jok would have his say.

Zack watched with a now-familiar sense of being in two places at once. He could just imagine his father bellowing out the Minnesota Vikings fight song in the same way, out to the world, whether or not anyone was listening.

Purple Pride is coming to get you. . . .

It wasn't homesickness he felt. Not really. Somehow, the longer he was in this world, the closer he felt to home and to everything back in Minnesota. How was that possible?

Could he feel closer to Jock by being around Jok? Zack didn't know. But the ache he had felt last time wasn't there anymore. The last time, he had longed every minute to get back to his friends and his father, even his sister, a little bit. Back to warm blankets and meatball subs. It was weird. There was no guarantee he was ever going back to everything he knew, or if he did, that he was going back to the same moment in time. But it was as if only part of him thought about it anymore. Part of him didn't—that was the strange thing. It was as if he was, what? Taking root in this place. Like he was being painted into the picture and not just passing through it anymore. Almost as if he had two homes. And two fathers.

"Lost Boy, let's have another look at that!" called out one of Jok's men. Zack shook his head, cleared his thoughts.

One thing I know. Right now, I'm here.

He went over to show the helmet to anyone who wanted to see. The soldiers gathered around. Sigurd reached over

Zack's shoulder and pointed mutely at the helmet's visor. Harald leaned in. "Runes," he said.

"What?" Zack asked.

"There's something there, written in runes."

Zask had seen some etching on the helmet before, but hadn't paid it much attention. Now he looked closer. The symbols were as plain as English to him. "It says 'Faith,'" he told the others.

He had seen this runic language before. The prophecy was carved into a stone Jok had once showed him, with the same kind of symbols. Without Yggdrasil's Key, Zack knew, it would all be a garble to his eyes. The key allowed him to understand and speak with everyone, and it allowed him to read this language as well.

As Zack stared at the word, a line from the Prophecy came into his head.

With the quest there comes a price: Courage, Faith, and Sacrifice.

"Jok!" Zack rushed to the front of the ship. He pointed to the symbols on the helmet.

Jok looked at them quizzically.

"Faith," Zack said. He had forgotten that Jok, like most of the tribe, couldn't read.

Asleif, Olaf, and several others gathered around. Zack turned to speak to them all. "It says 'Faith.'"

Jok's eyes narrowed. "Courage, Faith, and Sacrifice," he said.

"Exactly."

"Ha!" Jok slapped Zack roundly on the back. "Lost Boy, we are geniuses!" He roared with laughter. "Faith is ours! And Courage and Sacrifice await!"

Soon everyone was discussing what kind of treasures Courage and Sacrifice might be. Plans would be under way soon for the next legs of the quest—to Niflheim and Asgard.

The excitement was cut short when Helga called out sharply. "There he is!"

Everyone turned to look back where she was pointing. To their left, off the southern tip of Jotunheim, was Erik's ship. Its red-and-black sail waved like a warning beacon.

"We can't outpace them," Helga growled. "He's got half our number of people on board. But we can outfight them."

Zack looked at the exhausted soldiers around him.

Let's hope so.

The twins kept the ship on course. Hilda called out for the rowers to go easy. "Best to get as far from Jotunheim as possible," she said. "But we'll need our strength when the time comes." She looked back over her shoulder at the encroaching ship.

Jok and his men gathered what weapons they had. Zack watched them stand into a V-formation at the front of the ship, waiting grimly. He sidled up to Jok, speaking low.

"What if he tries to burn us out? Can we stop him?" All the weapons in the world would do them no good if the *Freya* went down in the middle of nowhere.

Jok stared straight ahead, saying nothing. Zack took the silence as his answer.

Helga had been right. Erik's ship was noticeably gaining on them. It still looked to be at least a half-mile away, but it was only a matter of time before he would be upon them.

"What now?" Asleif stood close to Zack. "This doesn't bode well."

Now it was Zack's turn to keep his mouth shut. No point in overstating the obvious. Olaf stood on his other side, growling and waving a fist at the enemy ship.

Asleif looked at the helmet Faith, clasped under Zack's arm. "Do you think it would be worth offering him something? Maybe he has a price for sailing on and leaving us. Not the key, maybe, but . . ." She trailed off.

Zack looked down at the helmet. "There's no way Jok would go for it. Besides, Erik's all about the key. And about . . . getting you back." He regretted the last part right away. Asleif didn't need to be reminded about her life as a slave. It could only scare her to bring it up now.

"Listen—" Zack began.

"It's all right," Asleif interrupted. "And you are right. There's no giving up."

They could see Erik himself now, standing on the deck of his ship. His dark red robes stood out from all the brown and black fur worn by the Bears of the North. Even though Erik was just a tiny figure several hundred yards away, Zack felt as if he were staring right into his beady little eyes.

Forget it, Erik. It's not going to happen. Not today.

Just like that, Zack moved into action. He crossed to the base of the ship's mast and looked up at it, carefully examining the ropes and the sail's rigging.

Looks like three lines, right across the top.

"What are you doing?" Asleif was at his side. She looked up the mast curiously.

Zack offered no answer. This was crazy risky, and if he said anything, they probably wouldn't let him try it. Not after what had happened with Sottar. For that matter, if he said it out loud, he would realize how impossible it was himself and chicken out.

He stepped up behind one of the rowers. The man's axe sat flat on the deck. Zack picked it up and raced to the back of the ship.

"What the . . . ?" The rower called out. "The Lost Boy just took my axe."

"Zack," Jok shouted to him. "Whatever you are thinking about—don't."

Zack looked across the length of the ship at Jok. He hated to go against Jok's orders, but this was the only thing that made sense.

Barely made sense.

Don't think about it.

He slipped Faith onto his head. The helmet fused there and he rose into the air.

"No!" Jok ran toward him. Several soldiers reached for Zack's feet but he was already beyond their outstretched hands.

Nice acceleration. Now careful. Just a little forward—

He shot straight into the *Freya*'s sail. The material caught him in the face. He flapped at it with his free arm, trying to get loose without slitting the material with his axe.

His hands found the shape of the mast through the cloth. He pushed against it and floated gently backward.

Okay. Now how do I . . . ?

He leaned to the left and shot away from the ship, out over the water. His sense of direction was mush. He spun around in the air, until he spotted Erik's ship off to his right. Zack used what little he had learned about this helmet so far, and angled his body before actually leaning the way he wanted to go.

Now—that way.

He leaned, more gently than ever, and sped off.

Yes!

The enemy ship grew closer. Zack could see most of the Bears looking at him, their mouths hanging slack. Erik also stood dumbfounded, frozen like an openmouthed statue on the deck.

Zack couldn't resist a little wave, palm held up flat, like he was rubbing something in Erik's face.

That's right, you twink. I'm back.

The stillness on board didn't last long. Erik shouted to the nearest soldiers. A moment later, half a dozen arrows sang through the air. Zack leaned hard and sped up. He sailed just over and past the ship, well away from the arrows' trajectories.

At least I'm a moving target.

He leaned a whisper to the right and banked slowly, coming around to face the ship again.

The expanse of water below was starting to look like an abyss just waiting to swallow him. One arrow was all it would take to bring him down for a permanent ocean nap. The problem with this world was you never got to really enjoy the good stuff. Like flying.

He banked again, circling to get a good look at Erik's rigging. Three lines of rope held the sail in place, just like on the *Freya*. They extended from the sides of the ship, meeting in a point near the top center of the sail. One good swing with the axe could take them out at once, if Zack could approach from the back.

But it has to be just right. No second chances here.

Another volley of arrows shot out toward him. Zack leaned back hard, pulling farther away, over the water. He was safely out of range again but he was going to have to get close—very close—to finish the job. And soon. Erik's ship seemed to have twice the speed as the *Freya*, and it was bearing down fast.

Zack could see Hilda's rowers stroking as quickly as they could. The rest of the tribe was yelling out to him, cheering him on.

He cocked his arm, raising the axe at the ready, and leaned toward the red-and-black of Erik's sail.

Speed and accuracy. Speed and accuracy.

His body moved through zero resistance, like a bullet. Erik's soldiers turned, fired, and missed again. With any luck, they would have no time to reload their bows.

Zack's thoughts dropped away. He saw nothing but his

target, felt nothing but the axe in his hand.

He was in over the ship.

He raised his arm and swung; the ropes snapped.

He flew straight into the sail. The black and red of the cloth obliterated his view. He pushed blindly on and the sail billowed loosely around him. Zack reached down with his axe and dragged its edge along the dark material. The sail opened up with a long, satisfying ripping sound as Zack pushed through it and soared away.

A moment later, he was in the clear. Zack leaned hard and flew faster than ever. When he was well away, he gritted his teeth and looked over his shoulder. Erik's sail hung loosely over the edge of his ship, trailing like a dead body, half in the water. Erik would be on oar power all the way back to Midgard.

Zack faced forward again and saw the *Freya* pulling away, fast increasing the distance between the two ships. Everyone on board was jumping in the air and waving. Zack sped back toward them. He circled the ship once just because he could. *Now* it felt good to fly. Amazing in fact. The water rushed by under him. He cut a wide arc, flying alongside as the *Freya* moved over the sea toward home.

When he finally landed on the deck, catching his feet on the ground and rolling once again to a stop, Zack found himself at the bottom of a pile-on. Two dozen of his tribemates leapt at—and onto—him with shouts and congratulations.

"Lost Boy has done it . . . again!" shouted Harald.

"Hail the Lost Boy!" shouted Jok.

"Hail the Lost Boy," they all repeated, still clamoring over one another.

He rolled out from under them, plucking the helmet from his head to keep from floating off into space again.

He raised his fists into the air and shouted the call he had taught them once before. "V–I–K–I–N–G–S!"

"Go, Vikings, let's go!" everyone screamed back.

In that moment, Zack knew just how proud Jock Gilman would be. There was, of course, the amazing flight he had just taken. Not to mention this entire journey to the land of the giants. But most of all, Zack knew, Jock would be stoked beyond belief knowing that his son had brought the Minnesota Vikings fight song to the ninth century.

❧

The *Freya* left Erik and the Bears of the North far behind. By nightfall, the enemy ship had long since disappeared on the horizon behind them.

The next morning they beached once again at the entrance to Midgard just below Mimir's well. "I don't know why," Zack said to Jok, "I just want to tell him what happened." Mimir had seemed so pleased to have visitors before. "And I want to thank him."

He climbed up into the glade, alone this time. The soft green light washed over him as he moved toward the pool. Mimir was already looking up from the water when Zack got there.

"So you found what you were seeking."

"Yeah," Zack said, holding up the helmet. "But how did you—"

"You forget," Mimir said.

"Oh right, you're all-knowing and everything."

"No," Mimir replied. The light darkened in the glade, and his voice reverberated around Zack like surround-sound stereo. "I am *ALL-KNOWING.*"

"Got it," Zack said. "So anyway, I just wanted to—I don't know. Thank you, I guess."

"Well, you are welcome. And congratulations to you as well. You have completed the two trials of Faith."

Zack cocked his head to the side. "Two trials? What do you mean?"

"Sit down," Mimir said.

Zack looked over his shoulder, toward the beach where everyone was waiting.

"Don't worry," Mimir scolded. "I won't keep you so long this time. Sit. You will want to hear this."

Zack sat down where he could still see Mimir's face floating in the water but not his bloody, severed neck.

"You are to gather the three treasures of Yggdrasil's Chest," Mimir said.

"Right," Zack said.

"Each of the three treasures is gained by the completion of two trials. One to begin the search, and one to end it. These were the trials of Faith."

"Trials of Faith?" Zack said, putting two and two together. "Do you mean like the leap you talked about?"

"The leap of faith, yes," Mimir answered.

"That definitely got me to the treasure," Zack said. "But

the trial to begin it?" He searched his mind. Everything about this place was a trial.

Mimir closed his eyes and the pool shimmered. Another image replaced his face. Zack saw Ollie in the woods at home. He saw the wolves in the fog and Ollie's flashlight playing across the trees. Then he saw himself as he turned back into the woods, away from Ollie, just before he passed through time.

Mimir's face returned to the pool. "You chose to begin this journey," he said. "You showed what was needed to begin the search for Faith, which, of course, was faith in the quest itself."

In its own way, it all made sense. But it didn't make the next steps in the quest seem too inviting. "So . . . more trials still to go, huh?" Zack asked.

"Yes," Mimir said simply.

"What comes next?"

"Ah, Lost Boy, I think you already know that you will have to find that out for yourself."

"That's what I was afraid of," Zack said. He sat in the silence of the glade for several minutes, trying to pull it all together—where this was leading him, what it all meant.

"Do not look for answers, Lost Boy," Mimir said quietly. "Do what seems to you to be the right thing. That *is* the answer."

Zack couldn't help laughing. He was suddenly conscious of sitting here, sharing deep thoughts with a severed head in a pool of water at the base of a giant tree root, in the ninth century. There were definitely better things to do than try to make sense of it all.

"Thanks, Mimir."

"Good luck, Lost Boy."

Zack emerged from the glade. As he turned to climb back down to the beach, something else caught his eye, farther up the slope. It was hard to see, but it looked as if there was another level above him. And it looked like a huge black bird wing was flapping over the edge.

Could it be?

His curiosity got the best of him. He dug into the slope and climbed up. Coming over another rise in the brown bark that covered the ground, he came face-to-face with his old raven friends.

"Huginn! Muninn!" Zack cried. "Man, I could have used you guys before."

The ravens, each as big as Zack, nodded their heads at him. Like with Hilda and Helga, Zack needed a clue as to which was which.

"It seems you've made a name for yourself," said one of the two.

"So, am I speaking raven right now?" Zack asked. "Or are you speaking my language?"

"I speak all languages," said the other bird.

"I speak all languages," mocked the first raven. "As if he's the only one."

"Lost Boy, will you please tell Muninn that we speak for ourselves?"

"Lost Boy," said Muninn, "will you please tell Huginn that he is an idiot?"

"Uh . . ." Zack trailed off, suddenly feeling some sympathy for what Jock went through when Zack and Valerie put him in the middle of their fights.

The two ravens turned at each other and began squawking and arguing in their high-pitched voices.

"Oh, *I'm* an idiot? Who's the one who . . ."

"Don't take that tone with me . . ."

Zack shouted over top of them. "Hey!" They stopped and looked at him. "Is something wrong?" It wasn't much of a question. Huginn and Muninn disagreed on just about everything. But their arguing was hard to listen to.

"Yes," Huginn said.

"No," Muninn answered at the same time.

"It's nothing," Huginn said.

"Nothing?" Muninn challenged.

"Well, it's certainly not why we're here," Huginn said quickly. They turned to Zack and began speaking at the same time.

"You've found the helmet," Huginn said.

"The helmet is yours," Muninn said.

"Yes," Zack said, answering both of them. "It's on the ship."

"Good," said Huginn. "Excellent work, Lost Boy."

"Thanks." Before they could start again, Zack asked, "So, can you tell me about the trials of Courage, or Sacrifice? Whatever I'm supposed to do next?"

"Yes," Muninn said.

"And no," Huginn corrected. "We *could* tell you. But we may not."

"It is forbidden," Muninn said.

"Forbidden?" Zack asked. "By who?"

"No one," they both said at the same time. Each nodded at the other. And the fact that they seemed to agree made Zack suspect even more strongly they were lying.

"Is someone . . . watching me?" Zack asked. "Watching all this?"

"We see almost everything that goes on in the world," Huginn said.

"That's not what I asked."

"Lost Boy," Muninn broke in. "It is good that you found the helmet Faith. We can tell you are doing well."

"And we can tell you that you should keep going," Huginn added.

"I know that," Zack said. "That's all anyone tells me. You guys, Mimir, the Free Man. Can't you tell me anything else?"

"Would you like to hear the prophecy again?" asked Muninn. The two ravens seemed to love reciting it.

"No," Zack said quickly and too loudly. "No," he repeated, more politely. "Thank you."

"Then we should go," Huginn said.

"We?" said Muninn haughtily. "Since when do you speak for me?"

"Never mind," snapped Huginn. He turned back to Zack. "I should go."

"Me, too," said Muninn. Both birds stood up higher on their thin legs, flapped their wings, and lifted into the air.

"Good luck, Lost Boy," they both called, and took off in

opposite directions. A moment later, one of them banked and flew to catch up with the other.

Zack waved after them with a sigh. This hadn't been nearly as helpful as his last meeting with the ravens. He climbed back down to his tribe and gave the go-ahead to leave, without a word about what had happened.

The trip back into Midgard was nearly as difficult as the trip out. The *Freya* navigated up the tunnel toward the back of the massive waterfall.

"Now I see why no one ever does this," Asleif said, tying herself in. Zack pressed himself down between her and Olaf, arms locked and determined not to let go of either one of them this time.

The extra weight from Jok's tribe on the ship seemed to help as they made their way back through the enormous deluge. The water seemed to flow toward the outside of the falls, which helped as well. The ship naturally moved through and popped out the other side, its crew and passengers soaking wet and beaten by the heavy water, but alive, safe, and home in Midgard once again.

CHAPTER THIRTEEN

The burned carcass of the *Winniferd* stood as it had when they left it, a dark reminder of a terrible day.

"There she is."

That was all Jok said, his voice thick. He stood straight and unmoving as Hilda navigated the *Freya* toward it.

"A small price to pay for a much bigger task," Helga offered. Jok nodded silently.

"There will be another ship," Sven said. "A new *Winniferd*—not to replace this one but to stand in its memory."

"Just as we will someday find the woman for whom it is named," Jok vowed quietly to himself.

Every time Jok mentioned his missing wife, Zack got a mental picture of his own mother. He had to guess that they looked alike, and also—as much as Jok obviously wanted to think otherwise—that Jok's wife was gone forever, just like Zack's mom.

The crew immediately set to finding the chest they had thrown into the lake.

"Right here," Jok said, pointing down at the cloudy water. "We bound it with a cord and anchored it with a stone."

Using two of the long oars from the *Freya*, they were able to haul the chest up on board. Lars and Sigurd set it on the deck in front of Zack.

"A part of our destiny completes itself today," Jok said. His jaw was set and his voice was firm, but it was tinged with anger and sadness. "As the Prophecy says, this quest has its price," he added, obviously thinking about the *Winniferd*.

Everyone stood in silence for a moment. Then Jok motioned for Zack to go ahead.

Zack set the golden helmet down next to the chest. He took Yggdrasil's Key from around his neck and put it to the first of the three locks, under Faith. What would happen when the treasure was placed inside?

He took a deep breath and turned the key. Nothing.

What?

He tried the key's other two stems but was unable to budge the lock.

"Something's happened," Zack said. "Are you sure this is it? The real chest?"

"Absolutely," Jok said. "No one could have known we left this here."

"Erik couldn't have possibly made it back here ahead of us, Ogmunder or no Ogmunder," Sven said. "He's still in the unknown sea, I'm sure of it."

"But how can this not work?" Zack said, his pulse rising. "Is it because it's been in the water all this time?" There had to be an explanation.

"That chest has seen much worse than water, over the years," Jok said. "Something is wrong here. Something is very, very wrong."

A sense of foreboding lay over everyone on board. Helga called the tribe back to their oars. "We're going back to Konur. Right now."

The *Freya* moved swiftly across the lake and back through the maze of waterways. Hilda called out to the rowers. No one else spoke the entire way.

Even before the ship reached land, Hilda, Helga, Jok, and several others leapt overboard and ran into the twins' village. Zack, Asleif, and Olaf were close behind.

A guard rushed out to meet them.

"What is it?" Helga asked right away.

"You've returned!" the guard said excitedly.

"But what's wrong? What's happened?" Hilda pressed.

"Where are my people?" Jok thundered, grabbing the soldier at the neck.

"Everyone is where they should be," choked the soldier. "All is well."

Jok stopped shaking the man. Hilda and Helga looked at each other. Villagers started streaming from all directions, hugging and welcoming the tribe home.

"Are you looking for this?" Valdis stood at the door of Hilda and Helga's house, another chest on the ground next to her.

"Valdis!" Jok went to her and pulled her off her feet in a hug, twirling her around. When he put her down again, Valdis pointed to the chest at her feet.

"I think you'll want this," she said.

"Yggdrasil's Chest?" Zack asked. "But . . ."

Valdis put her hands on her hips. "You didn't expect I

would let the tribe venture off with this chest, our fate, into who knew what kind of danger? After all we've been through to get it, just to send it off to the land of the giants? I don't think so."

No one answered. Jok and his crew looked dubiously from one to the other.

"It was a simple matter of switching the chests while you gorged yourselves at the feast before you left." She pointed to Jok. "He never pays attention to anything when he's eating."

Jok made an attempt at an angry face, but he couldn't pull it off. "Valdis, I should punish you."

"But you won't," she said, putting her arms around his waist again.

No one seemed prepared to breathe a sigh of relief just yet. Jok motioned for Zack to come over to the chest. Everyone gathered around as Zack once again took out the key. His curiosity returned in spite of the false alarm. The quest had proven so unpredictable, he was ready for anything now.

Zack handed the golden helmet to Jok as he fitted the key into the chest's first lock. With a soft and familiar click, the lid opened. He keyed all three sections of the chest and lifted the lids to reveal the carved interior map. The left-most section, under Faith, showed a depiction of the sharp peaks of Jotunheim and the towers of Utgard. The rest of the map showed them what they already knew—that the quest for Courage and Sacrifice would take them to Niflheim and Asgard.

Zack looked at it all with quiet awe. It was more beautiful than he remembered.

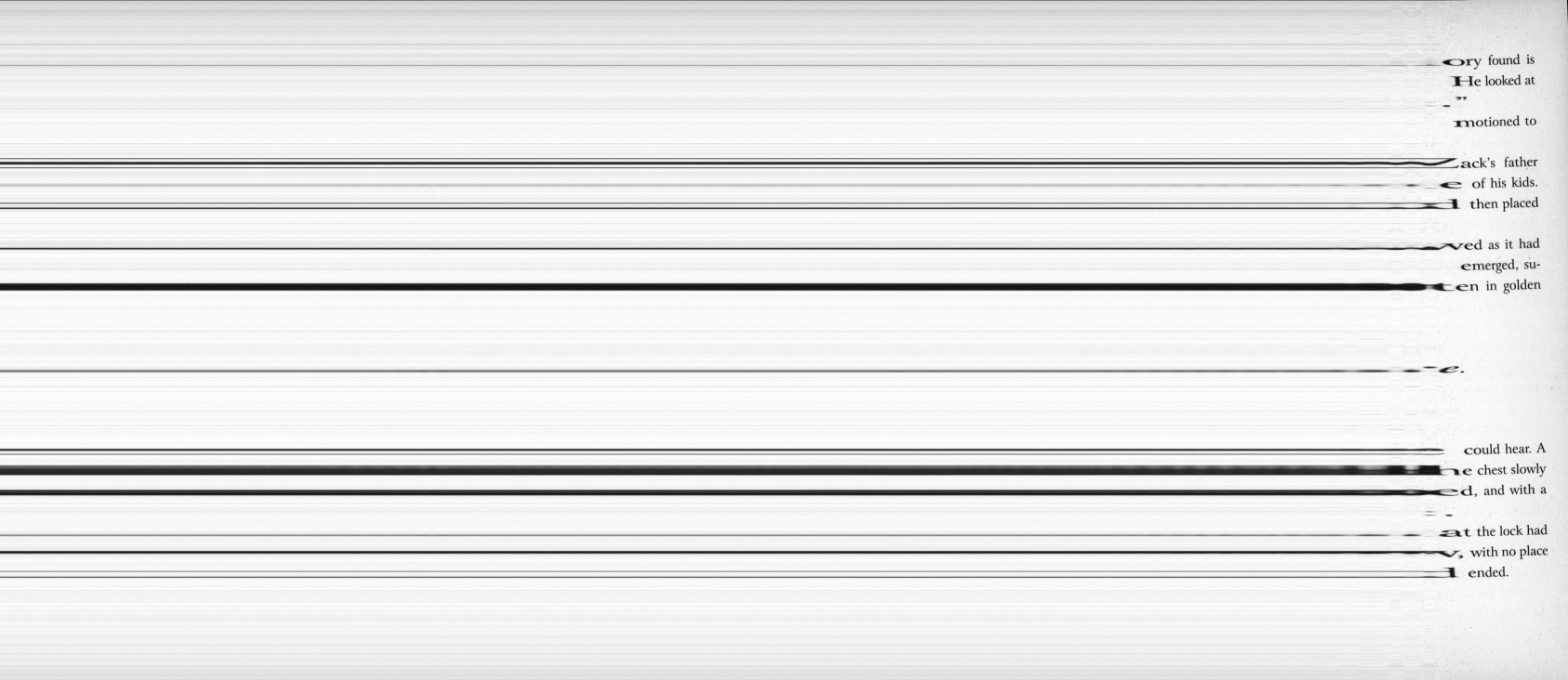

ory found is

He looked at

-"

motioned to

ack's father

e of his kids.

d then placed

ved as it had

emerged, su-

en in golden

e.

could hear. A

e chest slowly

d, and with a

-

at the lock had

, with no place

ended.

The feast that night

strategy session. Jok

Niflhim, and Asgard

lenges. At least they ha

land of the dead and th

matter. But one thing

be on the move. Some h

somehow, they had to f

"It has to be Ogmun

"The potions wiza

weapon, that one."

"True," said Hilda, "

using his magic someho

"Whatever he know

self, "we have to leave s

follows us, or we follow

that lies there."

"Somewhere," said S

"In Hel's realm," Jok

Niflheim and no doubt h

Asleif shivered next to

palace is said to be the w

Jok spoke quietly, quoting the Prophecy. "Glory found is glory earned, And what is lost must be returned." He looked at Zack. "It is time to return this to its rightful place."

He held out the helmet for Zack, but Zack motioned to the chest. "Go ahead," Zack said. "You do it."

Jok beamed, in exactly the same way Zack's father beamed when he was particularly proud of one of his kids. He held the helmet up for everyone to see, and then placed it gently in the first chamber of the chest.

Immediately, the map inside the chest glowed as it had once before. This time however, a new image emerged, superimposed over the map itself. Words, written in golden light burned out over the top of the helmet.

Faith you sought, as it should be,
And Faith you found, the first of three.
With the quest remains a price,
Courage now, then Sacrifice.

Zack read the words out loud so everyone could hear. A moment later, the lid to the first chamber of the chest slowly drew closed on its own force. The lock clicked, and with a slight hiss the golden light disappeared inside.

When Zack looked closely, he could see that the lock had fused over. Its metal was a smooth surface now, with no place for Yggdrasil's Key. This part of the quest had ended.

And the search for Courage had begun.

CHAPTER FOURTEEN

The feast that night in Konur was half-celebration, half-strategy session. Jok and the twins agreed that getting to Niflhim, and Asgard after that, would be formidable challenges. At least they had known how to sail to Jotunheim. The land of the dead and the home of the gods would be another matter. But one thing was for sure—Erik the Horrible would be on the move. Somehow, he was tracking their moves, and somehow, they had to find out how he was doing it.

"It has to be Ogmunder," Zack said.

"The potions wizard?" Lars asked. "Not a very strong weapon, that one."

"True," said Hilda, "but what else could it be? He must be using his magic somehow."

"Whatever he knows," Jok said, half-aloud, half to himself, "we have to leave soon for Niflheim. Whether or not he follows us, or we follow him, our goal must be the treasure that lies there."

"Somewhere," said Sven.

"In Hel's realm," Jok said. "I'm sure of it. She is queen of Niflheim and no doubt holds the secret of the second treasure."

Asleif shivered next to Zack. "I don't relish that trip. Hel's palace is said to be the worst place in all of the nine worlds."

A sense of foreboding lay over everyone on board. Helga called the tribe back to their oars. "We're going back to Konur. Right now."

The *Freya* moved swiftly across the lake and back through the maze of waterways. Hilda called out to the rowers. No one else spoke the entire way.

Even before the ship reached land, Hilda, Helga, Jok, and several others leapt overboard and ran into the twins' village. Zack, Asleif, and Olaf were close behind.

A guard rushed out to meet them.

"What is it?" Helga asked right away.

"You've returned!" the guard said excitedly.

"But what's wrong? What's happened?" Hilda pressed.

"Where are my people?" Jok thundered, grabbing the soldier at the neck.

"Everyone is where they should be," choked the soldier. "All is well."

Jok stopped shaking the man. Hilda and Helga looked at each other. Villagers started streaming from all directions, hugging and welcoming the tribe home.

"Are you looking for this?" Valdis stood at the door of Hilda and Helga's house, another chest on the ground next to her.

"Valdis!" Jok went to her and pulled her off her feet in a hug, twirling her around. When he put her down again, Valdis pointed to the chest at her feet.

"I think you'll want this," she said.

"Yggdrasil's Chest?" Zack asked. "But . . ."

Valdis put her hands on her hips. "You didn't expect I

would let the tribe venture off with this chest, our fate, into who knew what kind of danger? After all we've been through to get it, just to send it off to the land of the giants? I don't think so."

No one answered. Jok and his crew looked dubiously from one to the other.

"It was a simple matter of switching the chests while you gorged yourselves at the feast before you left." She pointed to Jok. "He never pays attention to anything when he's eating."

Jok made an attempt at an angry face, but he couldn't pull it off. "Valdis, I should punish you."

"But you won't," she said, putting her arms around his waist again.

No one seemed prepared to breathe a sigh of relief just yet. Jok motioned for Zack to come over to the chest. Everyone gathered around as Zack once again took out the key. His curiosity returned in spite of the false alarm. The quest had proven so unpredictable, he was ready for anything now.

Zack handed the golden helmet to Jok as he fitted the key into the chest's first lock. With a soft and familiar click, the lid opened. He keyed all three sections of the chest and lifted the lids to reveal the carved interior map. The left-most section, under Faith, showed a depiction of the sharp peaks of Jotunheim and the towers of Utgard. The rest of the map showed them what they already knew—that the quest for Courage and Sacrifice would take them to Niflheim and Asgard.

Zack looked at it all with quiet awe. It was more beautiful than he remembered.

should be able to stay on course and make good time."

There was no conversation of postponing the trip. Zack and Olaf would set off on foot from Lykill to find the Free Man and, hopefully, learn whatever they needed to know about reaching Niflheim as soon as possible. The mood among the combined tribes was jovial and excited, and a little nervous.

"Where do you suppose Erik is now?" Asleif asked Zack. She had kept true to her word and had stuck close by him. Olaf would accompany Zack to the Free Man, but Asleif would see him as far as Lykill.

"Hopefully still lost at sea," Zack said with a smile. Danger remained a big part of the equation, but it was hard not to feel ahead of the game. For once, Erik didn't seem like a threat.

The fog settled thickly around the ship.

"Is like riding in clouds," Olaf remarked. Zack could barely see the outline of Olaf's three-foot body just a short distance away. Even with the wind picking up, using the sail was out of the question. Oars helped them gauge the water's depth. Hilda called out to the rowers in a slow steady rhythm.

"How can there be this much wind and still so much fog?" Sven said.

Almost immediately, the key around Zack's neck grew warm. This time there was no mistaking what was happening.

Oh no! Not yet. Not now.

He felt it quickly heating up against his chest, just as it

Everyone raised their drinking horns to the search for Courage, and the trip to Niflheim. And to finding the second great root of Yggdrasil, where the road to the land of the dead was said to begin.

"Is question for Free Man," Olaf said through a mouthful of fish. "Free Man knows many things."

"I'll go see him," Zack said. He didn't have to think about it.

"Thank you, Zack," Jok said. "If there is one thing we know, it is that this glory quest happens with, and only with, the Lost Boy. 'The Boy shall lead until the end.' We all know this from the Prophecy. Now we know it from our experience as well."

Zack knew it, too. It was up to him to help lead this quest. And he would.

Jok waved a large leg of venison, shaking it for emphasis. "There is nothing more important than continuing the quest. If the Free Man is our best answer for finding the way to Niflheim, then that is where we will go."

Zack looked around the room. Everyone was glancing his way. He cleared his throat. "And by 'we,' you mean—"

"You." Jok said. It was not a question or a request.

"Okay," Zack said. "Just so we're clear. Olaf, you up for another trip?"

Olaf's little red eyes blazed. "Trolls always ready."

෧ৡঔ

The *Freya* set sail for Lykill the next morning, heading into a dense fog.

"We won't sail far from the shore," Hilda said. "We

181

had every time he traveled between the ninth century and home. It was a possibility he hadn't even allowed for.

I'm not ready.

At the same instant, an even thicker fog rolled over him like a blanket. The wind picked up to a howl, a shriek. The fog swirled around Zack until he felt lost in it.

He stood up and felt around blindly. He definitely wasn't on the ship anymore. It was a blank nowhere, with nothing but mist and the high-pitched sound of the wind.

Moving was pointless but he walked on anyway. The light began to fade as if the sun behind the clouds was sinking at high speed. Zack found he was quickly surrounded by darkness, in addition to the fog. He stopped walking.

"Hello?" he shouted. "Jok! Asleif! Olaf!"

No answer.

He took another step forward and his knee hit something hard. He reached out and touched what felt like the rough bark of a tree.

The fog began to dissipate. The wind died down. The key grew cool around his neck.

He was in the forest. A light played across his feet. He looked down and saw a flashlight on the ground.

He was home. Again.

A rush of disappointment came over Zack. It was exactly the opposite feeling as the last time he had been sent back home.

He stooped down and picked up the flashlight. The beam stretched out and lit on the awestruck face of Ollie Grossberg.

"Ollie?"

Ollie stood staring at Zack, his eyes as big as cheeseburgers. He was in the exact same position he had been standing in when Zack left, forever ago. His arm was extended, as if he were still holding the flashlight which he had obviously dropped.

"Ollie? What's going on? How long have you been standing there?" Zack stared back at his friend. "How long have I been gone?"

Ollie gulped audibly. He came over to Zack and punched him in the arm. "Yeah, it's you all right."

"What did you expect?" Zack said, lightly tapping him back.

"Well, uh . . . I don't know. I've never seen someone disappear and then come back again." Ollie was still looking at him as if he didn't quite believe it really was Zack.

"So, it was just for a minute? A second?"

"Hard to say," Ollie said, his voice evening out. "It was pretty dark out here. A second or two, I guess."

They walked back toward Zack's house. Zack tried to find the words to explain everything that had happened in those two seconds he had been away. More than ever, he could see how crazy it all seemed, but Ollie listened silently.

"Well," Ollie said simply, "you sure stink like you've been gone a long time." Zack hadn't noticed how dirty he was until now. He could even smell himself.

When they got to Zack's window, it was still open.

Ollie turned to him. "I will never doubt you again. Ever."

He thought for a second. "Of course, I'll probably never see you again either—now that I've lost my mind and all."

Zack knew just how his friend felt—he'd questioned his own sanity a few times when he had first landed in the Viking world. But it was such a relief now that someone else in his life knew that all of this was real. Finally he could tell Ollie about Jok and Erik the Horrible and all the others without Ollie thinking he was crazy.

"I'll talk to you tomorrow," Zack said, but then smacked his forehead. "I just remembered, I'm supposed to go to Green Bay this weekend."

"I'm coming," Ollie said definitively. "I'm going to go home, get some stuff, and come back. I'll tell my parents we'll be back on Sunday. They can call your dad, okay?"

"Uh, sure." Zack was still processing it all.

"I want to hear all about this and I want to hear about it soon," Ollie said. He ducked off into the darkness. "I won't be gone long."

Zack shook his head.

Yeah—that's what I thought, too.

He climbed through the window back into his room and—at least for the time being—back into his regular life.

EPILOGUE

Erik paced the deck. "Faster, you idiots. Do you think this ship will bring itself home?" The ship had been slowly making its way through the unknown sea toward Midgard for several days, with high winds mocking the useless sail piled on the deck.

Next to the sail lay the splintered remains of the decoy chest. Erik kicked at the pieces every time he passed by. "Those idiots," he snarled. "How long did they think this ridiculous copy would hold up?"

"It fooled you long enough," Ogmunder told him.

"Oh, shut up," said Erik.

The exhausted rowers pulled lazily at their oars, making almost no headway at all.

"I should never have gotten onto this ship in the first place," fumed Ogmunder.

"You'll be paid," Erik seethed back. "Have a scrap of vision for once. Things take time."

Ogmunder sat crouched on a low trunk, ducking his long body out of the wind and squeezing under the ship rail. He cast a leery sideways glance toward Erik. "You said we would be in and out of Jotunheim, then back to Midgard in a few short days. This is not how I planned to spend my time."

"Oh," Erik said, walking over to him. "And you have so much to do there, more important than Yggdrasil's Treasure?"

A weak moan came from the front of the ship. "Sire?" Orn sat, clutching himself with his one arm, shivering in the cold. "Sire? Might we have a bit more ration?"

"Certainly," said Erik. He pointed to a heavy wooden food locker. "Pick that up and bring it over to me. Then you can have all you like."

Orn looked mournfully at the dried green slime that marked the place where his right arm had once met his shoulder. He looked at the bulky locker, then slumped back down again, grumbling to himself. Erik rolled his eyes and turned back to Ogmunder.

"I expect to be paid before I begin work on any new arm," Ogmunder said, "or anything else at all for that matter."

"Fine," Erik said. "I'm sure we can find someone else. Someone who has the tiniest modicum"— he poked at the wizard with his skull-tipped staff—"of patience." He motioned to the expanse of water all around them. "So, Ogmunder, I'm sorry you'll be leaving us, but you can get off at any time."

Ogmunder stood up. He towered over Erik, who looked defiantly up into the wizard's eyes.

Ogmunder broke first. "Well," he said between clenched teeth, "I never said we couldn't negotiate *something*."

Erik puffed out his narrow chest, preening like a small

rooster. "I thought as much."

Orn moaned again, a single long whine. "How long until we reach Midgard?"

Erik walked away without a word. He pivoted back on both of them, speaking in a taunting, whining tone. "My arm, my arm. My payment, my payment. Is it too much to ask for a little cooperation in all this? A drop of faith?" His voice broke in a gurgle. He cleared his throat and turned to address the crew at large. "Does anyone here doubt that I know exactly what I'm doing?" he shouted.

The Bear soldiers looked up, their eyes glazed. No one answered or seemed to want to.

Erik advanced on the nearest rower. He used his staff to chuck the tired man roughly under the chin. "You," he snapped. "Where do you suppose we go from here?"

The soldier looked perplexed.

"Speak up," Erik demanded.

"Lykill, sire?" the man asked timidly.

"No!" Erik swung the heavy end of his staff against the man's temple, sending him to the ground. "But a good guess," he added.

Ogmunder spoke again. "Don't you imagine they'll head straight out for the second treasure? To Niflheim or to Asgard? We'll never be there in time."

"Oh, but we already are," Erik said, a smirk creeping over his face. "Do you think I have no more resources than this pathetic little tribe of hired hands?"

"Well, actually . . ." Ogmunder sat up. Erik crossed slowly

toward him, and the wizard deflated just slightly. "No, of course not," he finished.

"Of course not," Erik repeated. "True, I would like to be there myself to take back the treasure, kill Jok, and kill the Lost Boy when he's no longer useful to us. But it's not absolutely necessary that I be there to see it happen."

No one spoke. Ogmunder sat down again with a disgusted groan.

"Isn't anyone going to ask me why?" Erik said, stomping his foot. He turned on another rower.

"Why, sire?" the man asked quietly and quickly.

"Because . . ." Erik spoke slowly, barely hiding his enjoyment of the attention he was drawing out. "Because we have someone on the inside."

"A spy?" Ogmunder asked with a scoff. "You've said yourself. Everyone has spies. They are everywhere."

"Oh, more than a spy," Erik said coolly. "We have a member of their own tribe. A trusted friend to Jok of Lykill. Someone who not only keeps us informed, but someone who will finish the job if necessary." Erik's eyes narrowed to slits as he turned away, speaking more to himself than anyone. "It won't be long now. Not long at all. Just a matter of time."

Don't miss the third hilarious, action-packed Viking Saga, LAND OF THE DEAD!

Zack, Jok, Olaf, and the rest of the Vikings are off to the mysterious world of Niflheim, where they must recover the next treasure of Yggdrasil's Chest. They know it won't be easy, but they find a lot more trouble than they'd bargained for when they get there. Hel, the ruler of the Viking land of the dead, is bound and determined to keep her new guests imprisoned in her freaky palace forever. She has many tricks up her sleeve—from a hideous flesh-eating dragon to a maze of moving walls to an army of undead warriors—and she'll use everything she's got to make sure Zack never makes it out alive. . . .

CLAMP

1

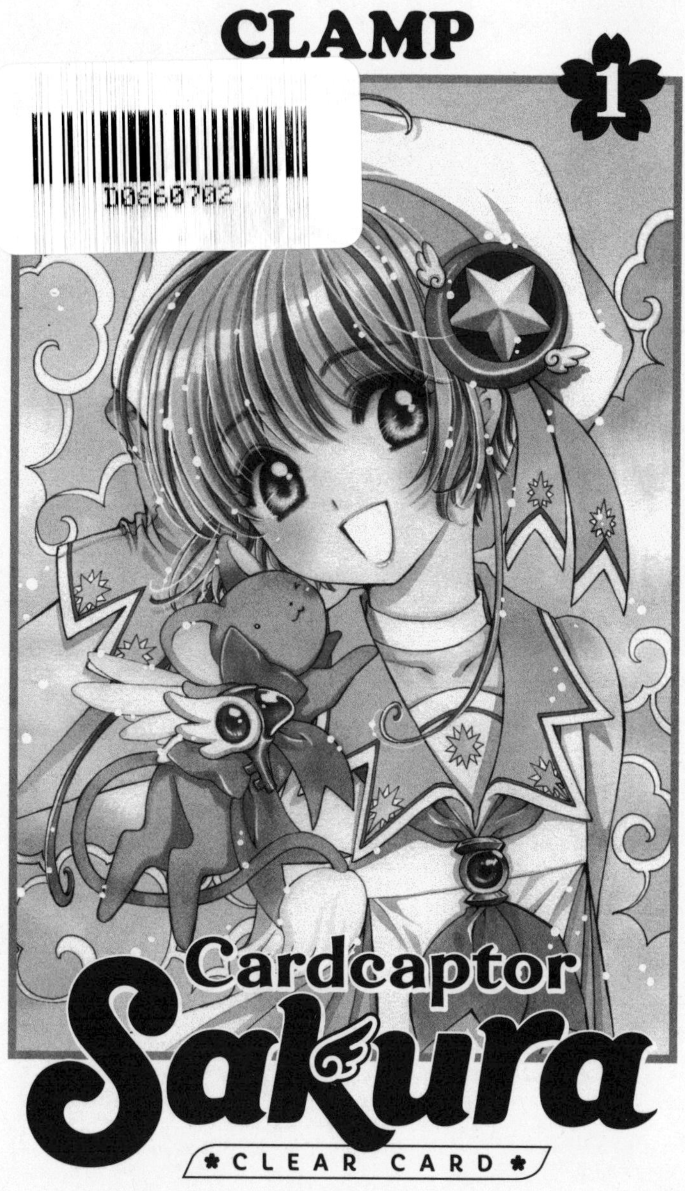

Cardcaptor Sakura

CLEAR CARD

CARDCAPTOR SAKURA CHARACTERS

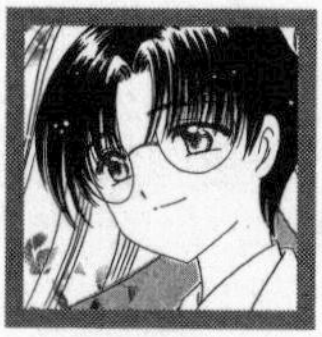

ERIOL HIIRAGIZAWA

AN EXCHANGE STUDENT FROM ENGLAND WHO WAS SAKURA'S CLASSMATE. ONCE ALL THE CLOW CARDS WERE TRANSFORMED INTO SAKURA CARDS, HE RETURN TO ENGLAND. HOWEVER...

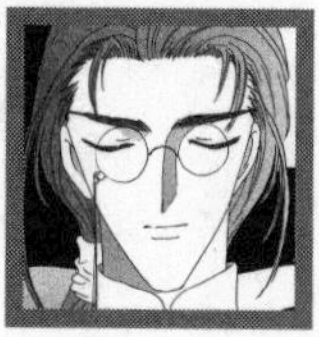

CLOW REED

A MAGICIAN AND FORTUNE TELLER WITH EXTRAORDINARY MAGICAL POWER. EVERYTHING WAS SET INTO MOTION WHEN HE CREATED THE CLOW CARDS.

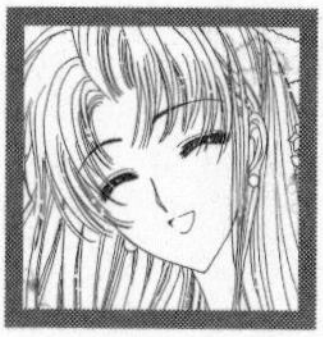

KAHO MIZUKI

FOR A SHORT TIME, SHE WAS SAKURA'S SUBSTITUTE MATH TEACHER. SHE SUPPORTED SAKURA DURING THE FINAL TRIAL.

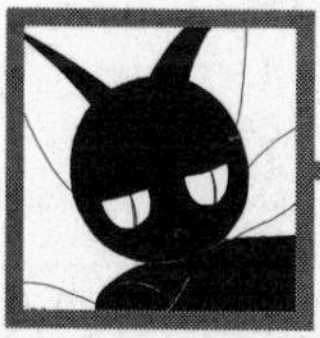

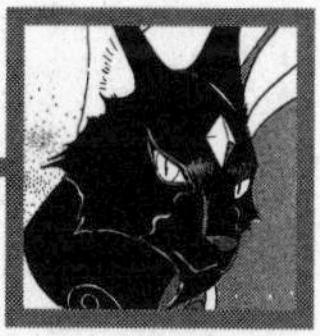

SPINEL SUN

SPINEL SUN'S SECRET IDENTITY. "SOUPY" FOR SHORT.

A FAMILIAR SERVANT CREATED BY ERIOL.

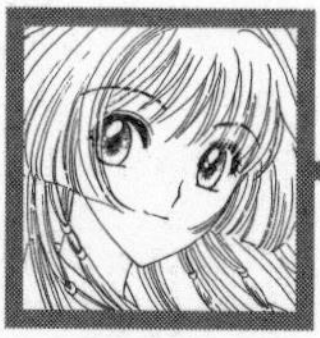

NAKURU AKIZUKI

RUBY MOON'S SECRET IDENTITY.

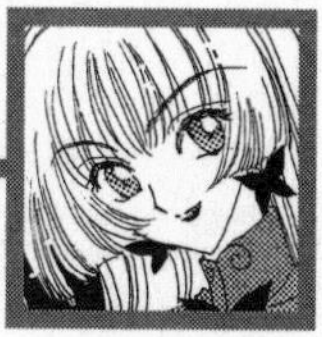

RUBY MOON

A FAMILIAR SERVANT CREATED BY ERIOL. SPINEL'S COUNTERPART.

SAKURA'S FRIENDS

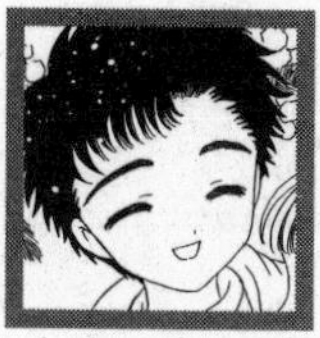

TAKASHI YAMAZAKI

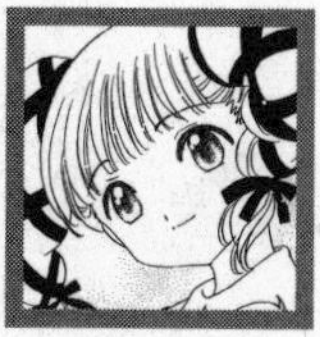

CHIHARU MIHARA

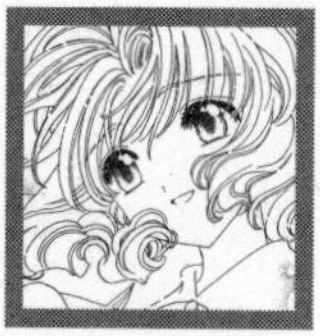

RIKA SASAKI

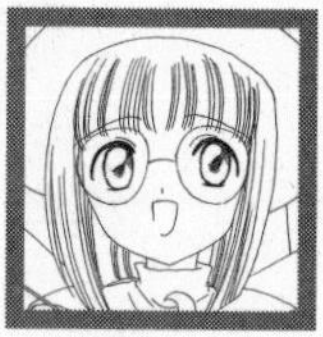

NAOKO YANAGISAWA

FOR DETAILS, PLEASE READ *CARDCAPTOR SAKURA!*

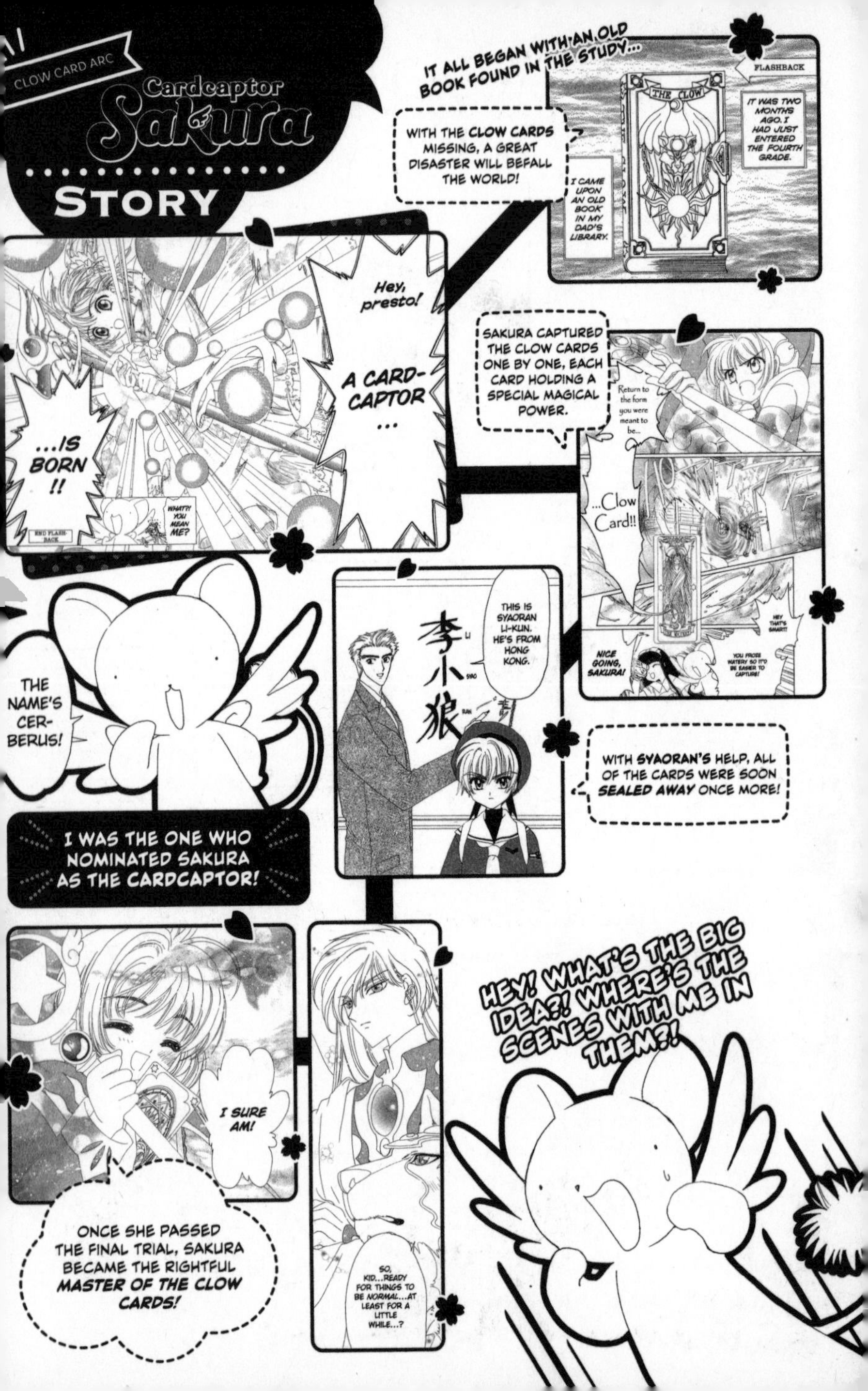

CLOW CARD ARC
Cardcaptor Sakura
STORY
IT ALL BEGAN WITH AN OLD BOOK FOUND IN THE STUDY...
FLASHBACK
IT WAS TWO MONTHS AGO. I HAD JUST ENTERED THE FOURTH GRADE.
I CAME UPON AN OLD BOOK IN MY DAD'S LIBRARY.
THE CLOW
WITH THE CLOW CARDS MISSING, A GREAT DISASTER WILL BEFALL THE WORLD!
Hey, presto!
A CARD-CAPTOR...
...IS BORN!!
WHAT?! YOU MEAN ME?
END FLASH-BACK
THE NAME'S CER-BERUS!
I WAS THE ONE WHO NOMINATED SAKURA AS THE CARDCAPTOR!
SAKURA CAPTURED THE CLOW CARDS ONE BY ONE, EACH CARD HOLDING A SPECIAL MAGICAL POWER.
Return to the form you were meant to be...
...Clow Card!!
HEY THAT'S SMART!
YOU FROZE WATERY SO IT'D BE EASIER TO CAPTURE!
NICE GOING, SAKURA!
THIS IS SYAORAN LI-KUN. HE'S FROM HONG KONG.
李 LI
小 SIAO
狼 RAN
WITH SYAORAN'S HELP, ALL OF THE CARDS WERE SOON SEALED AWAY ONCE MORE!
I SURE AM!
ONCE SHE PASSED THE FINAL TRIAL, SAKURA BECAME THE RIGHTFUL MASTER OF THE CLOW CARDS!
SO, KID...READY FOR THINGS TO BE NORMAL...AT LEAST FOR A LITTLE WHILE...?
HEY! WHAT'S THE BIG IDEA?! WHERE'S THE SCENES WITH ME IN THEM?!

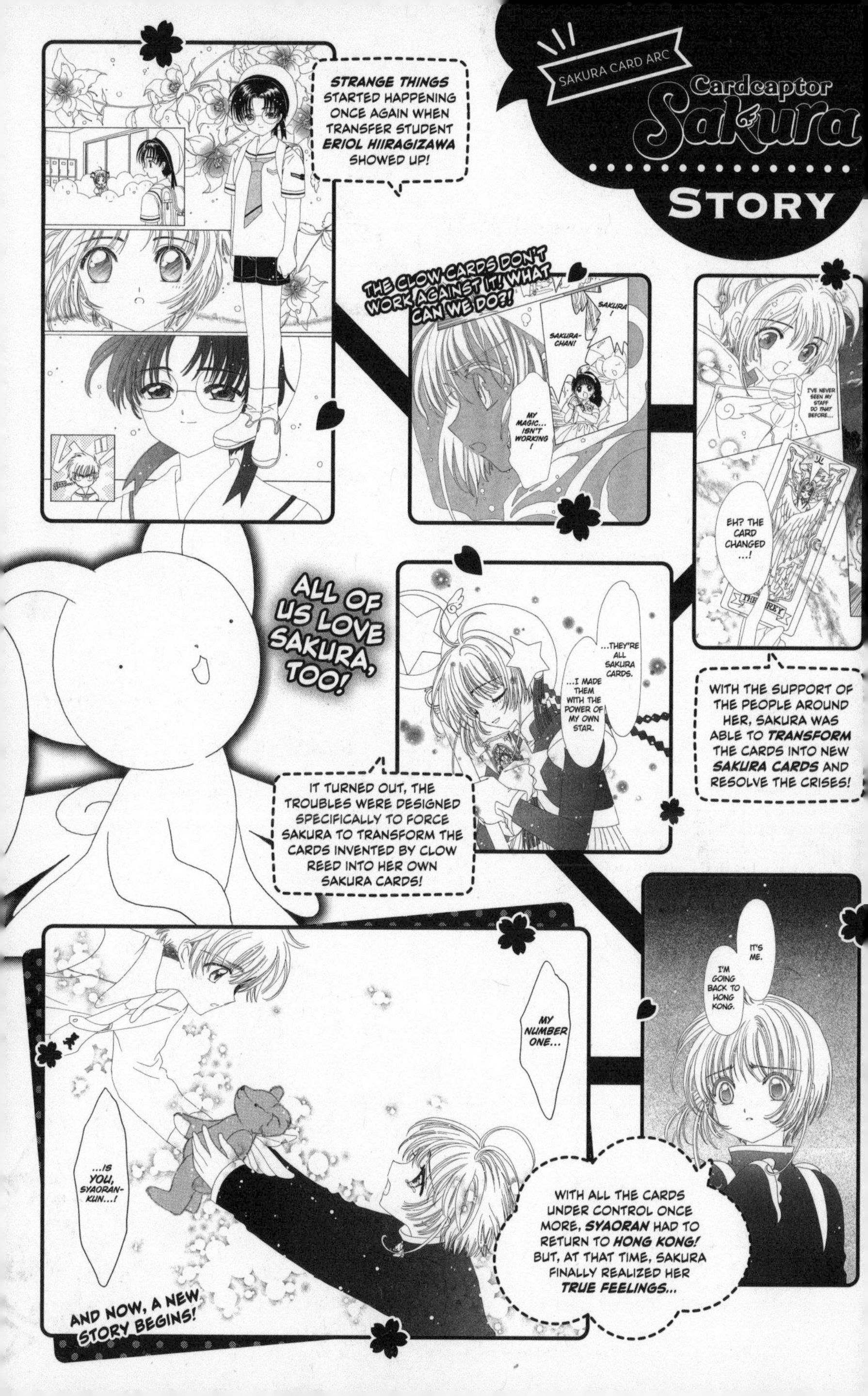
SAKURA CARD ARC
Cardcaptor Sakura
STORY
STRANGE THINGS STARTED HAPPENING ONCE AGAIN WHEN TRANSFER STUDENT ERIOL HIIRAGIZAWA SHOWED UP!
THE CLOW CARDS DON'T WORK AGAINST IT! WHAT CAN WE DO?!
SAKURA!
SAKURA-CHAN!
MY MAGIC... ISN'T WORKING!
I'VE NEVER SEEN MY STAFF DO THAT BEFORE...
EH? THE CARD CHANGED...!
WITH THE SUPPORT OF THE PEOPLE AROUND HER, SAKURA WAS ABLE TO TRANSFORM THE CARDS INTO NEW SAKURA CARDS AND RESOLVE THE CRISES!
...THEY'RE ALL SAKURA CARDS.
...I MADE THEM WITH THE POWER OF MY OWN STAR.
IT TURNED OUT, THE TROUBLES WERE DESIGNED SPECIFICALLY TO FORCE SAKURA TO TRANSFORM THE CARDS INVENTED BY CLOW REED INTO HER OWN SAKURA CARDS!
ALL OF US LOVE SAKURA, TOO!
IT'S ME.
I'M GOING BACK TO HONG KONG.
WITH ALL THE CARDS UNDER CONTROL ONCE MORE, SYAORAN HAD TO RETURN TO HONG KONG! BUT, AT THAT TIME, SAKURA FINALLY REALIZED HER TRUE FEELINGS...
MY NUMBER ONE...
...IS YOU, SYAORAN-KUN...!
AND NOW, A NEW STORY BEGINS!

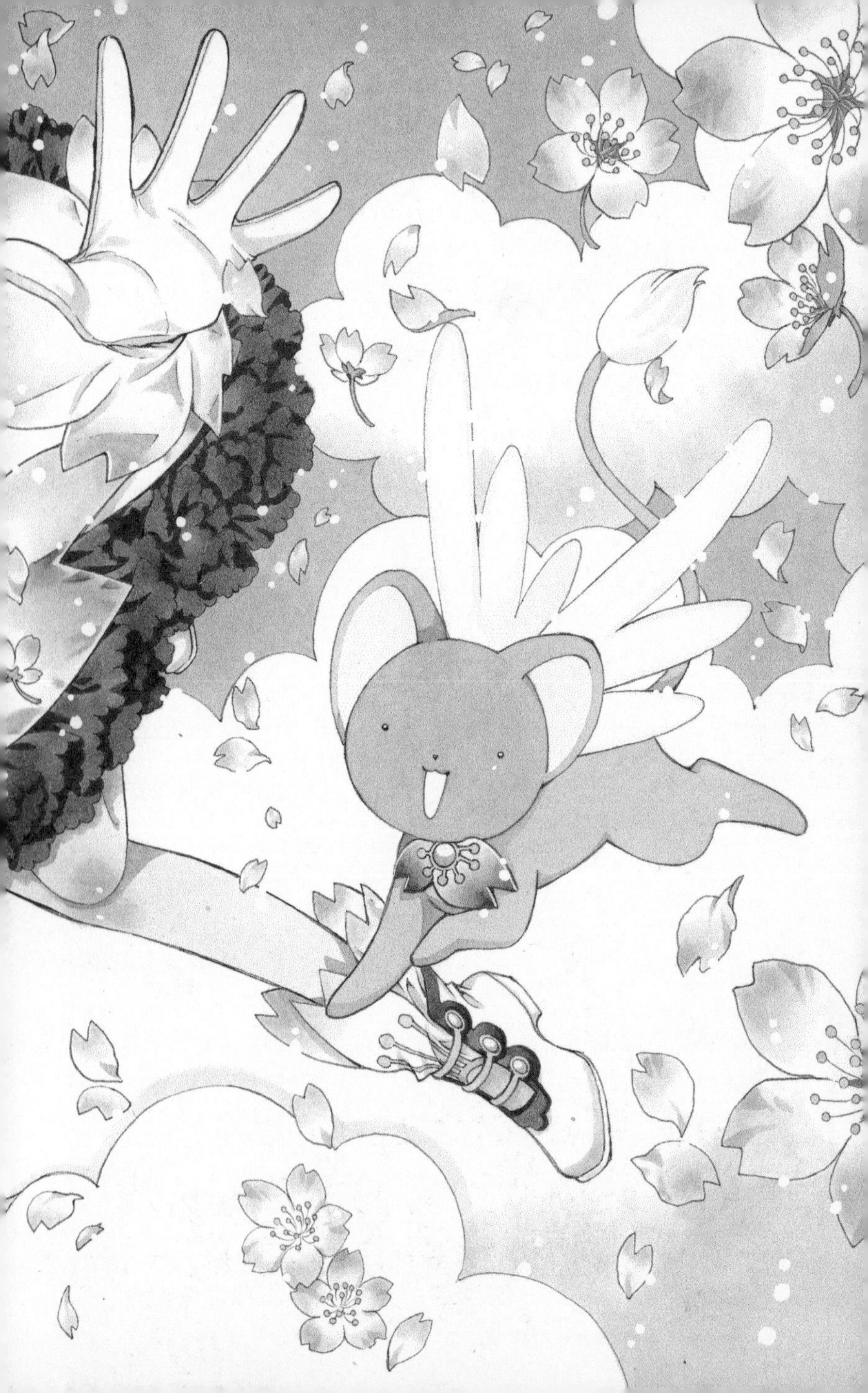

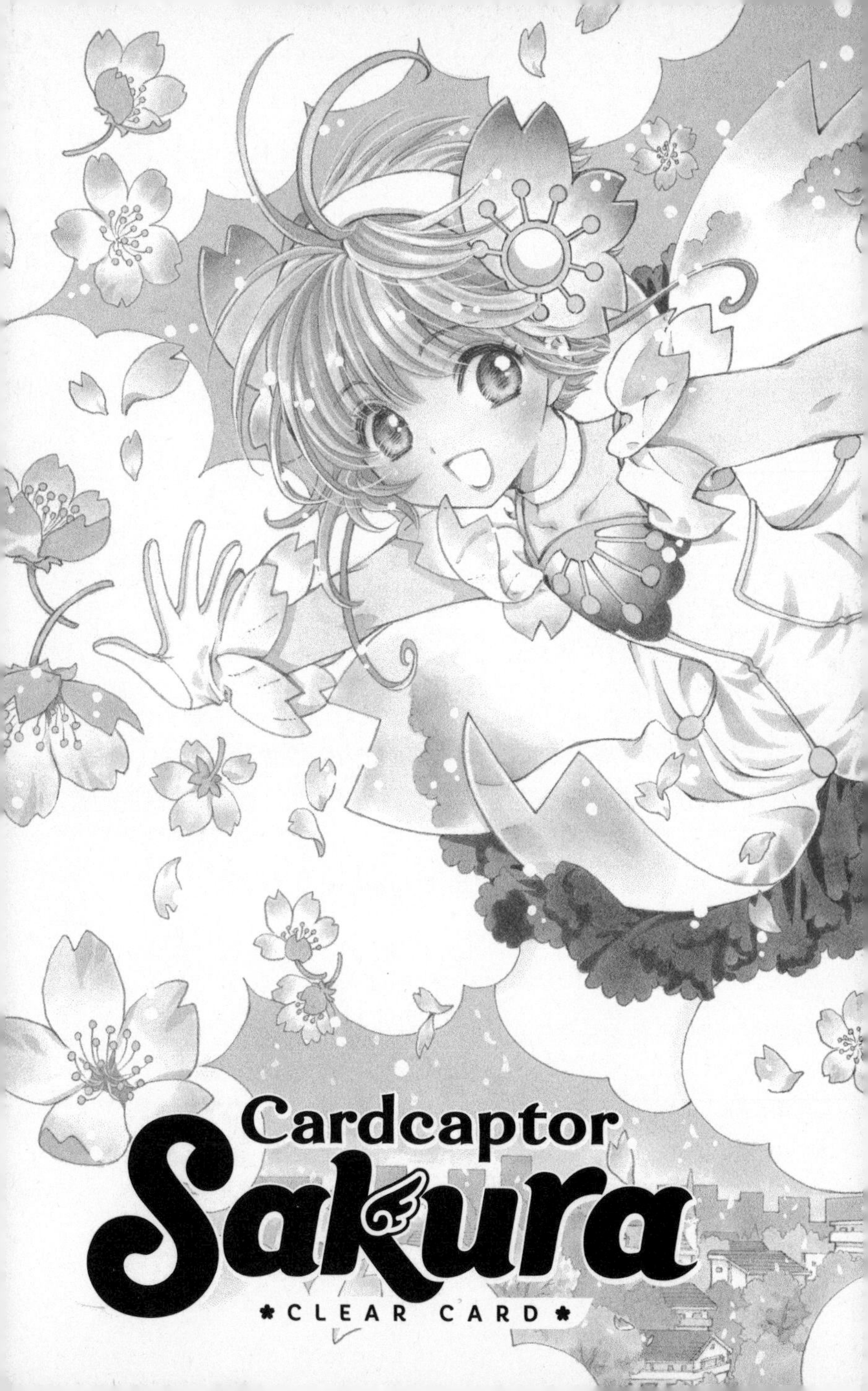
Cardcaptor
Sakura
CLEAR CARD

Cardcaptor Sakura

CLEAR CARD

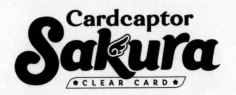

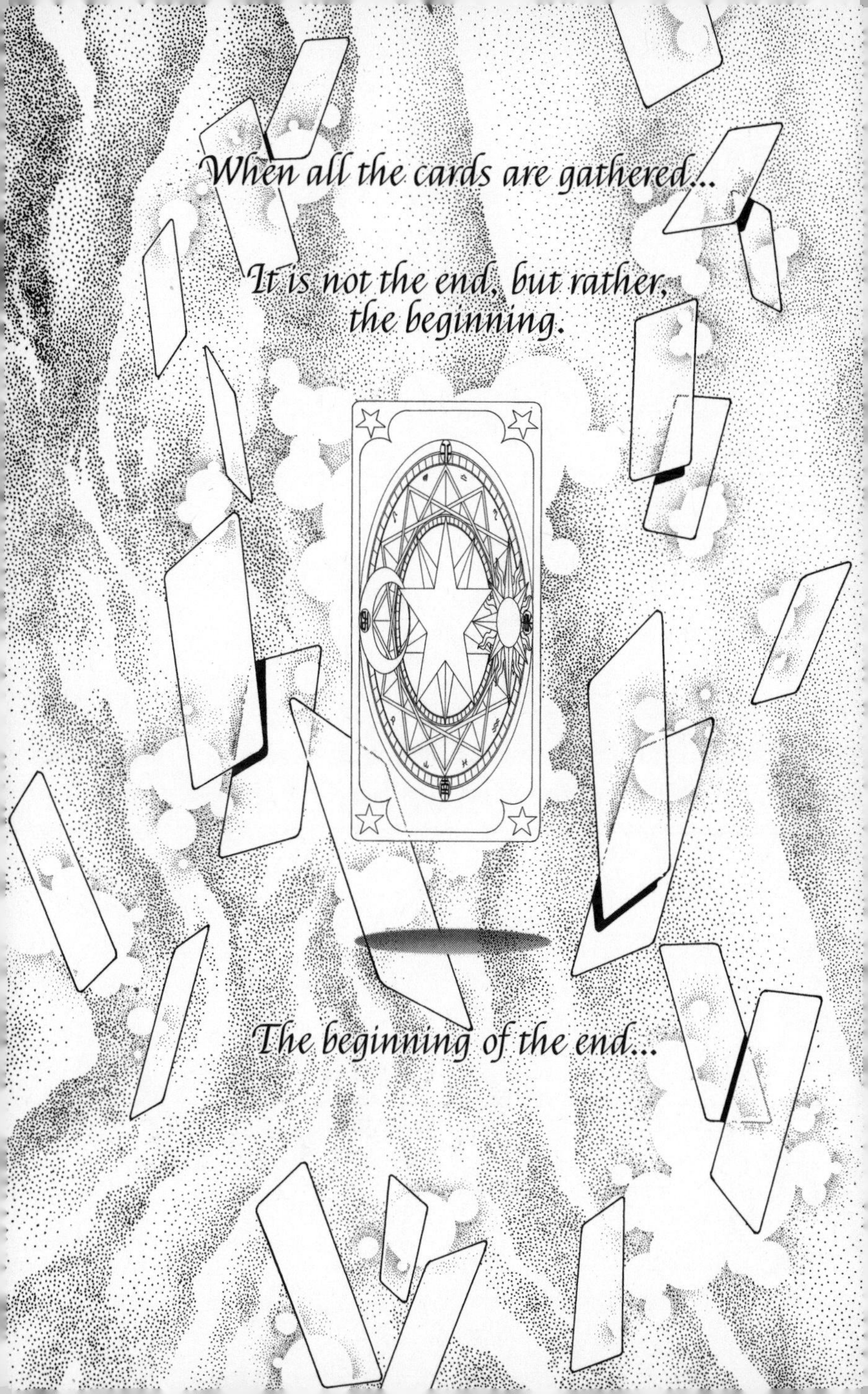
When all the cards are gathered...
It is not the end, but rather, the beginning.
The beginning of the end...

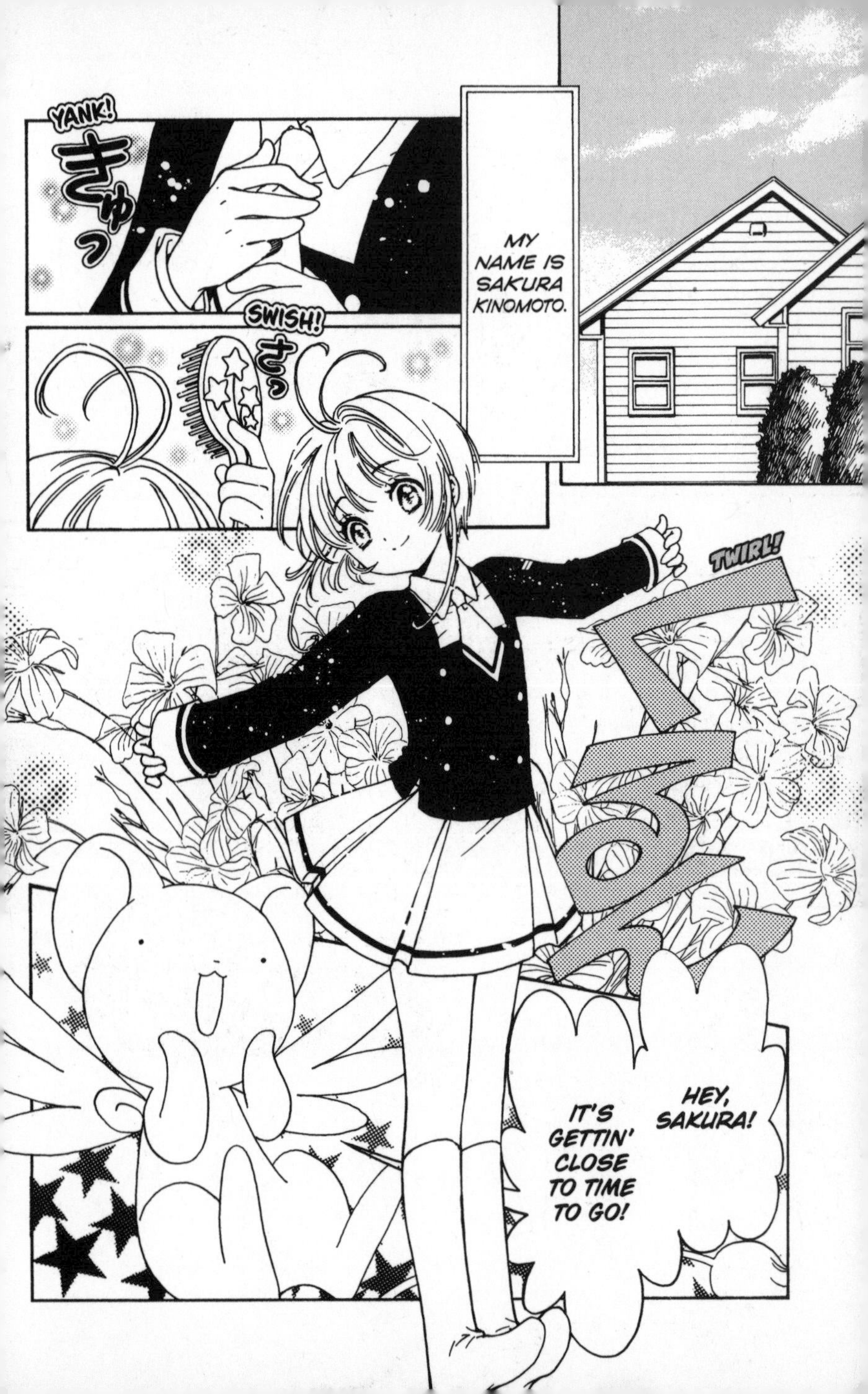
MY NAME IS SAKURA KINOMOTO.
YANK!
きゅっ
SWISH!
さっ
TWIRL!
くるっ
HEY, SAKURA!
IT'S GETTIN' CLOSE TO TIME TO GO!

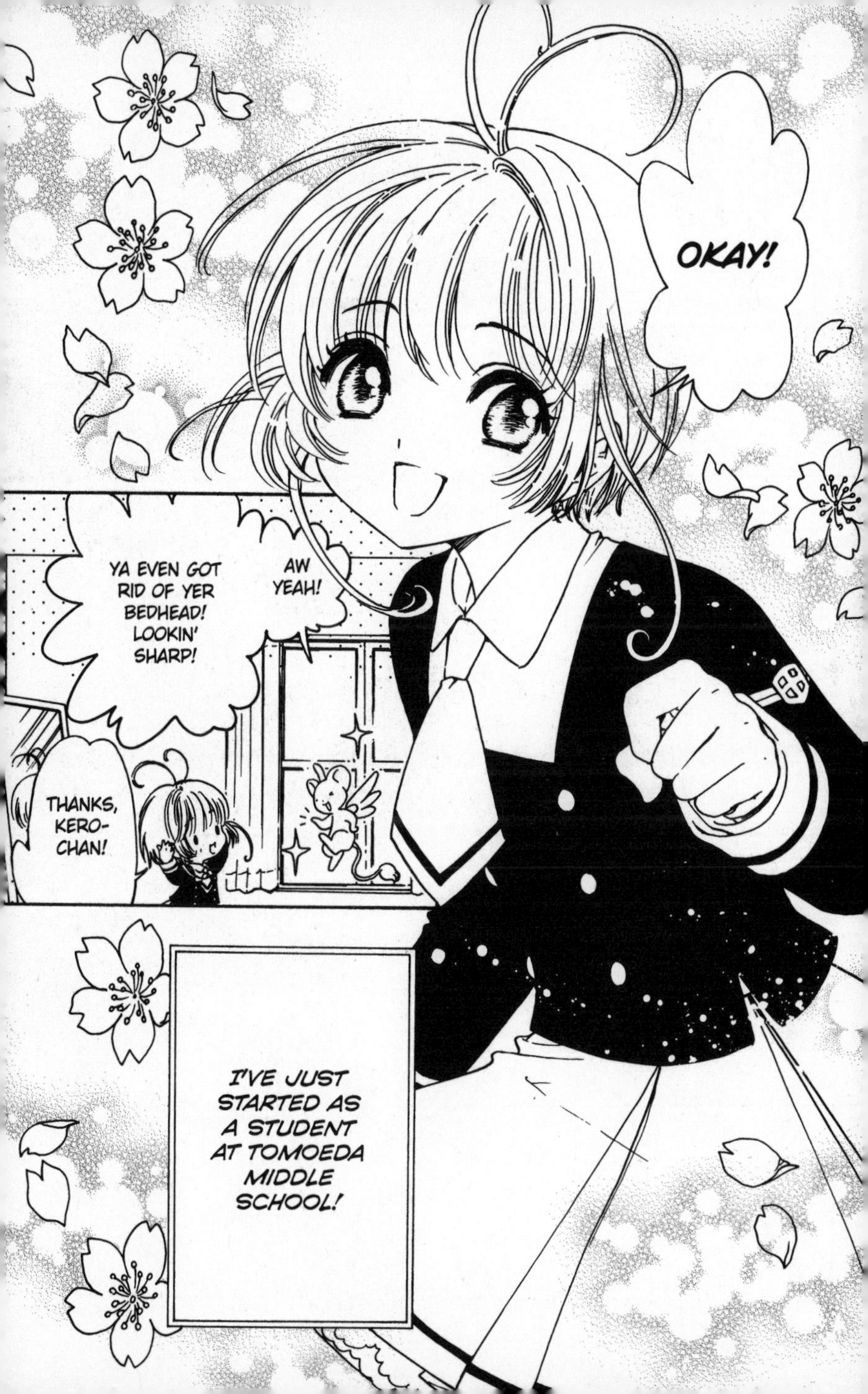
OKAY!
AW YEAH!
YA EVEN GOT RID OF YER BEDHEAD! LOOKIN' SHARP!
THANKS, KERO-CHAN!
I'VE JUST STARTED AS A STUDENT AT TOMOEDA MIDDLE SCHOOL!

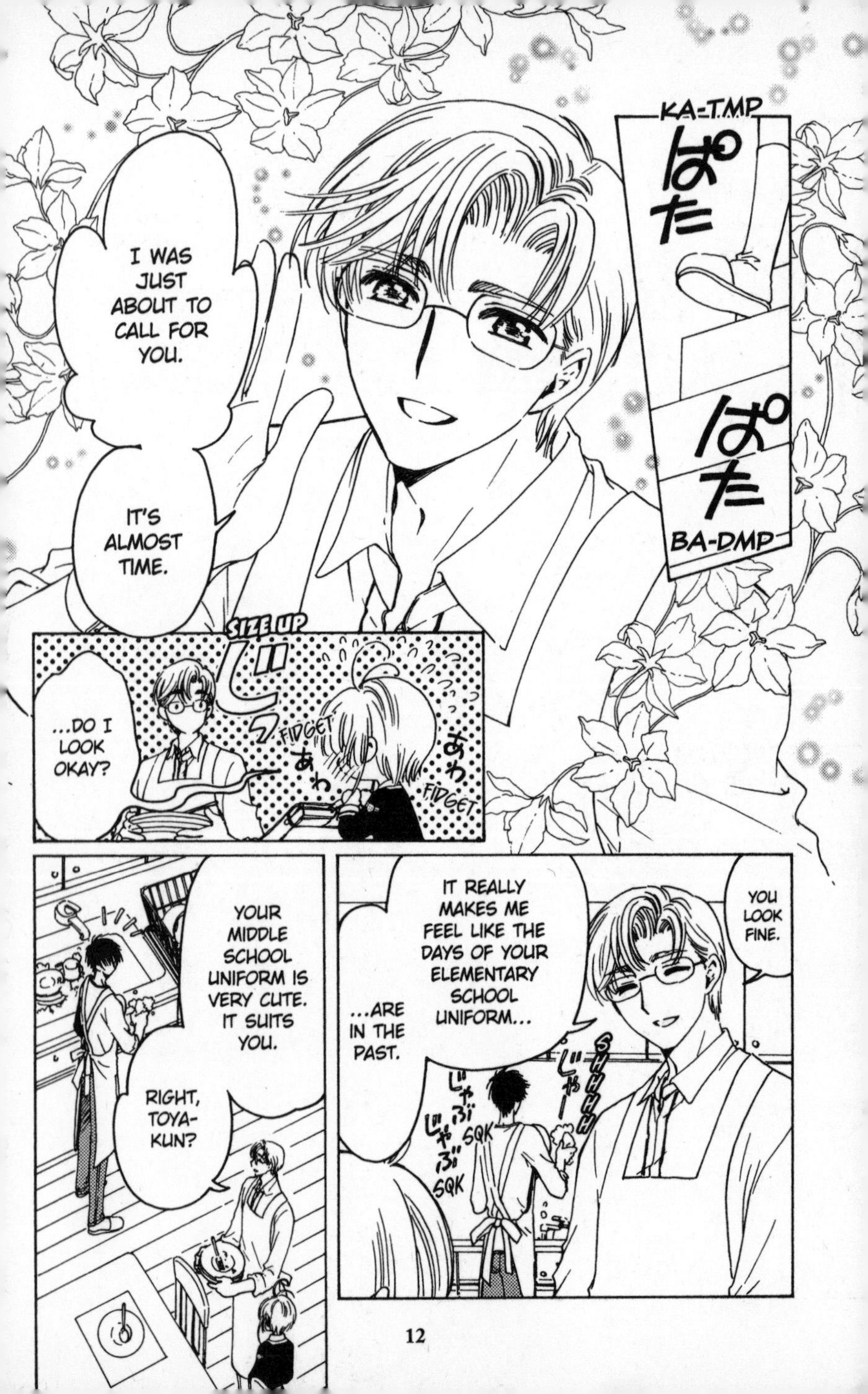
KA-TMP
ぱた
ぱた
BA-DMP
I WAS JUST ABOUT TO CALL FOR YOU.
IT'S ALMOST TIME.
SIZE UP
じー
FIDGET
あわ
あわ
FIDGET
...DO I LOOK OKAY?
YOU LOOK FINE.
IT REALLY MAKES ME FEEL LIKE THE DAYS OF YOUR ELEMENTARY SCHOOL UNIFORM...
...ARE IN THE PAST.
SHHHH
じゃー
じゃぶ
じゃぶ
SQK
SQK
YOUR MIDDLE SCHOOL UNIFORM IS VERY CUTE. IT SUITS YOU.
RIGHT, TOYA-KUN?

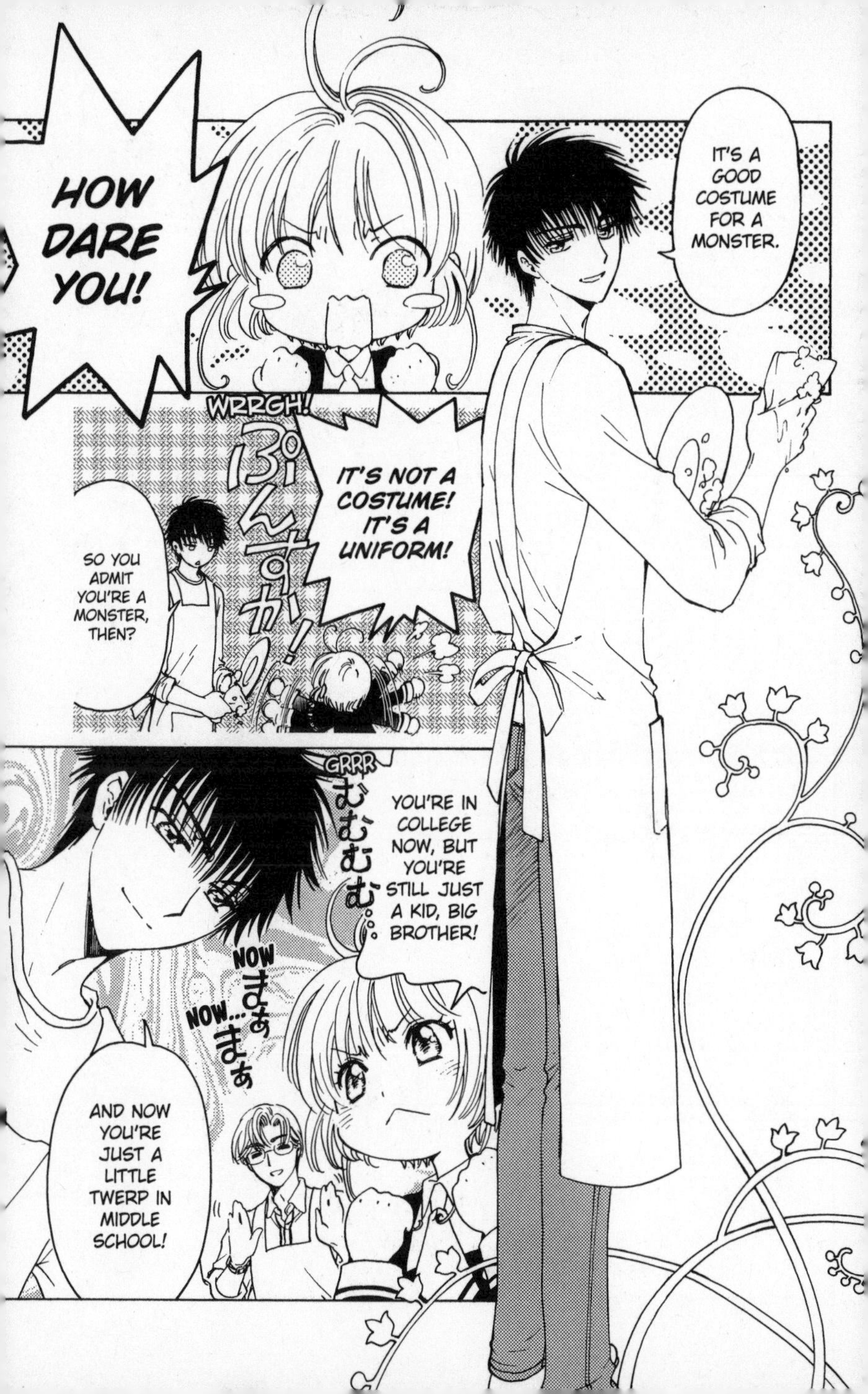
IT'S A GOOD COSTUME FOR A MONSTER.
HOW DARE YOU!
WRRGH!
ぷんすか!
IT'S NOT A COSTUME! IT'S A UNIFORM!
SO YOU ADMIT YOU'RE A MONSTER, THEN?
GRRR
むむむ。。
YOU'RE IN COLLEGE NOW, BUT YOU'RE STILL JUST A KID, BIG BROTHER!
NOW まぁ
NOW... まぁ
AND NOW YOU'RE JUST A LITTLE TWERP IN MIDDLE SCHOOL!

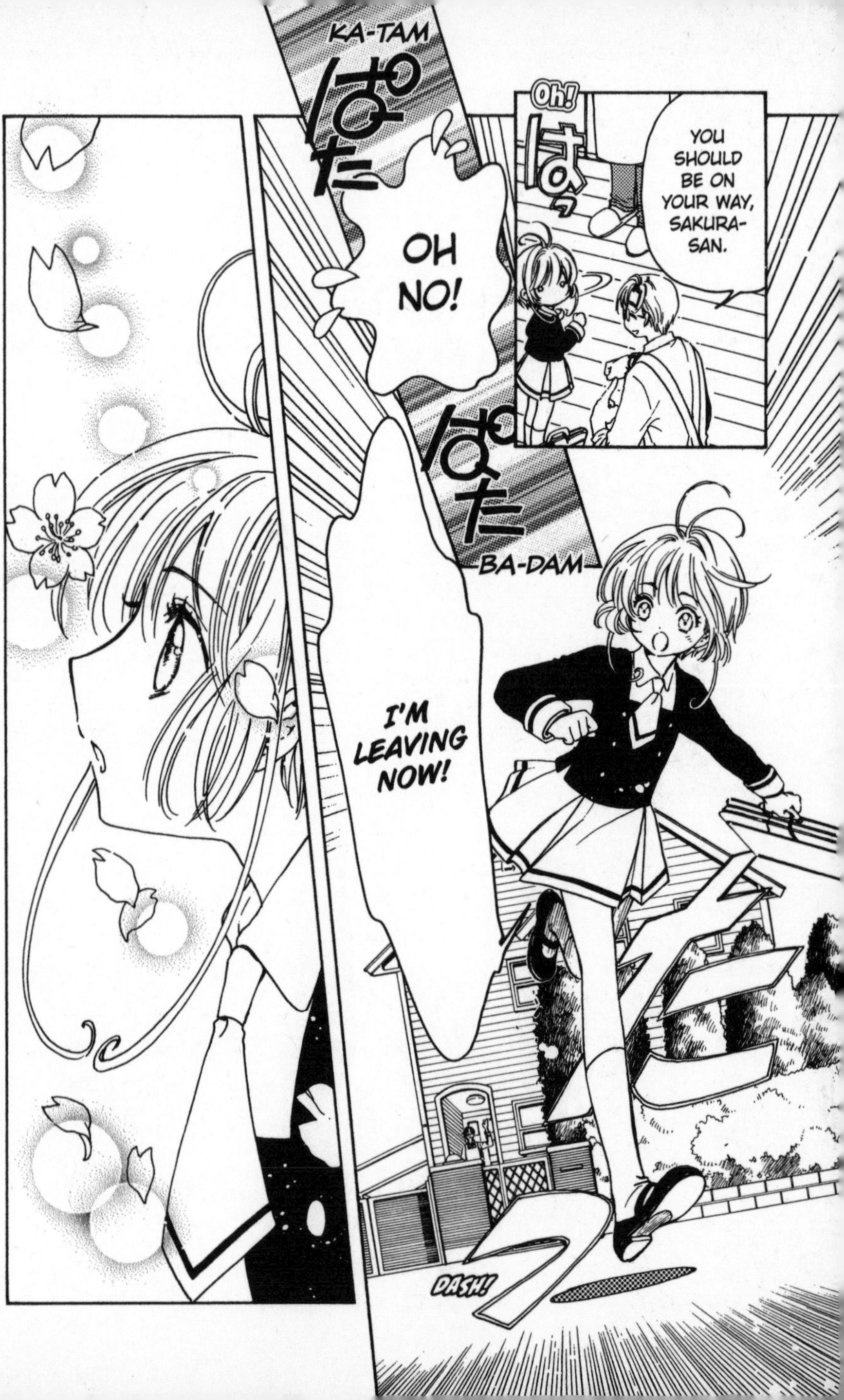
Oh!
はっ
YOU SHOULD BE ON YOUR WAY, SAKURA-SAN.
KA-TAM
ぱた
OH NO!
ぱた
BA-DAM
I'M LEAVING NOW!
DASH!

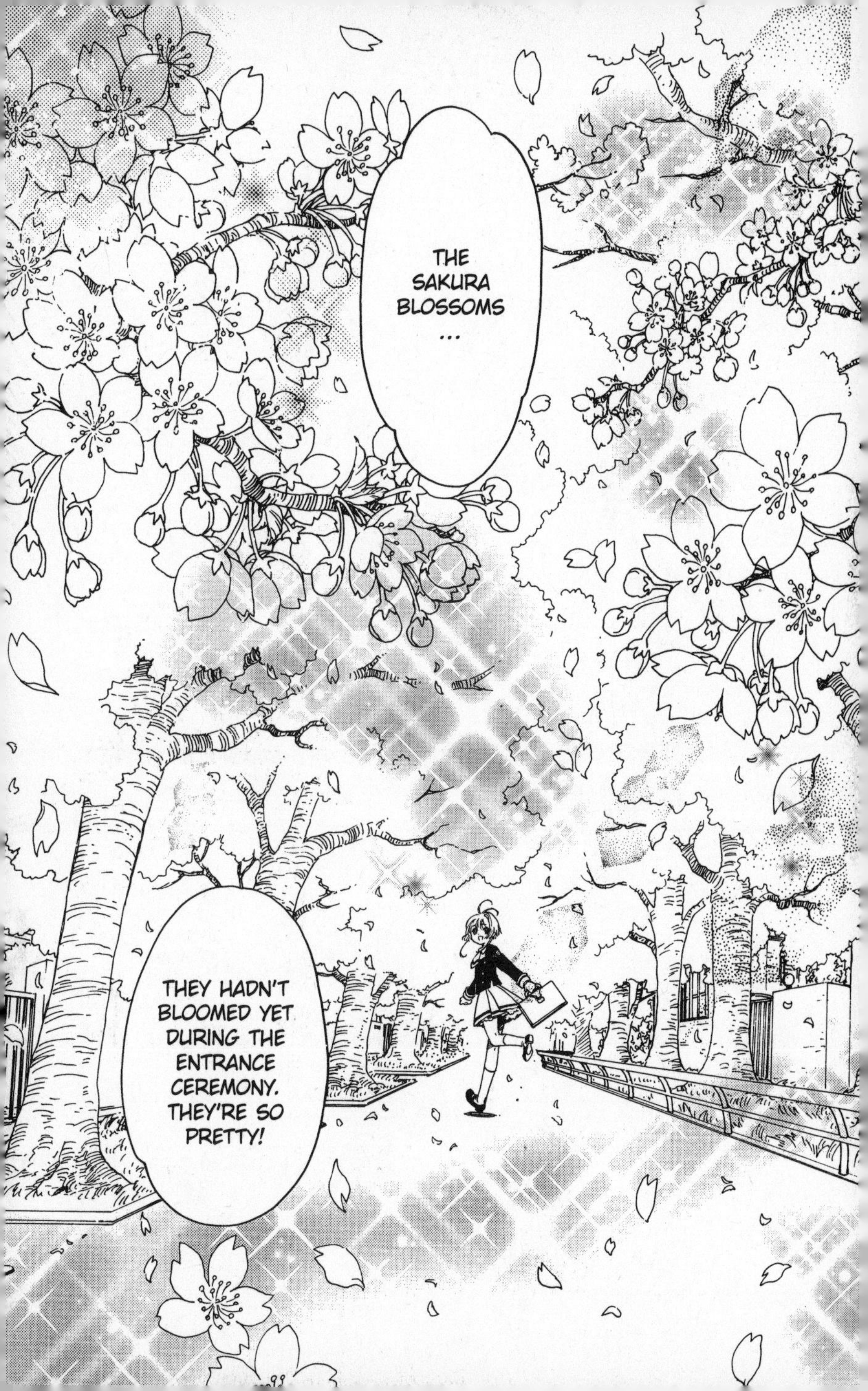
THE SAKURA BLOSSOMS ...
THEY HADN'T BLOOMED YET DURING THE ENTRANCE CEREMONY. THEY'RE SO PRETTY!

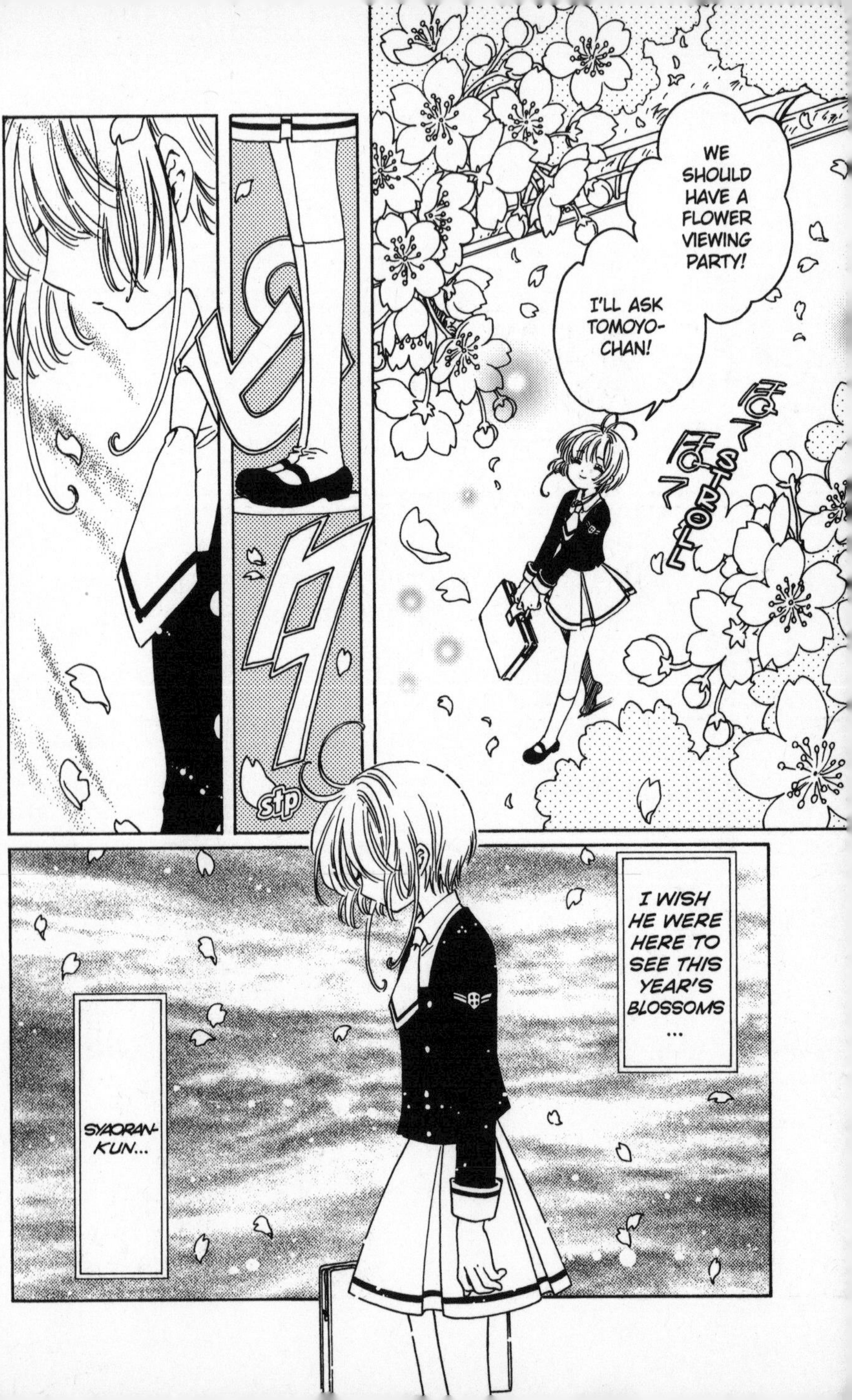
WE SHOULD HAVE A FLOWER VIEWING PARTY!
I'LL ASK TOMOYO-CHAN!
STROLL
stp
I WISH HE WERE HERE TO SEE THIS YEAR'S BLOSSOMS ...
SYAORAN-KUN...

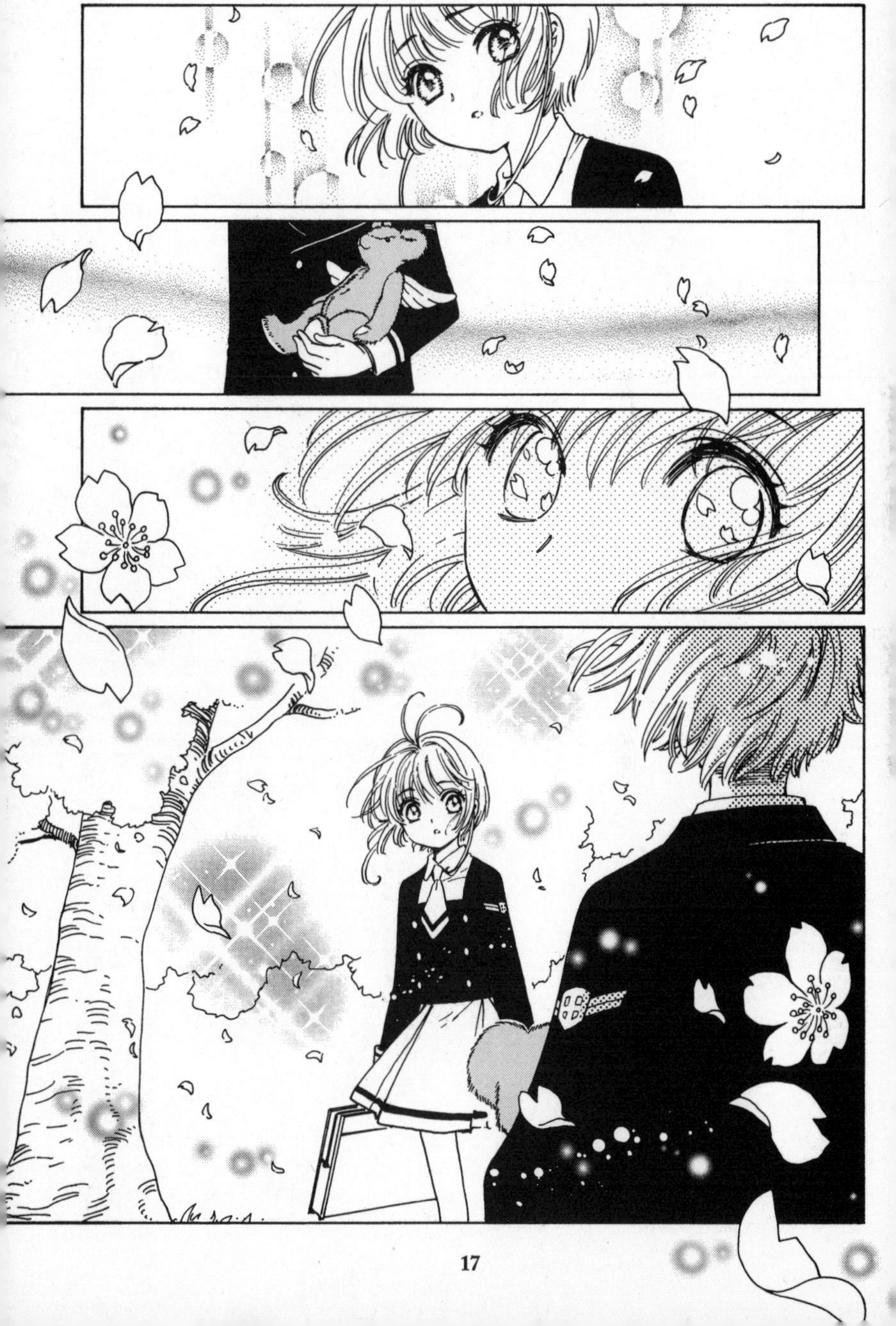

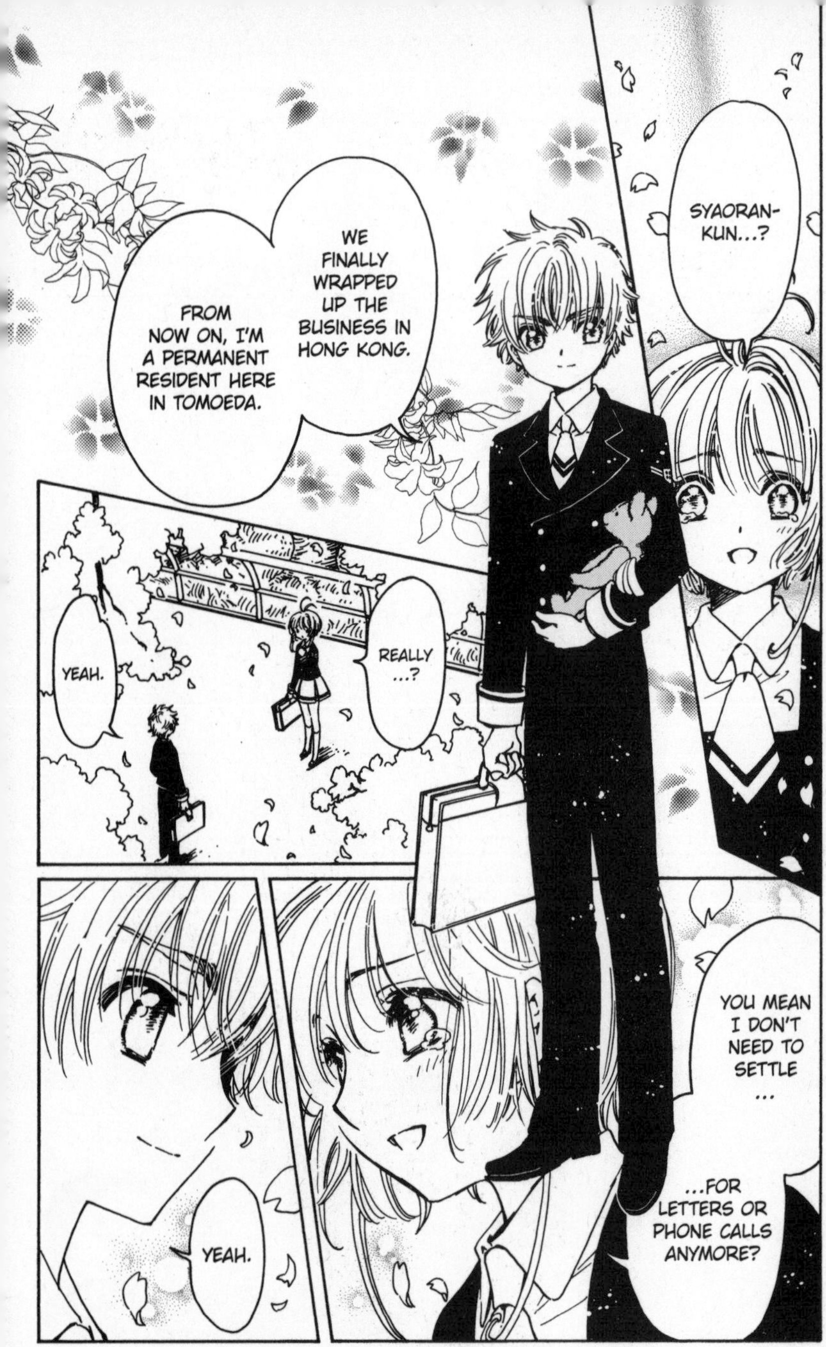
SYAORAN-KUN...?
WE FINALLY WRAPPED UP THE BUSINESS IN HONG KONG.
FROM NOW ON, I'M A PERMANENT RESIDENT HERE IN TOMOEDA.
REALLY ...?
YEAH.
YOU MEAN I DON'T NEED TO SETTLE ...
...FOR LETTERS OR PHONE CALLS ANYMORE?
YEAH.

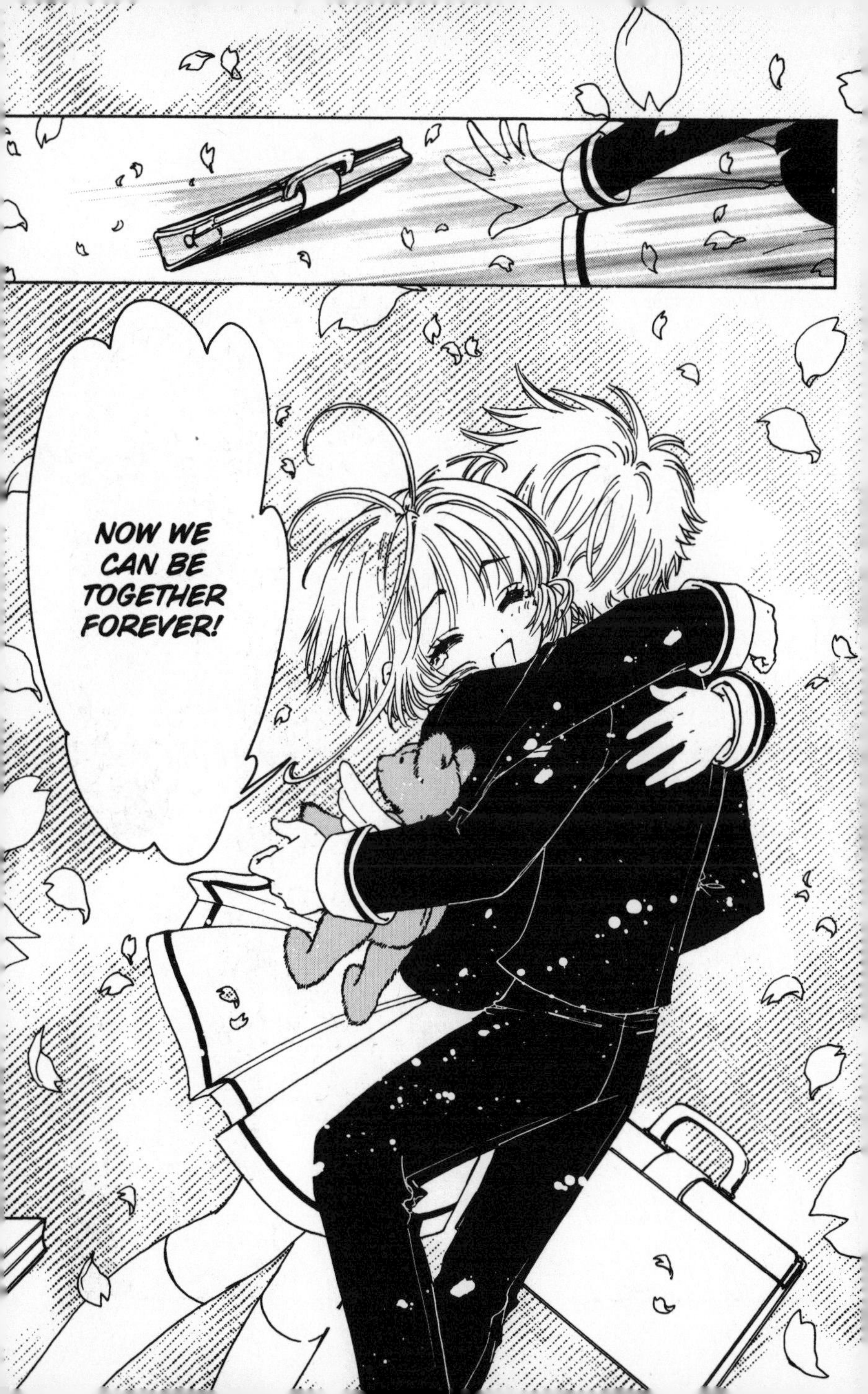
NOW WE CAN BE TOGETHER FOREVER!

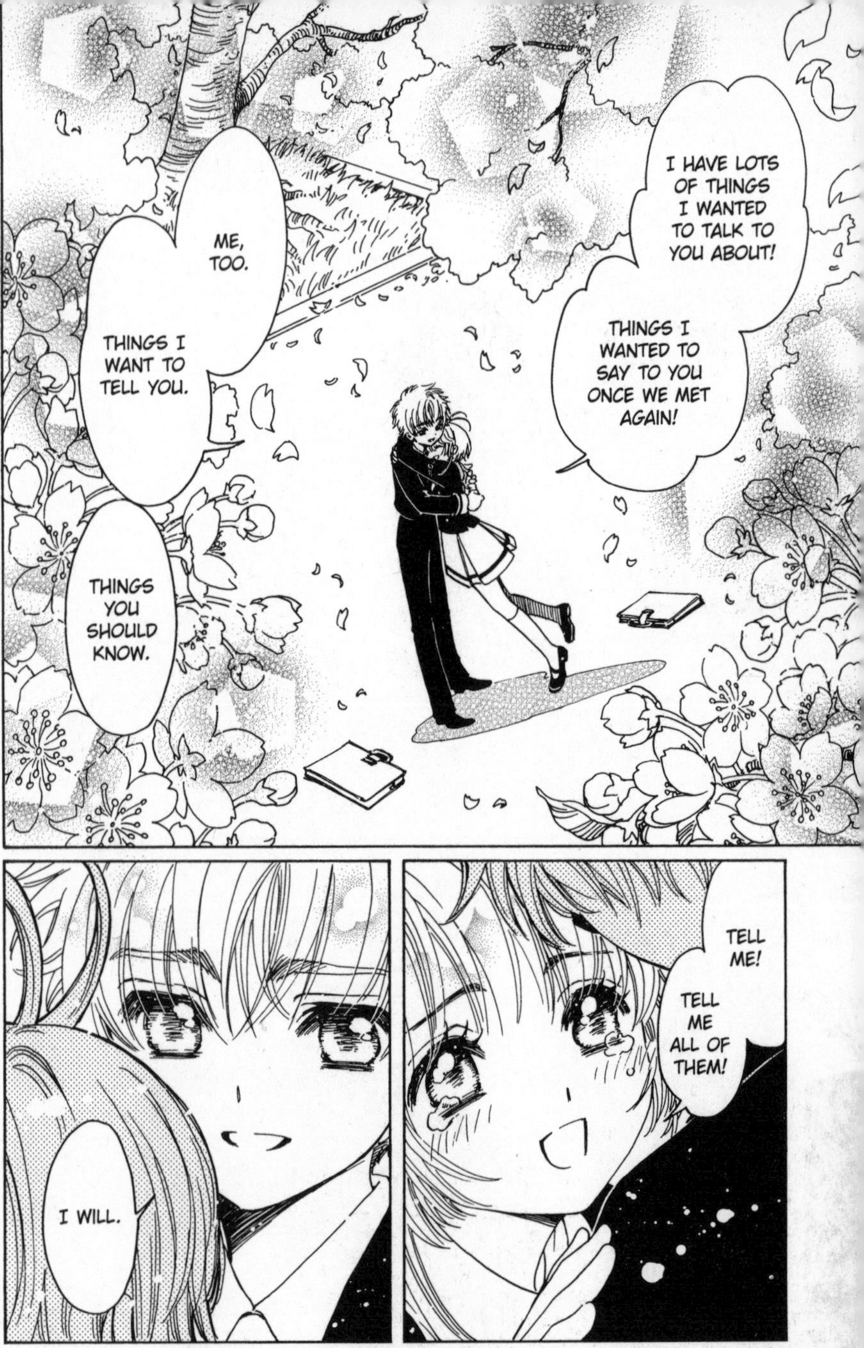
I HAVE LOTS OF THINGS I WANTED TO TALK TO YOU ABOUT!
THINGS I WANTED TO SAY TO YOU ONCE WE MET AGAIN!
ME, TOO.
THINGS I WANT TO TELL YOU.
THINGS YOU SHOULD KNOW.
TELL ME!
TELL ME ALL OF THEM!
I WILL.

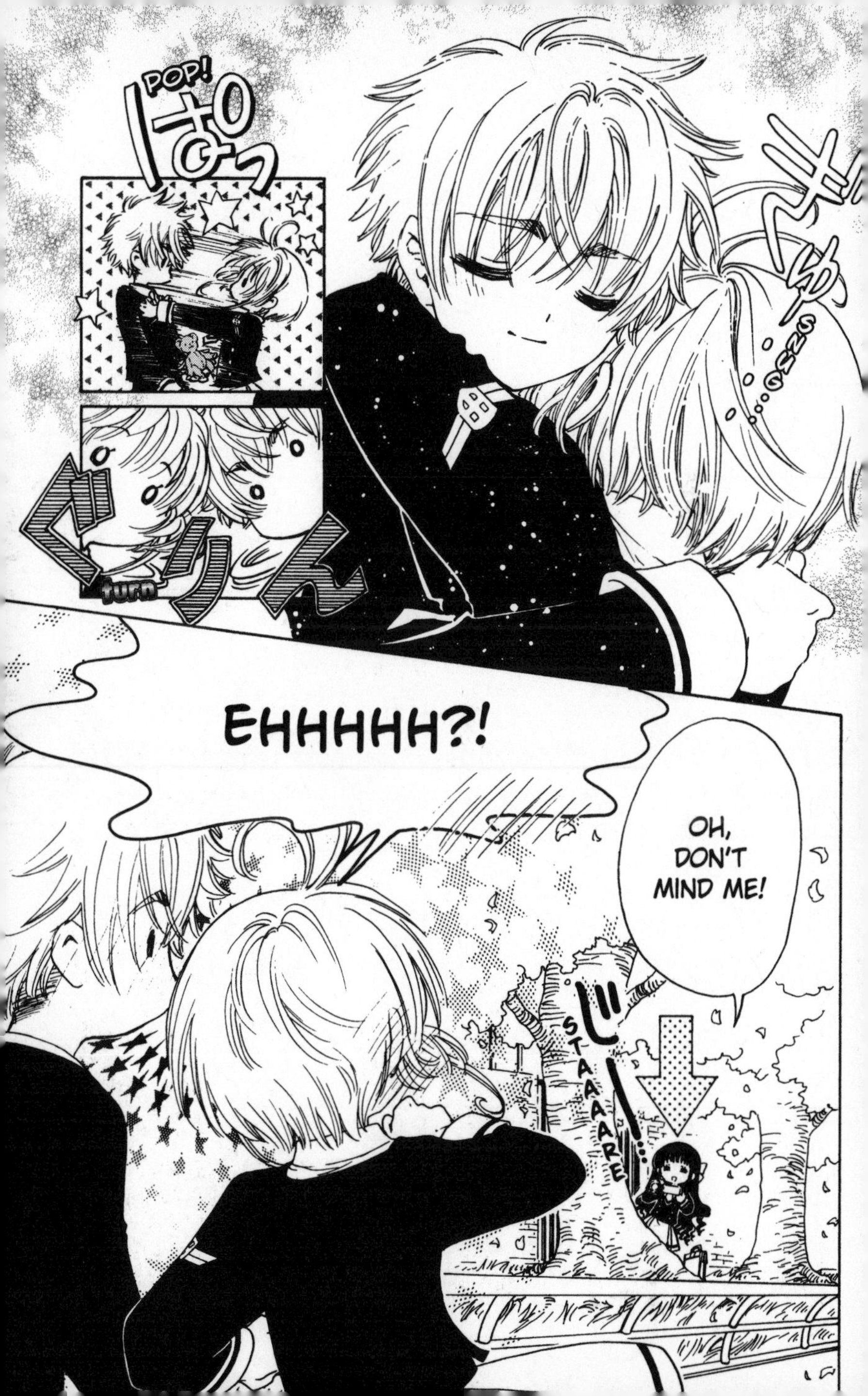
SNUG...
POP!
turn
EHHHHH?!
OH, DON'T MIND ME!
STAAAARE

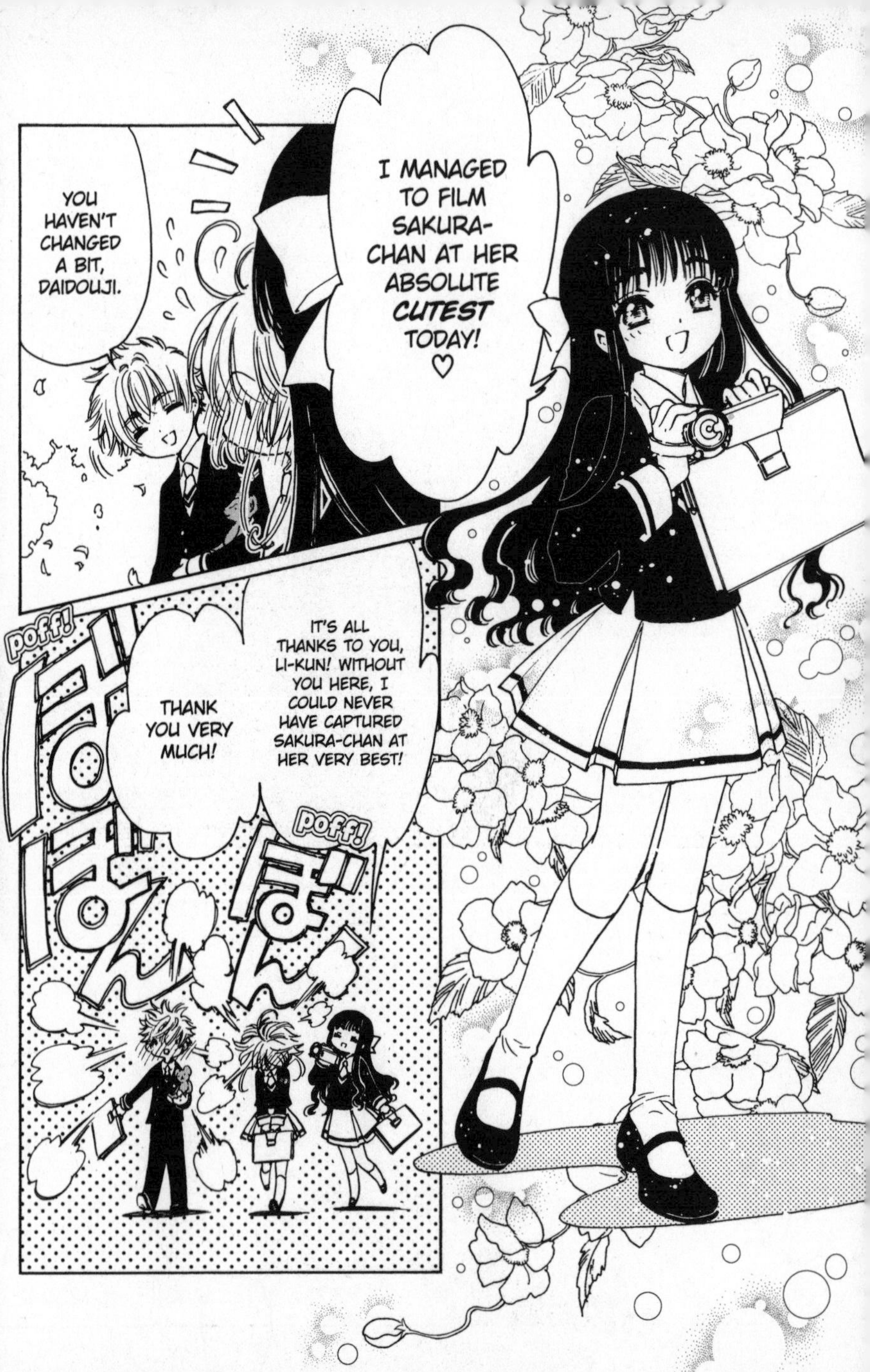
I MANAGED TO FILM SAKURA-CHAN AT HER ABSOLUTE CUTEST TODAY! ♡
YOU HAVEN'T CHANGED A BIT, DAIDOUJI.
IT'S ALL THANKS TO YOU, LI-KUN! WITHOUT YOU HERE, I COULD NEVER HAVE CAPTURED SAKURA-CHAN AT HER VERY BEST!
THANK YOU VERY MUCH!
poff!
poff!

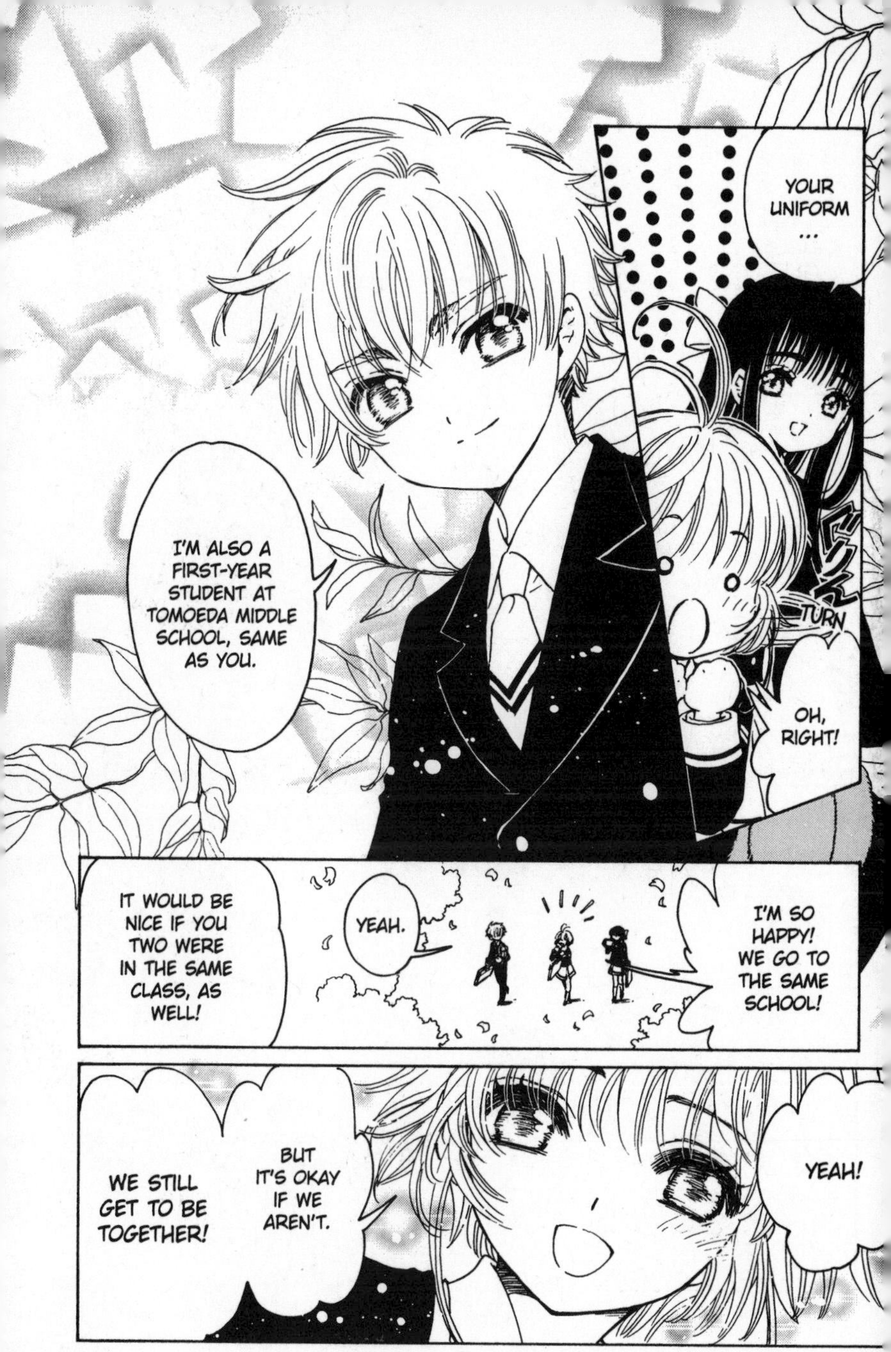
YOUR UNIFORM ...
TURN
OH, RIGHT!
I'M ALSO A FIRST-YEAR STUDENT AT TOMOEDA MIDDLE SCHOOL, SAME AS YOU.
I'M SO HAPPY! WE GO TO THE SAME SCHOOL!
YEAH.
IT WOULD BE NICE IF YOU TWO WERE IN THE SAME CLASS, AS WELL!
YEAH!
BUT IT'S OKAY IF WE AREN'T.
WE STILL GET TO BE TOGETHER!

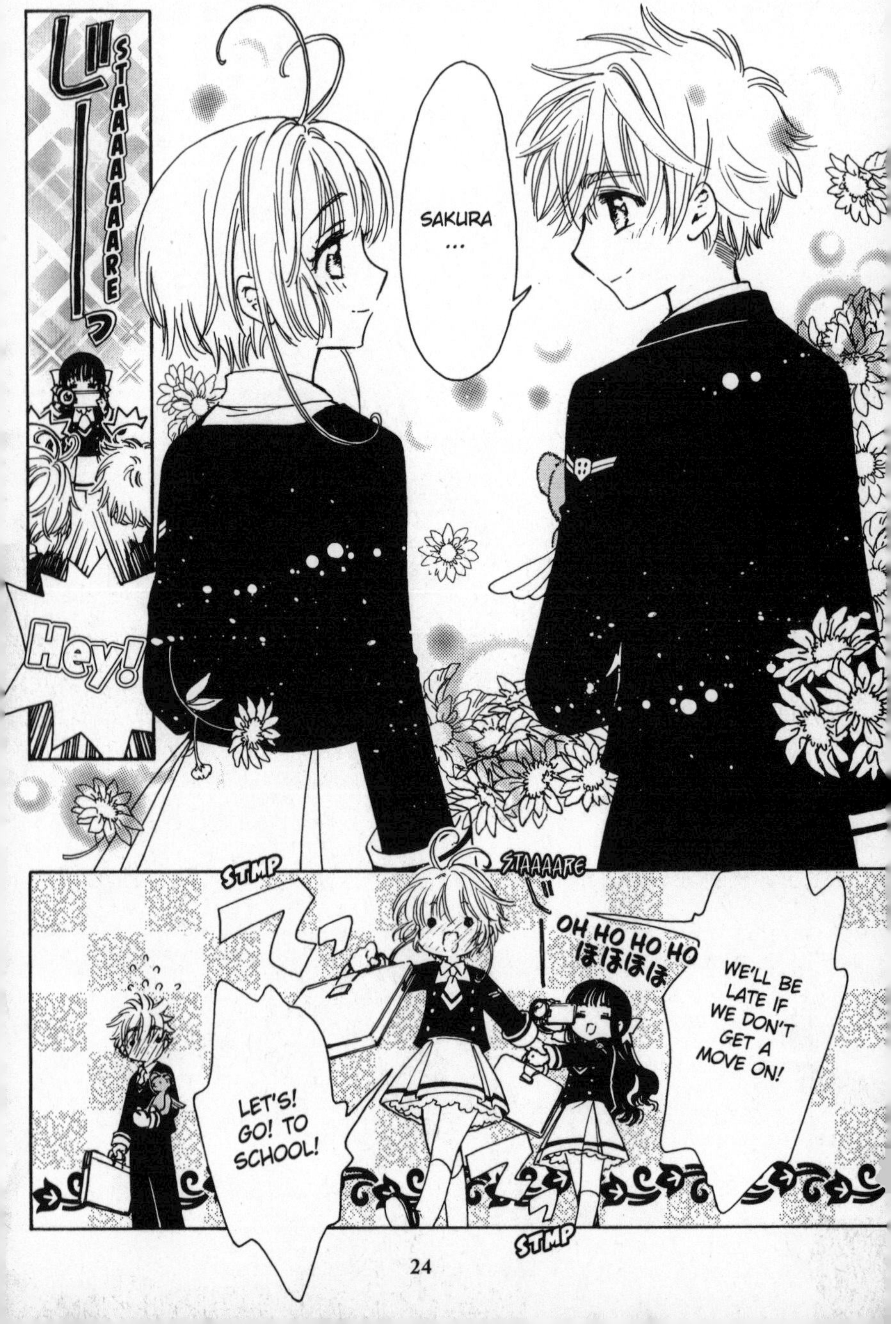
SAKURA ...
STAAAAAAARE
じーっ
Hey!
STAAAARE
じ
OH HO HO HO
ほほほほ
WE'LL BE LATE IF WE DON'T GET A MOVE ON!
STMP
LET'S! GO! TO SCHOOL!
STMP

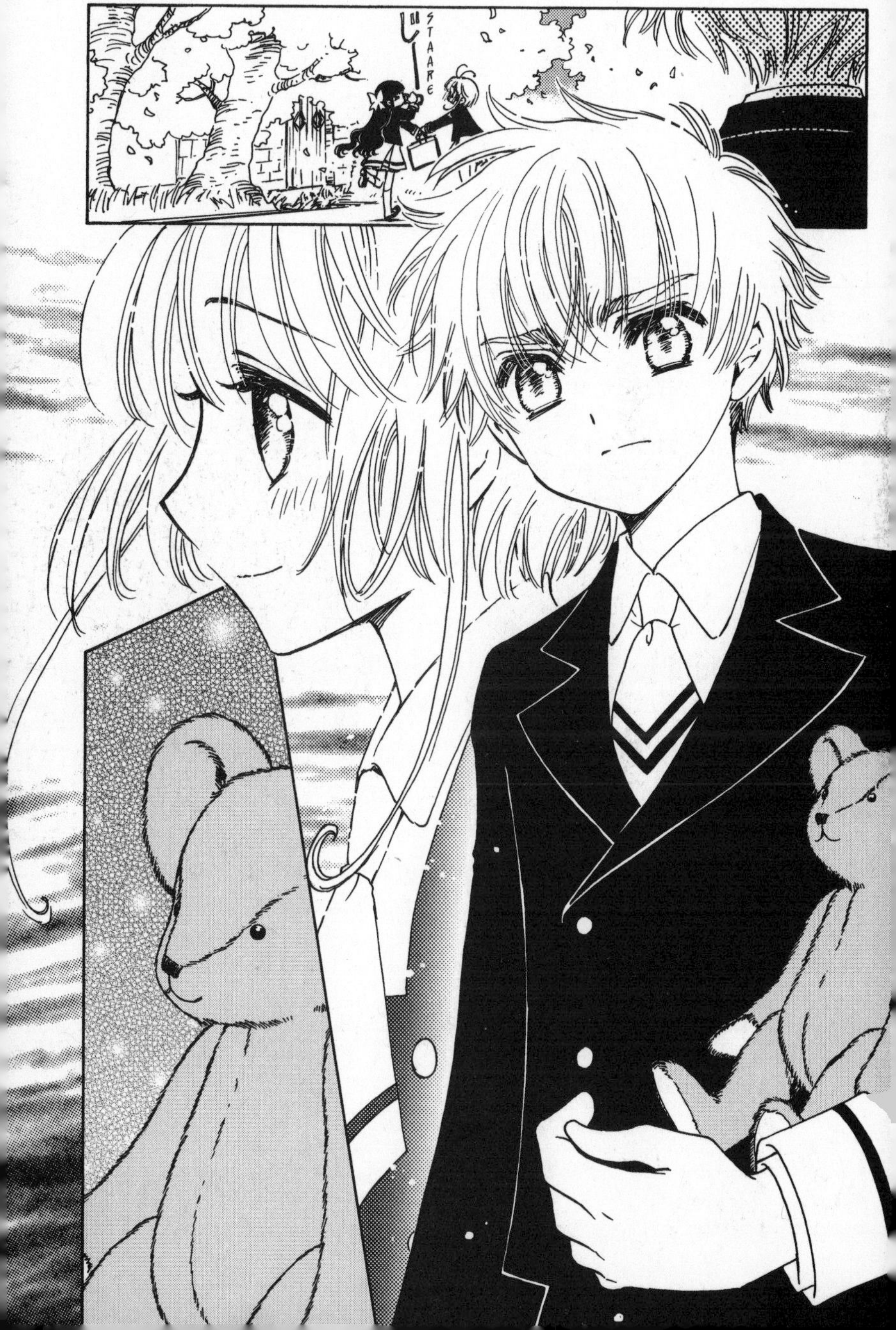
じー
STAARE

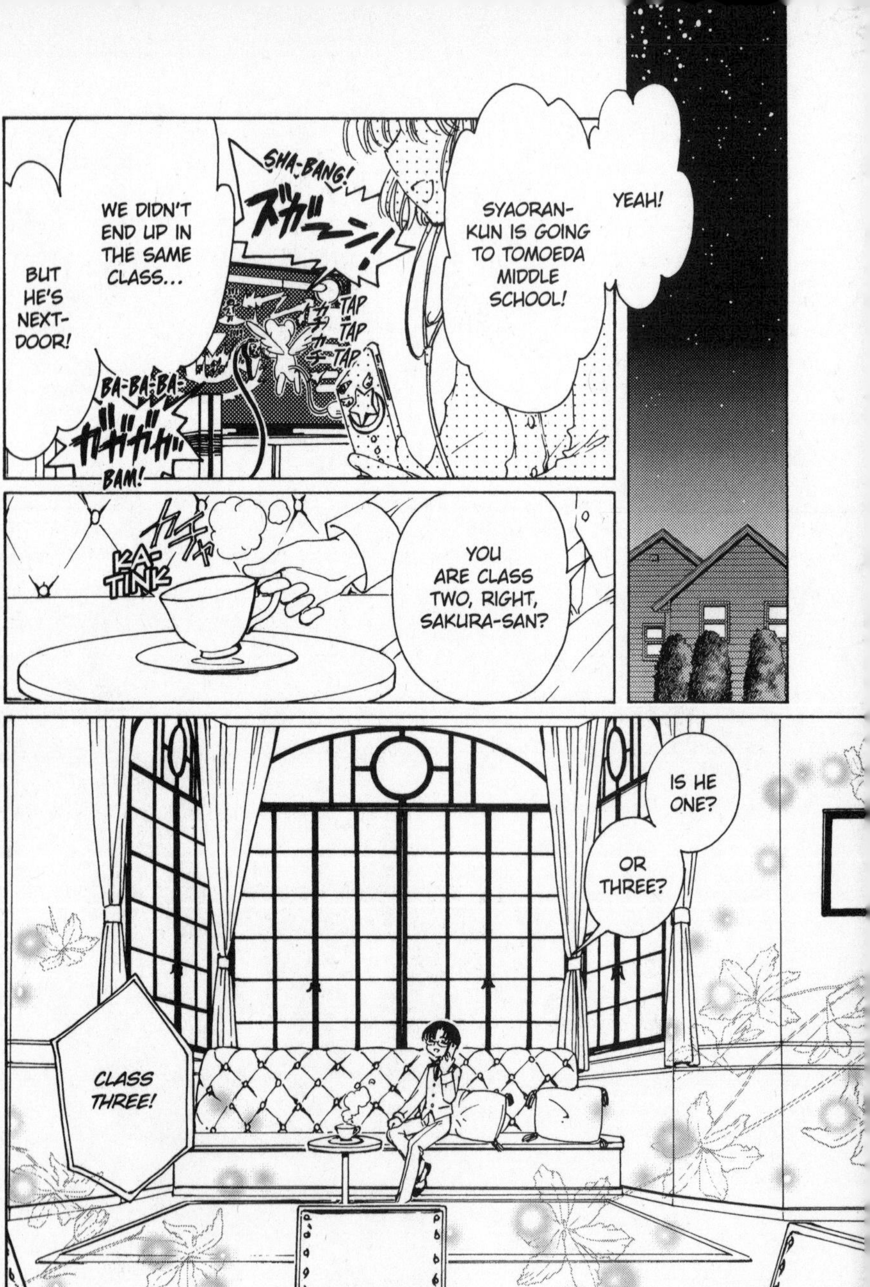
YEAH!
SYAORAN-KUN IS GOING TO TOMOEDA MIDDLE SCHOOL!
SHA-BANG!
TAP TAP TAP
WE DIDN'T END UP IN THE SAME CLASS...
BUT HE'S NEXT-DOOR!
BA-BA-BA
BAM!
YOU ARE CLASS TWO, RIGHT, SAKURA-SAN?
KA-TINK
IS HE ONE?
OR THREE?
CLASS THREE!

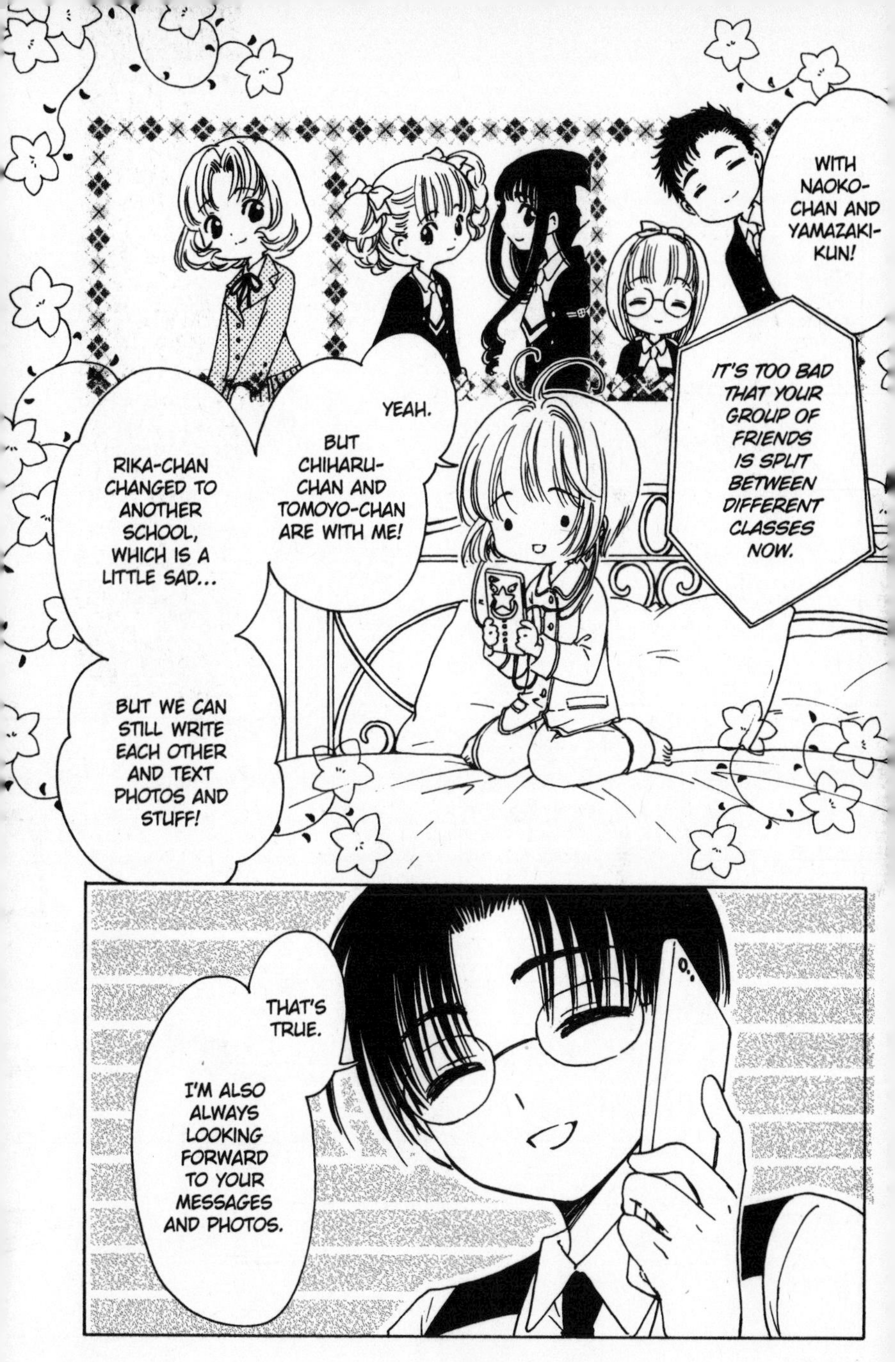
WITH NAOKO-CHAN AND YAMAZAKI-KUN!
IT'S TOO BAD THAT YOUR GROUP OF FRIENDS IS SPLIT BETWEEN DIFFERENT CLASSES NOW.
YEAH.
BUT CHIHARU-CHAN AND TOMOYO-CHAN ARE WITH ME!
RIKA-CHAN CHANGED TO ANOTHER SCHOOL, WHICH IS A LITTLE SAD...
BUT WE CAN STILL WRITE EACH OTHER AND TEXT PHOTOS AND STUFF!
THAT'S TRUE.
I'M ALSO ALWAYS LOOKING FORWARD TO YOUR MESSAGES AND PHOTOS.

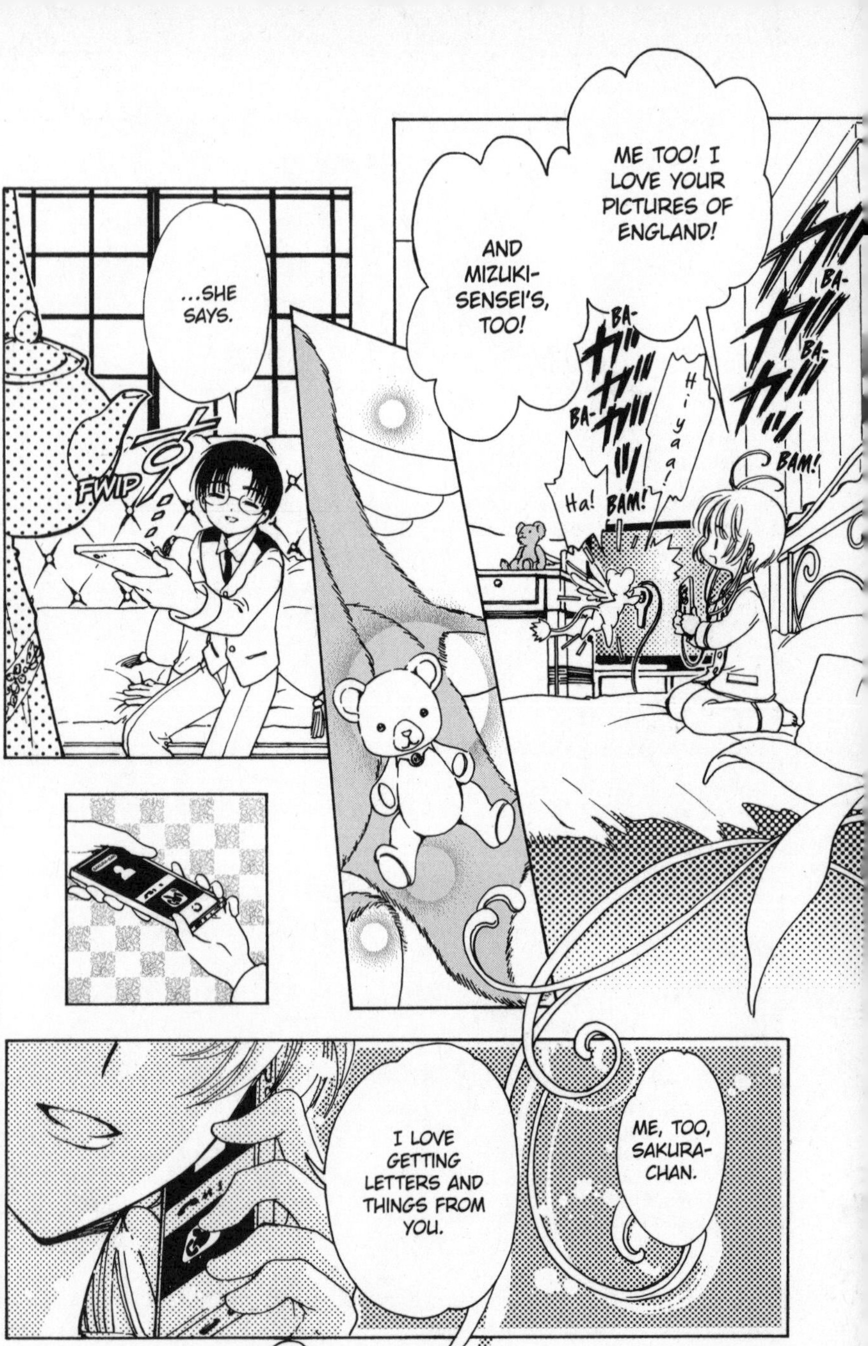
ME TOO! I LOVE YOUR PICTURES OF ENGLAND!
BA-
BA-
BAM!
Hi yaa!
AND MIZUKI-SENSEI'S, TOO!
BA-
BA-
BAM!
Ha!
...SHE SAYS.
FWIP
ME, TOO, SAKURA-CHAN.
I LOVE GETTING LETTERS AND THINGS FROM YOU.

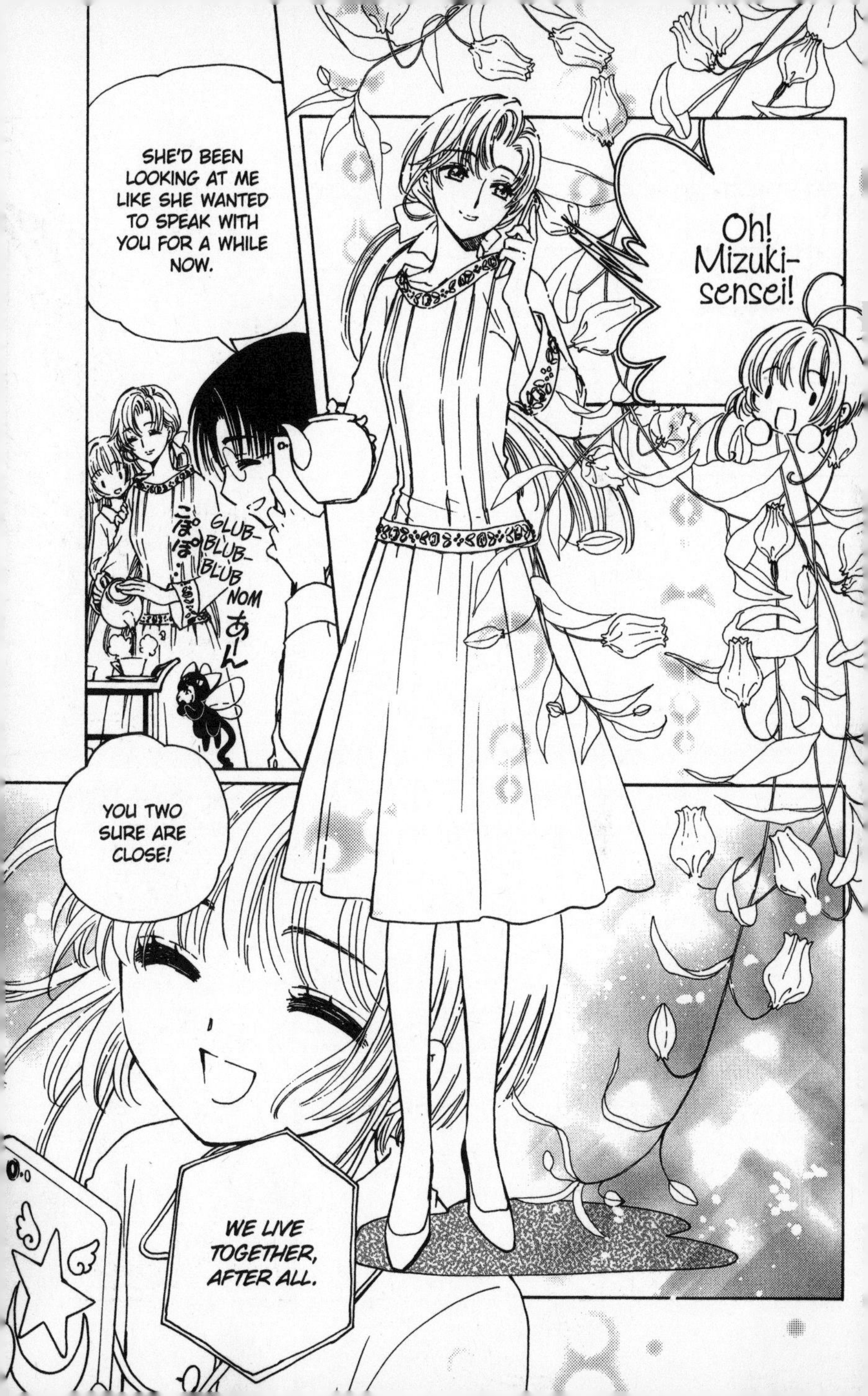
Oh! Mizuki-sensei!
SHE'D BEEN LOOKING AT ME LIKE SHE WANTED TO SPEAK WITH YOU FOR A WHILE NOW.
こぽぽ…
GLUB-BLUB-BLUB
あーん
NOM
YOU TWO SURE ARE CLOSE!
WE LIVE TOGETHER, AFTER ALL.

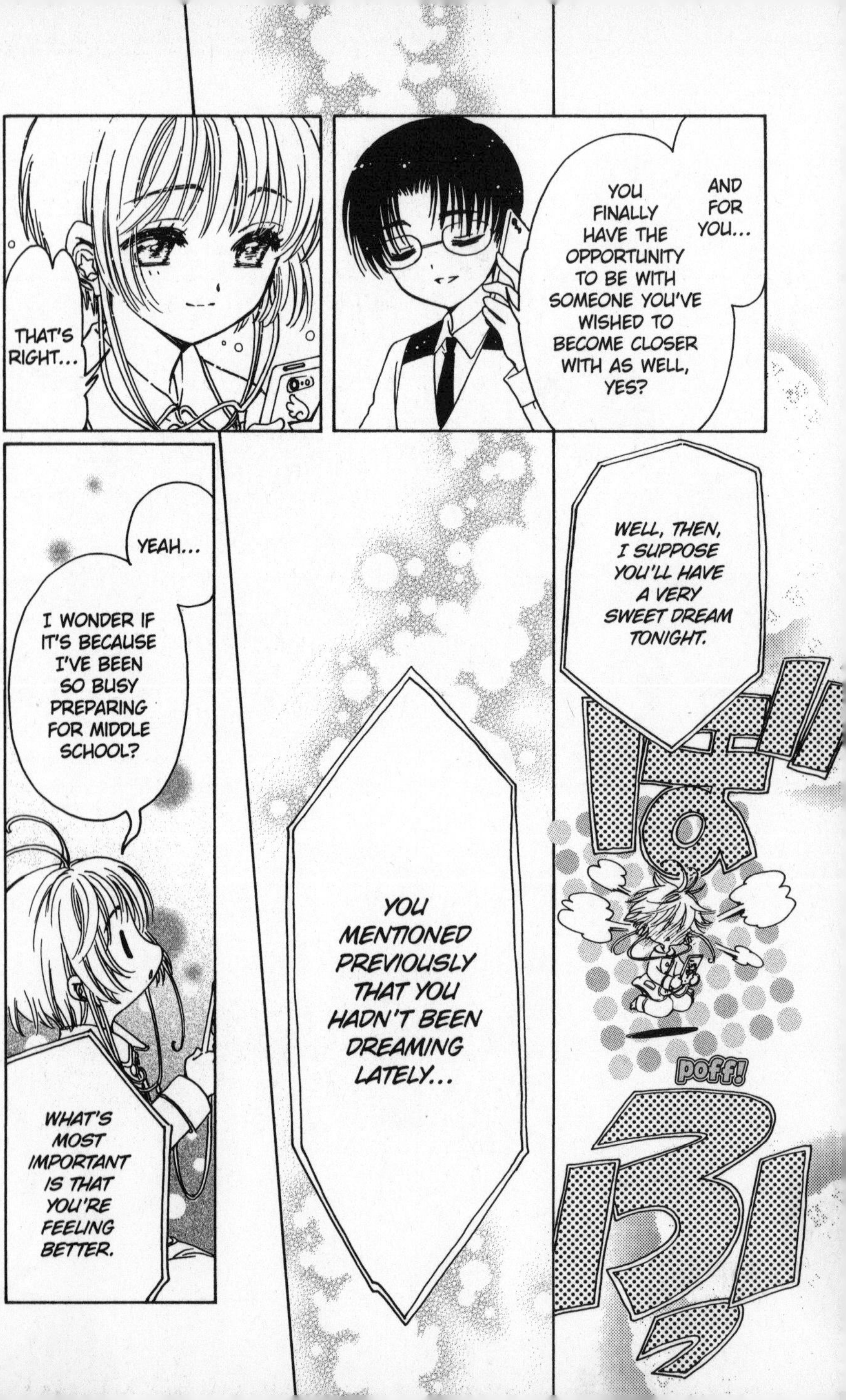
AND FOR YOU...
YOU FINALLY HAVE THE OPPORTUNITY TO BE WITH SOMEONE YOU'VE WISHED TO BECOME CLOSER WITH AS WELL, YES?
THAT'S RIGHT...
WELL, THEN, I SUPPOSE YOU'LL HAVE A VERY SWEET DREAM TONIGHT.
poff!
YOU MENTIONED PREVIOUSLY THAT YOU HADN'T BEEN DREAMING LATELY...
YEAH...
I WONDER IF IT'S BECAUSE I'VE BEEN SO BUSY PREPARING FOR MIDDLE SCHOOL?
WHAT'S MOST IMPORTANT IS THAT YOU'RE FEELING BETTER.

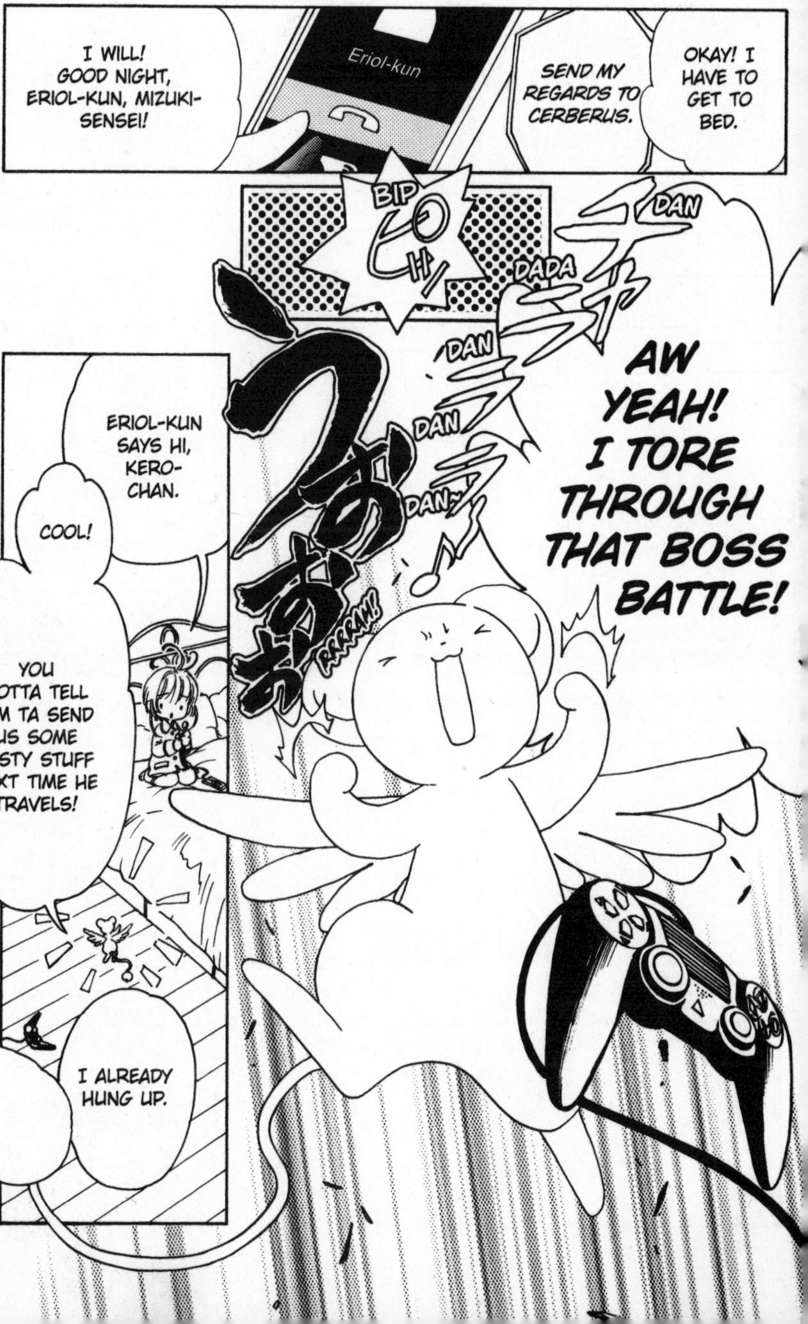
Eriol-kun
OKAY! I HAVE TO GET TO BED.
SEND MY REGARDS TO CERBERUS.
I WILL! GOOD NIGHT, ERIOL-KUN, MIZUKI-SENSEI!
BIP
DAN
DADA
DAN
DAN
DAN~
AW YEAH! I TORE THROUGH THAT BOSS BATTLE!
BRRRAM!
ERIOL-KUN SAYS HI, KERO-CHAN.
COOL!
YOU GOTTA TELL HIM TA SEND US SOME TASTY STUFF NEXT TIME HE TRAVELS!
I ALREADY HUNG UP.

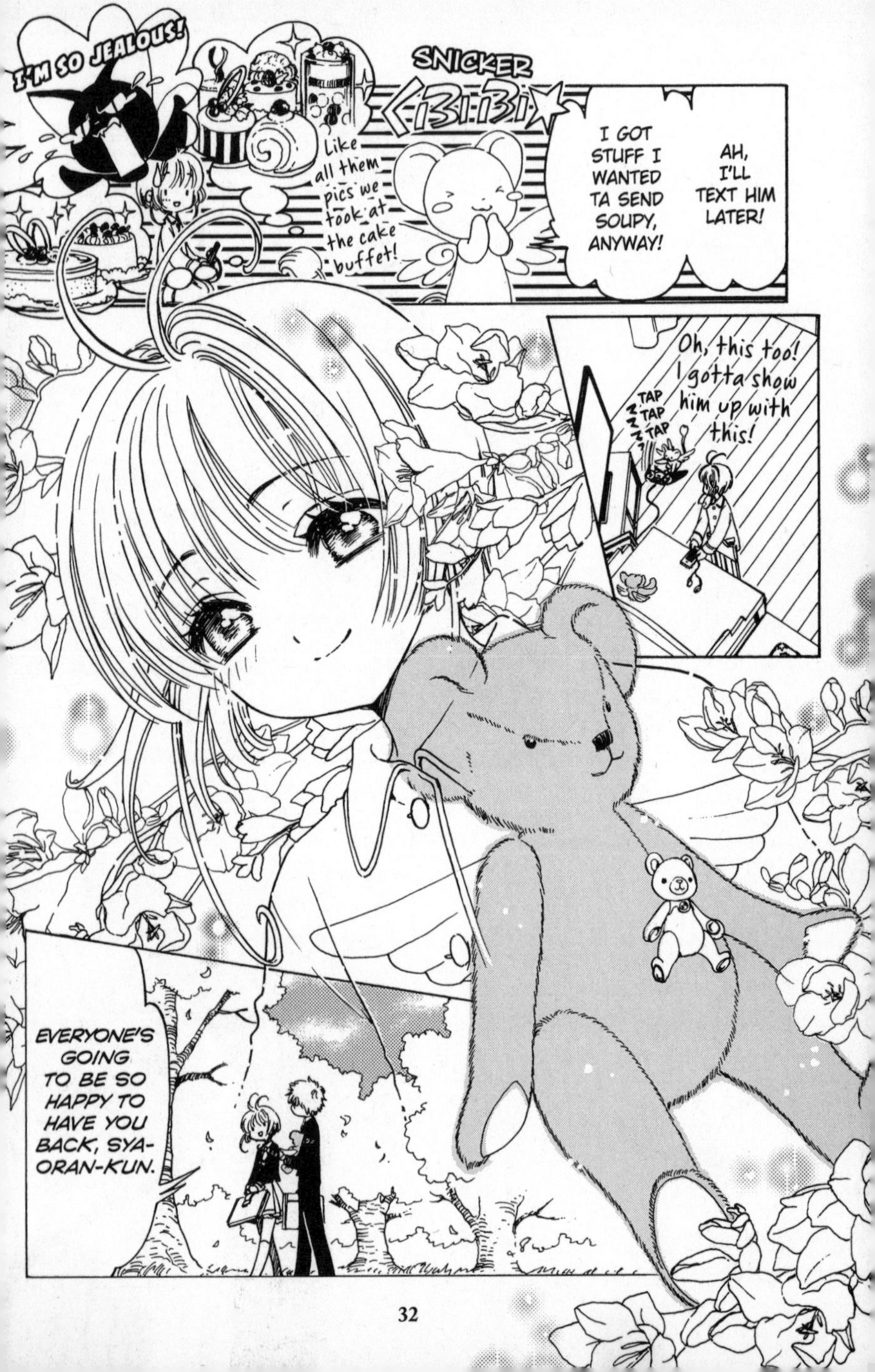
AH, I'LL TEXT HIM LATER!
I GOT STUFF I WANTED TA SEND SOUPY, ANYWAY!
Like all them pics we took at the cake buffet!
SNICKER
I'M SO JEALOUS!
Oh, this too! I gotta show him up with this!
TAP TAP TAP
EVERYONE'S GOING TO BE SO HAPPY TO HAVE YOU BACK, SYA-ORAN-KUN.

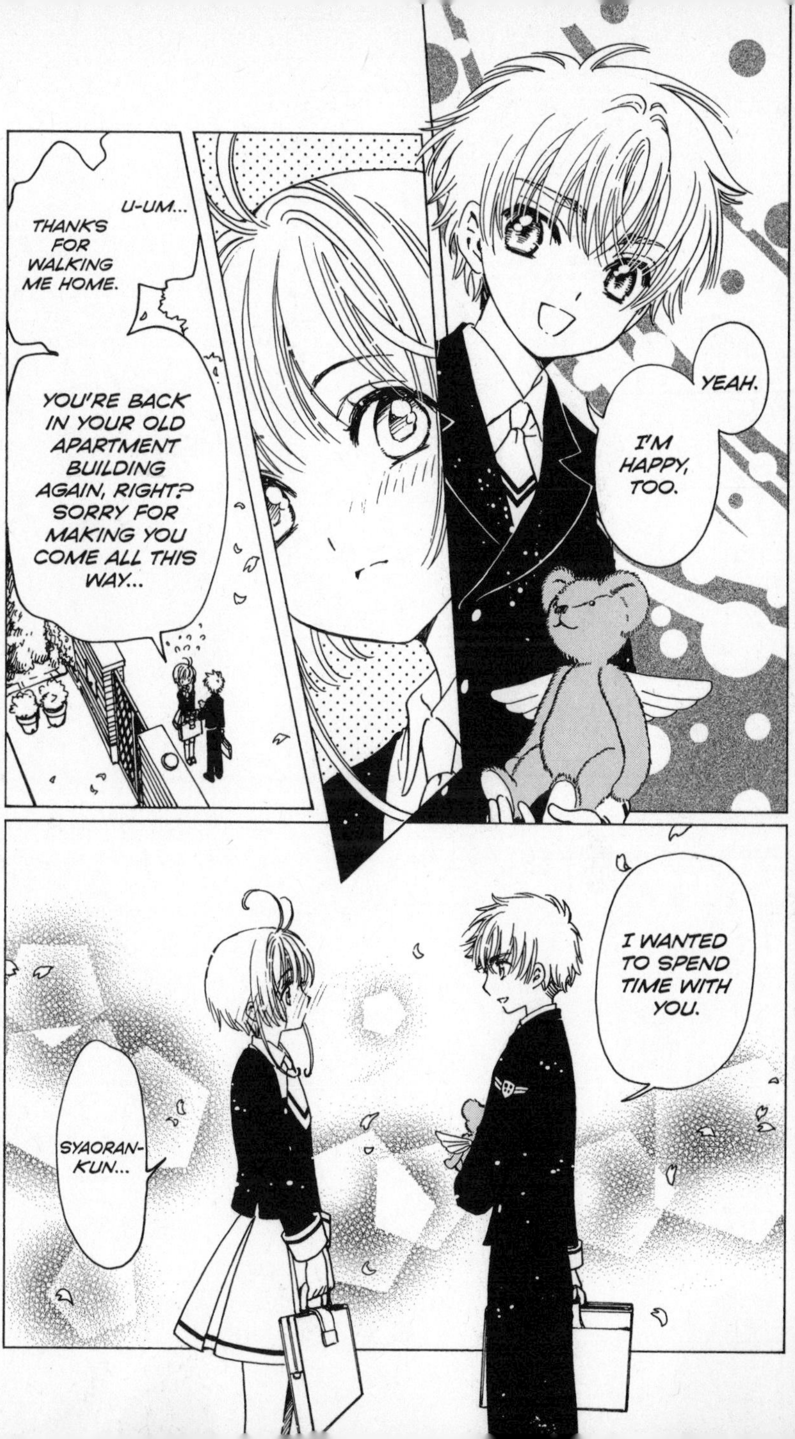
YEAH.
I'M HAPPY, TOO.
U-UM... THANKS FOR WALKING ME HOME.
YOU'RE BACK IN YOUR OLD APARTMENT BUILDING AGAIN, RIGHT? SORRY FOR MAKING YOU COME ALL THIS WAY...
I WANTED TO SPEND TIME WITH YOU.
SYAORAN-KUN...

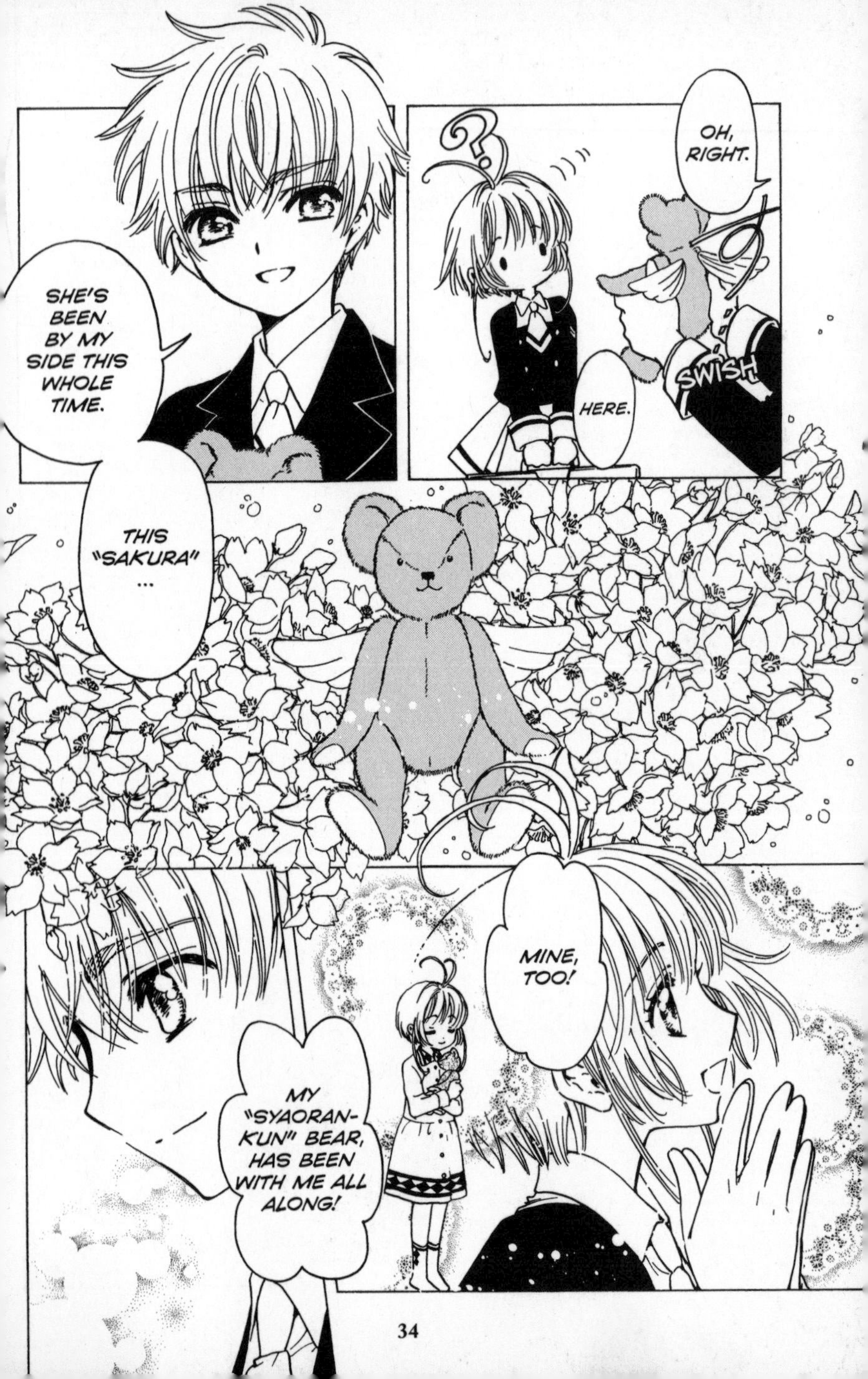
OH, RIGHT.
SWISH
HERE.
SHE'S BEEN BY MY SIDE THIS WHOLE TIME.
THIS "SAKURA" ...
MINE, TOO!
MY "SYAORAN-KUN" BEAR, HAS BEEN WITH ME ALL ALONG!

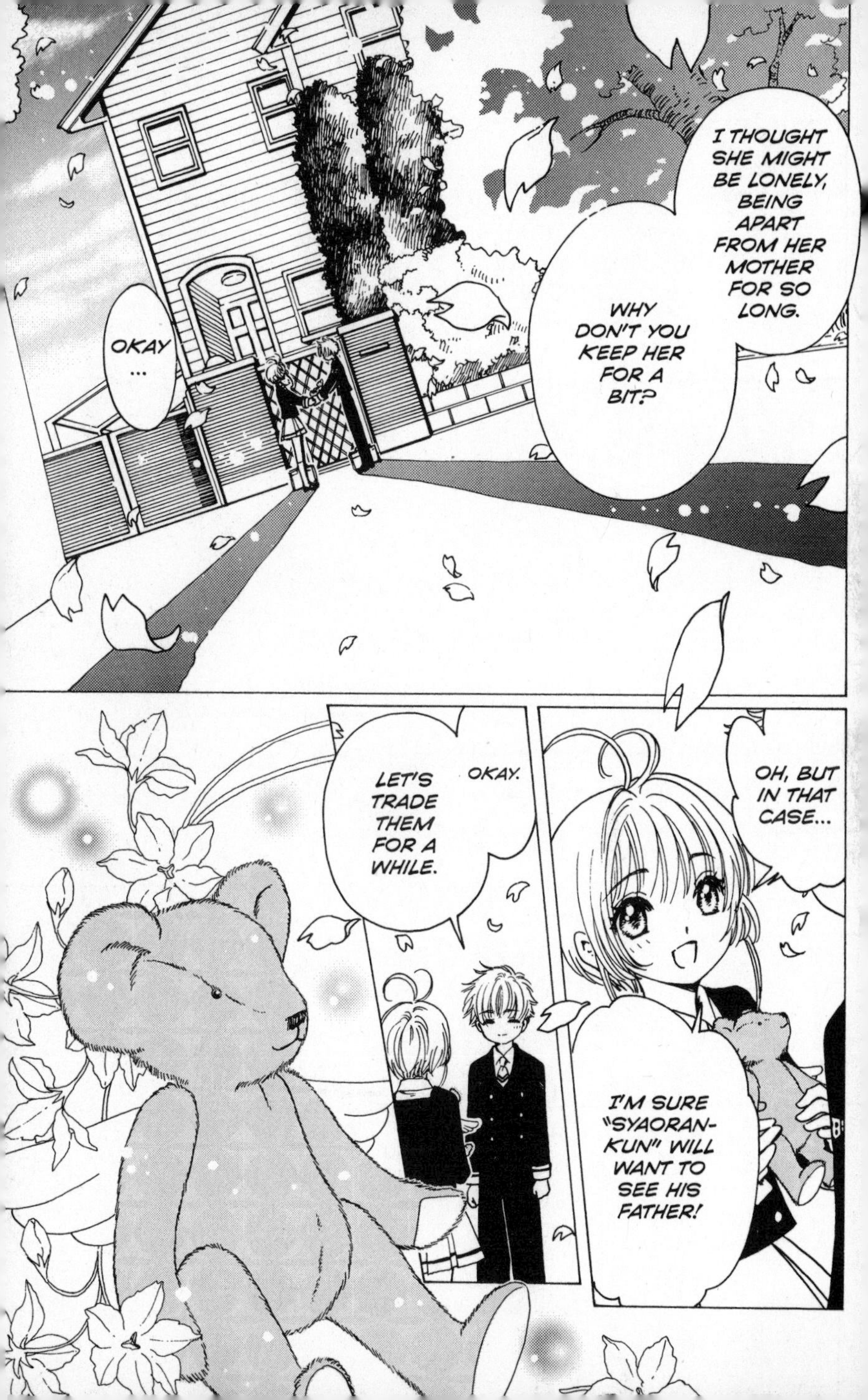
I THOUGHT SHE MIGHT BE LONELY, BEING APART FROM HER MOTHER FOR SO LONG.
WHY DON'T YOU KEEP HER FOR A BIT?
OKAY ...
OH, BUT IN THAT CASE...
I'M SURE "SYAORAN-KUN" WILL WANT TO SEE HIS FATHER!
OKAY.
LET'S TRADE THEM FOR A WHILE.

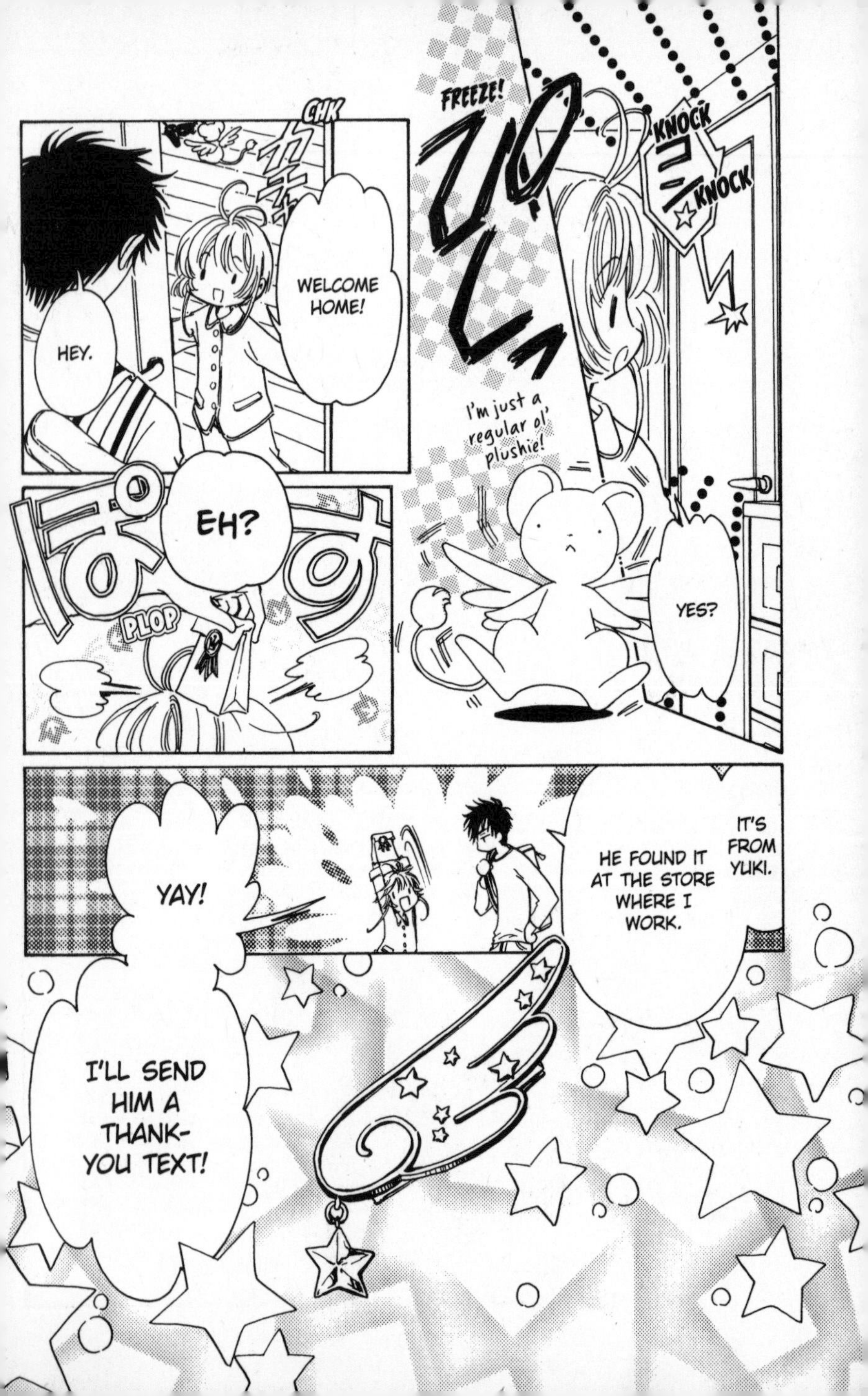
KNOCK
KNOCK
YES?
FREEZE!
I'm just a regular ol' plushie!
CHK
WELCOME HOME!
HEY.
EH?
PLOP
IT'S FROM YUKI.
HE FOUND IT AT THE STORE WHERE I WORK.
YAY!
I'LL SEND HIM A THANK-YOU TEXT!

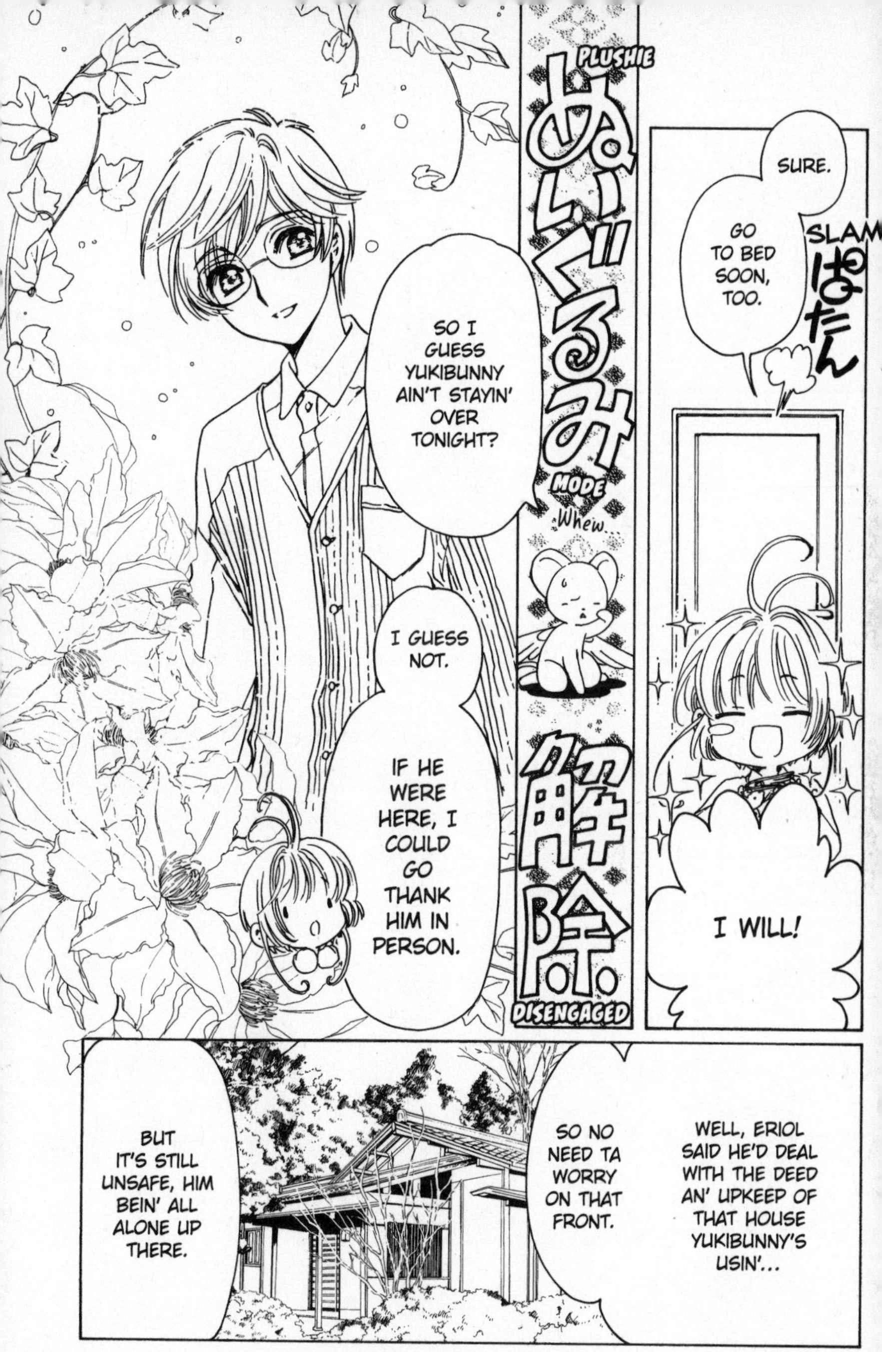
SURE.
GO TO BED SOON, TOO.
SLAM
ぱたん
I WILL!
PLUSHIE
ぬいぐるみ
MODE
解除。
DISENGAGED
Whew...
SO I GUESS YUKIBUNNY AIN'T STAYIN' OVER TONIGHT?
I GUESS NOT.
IF HE WERE HERE, I COULD GO THANK HIM IN PERSON.
WELL, ERIOL SAID HE'D DEAL WITH THE DEED AN' UPKEEP OF THAT HOUSE YUKIBUNNY'S USIN'...
SO NO NEED TA WORRY ON THAT FRONT.
BUT IT'S STILL UNSAFE, HIM BEIN' ALL ALONE UP THERE.

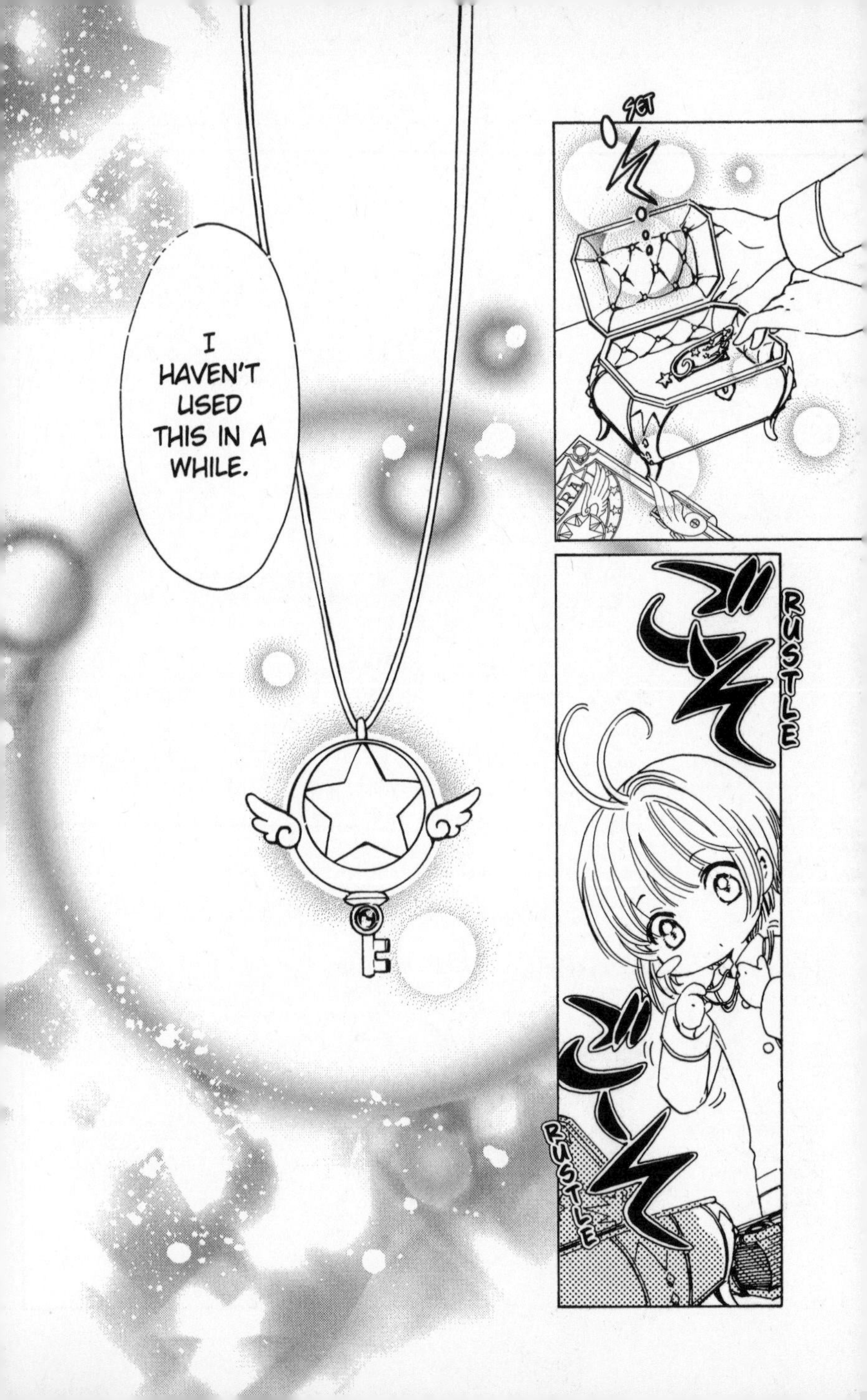
SET
RUSTLE
RUSTLE
I HAVEN'T USED THIS IN A WHILE.

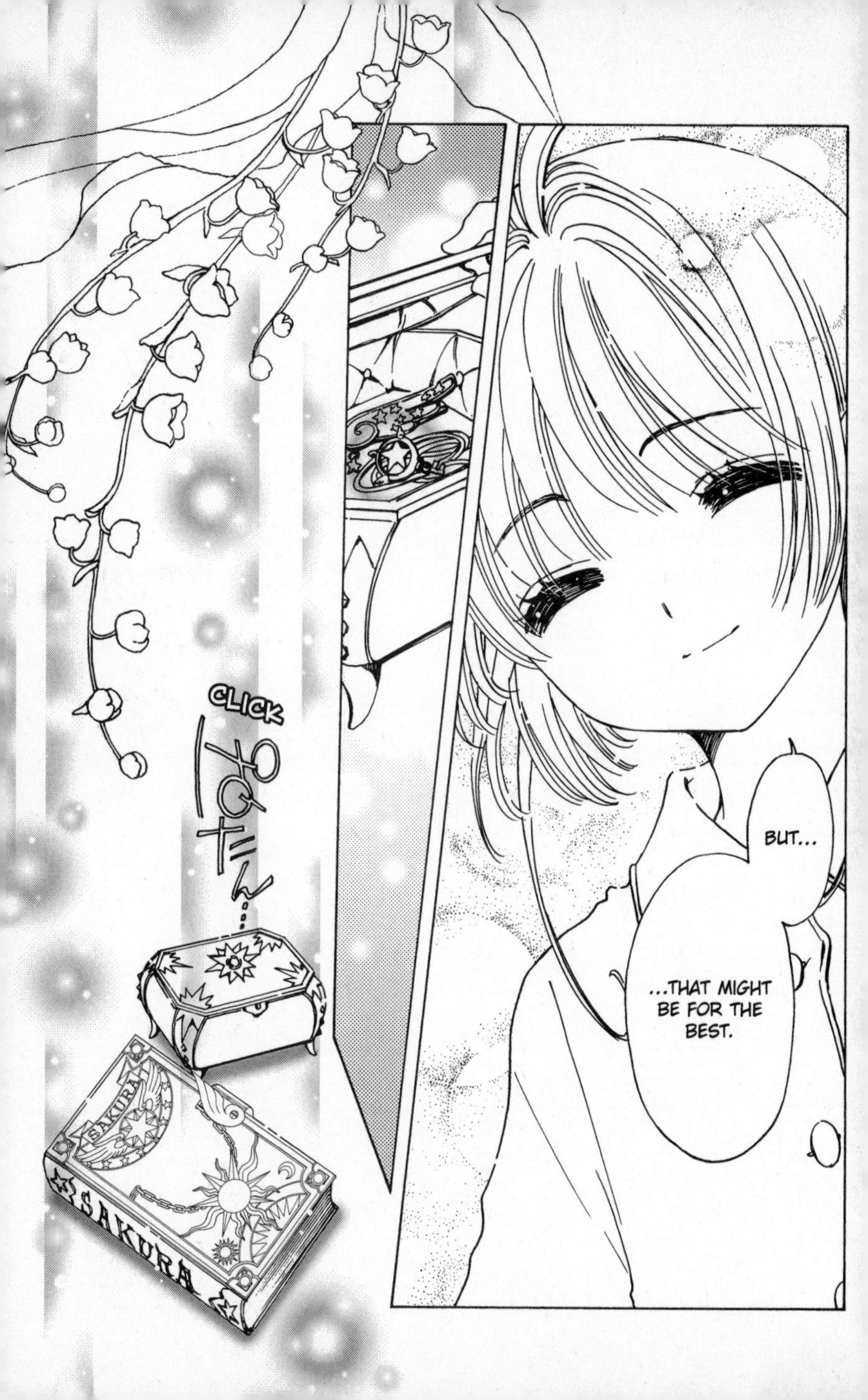
BUT...
...THAT MIGHT BE FOR THE BEST.
CLICK

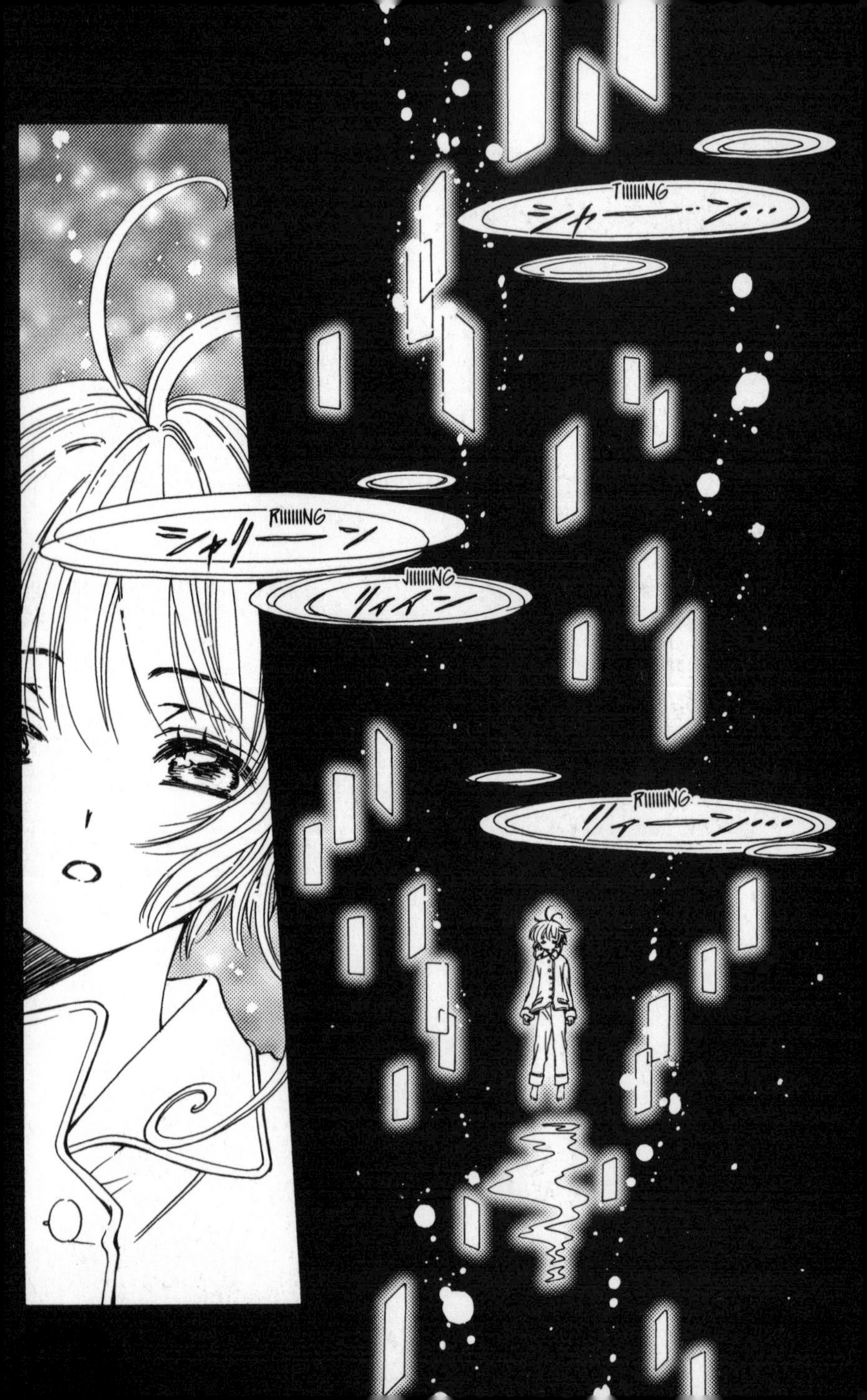
TIIIIING
RIIIIING.
RIIIIING
JIIIIING

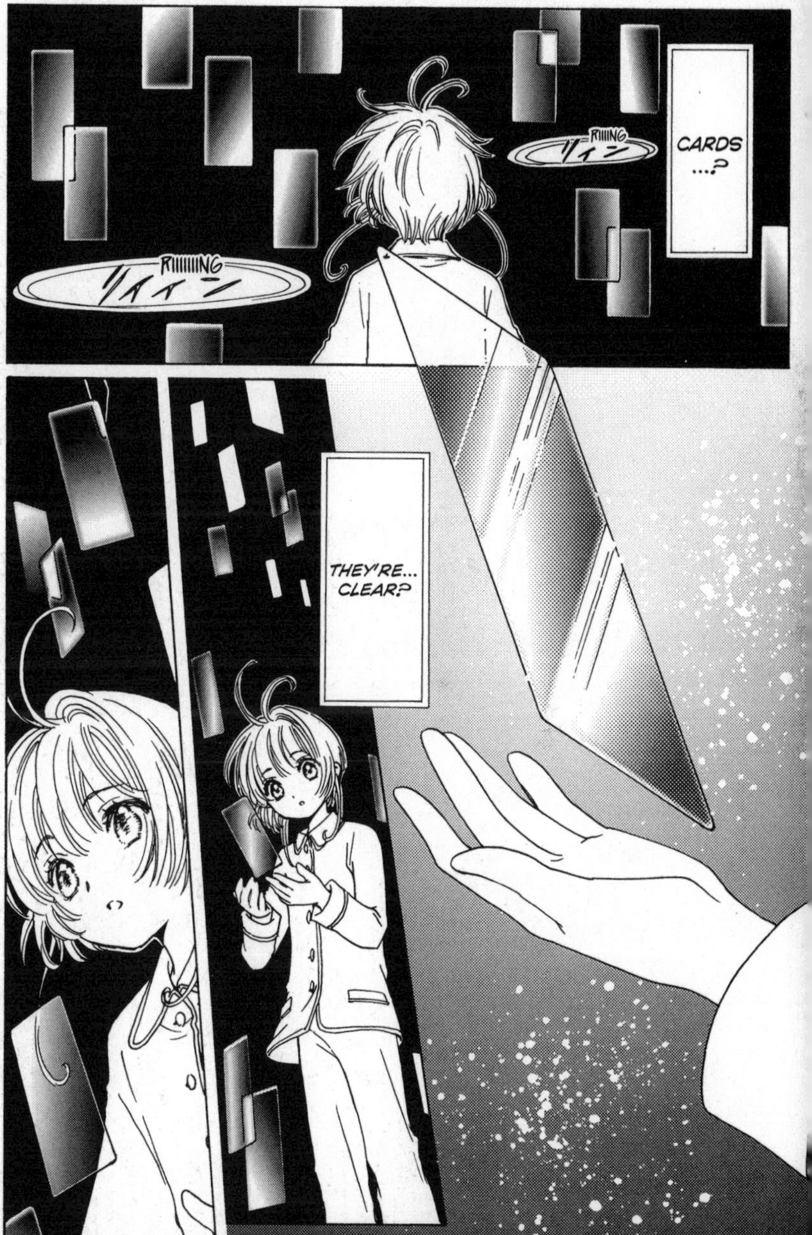
CARDS ...?
RIIING
リィン
RIIIIIING
リィィーン
THEY'RE... CLEAR?

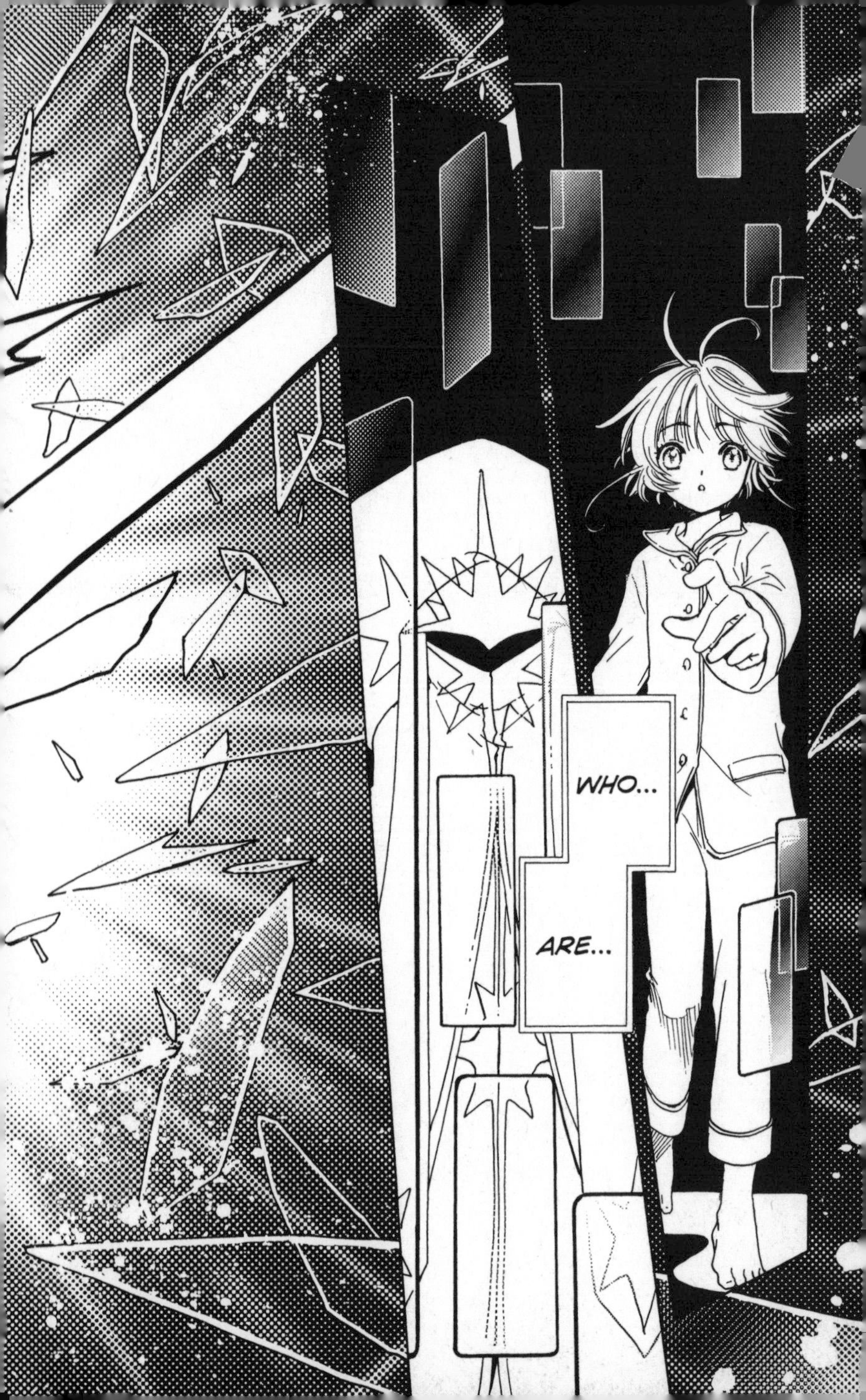
WHO...
ARE...

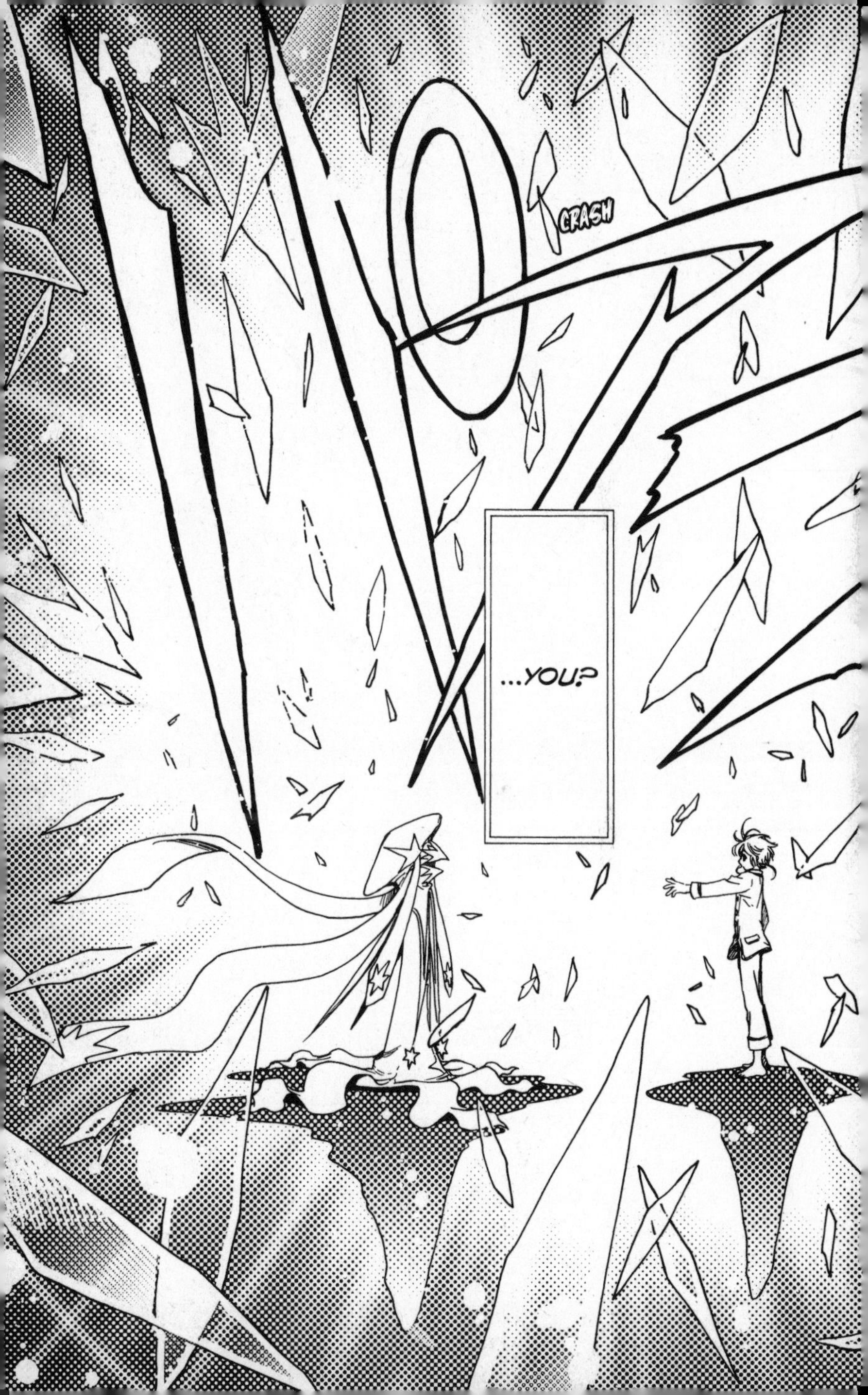
CRASH
...YOU?

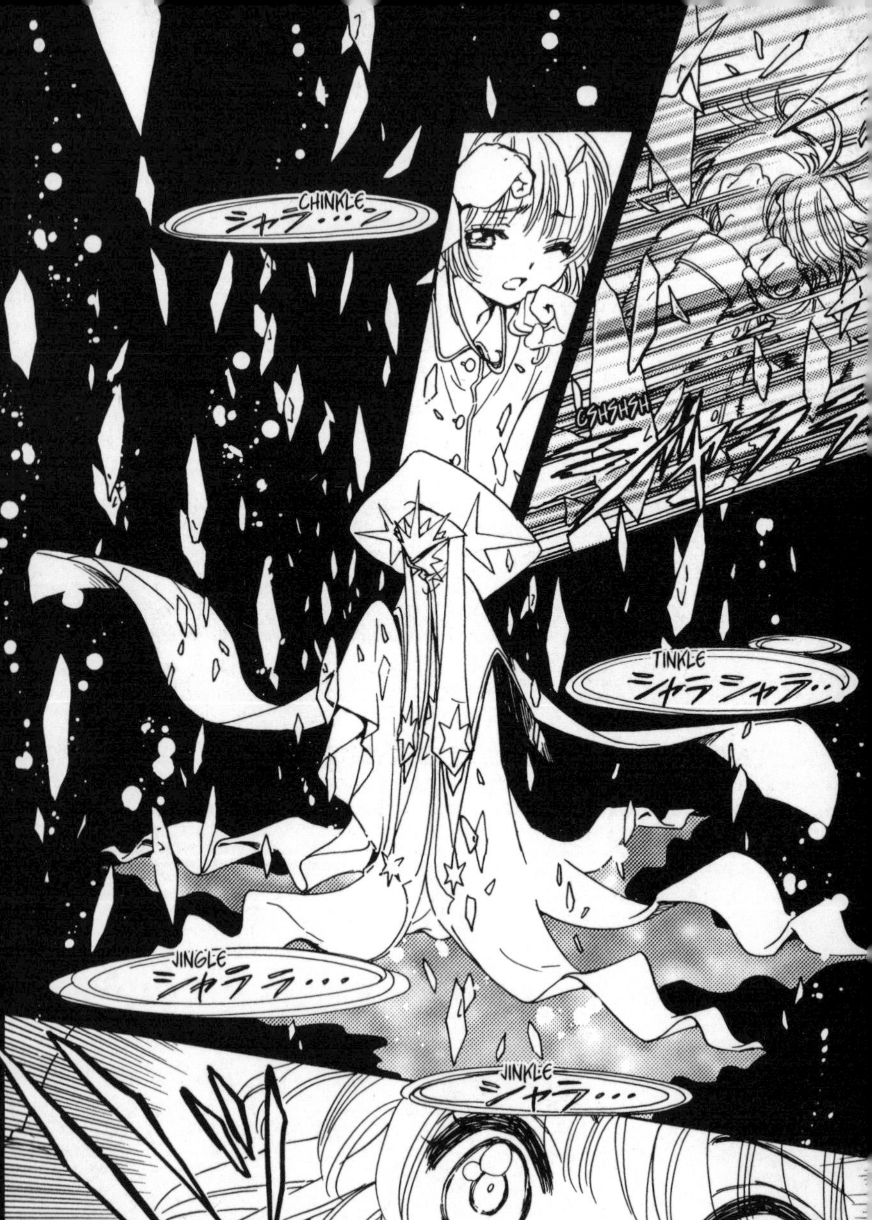
CSHSHSH
CHINKLE
シャラ…
TINKLE
シャラシャラ…
JINGLE
シャララ…
JINKLE
シャラ…
OH!

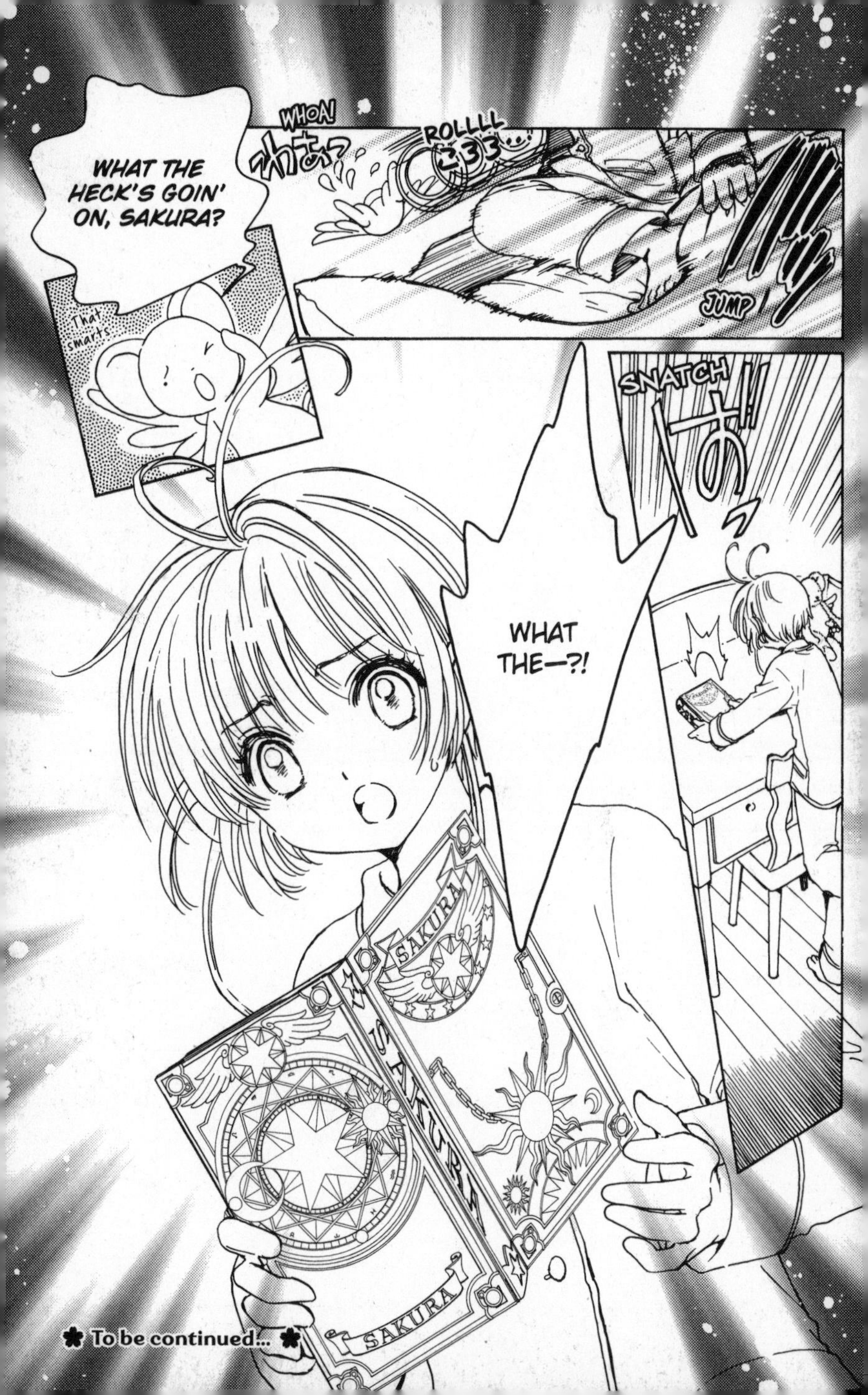
WHOA!
ROLLLL
JUMP
WHAT THE HECK'S GOIN' ON, SAKURA?
That smarts.
SNATCH
WHAT THE—?!
To be continued...

Cardcaptor Sakura

CLEAR CARD

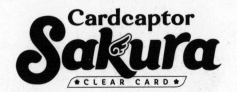

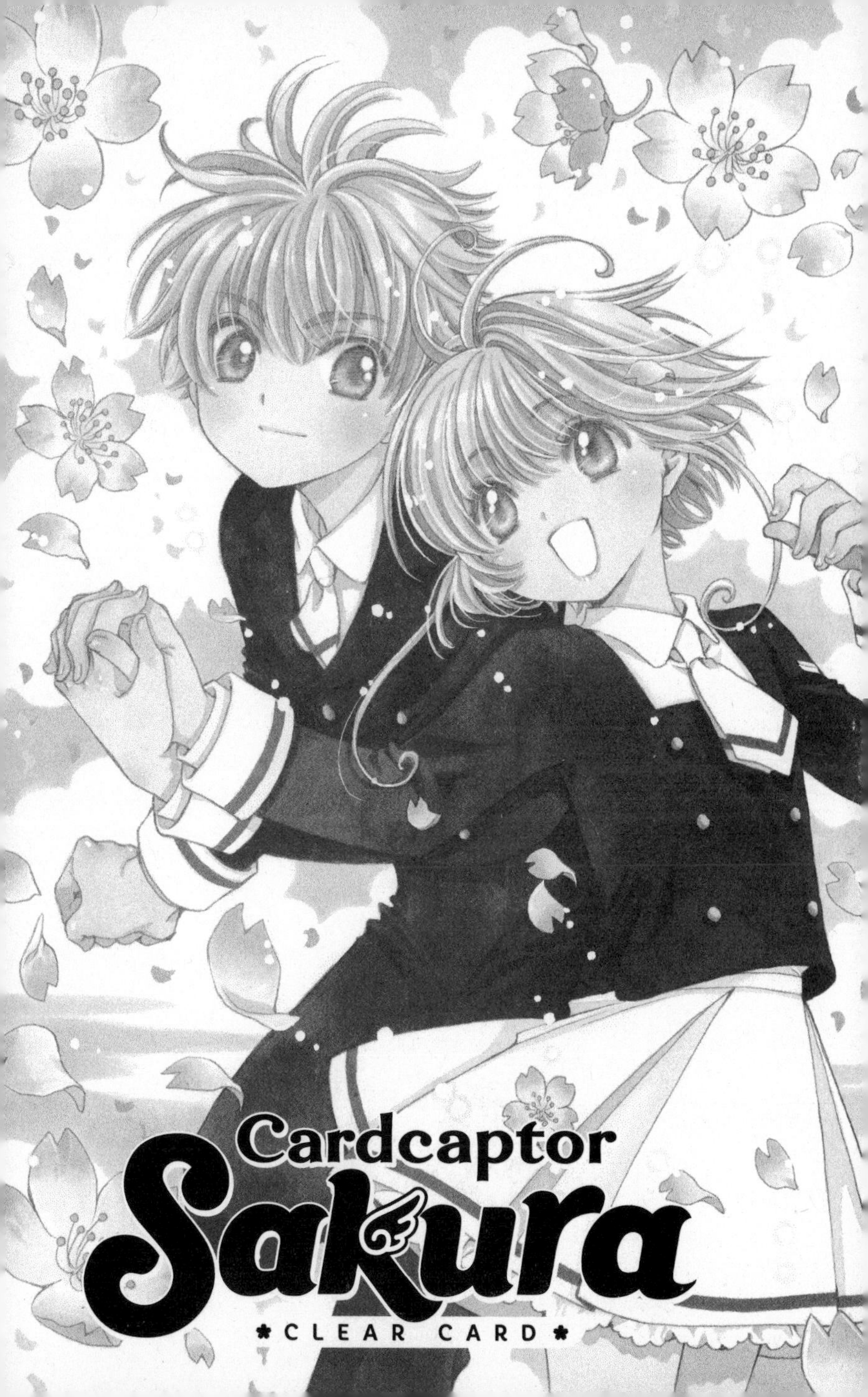
Cardcaptor
Sakura
CLEAR CARD

Cardcaptor Sakura

CLEAR CARD

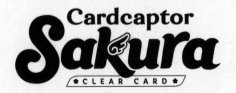

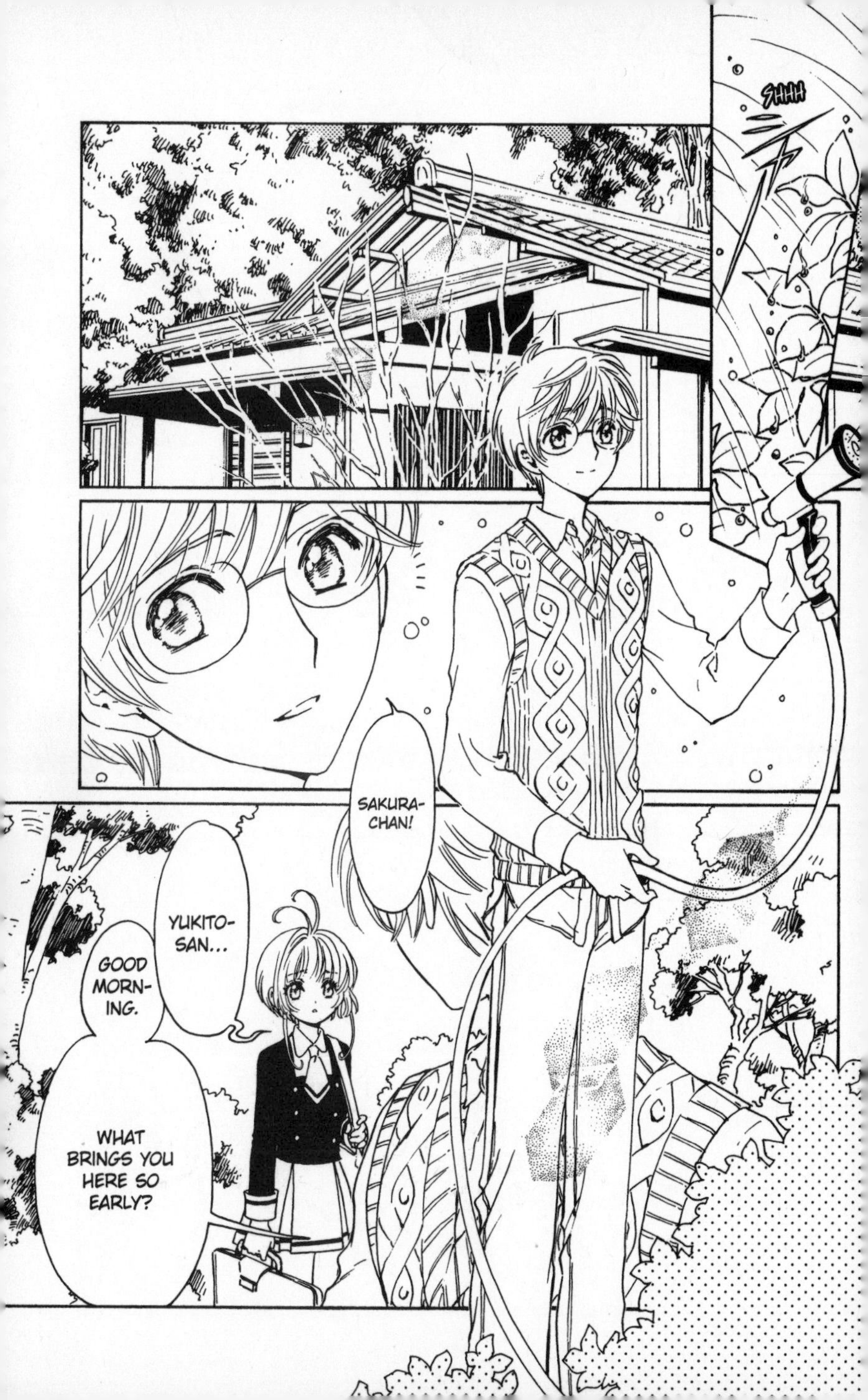
SHHH
SAKURA-CHAN!
YUKITO-SAN...
GOOD MORN-ING.
WHAT BRINGS YOU HERE SO EARLY?

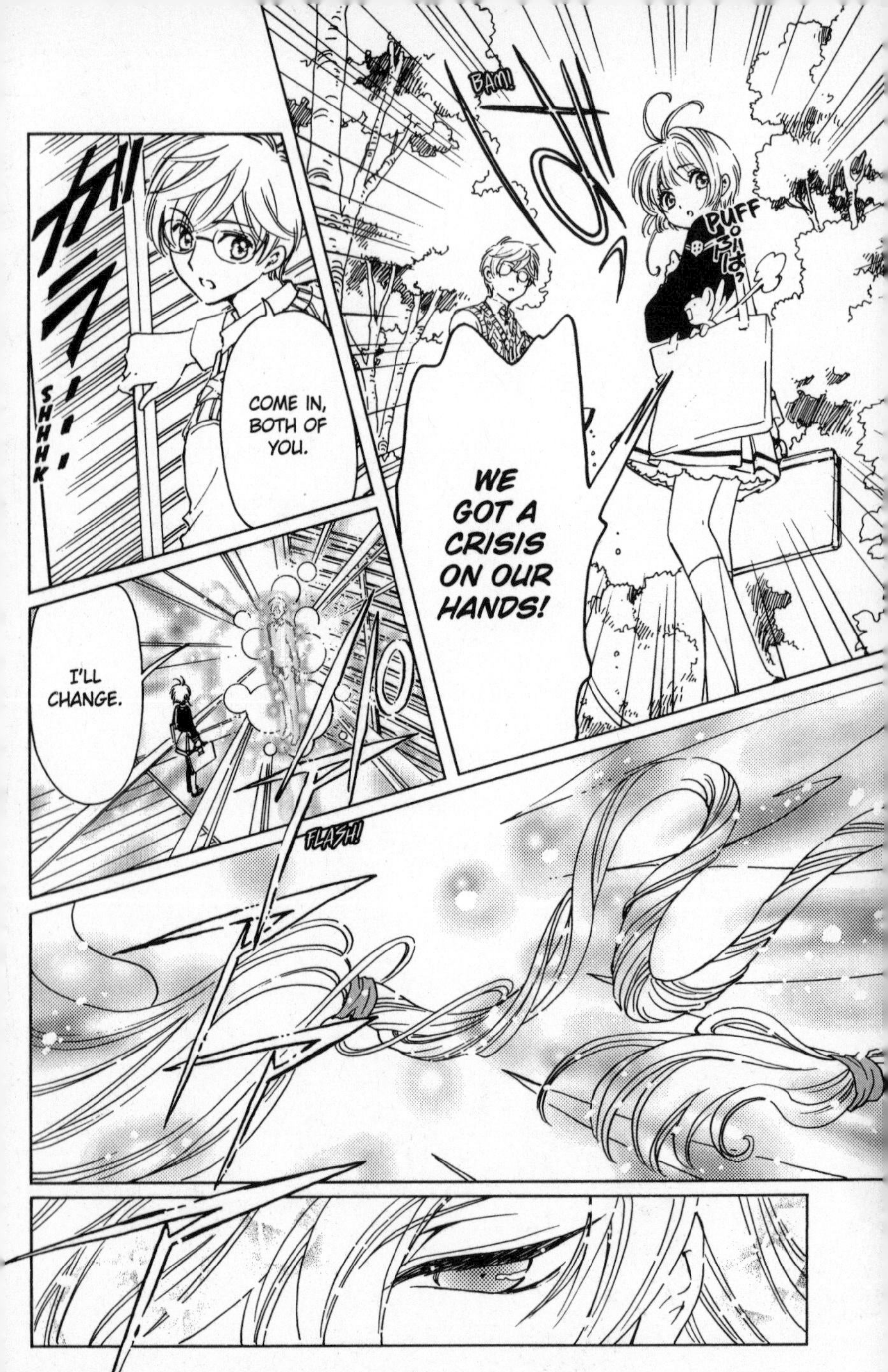
BAM!
WE GOT A CRISIS ON OUR HANDS!
PUFF
SHHHK
COME IN, BOTH OF YOU.
I'LL CHANGE.
FLASH!

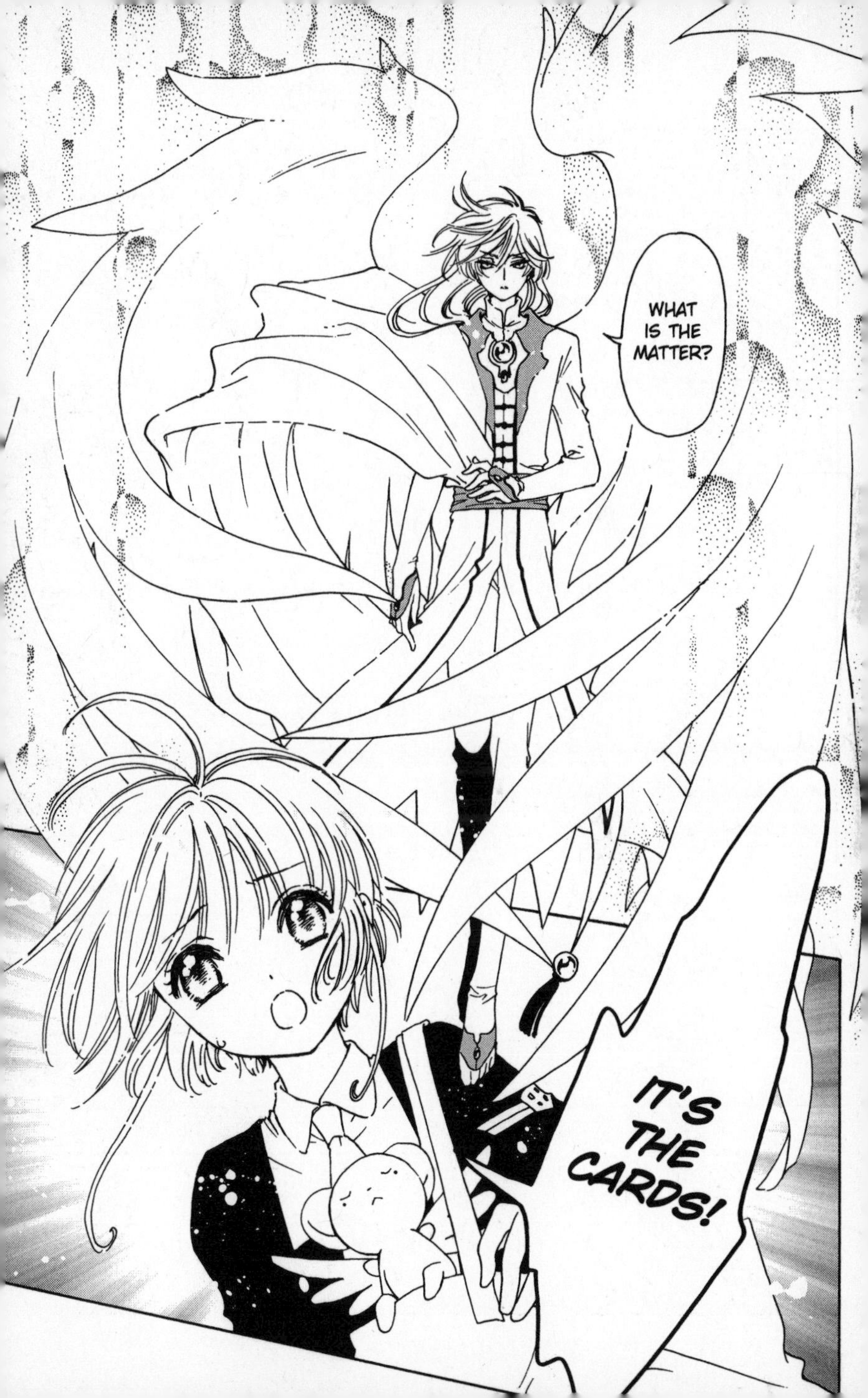
WHAT IS THE MATTER?
IT'S THE CARDS!

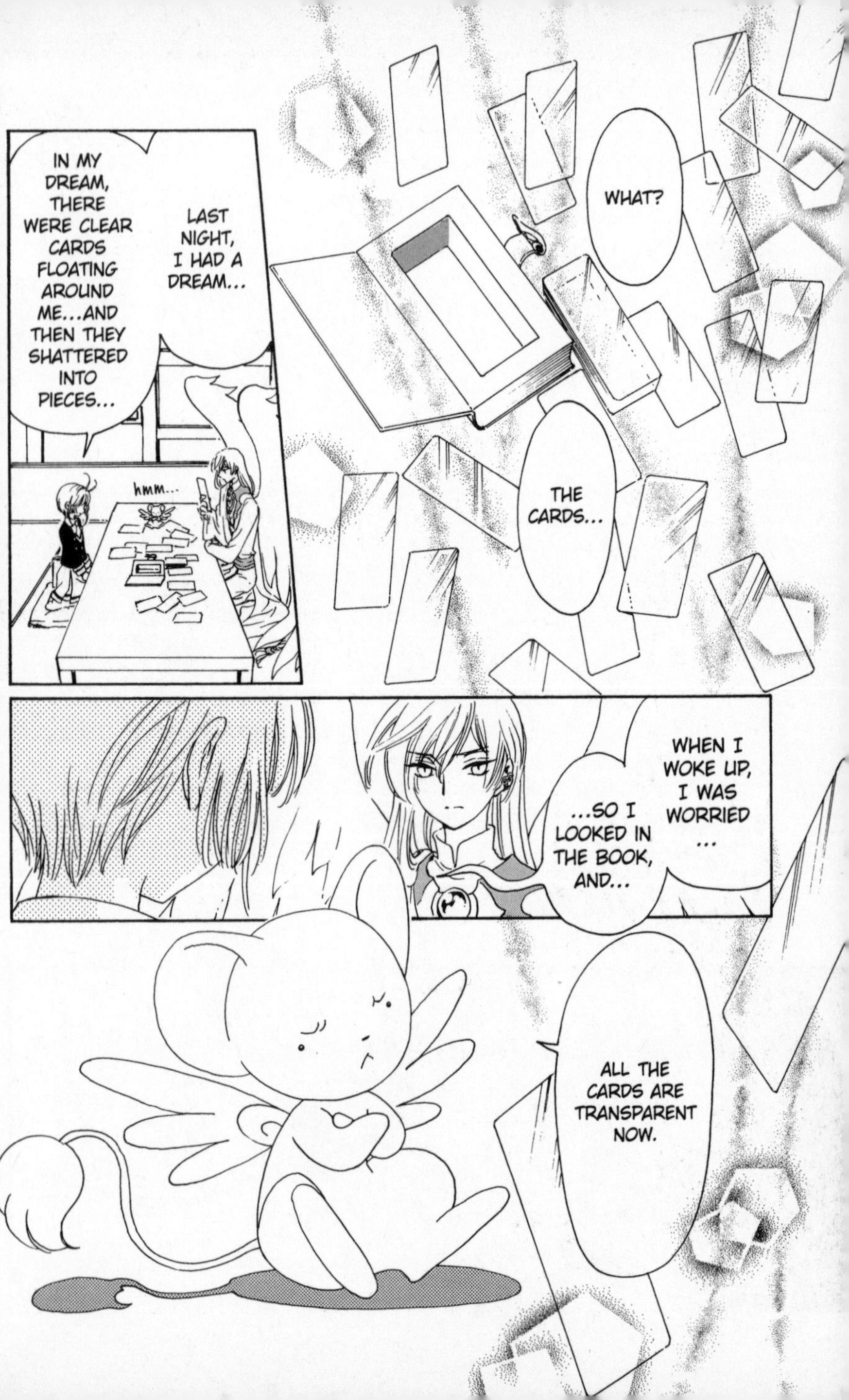
WHAT?
THE CARDS...
LAST NIGHT, I HAD A DREAM...
IN MY DREAM, THERE WERE CLEAR CARDS FLOATING AROUND ME...AND THEN THEY SHATTERED INTO PIECES...
hmm...
WHEN I WOKE UP, I WAS WORRIED ...
...SO I LOOKED IN THE BOOK, AND...
ALL THE CARDS ARE TRANSPARENT NOW.

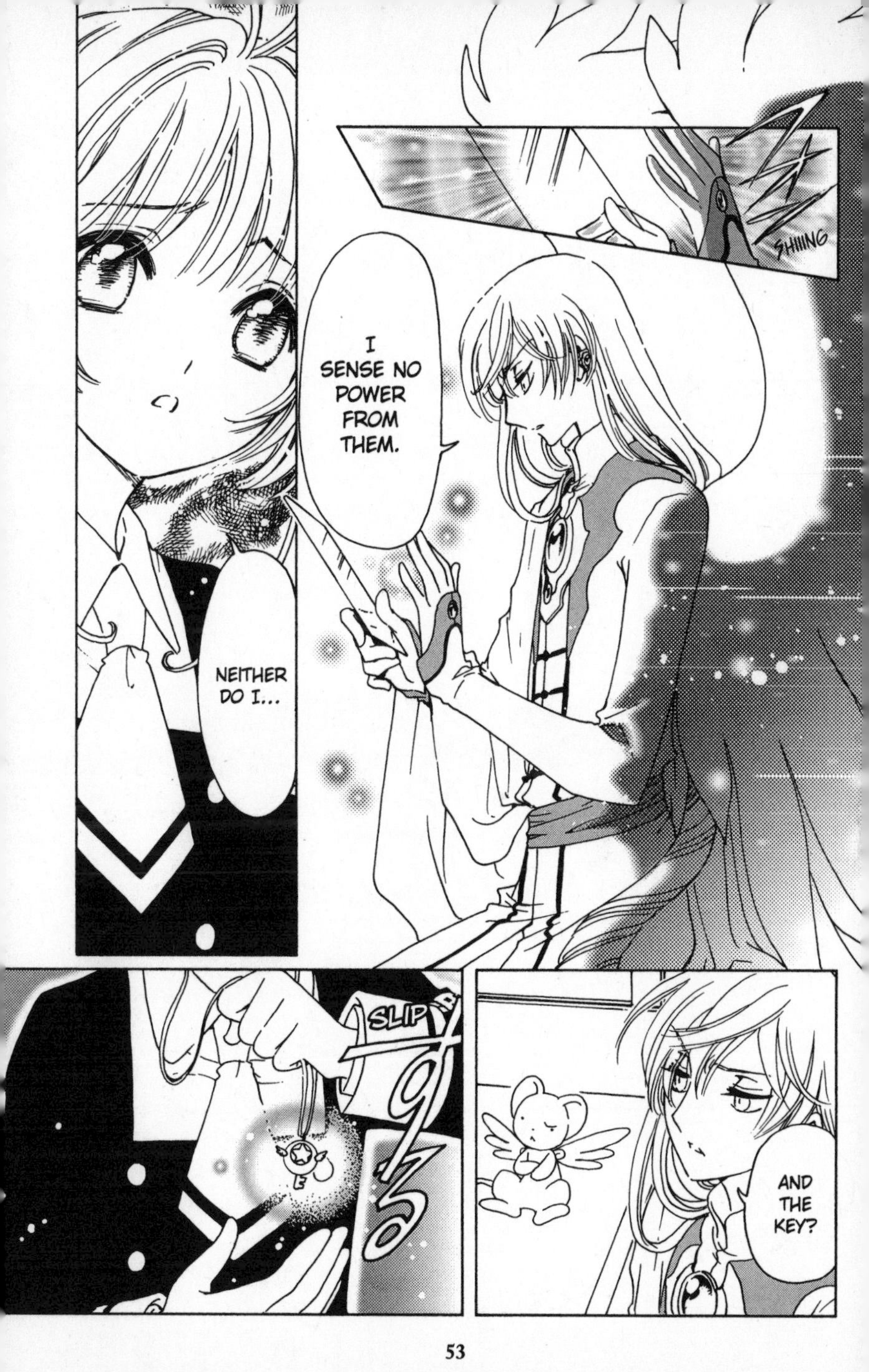
SHIING
I SENSE NO POWER FROM THEM.
NEITHER DO I...
AND THE KEY?
SLIP

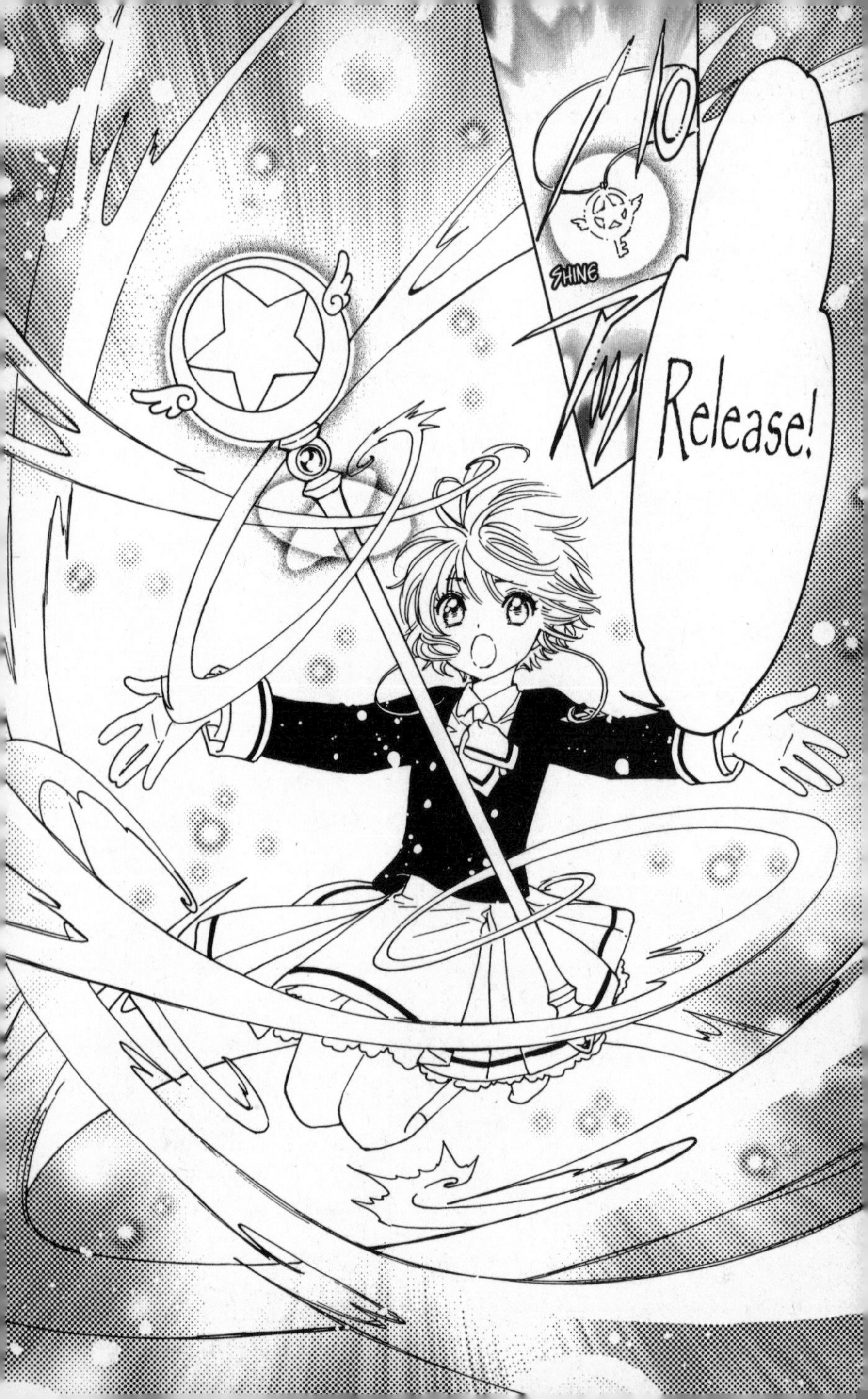
SHINE
Release!

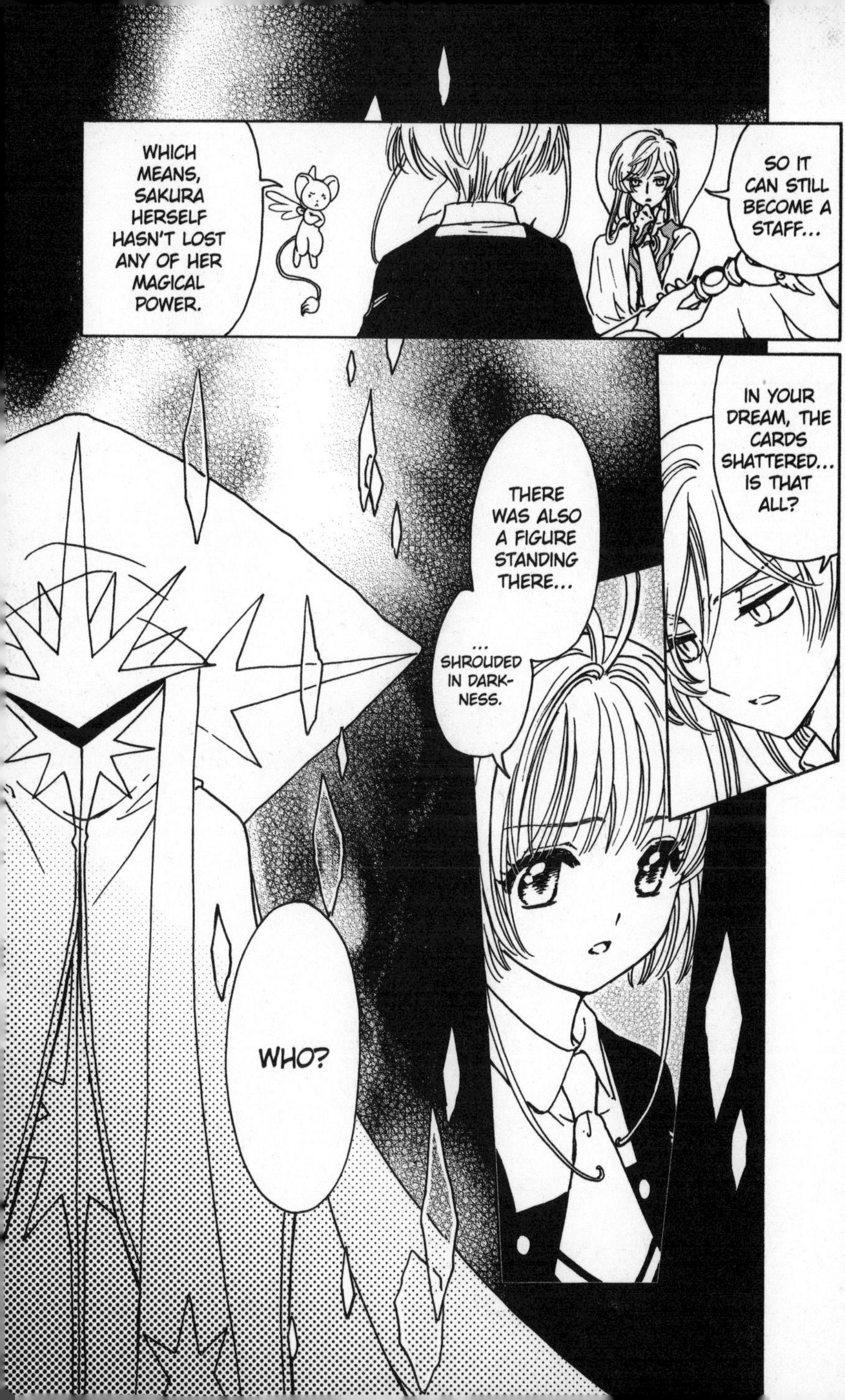
SO IT CAN STILL BECOME A STAFF...
WHICH MEANS, SAKURA HERSELF HASN'T LOST ANY OF HER MAGICAL POWER.
IN YOUR DREAM, THE CARDS SHATTERED... IS THAT ALL?
THERE WAS ALSO A FIGURE STANDING THERE...
...SHROUDED IN DARK-NESS.
WHO?

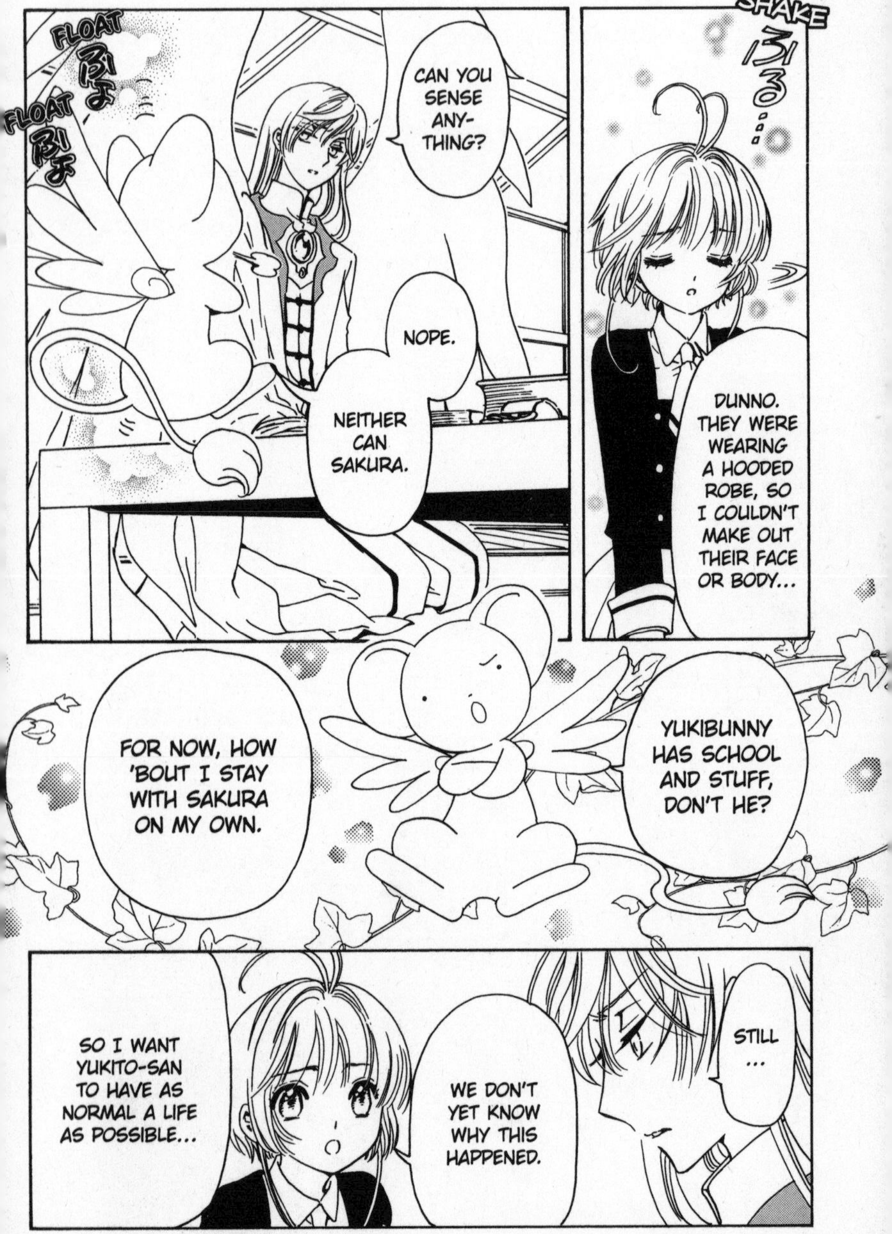
SHAKE
DUNNO. THEY WERE WEARING A HOODED ROBE, SO I COULDN'T MAKE OUT THEIR FACE OR BODY...
FLOAT
FLOAT
CAN YOU SENSE ANY-THING?
NOPE.
NEITHER CAN SAKURA.
YUKIBUNNY HAS SCHOOL AND STUFF, DON'T HE?
FOR NOW, HOW 'BOUT I STAY WITH SAKURA ON MY OWN.
STILL ...
WE DON'T YET KNOW WHY THIS HAPPENED.
SO I WANT YUKITO-SAN TO HAVE AS NORMAL A LIFE AS POSSIBLE...

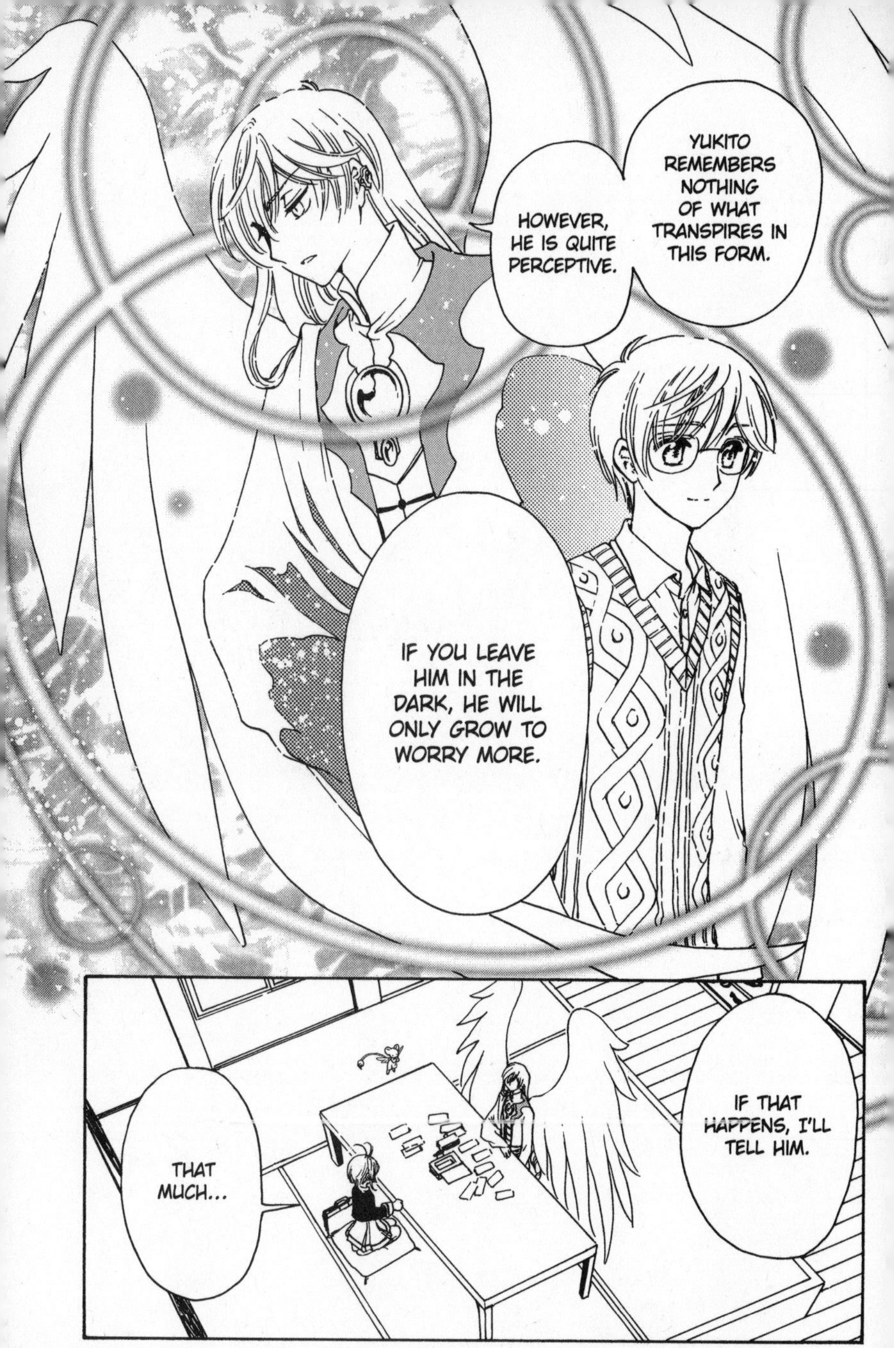
YUKITO REMEMBERS NOTHING OF WHAT TRANSPIRES IN THIS FORM.
HOWEVER, HE IS QUITE PERCEPTIVE.
IF YOU LEAVE HIM IN THE DARK, HE WILL ONLY GROW TO WORRY MORE.
IF THAT HAPPENS, I'LL TELL HIM.
THAT MUCH...

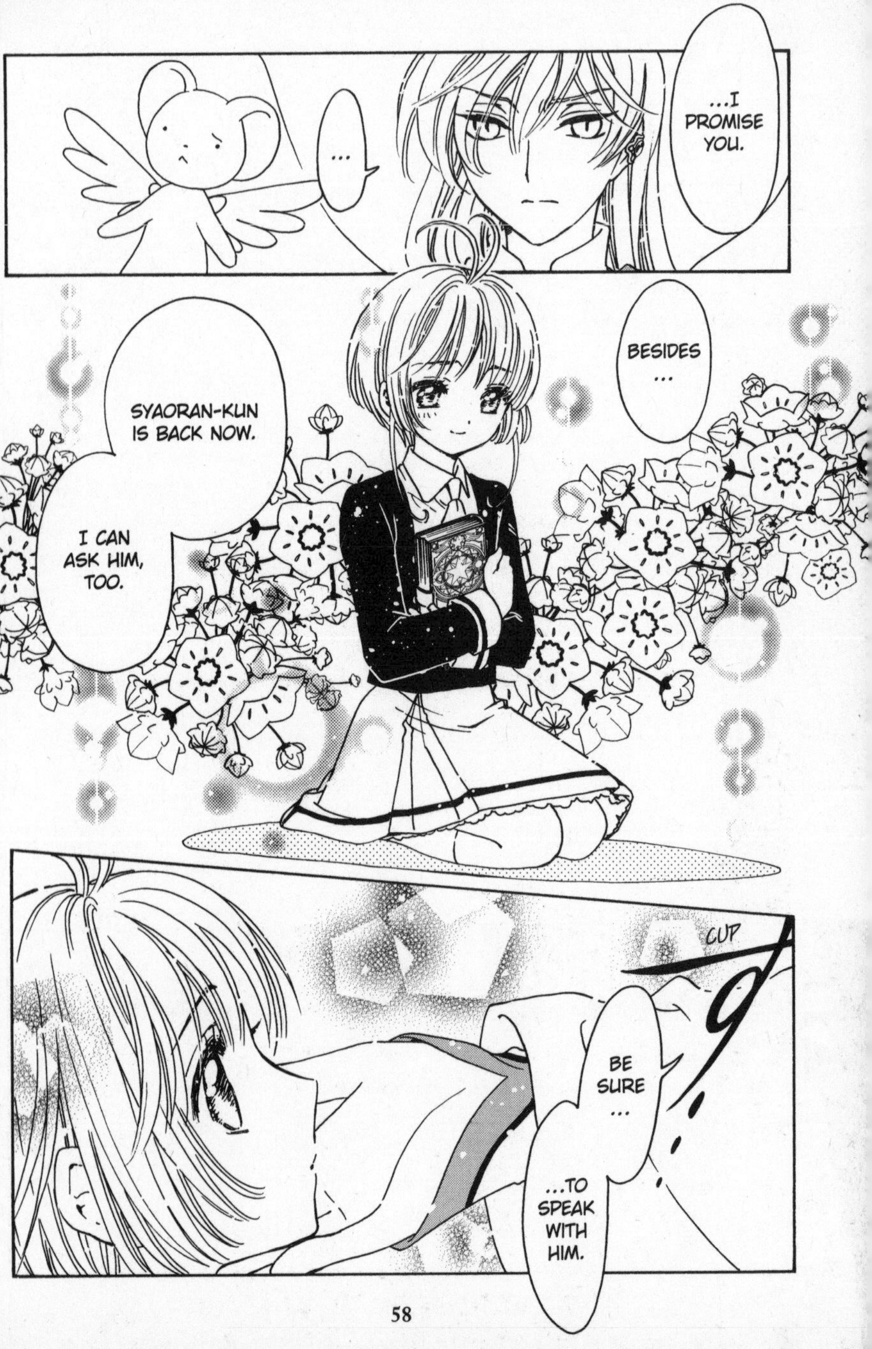
...I PROMISE YOU.
...
BESIDES ...
SYAORAN-KUN IS BACK NOW.
I CAN ASK HIM, TOO.
CUP
BE SURE ...
...TO SPEAK WITH HIM.

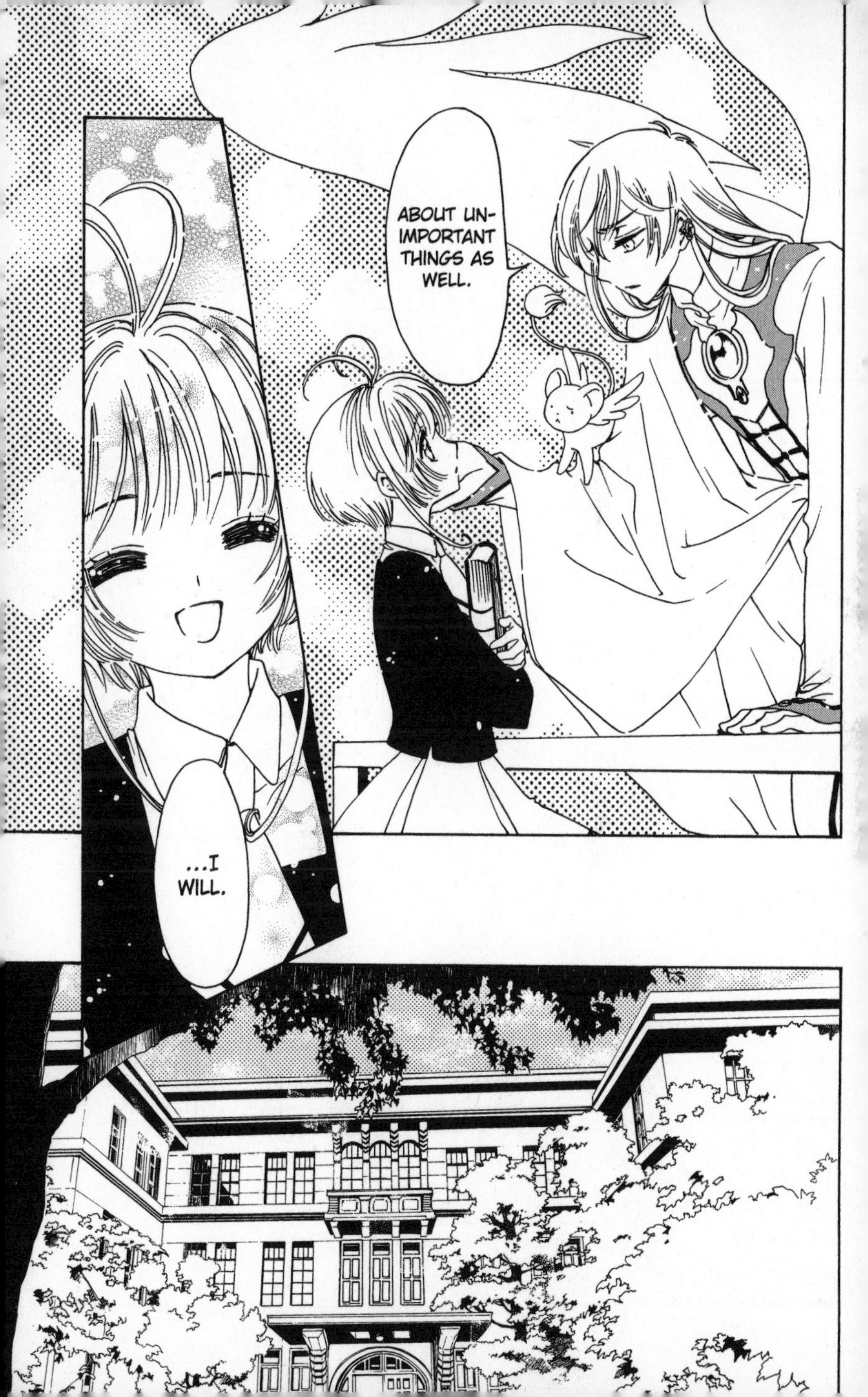
ABOUT UN-IMPORTANT THINGS AS WELL.
...I WILL.

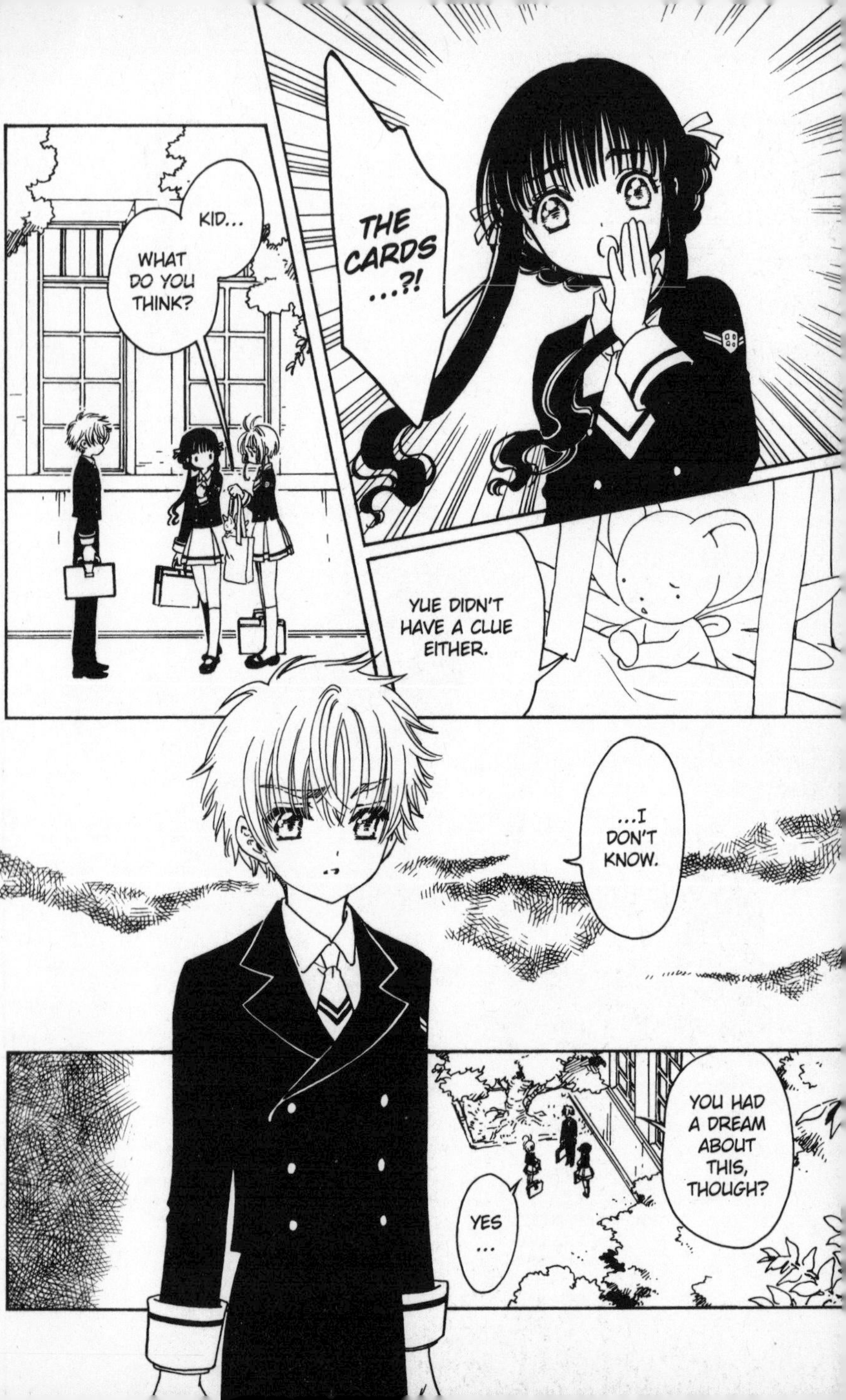
THE CARDS ...?!
YUE DIDN'T HAVE A CLUE EITHER.
KID... WHAT DO YOU THINK?
...I DON'T KNOW.
YOU HAD A DREAM ABOUT THIS, THOUGH?
YES ...

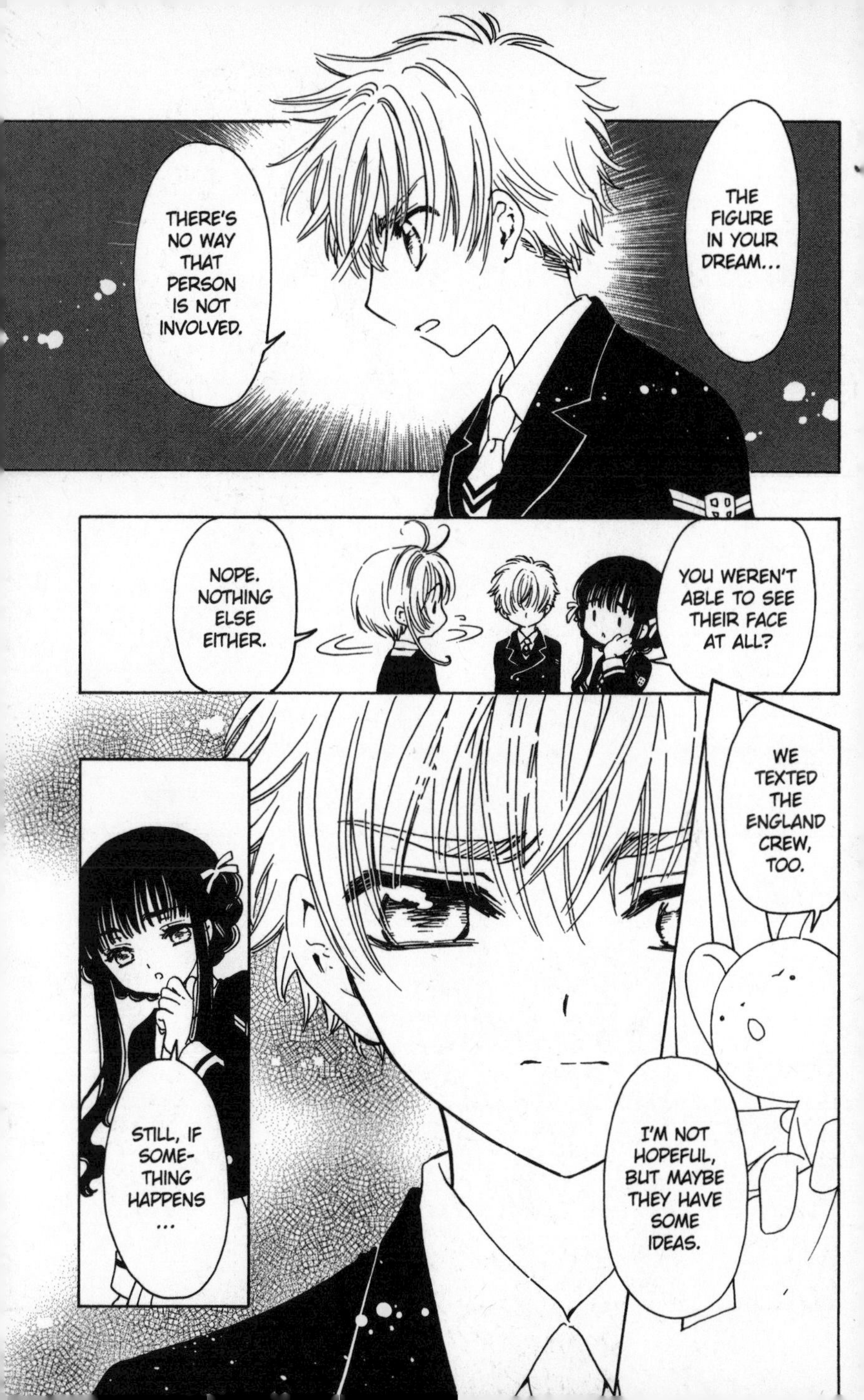
THE FIGURE IN YOUR DREAM...
THERE'S NO WAY THAT PERSON IS NOT INVOLVED.
YOU WEREN'T ABLE TO SEE THEIR FACE AT ALL?
NOPE. NOTHING ELSE EITHER.
WE TEXTED THE ENGLAND CREW, TOO.
I'M NOT HOPEFUL, BUT MAYBE THEY HAVE SOME IDEAS.
STILL, IF SOME-THING HAPPENS ...

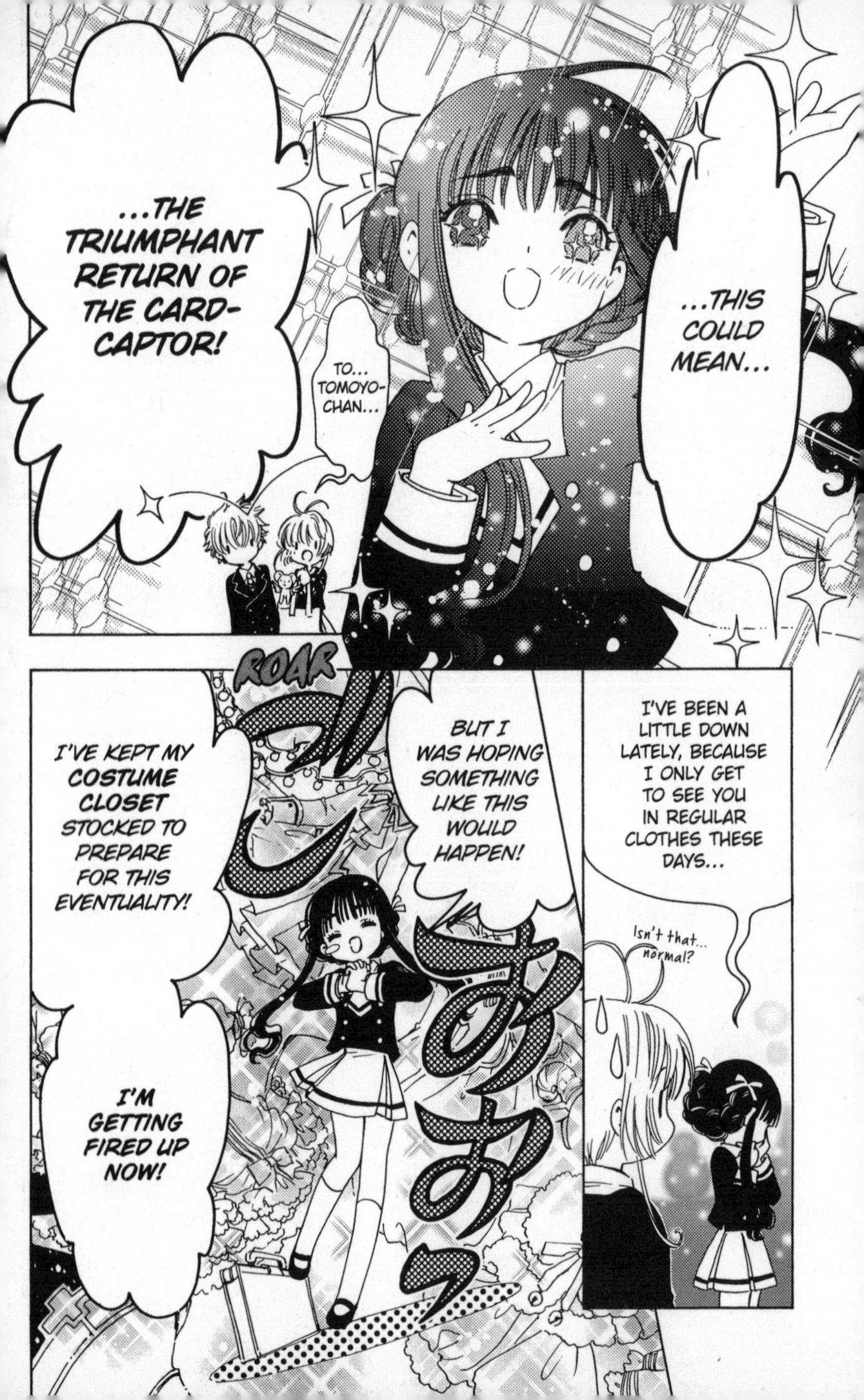
...THIS COULD MEAN...
...THE TRIUMPHANT RETURN OF THE CARD-CAPTOR!
TO... TOMOYO-CHAN...
I'VE BEEN A LITTLE DOWN LATELY, BECAUSE I ONLY GET TO SEE YOU IN REGULAR CLOTHES THESE DAYS...
Isn't that... normal?
ROAR
BUT I WAS HOPING SOMETHING LIKE THIS WOULD HAPPEN!
I'VE KEPT MY COSTUME CLOSET STOCKED TO PREPARE FOR THIS EVENTUALITY!
I'M GETTING FIRED UP NOW!

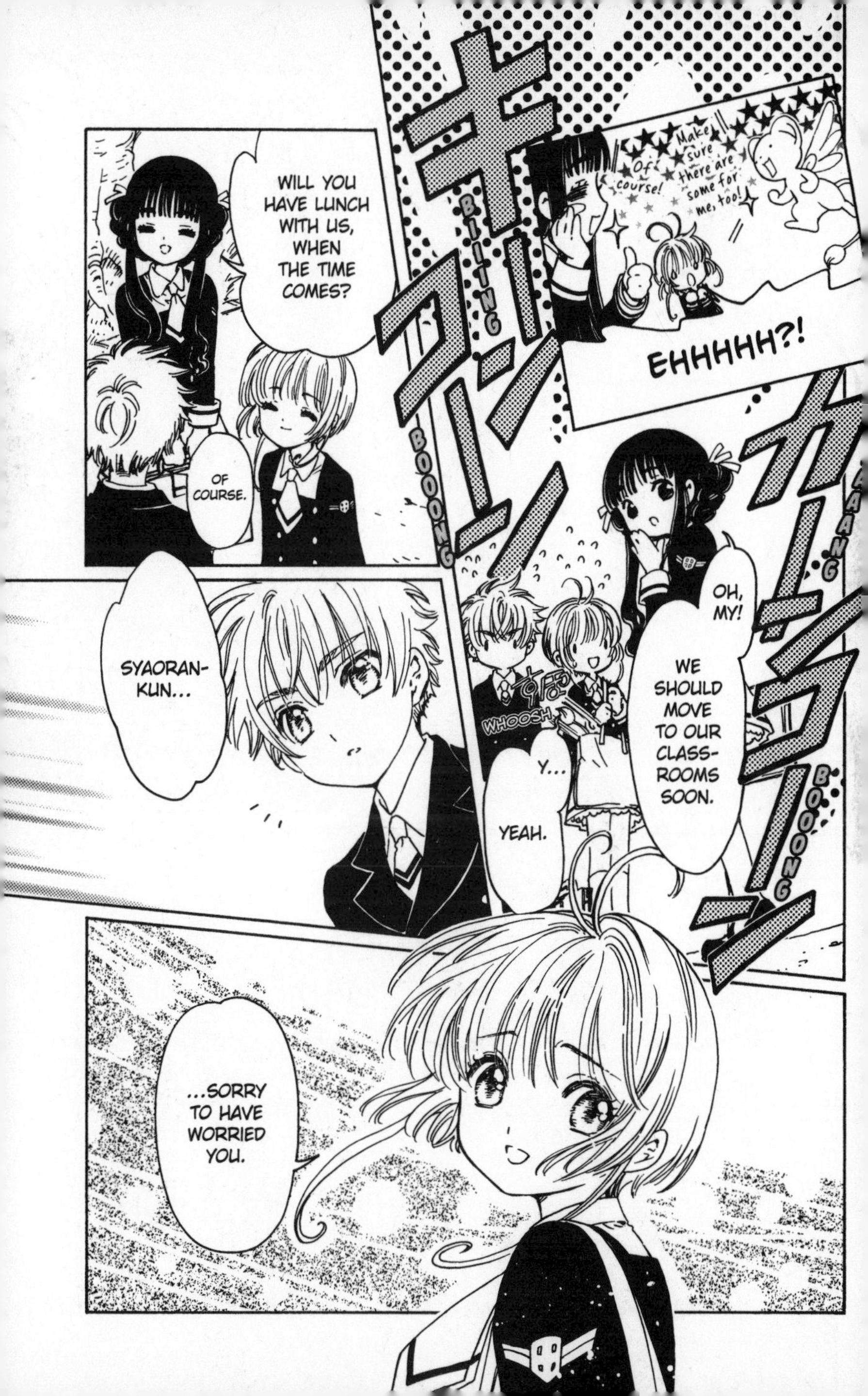
WILL YOU HAVE LUNCH WITH US, WHEN THE TIME COMES?
OF COURSE.
BIIING
BOOONG
Of course!
Make sure there are some for me, too!
EHHHHH?!
AAANG
BOOOONG
OH, MY!
WE SHOULD MOVE TO OUR CLASS- ROOMS SOON.
WHOOSH
Y...
YEAH.
SYAORAN- KUN...
...SORRY TO HAVE WORRIED YOU.

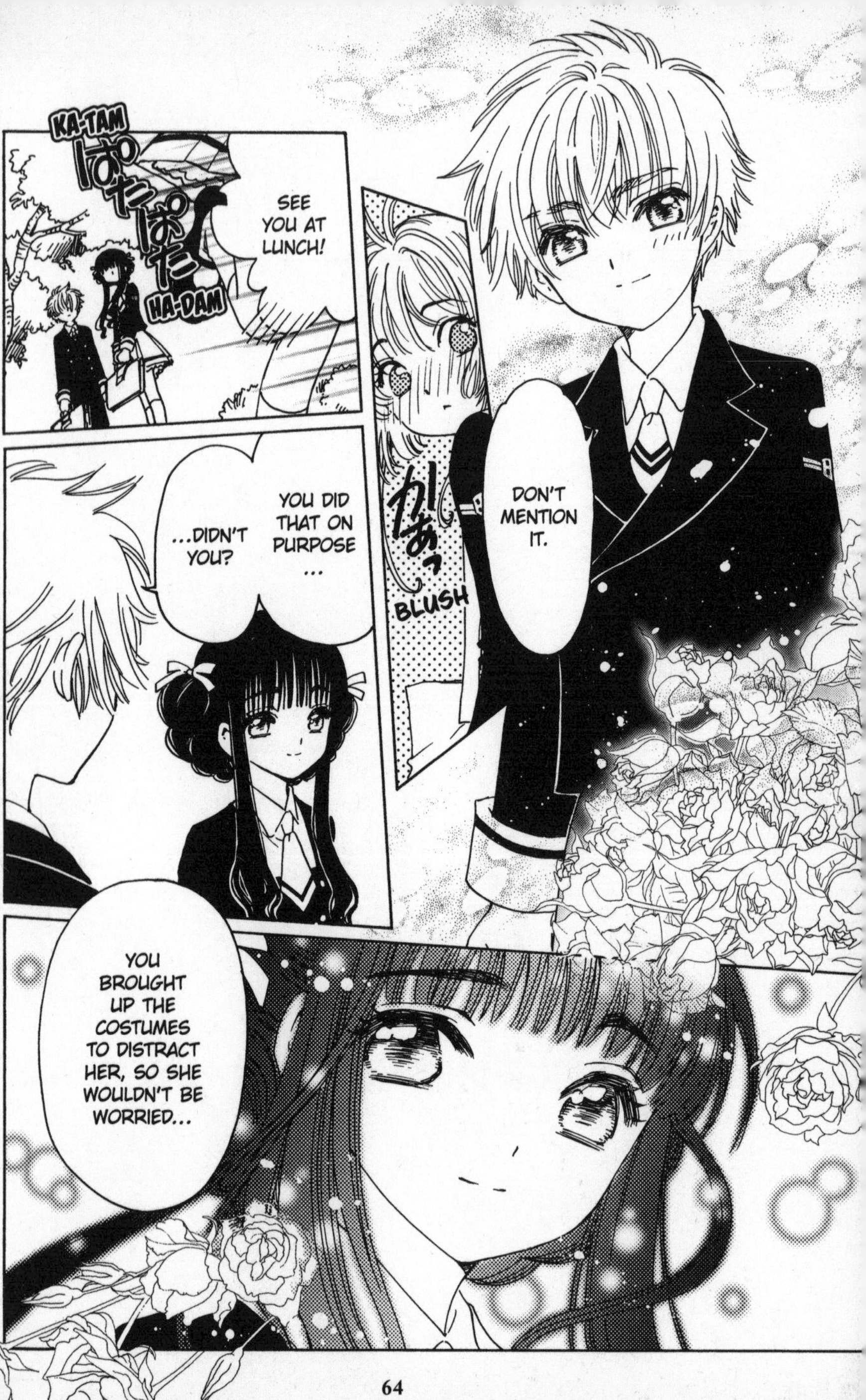
かぁっ
BLUSH
DON'T MENTION IT.
KA-TAM
ぱたぱた
HA-DAM
SEE YOU AT LUNCH!
YOU DID THAT ON PURPOSE ...
...DIDN'T YOU?
YOU BROUGHT UP THE COSTUMES TO DISTRACT HER, SO SHE WOULDN'T BE WORRIED...

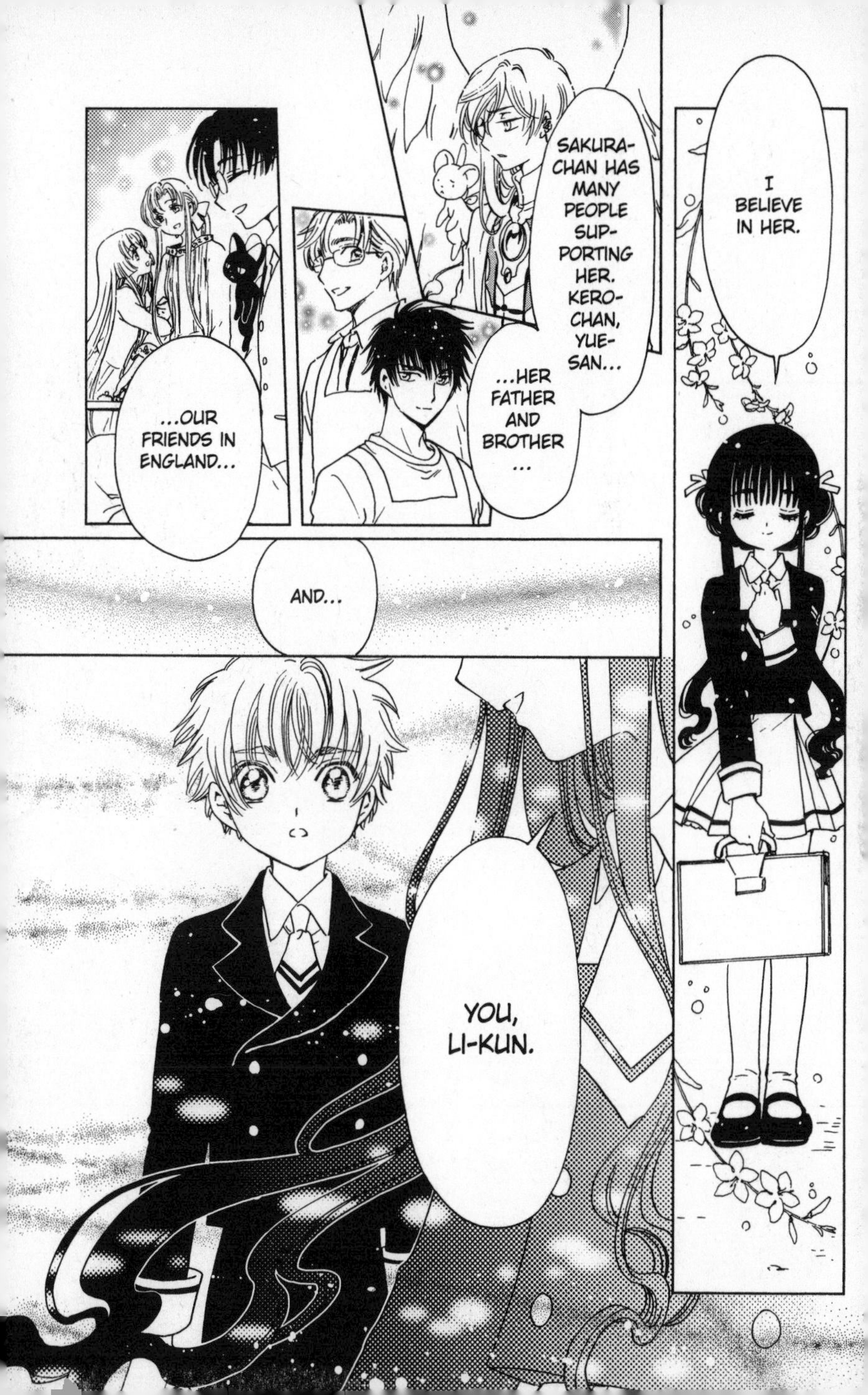
I BELIEVE IN HER.
SAKURA-CHAN HAS MANY PEOPLE SUP-PORTING HER. KERO-CHAN, YUE-SAN...
...HER FATHER AND BROTHER ...
...OUR FRIENDS IN ENGLAND...
AND...
YOU, LI-KUN.

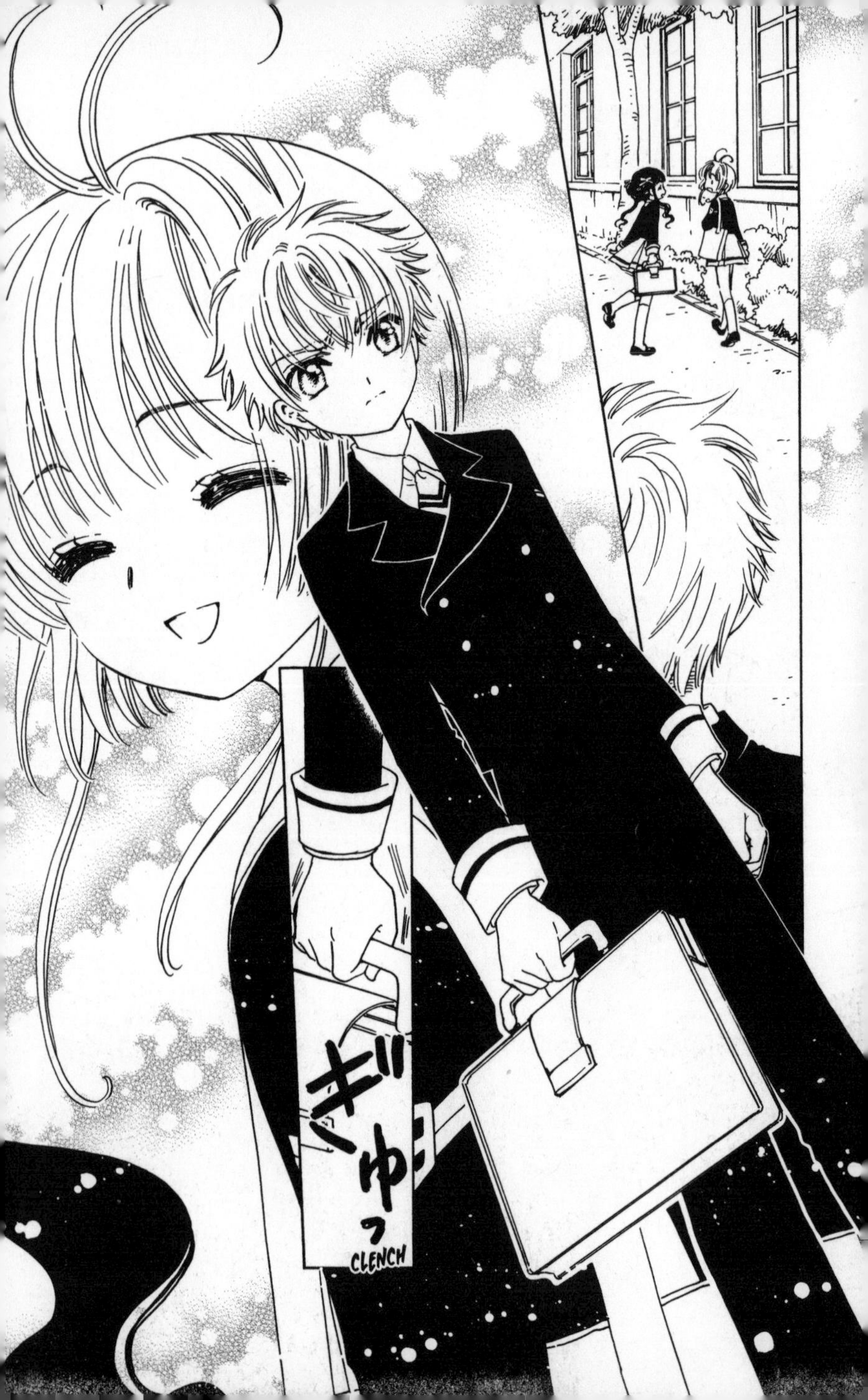
ぎゅっ
CLENCH

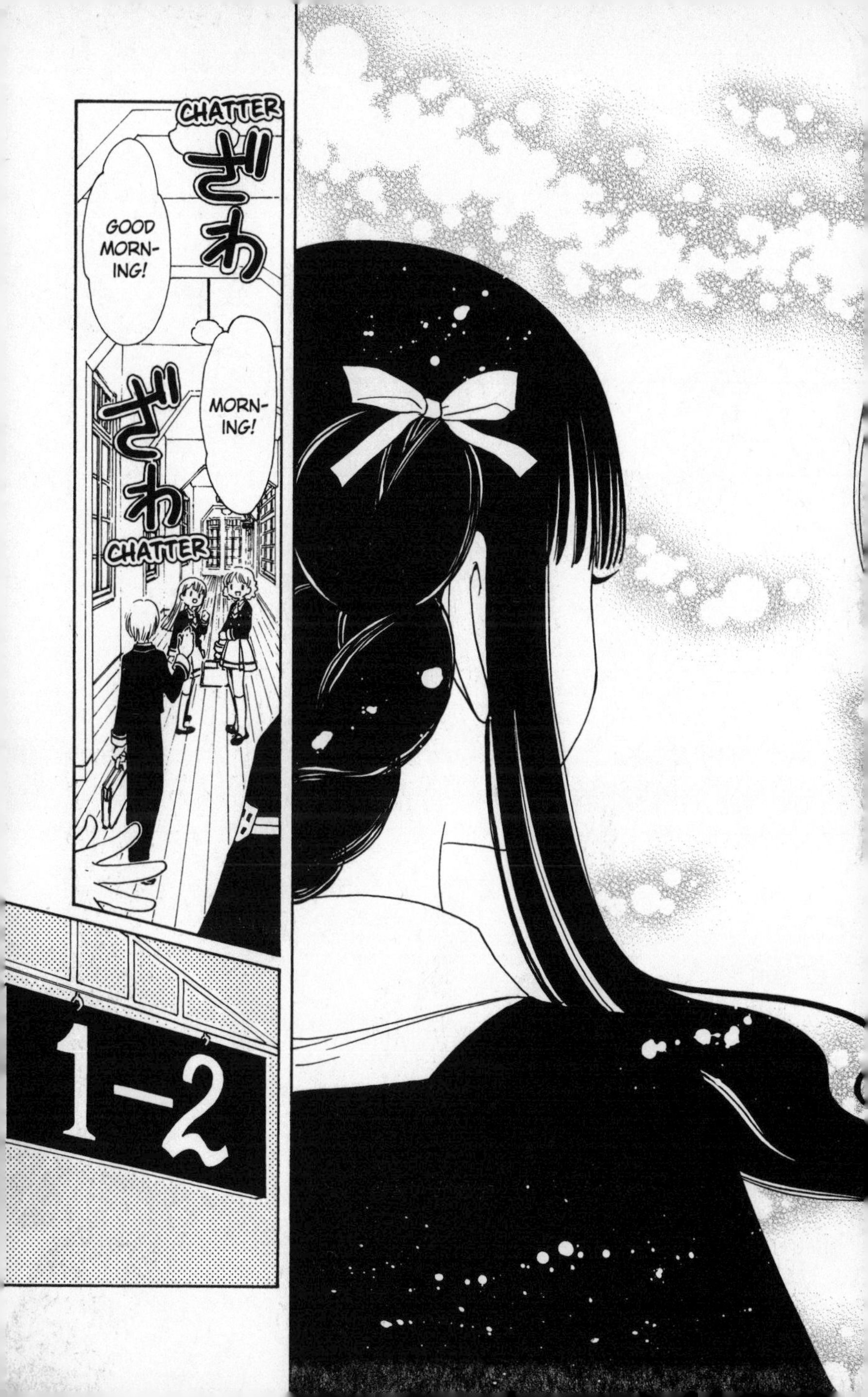
CHATTER
ざわ
GOOD MORNING!
MORNING!
ざわ
CHATTER
1-2

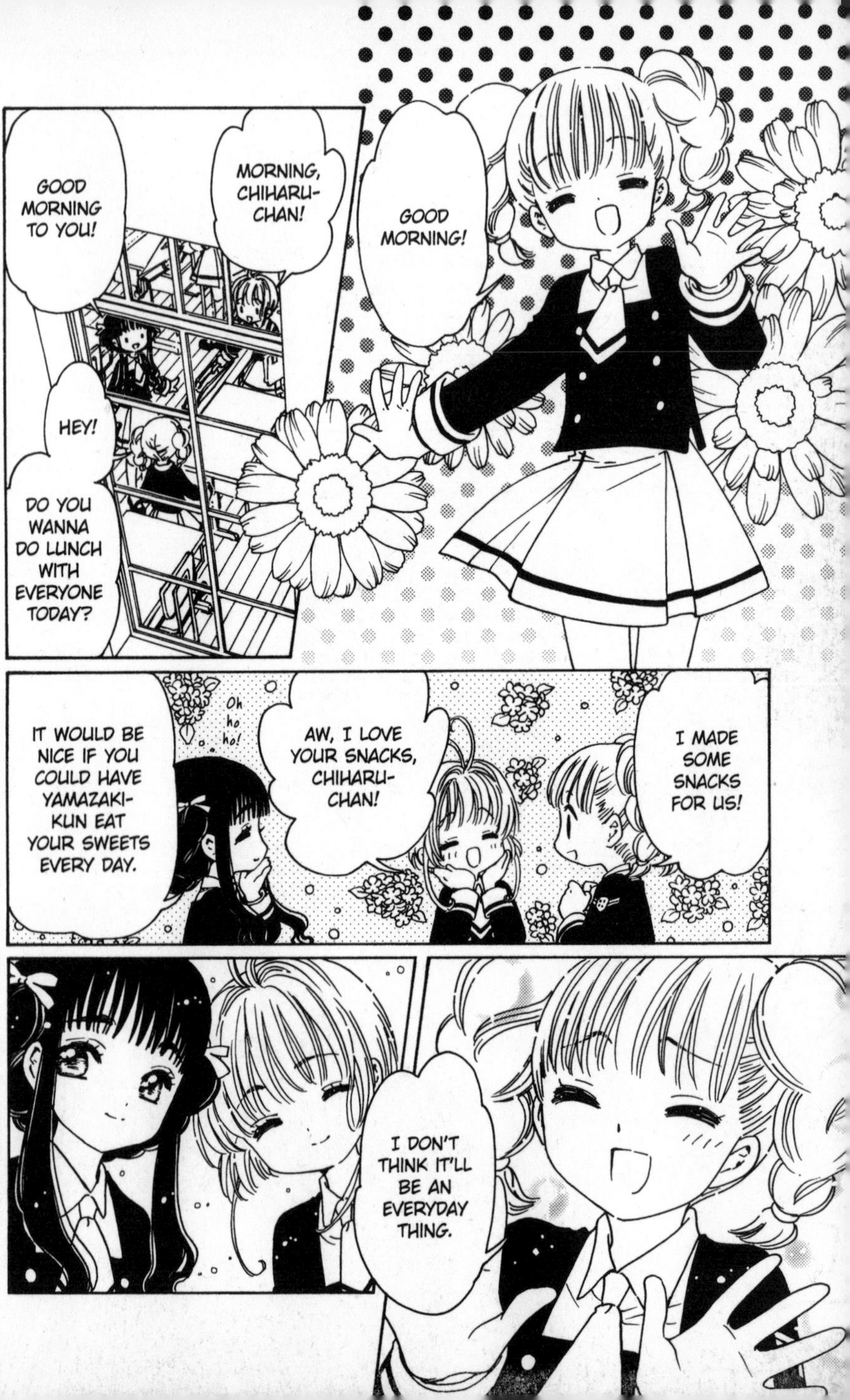
GOOD MORNING!
MORNING, CHIHARU-CHAN!
GOOD MORNING TO YOU!
HEY!
DO YOU WANNA DO LUNCH WITH EVERYONE TODAY?
I MADE SOME SNACKS FOR US!
AW, I LOVE YOUR SNACKS, CHIHARU-CHAN!
Oh ho ho!
IT WOULD BE NICE IF YOU COULD HAVE YAMAZAKI-KUN EAT YOUR SWEETS EVERY DAY.
I DON'T THINK IT'LL BE AN EVERYDAY THING.

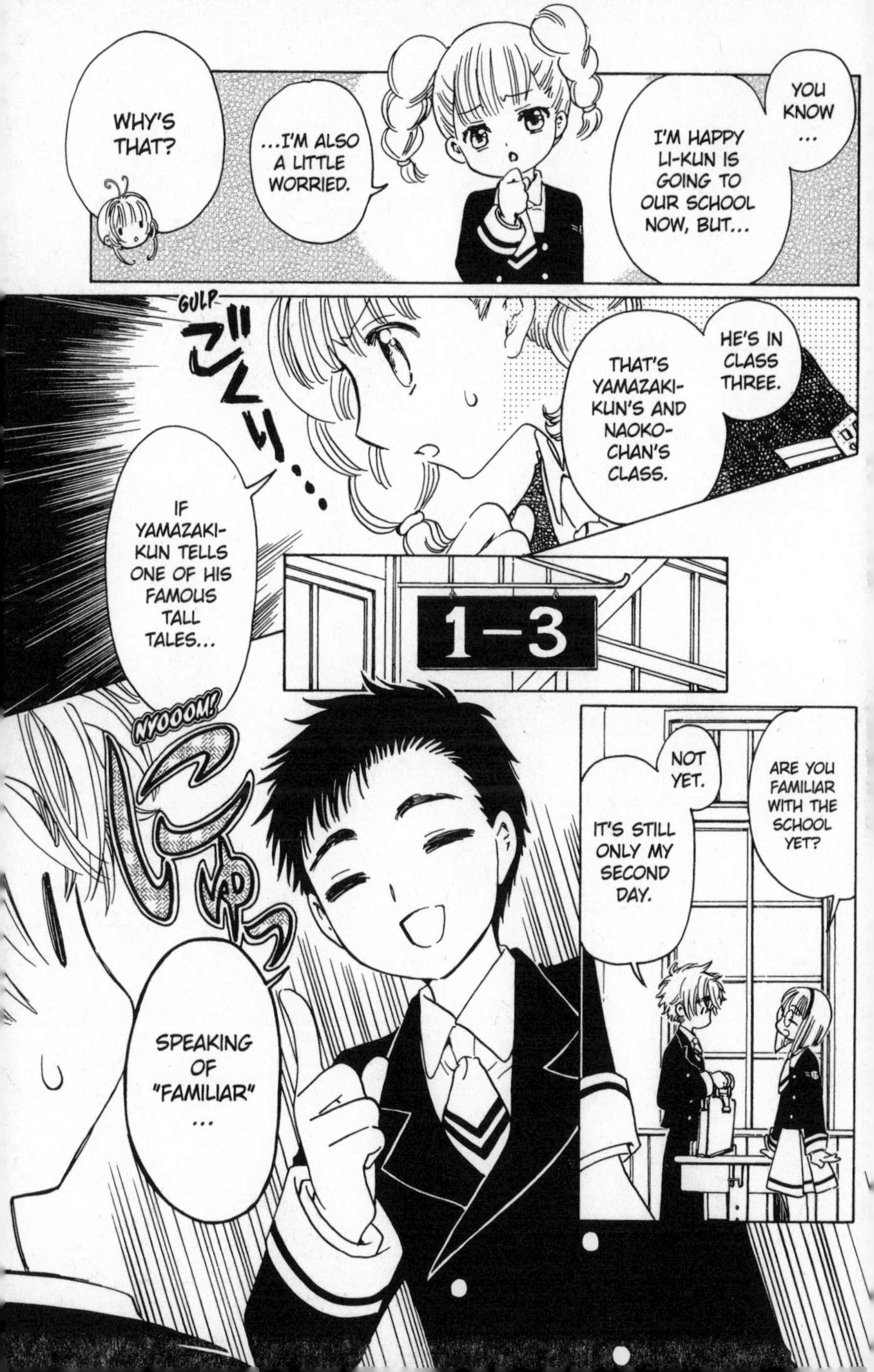
YOU KNOW ...
I'M HAPPY LI-KUN IS GOING TO OUR SCHOOL NOW, BUT...
...I'M ALSO A LITTLE WORRIED.
WHY'S THAT?
HE'S IN CLASS THREE.
THAT'S YAMAZAKI-KUN'S AND NAOKO-CHAN'S CLASS.
GULP
ごくり...
IF YAMAZAKI-KUN TELLS ONE OF HIS FAMOUS TALL TALES...
1-3
ARE YOU FAMILIAR WITH THE SCHOOL YET?
NOT YET.
IT'S STILL ONLY MY SECOND DAY.
NYOOOM!
SPEAKING OF "FAMILIAR" ...

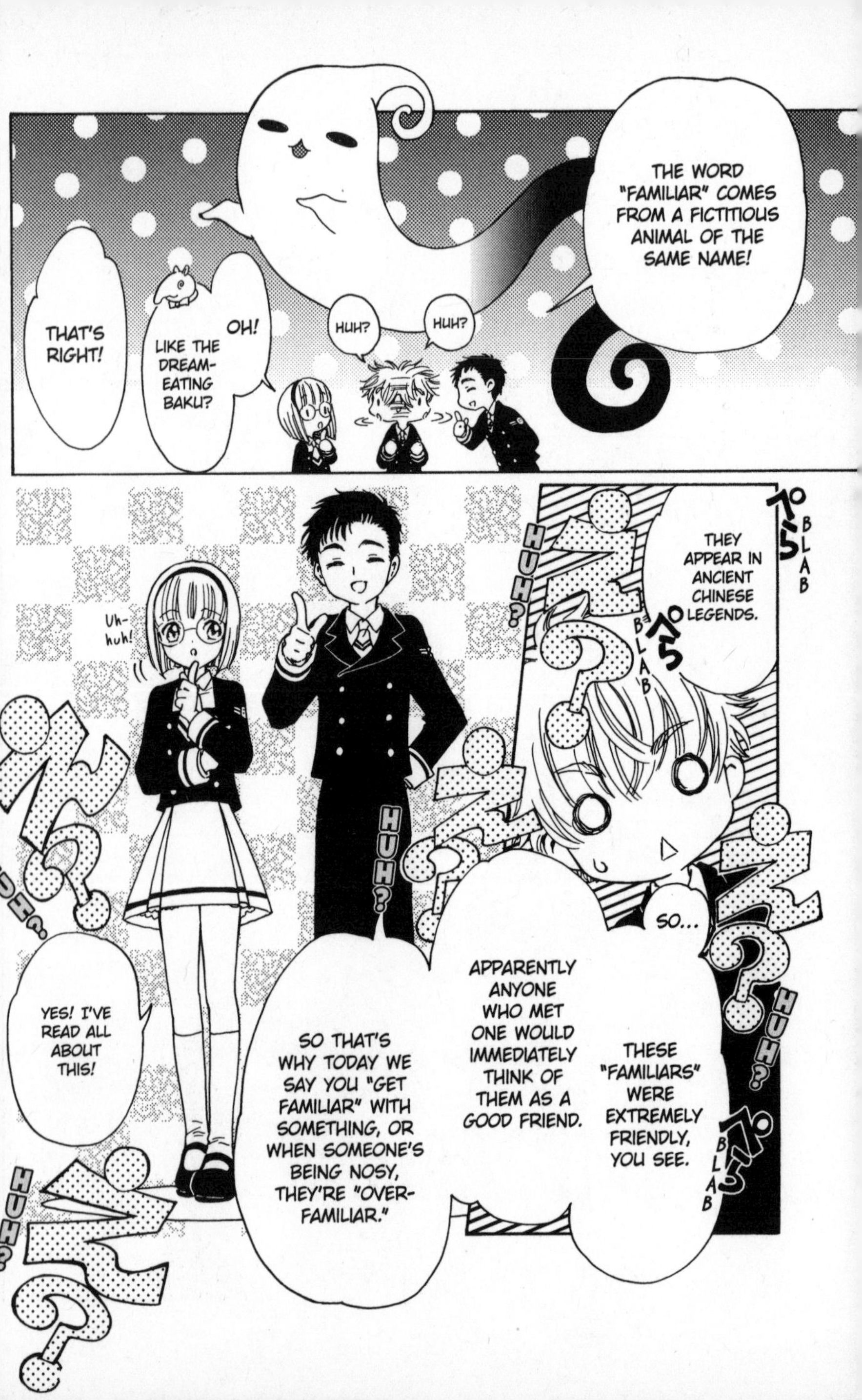
THE WORD "FAMILIAR" COMES FROM A FICTITIOUS ANIMAL OF THE SAME NAME!
HUH?
HUH?
OH! LIKE THE DREAM-EATING BAKU?
THAT'S RIGHT!
BLAB
THEY APPEAR IN ANCIENT CHINESE LEGENDS.
BLAB
HUH?
SO...
HUH?
THESE "FAMILIARS" WERE EXTREMELY FRIENDLY, YOU SEE.
BLAB
APPARENTLY ANYONE WHO MET ONE WOULD IMMEDIATELY THINK OF THEM AS A GOOD FRIEND.
SO THAT'S WHY TODAY WE SAY YOU "GET FAMILIAR" WITH SOMETHING, OR WHEN SOMEONE'S BEING NOSY, THEY'RE "OVER-FAMILIAR."
HUH?
Uh-huh!
YES! I'VE READ ALL ABOUT THIS!
HUH?

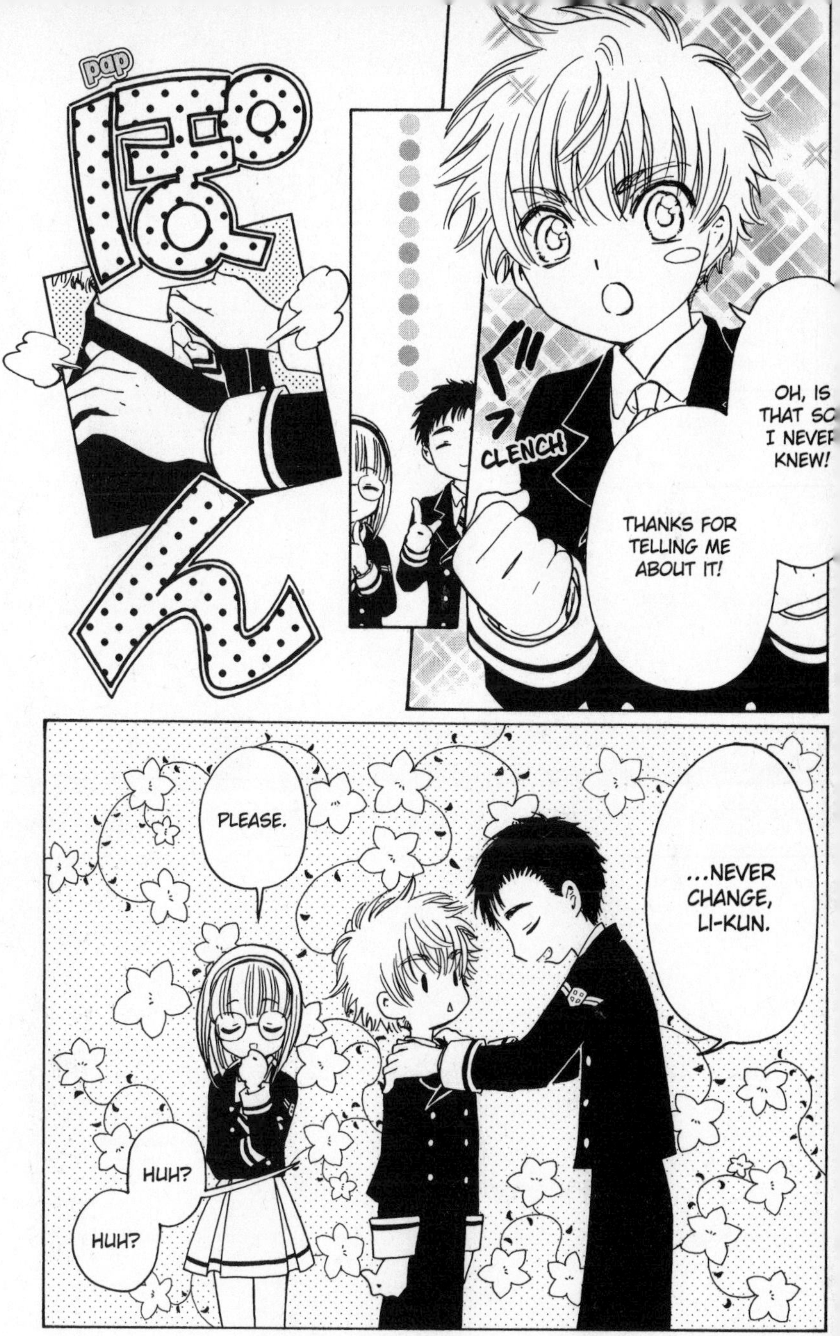
OH, IS THAT SO I NEVER KNEW!
THANKS FOR TELLING ME ABOUT IT!
CLENCH
pap
ぽん
...NEVER CHANGE, LI-KUN.
PLEASE.
HUH?
HUH?

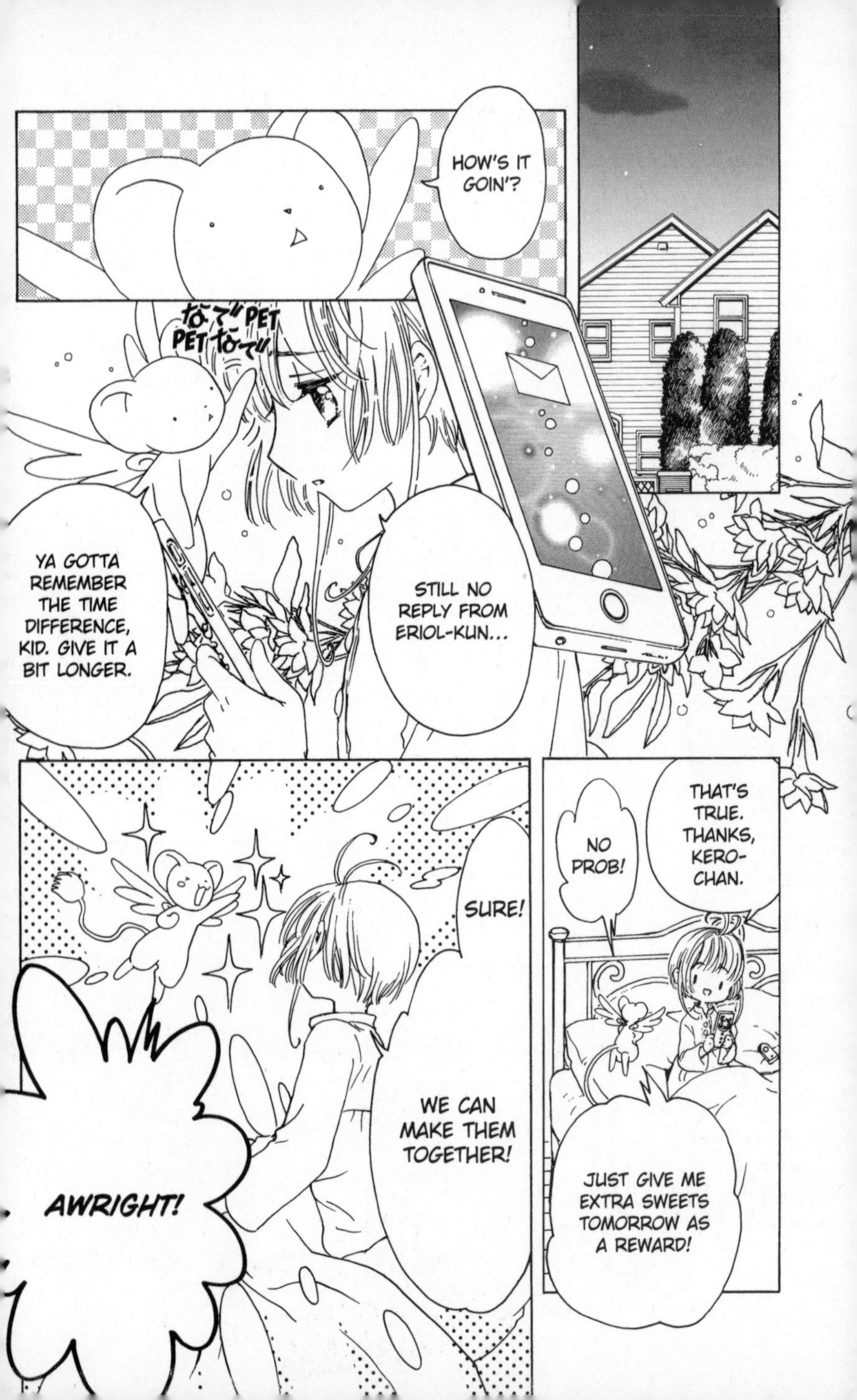
HOW'S IT GOIN'?
なで PET
PET なで
STILL NO REPLY FROM ERIOL-KUN...
YA GOTTA REMEMBER THE TIME DIFFERENCE, KID. GIVE IT A BIT LONGER.
THAT'S TRUE. THANKS, KERO-CHAN.
NO PROB!
JUST GIVE ME EXTRA SWEETS TOMORROW AS A REWARD!
SURE!
WE CAN MAKE THEM TOGETHER!
AWRIGHT!

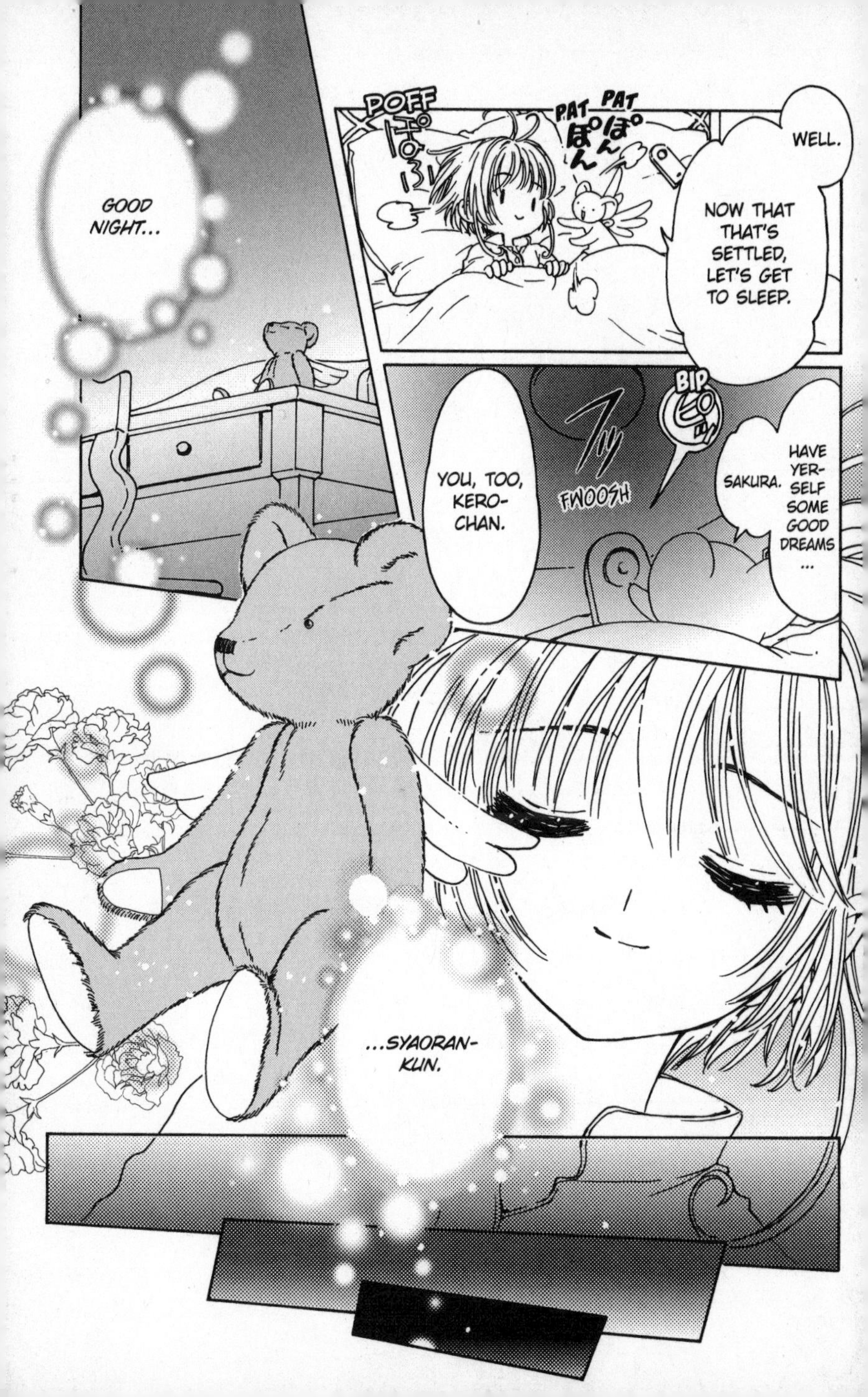

PAT PAT
POFF
WELL.
NOW THAT THAT'S SETTLED, LET'S GET TO SLEEP.
BIP
SAKURA.
HAVE YER-SELF SOME GOOD DREAMS ...
FWOOSH
YOU, TOO, KERO-CHAN.
GOOD NIGHT...
...SYAORAN-KUN.

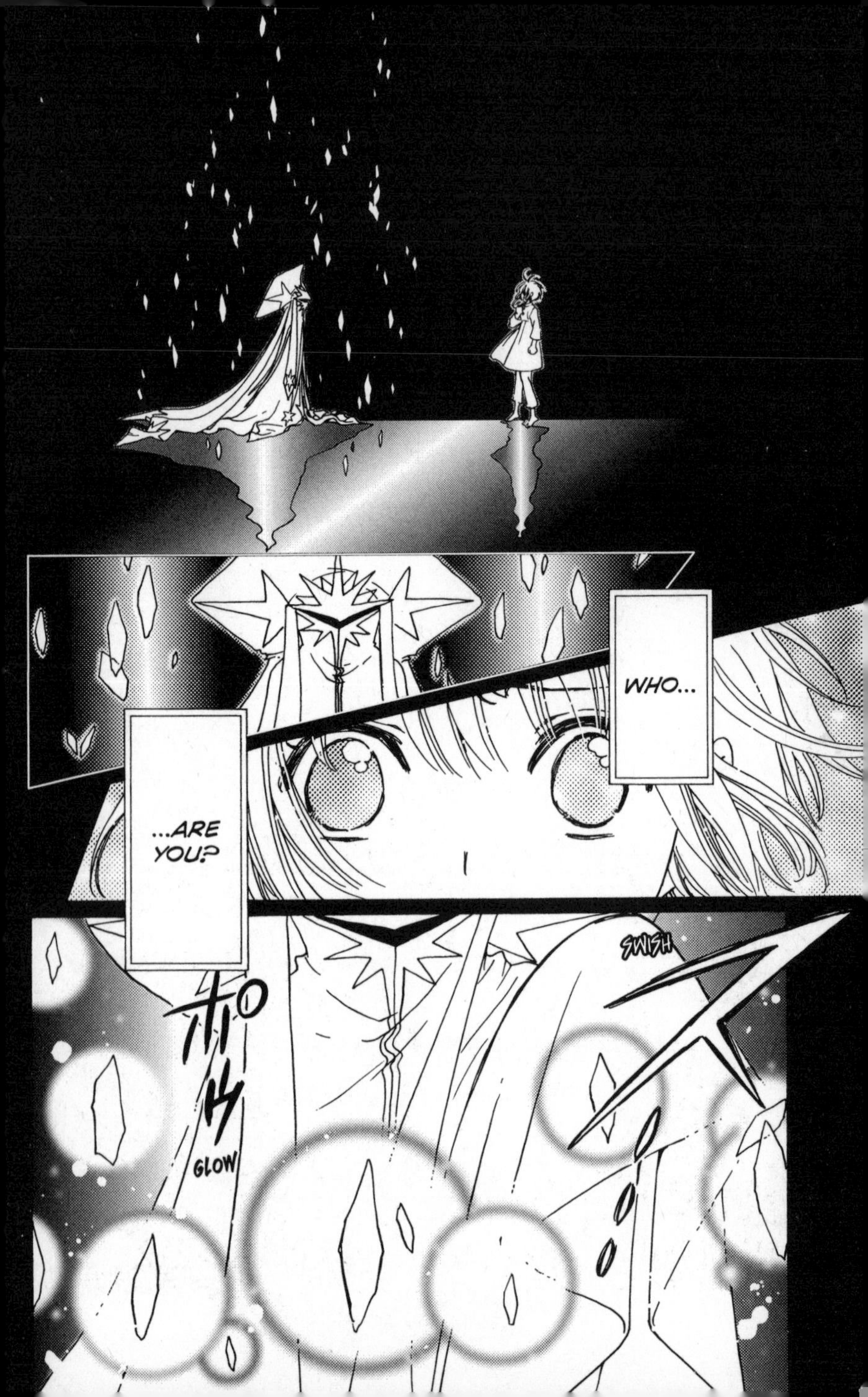
WHO...
...ARE YOU?
SWISH
GLOW

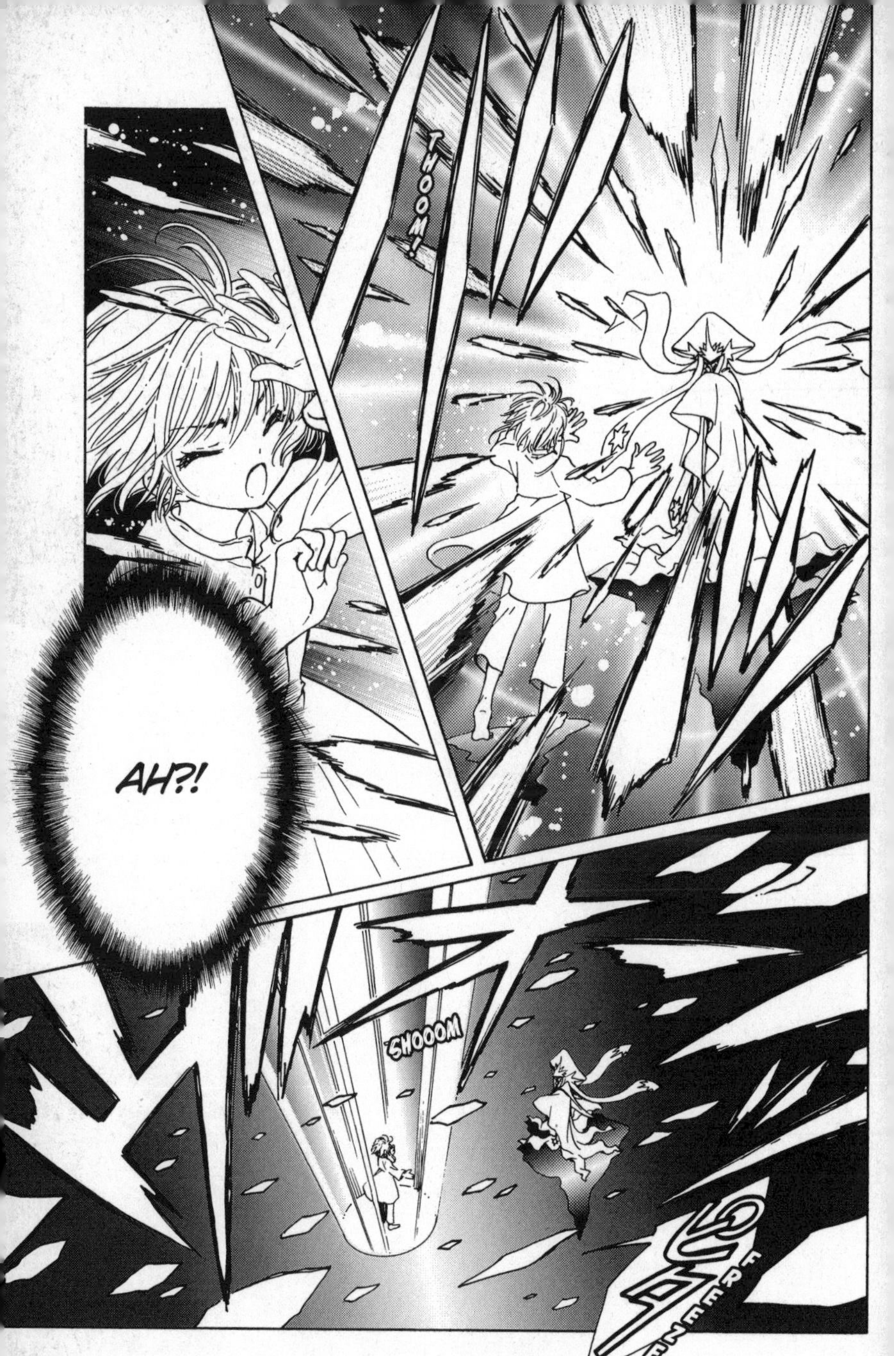
THOOOM!
AH?!
SHOOOM
FREEEZE

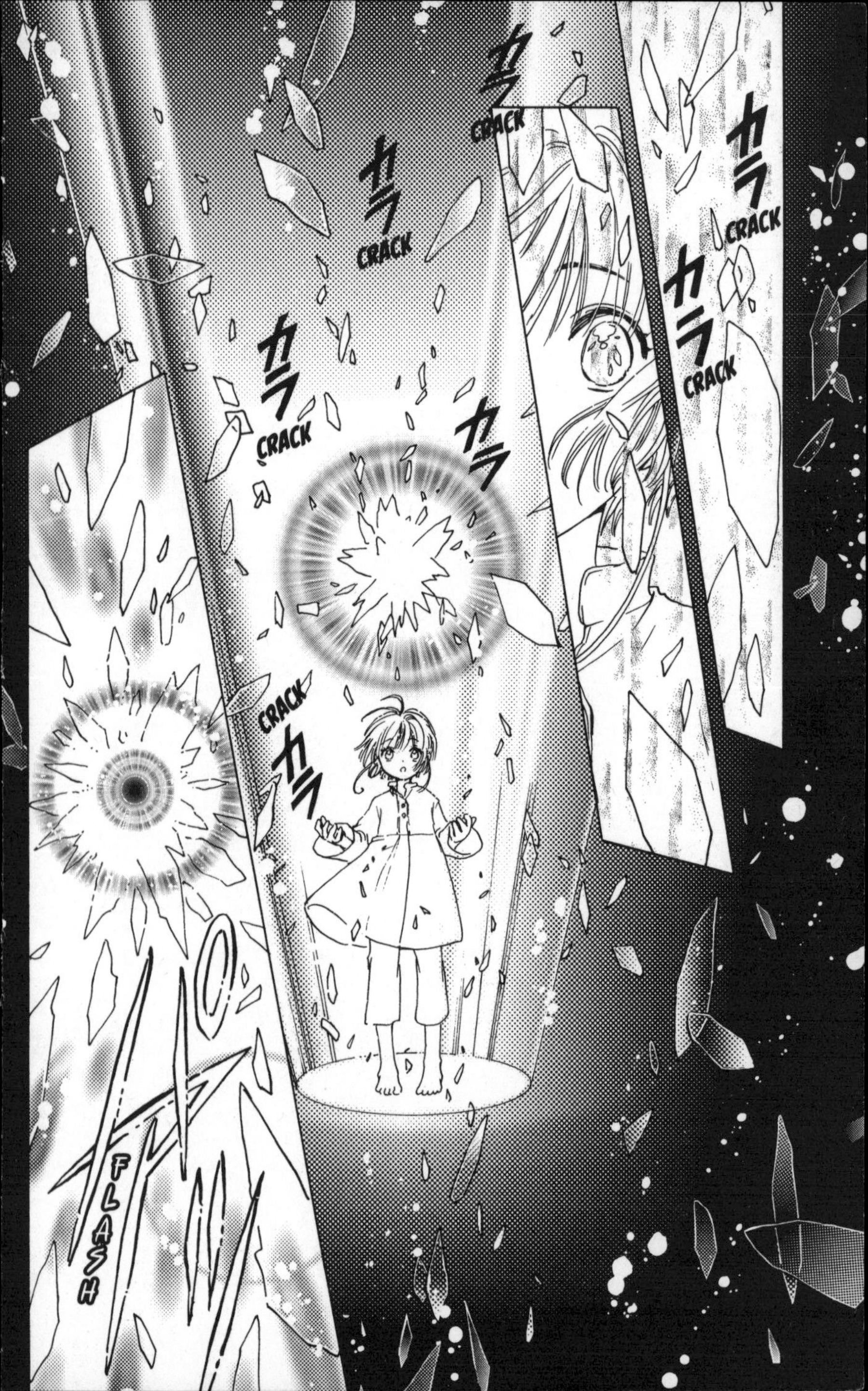

カラ
CRACK
カラ
CRACK
カラ
CRACK
カラ
CRACK
カラ
CRACK
カラ
CRACK
カラ
FLASH

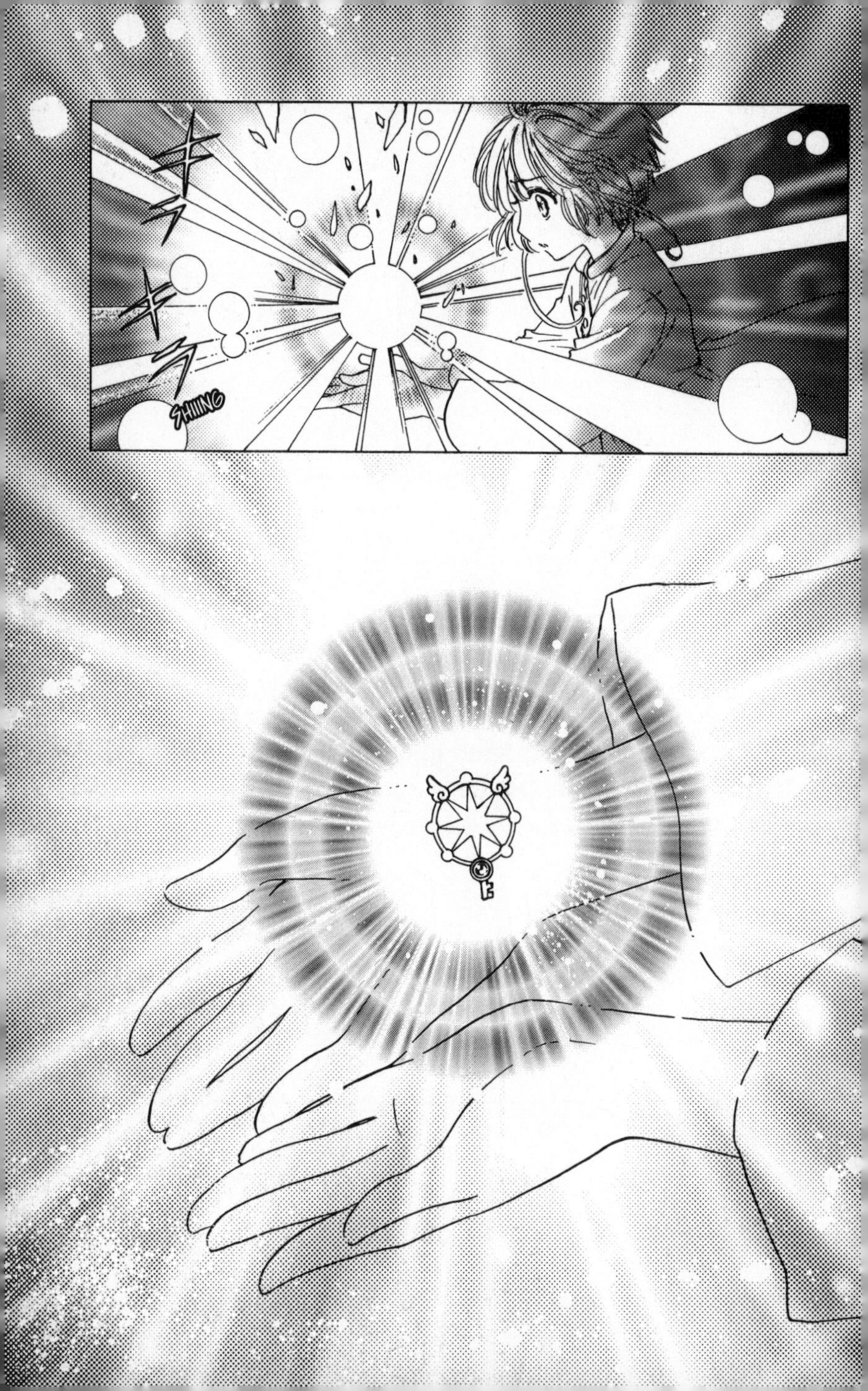
キラ
キラ
SHIIING

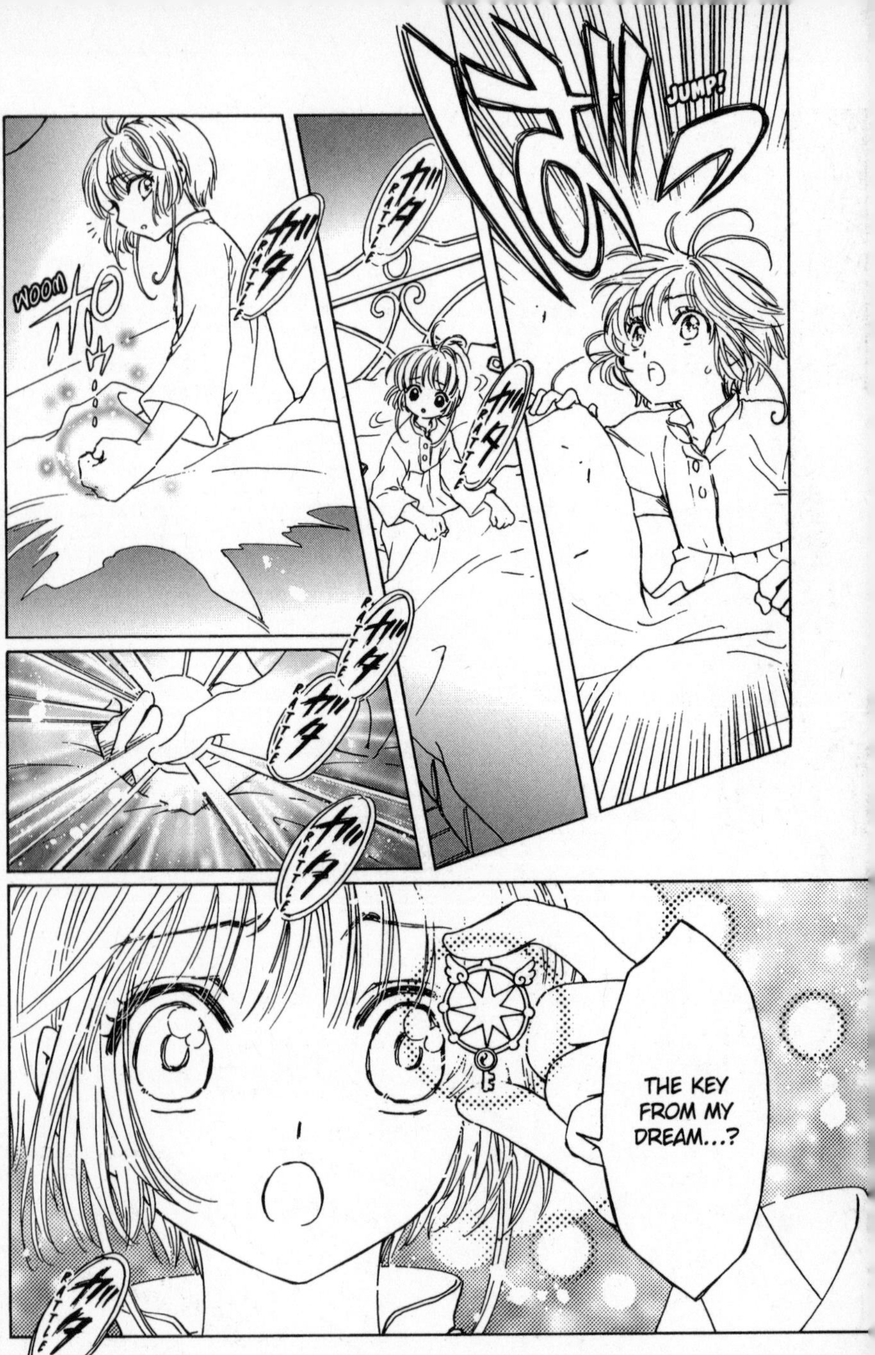
JUMP!
RATTLE
RATTLE
WOOM
RATTLE
RATTLE
RATTLE
RATTLE
THE KEY FROM MY DREAM...?
RATTLE

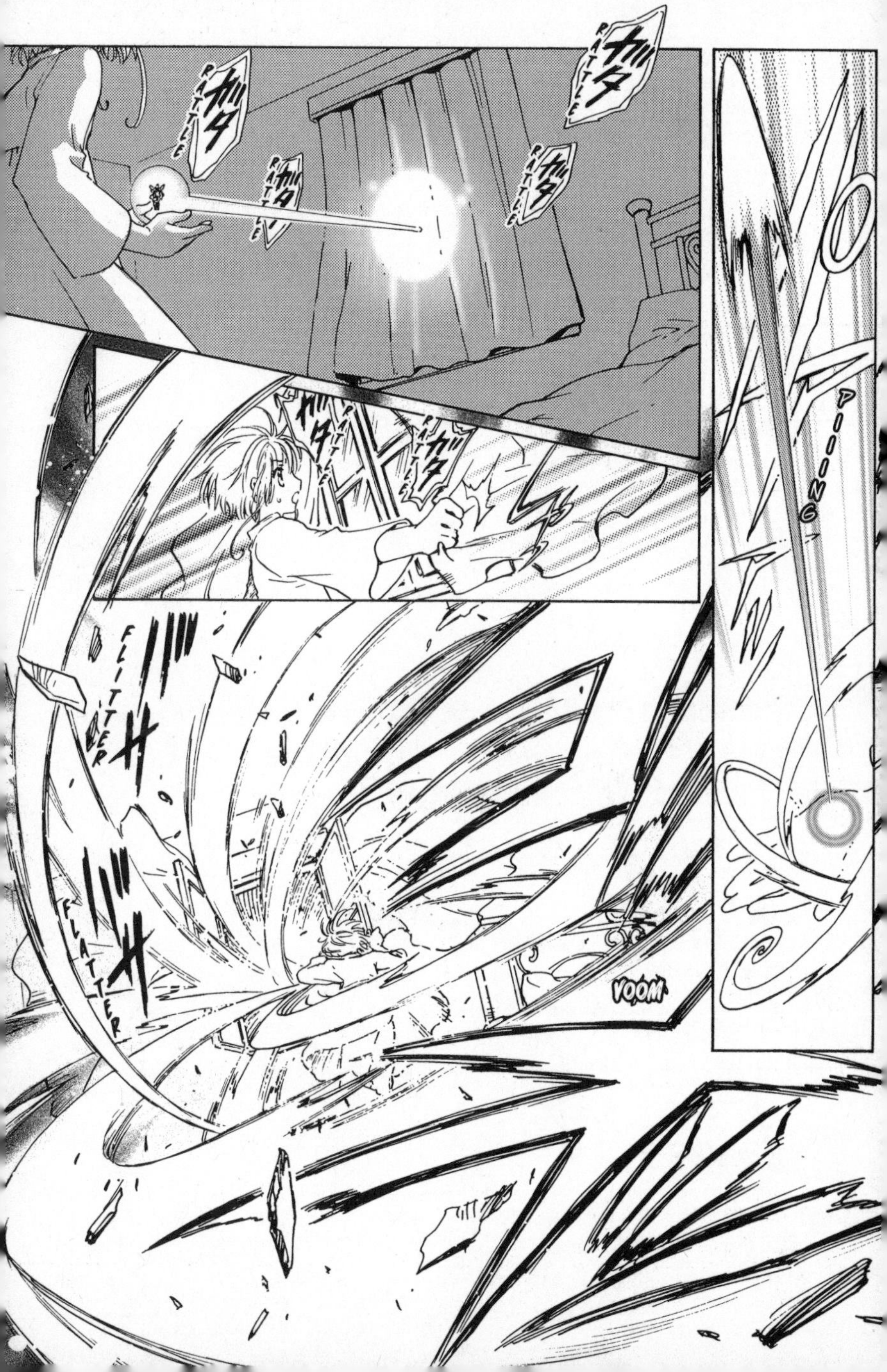
RATTLE
RATTLE
RATTLE
RATTLE
RATTLE
RATTLE
PIIIING
VOOM
FLITTER
FLATTER

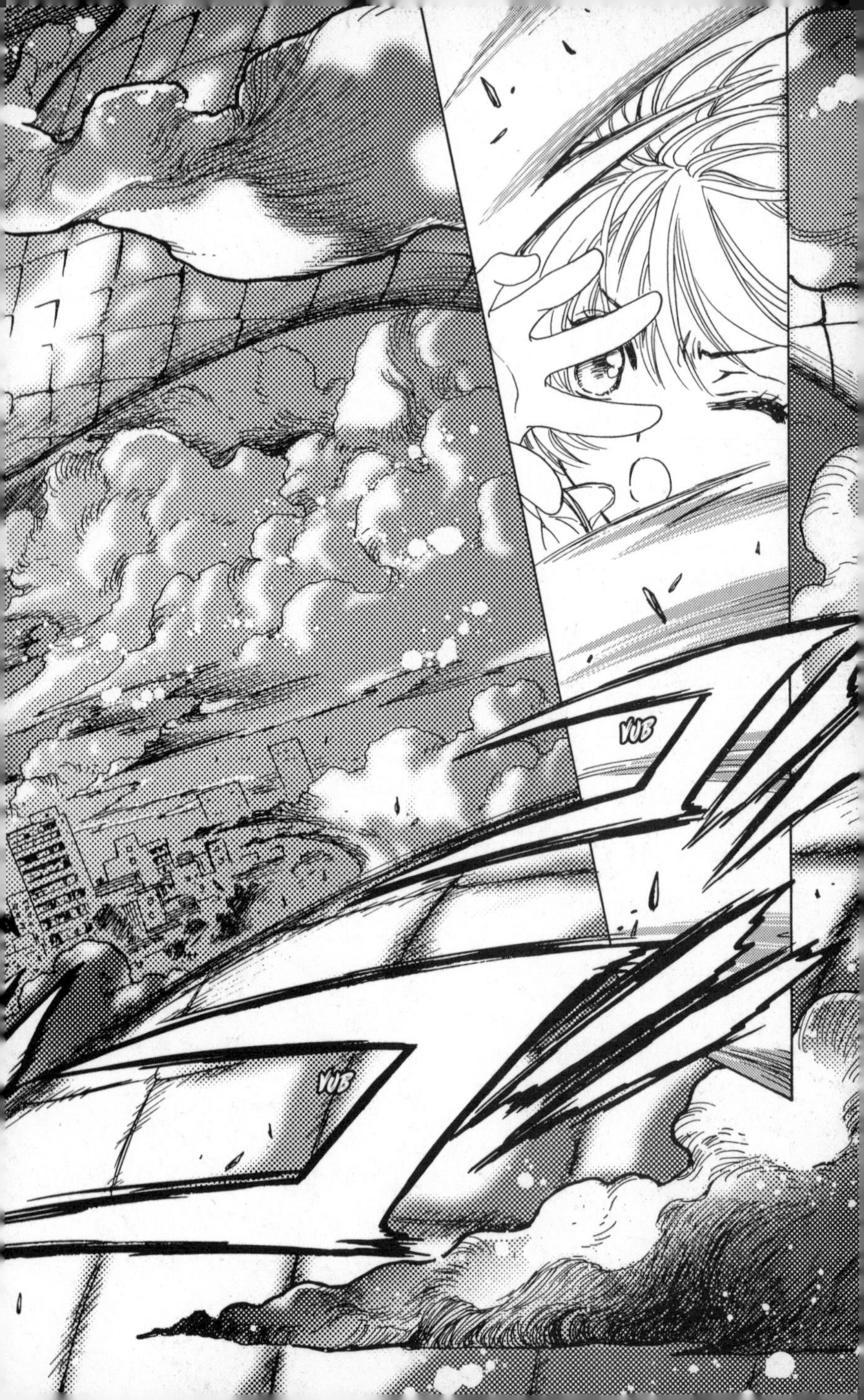
VUB
VUB

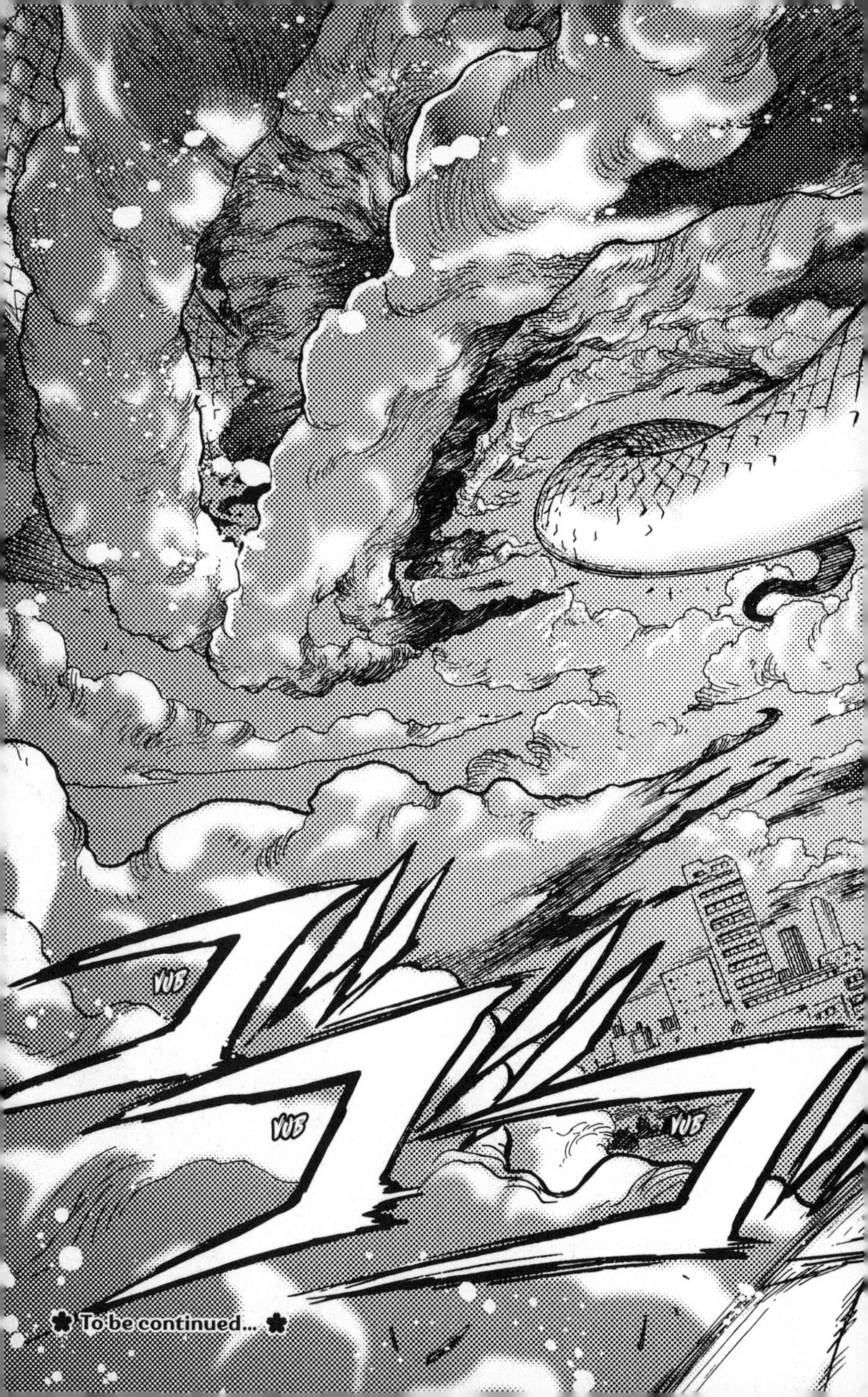
VUB
VUB
VUB

✿ To be continued... ✿

Cardcaptor Sakura
CLEAR CARD

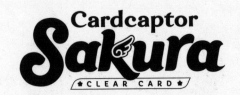

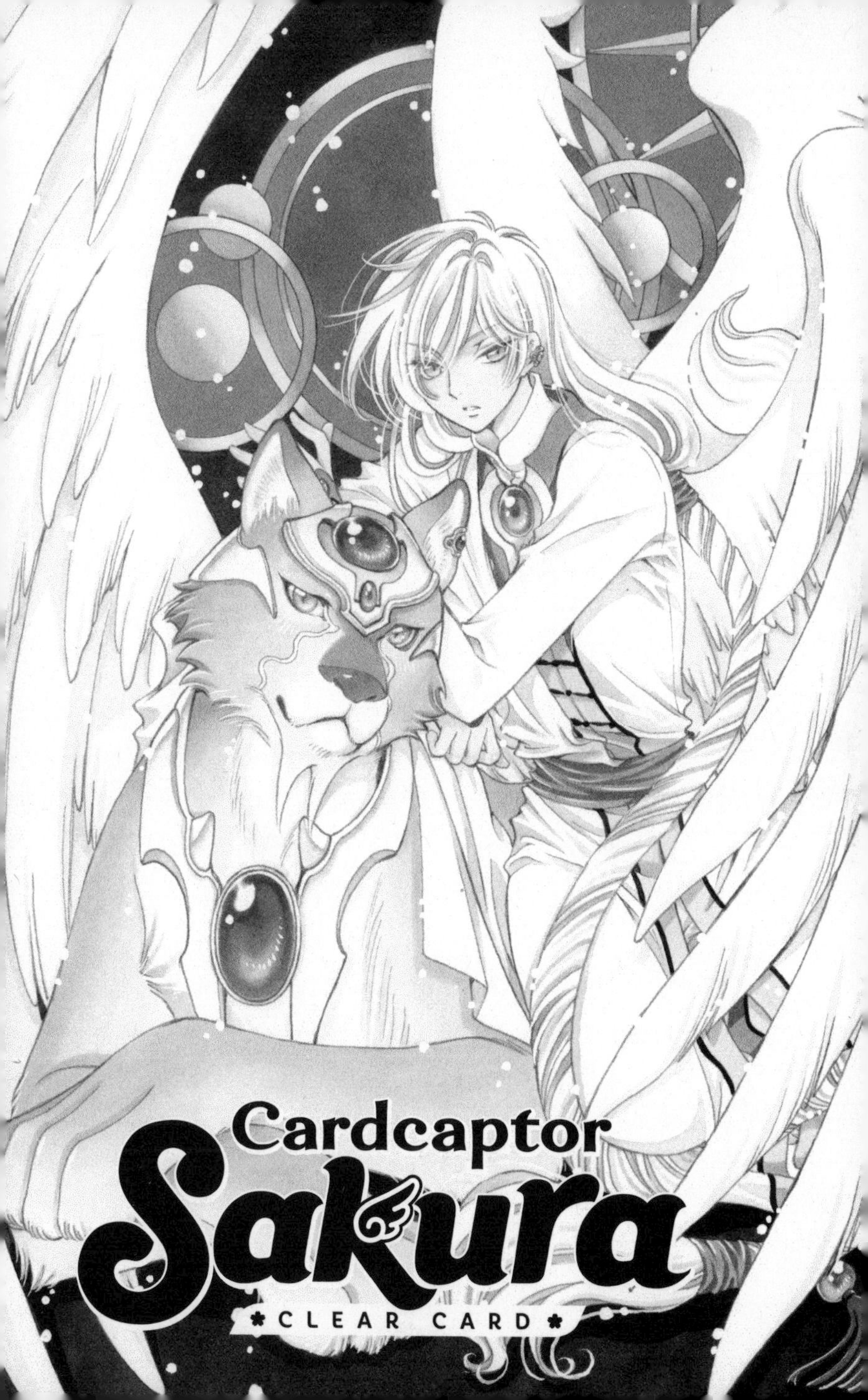
Cardcaptor
Sakura
CLEAR CARD

Cardcaptor Sakura

CLEAR CARD

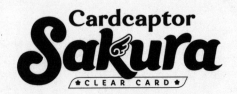

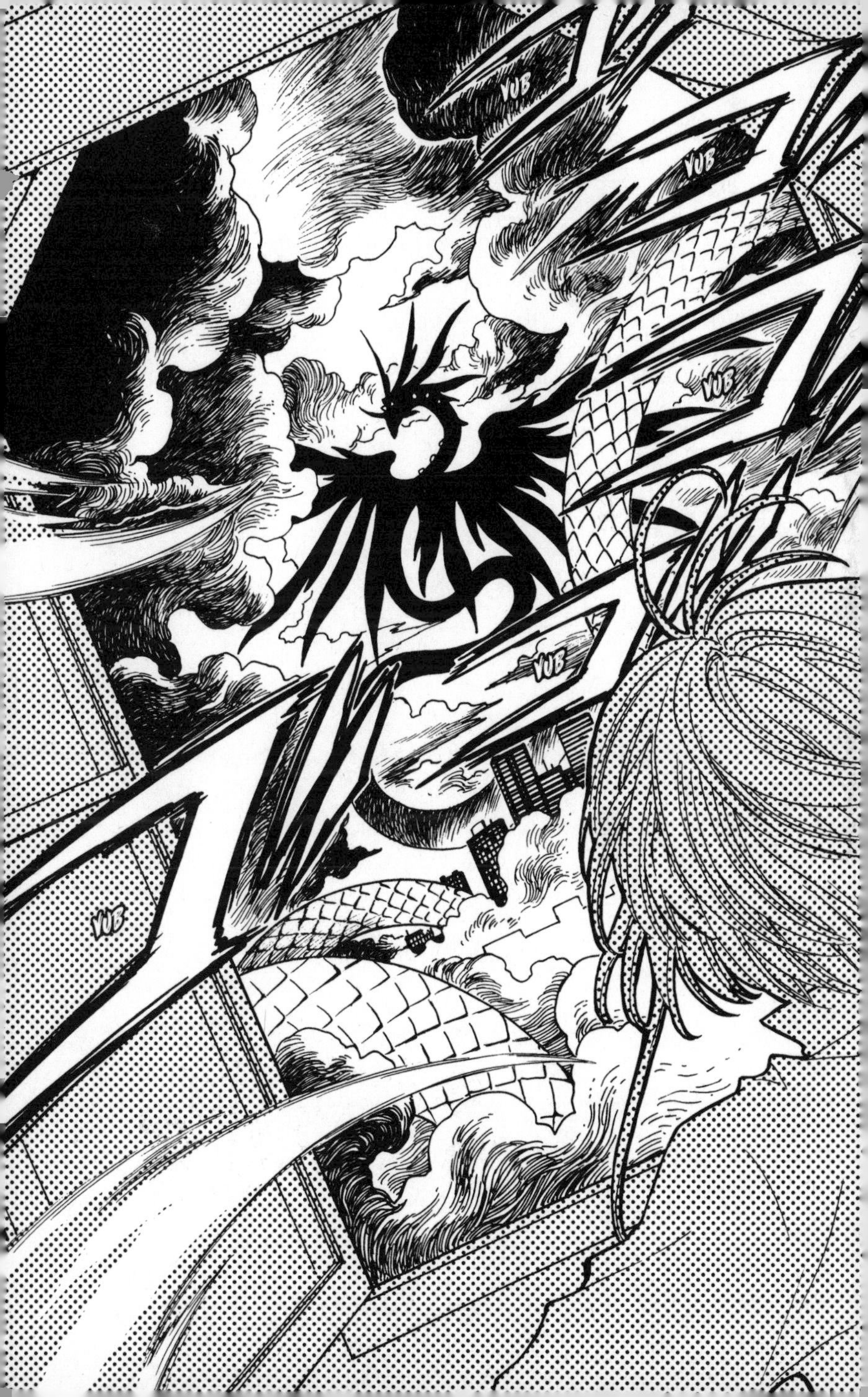
VUB
VUB
VUB
VUB
VUB
VUB

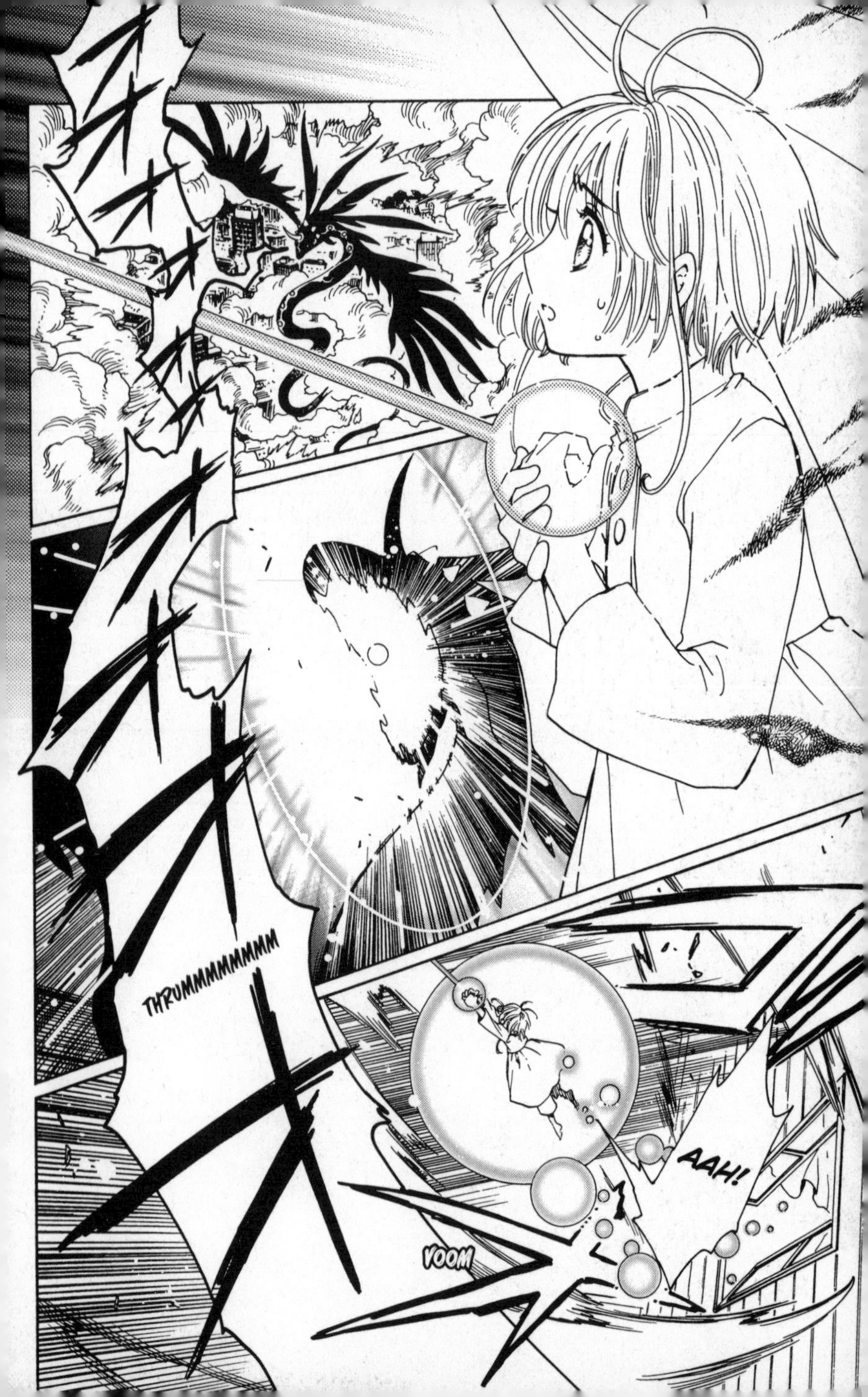
THRUMMMMMMMMM
AAH!
VOOM

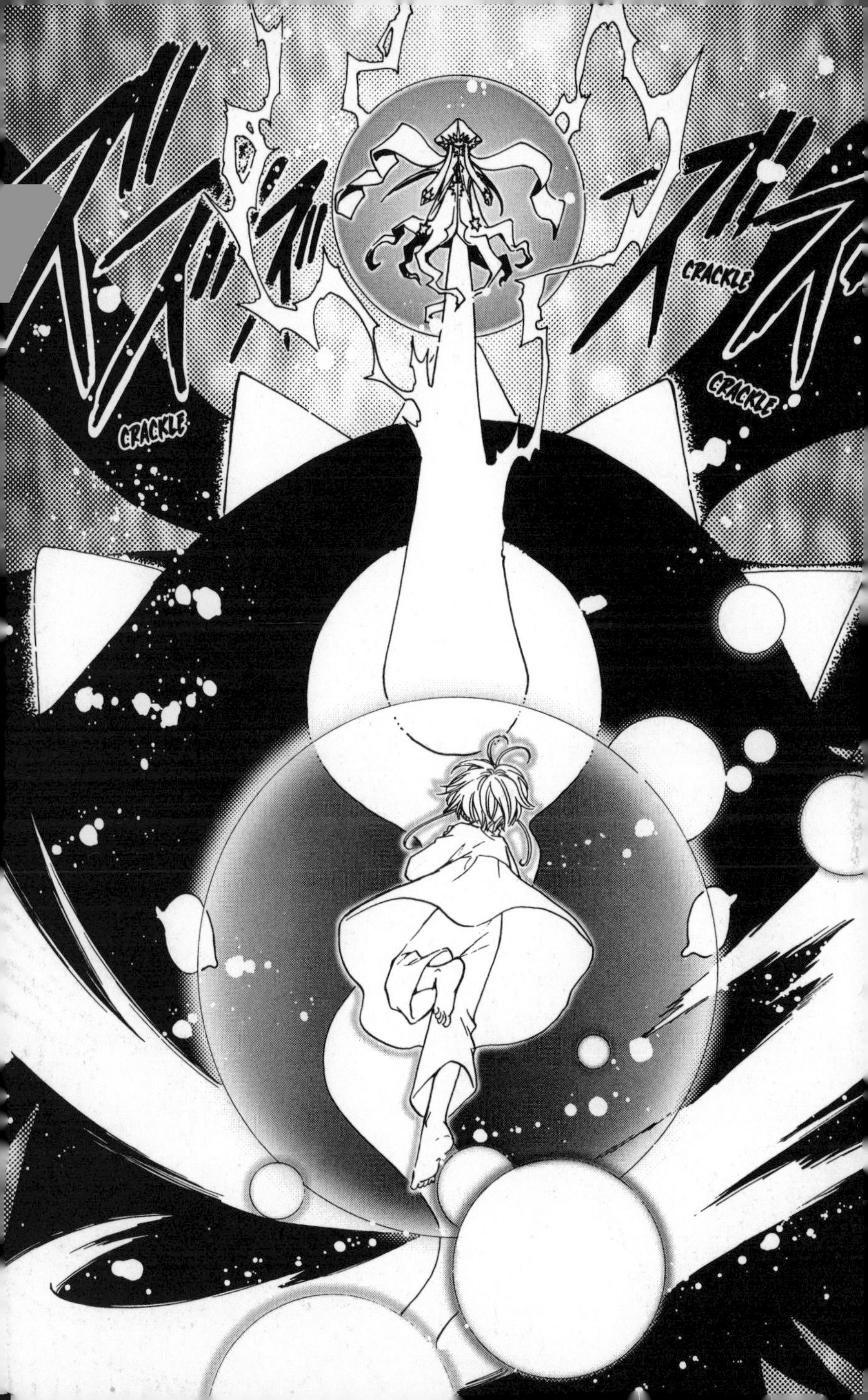
CRACKLE
CRACKLE
CRACKLE

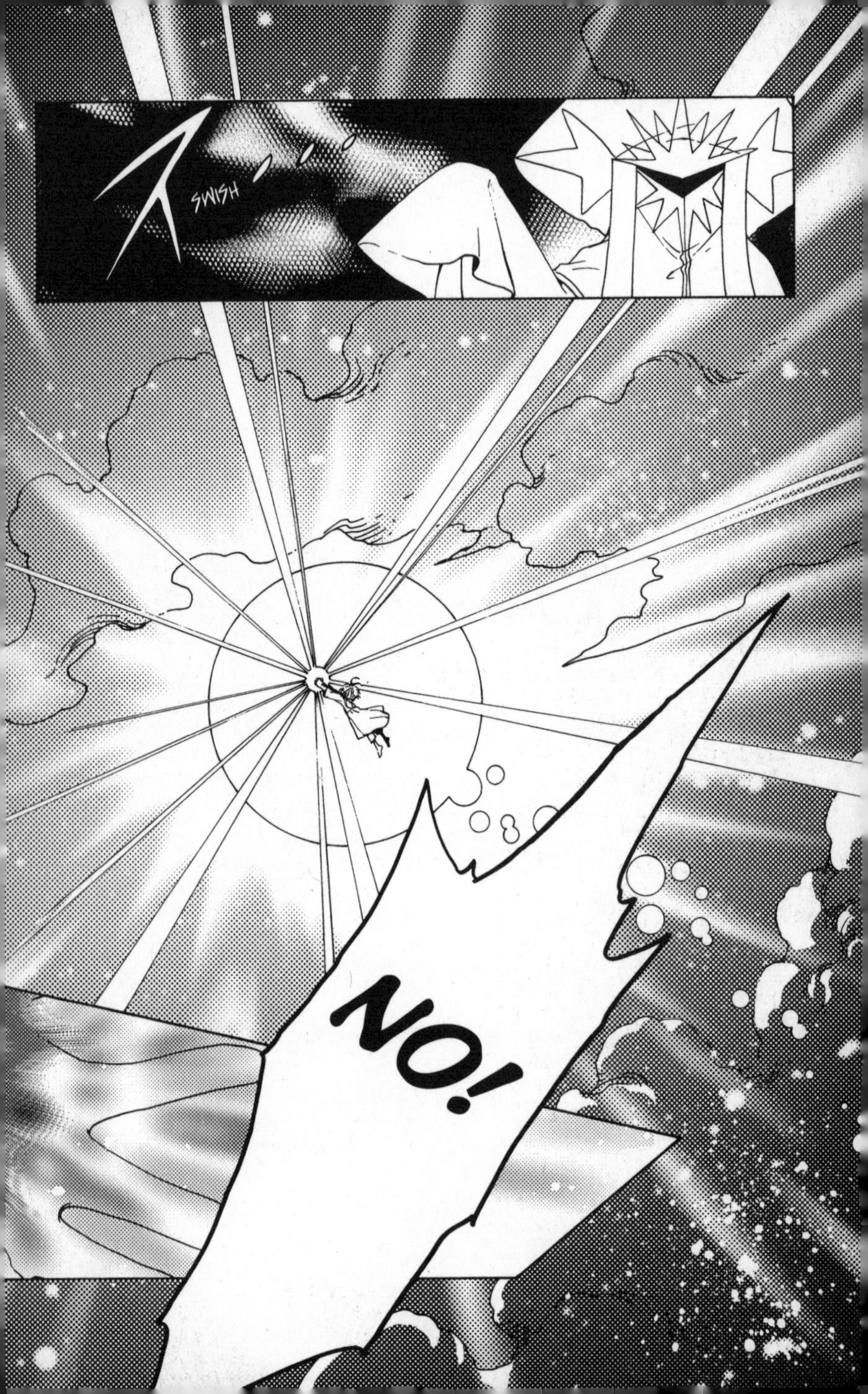
SWISH
NO!

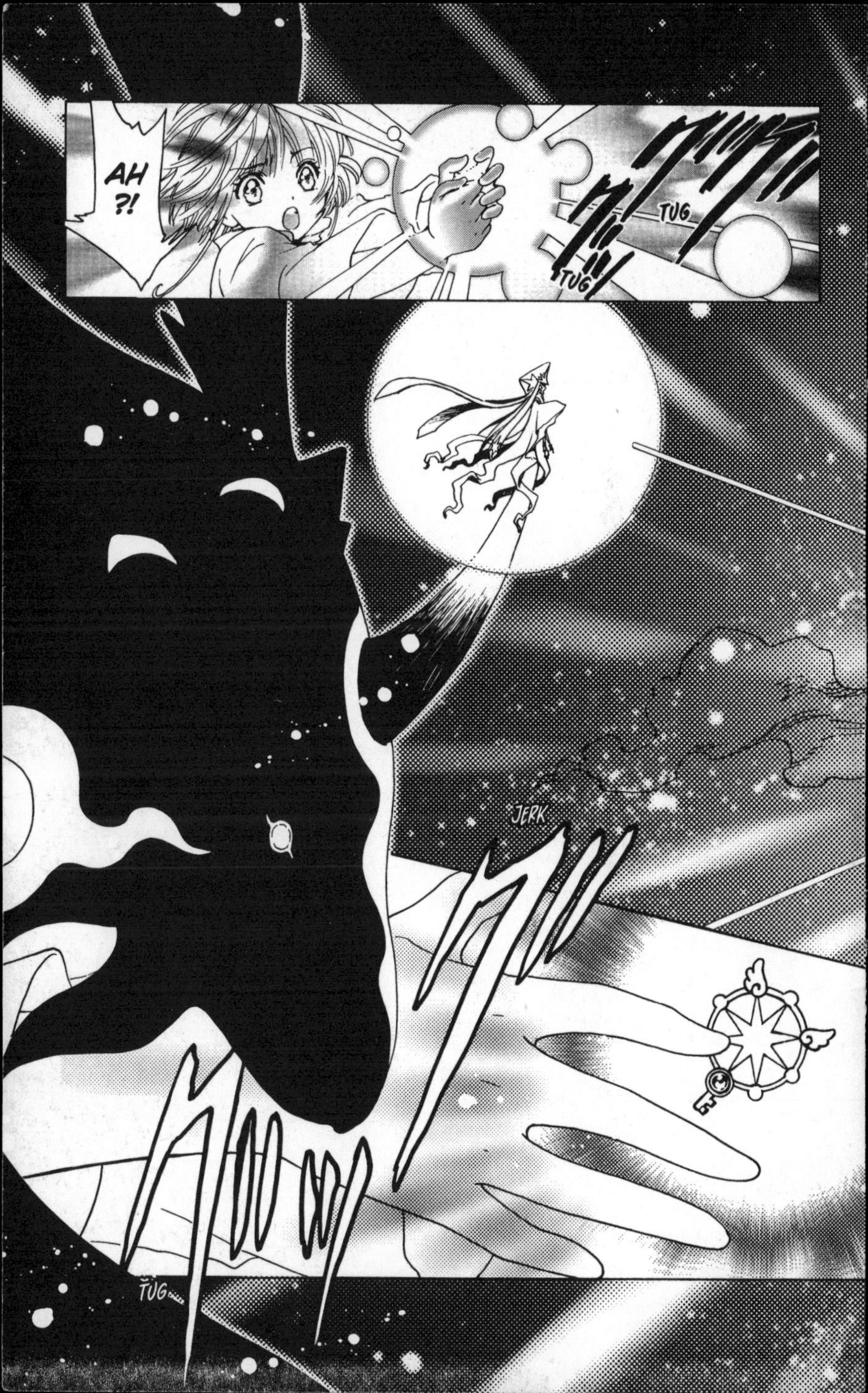
AH ?!
TUG
TUG
JERK
TUG...

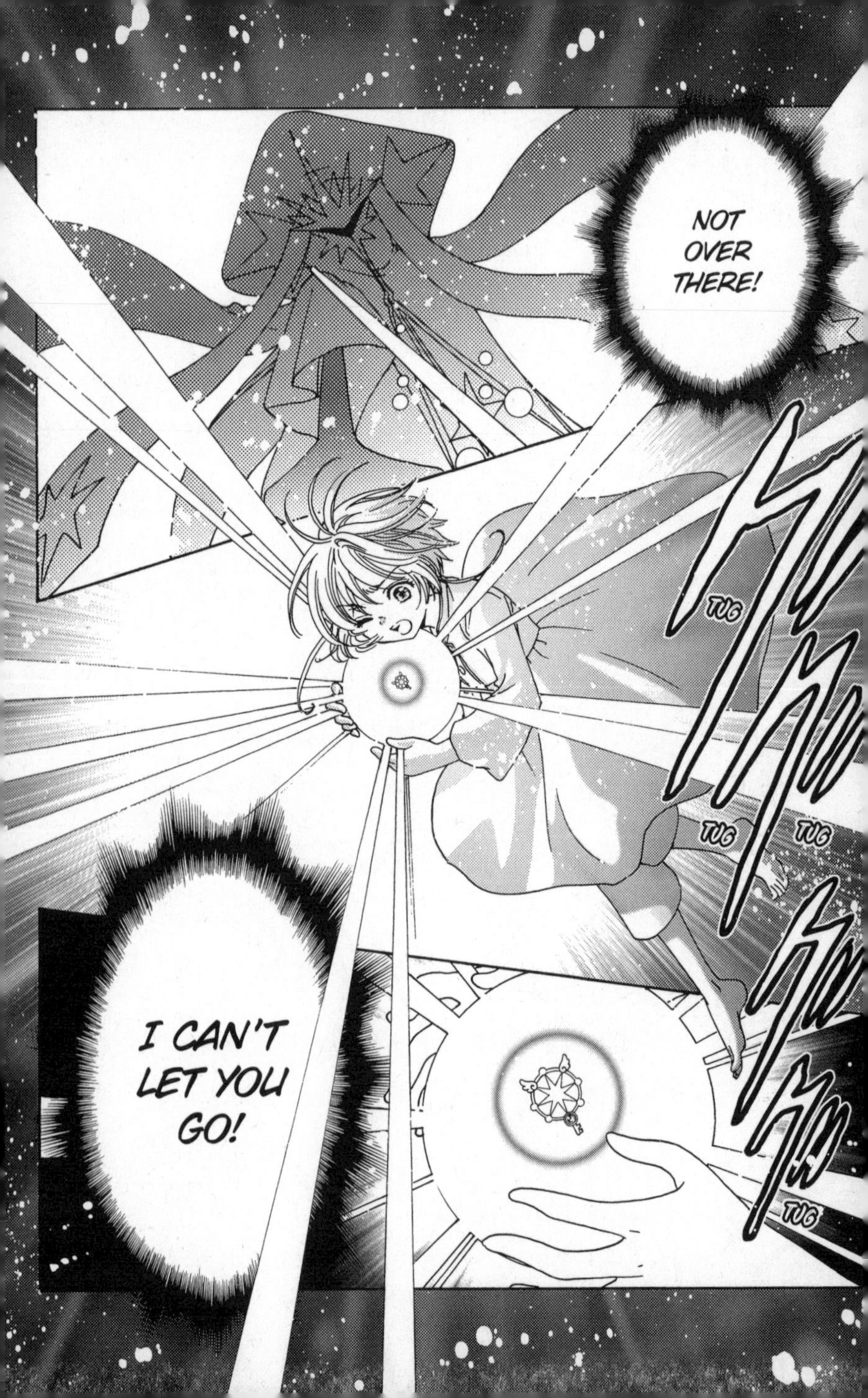
NOT OVER THERE!
TUG
TUG
TUG
TUG
I CAN'T LET YOU GO!

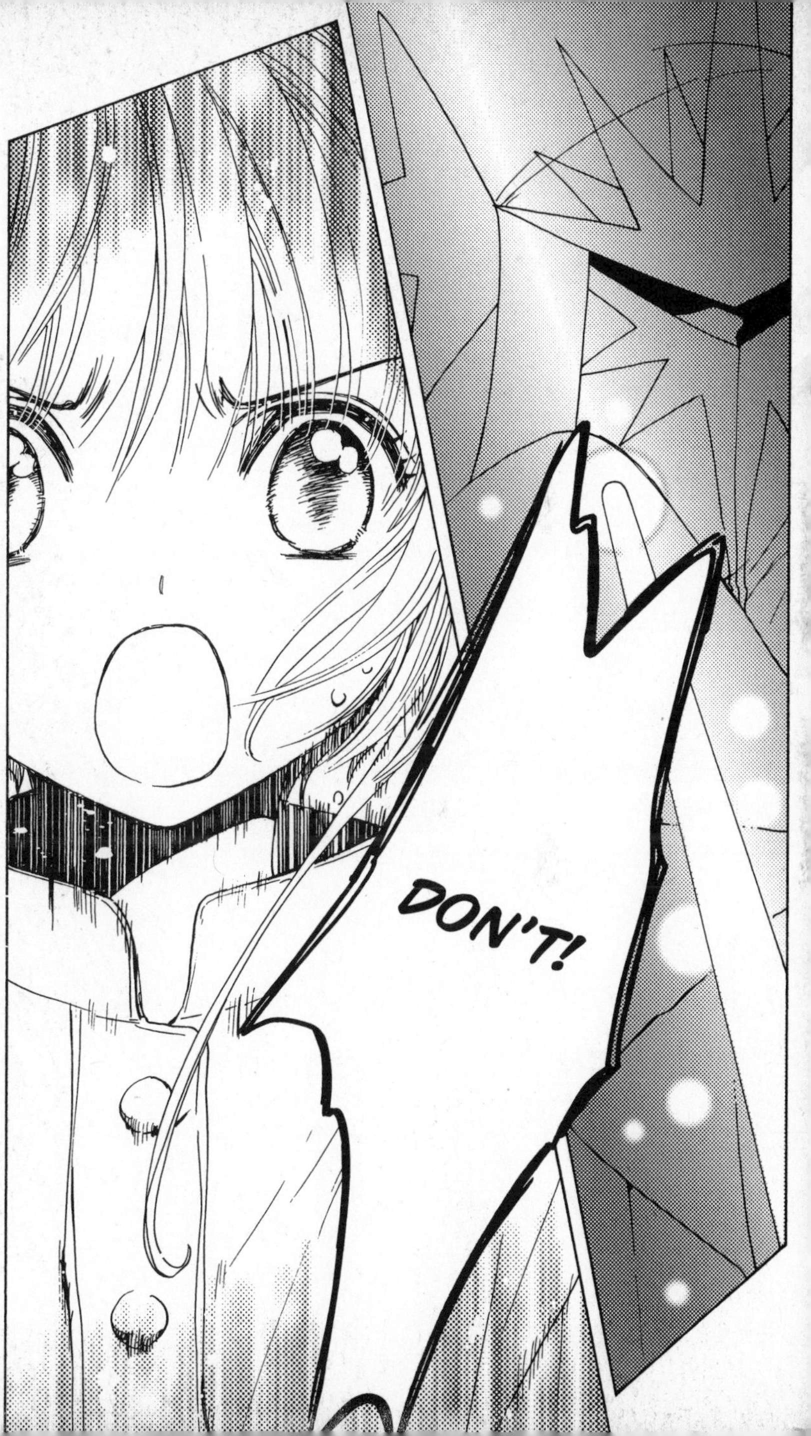
DON'T!

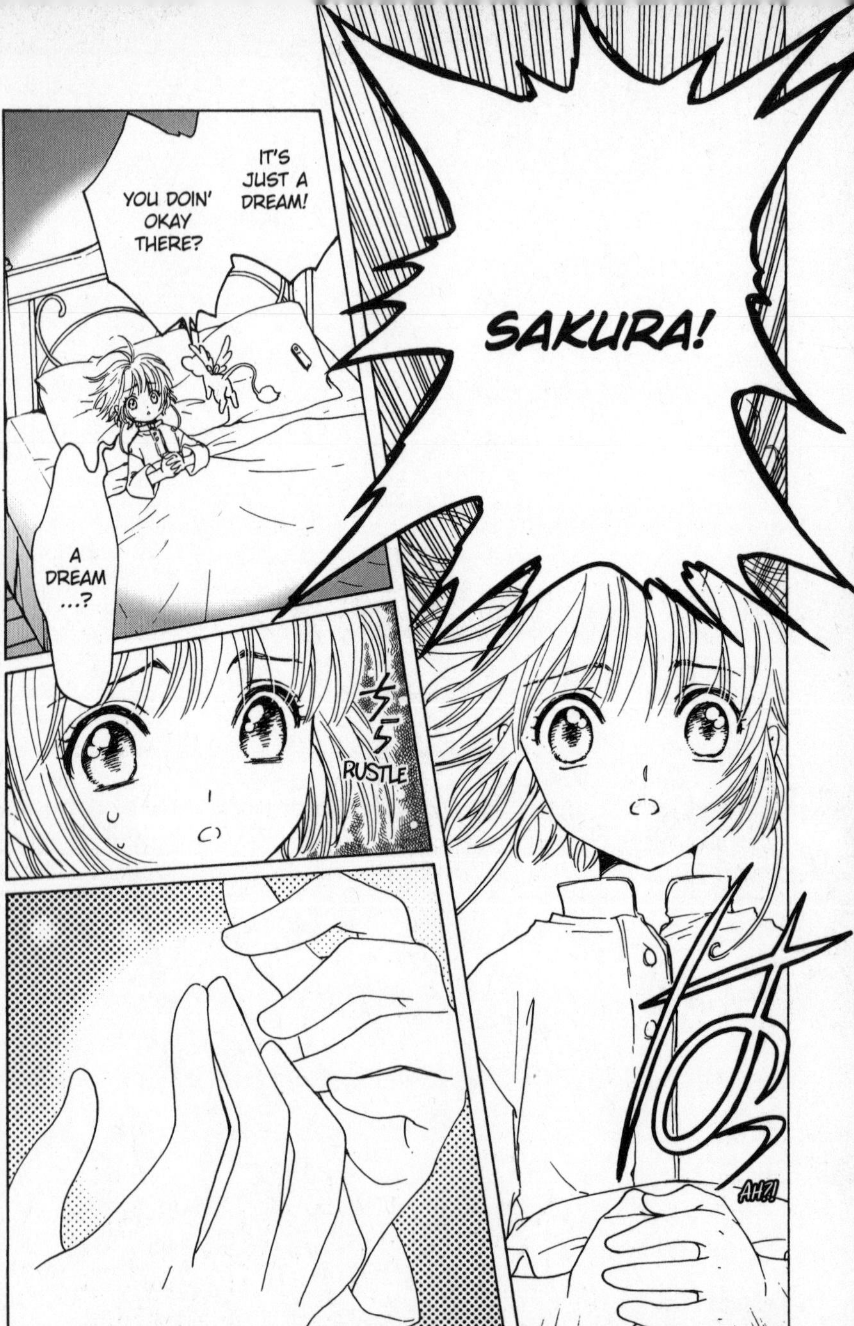
SAKURA!
AH?!
IT'S JUST A DREAM!
YOU DOIN' OKAY THERE?
A DREAM ...?
RUSTLE

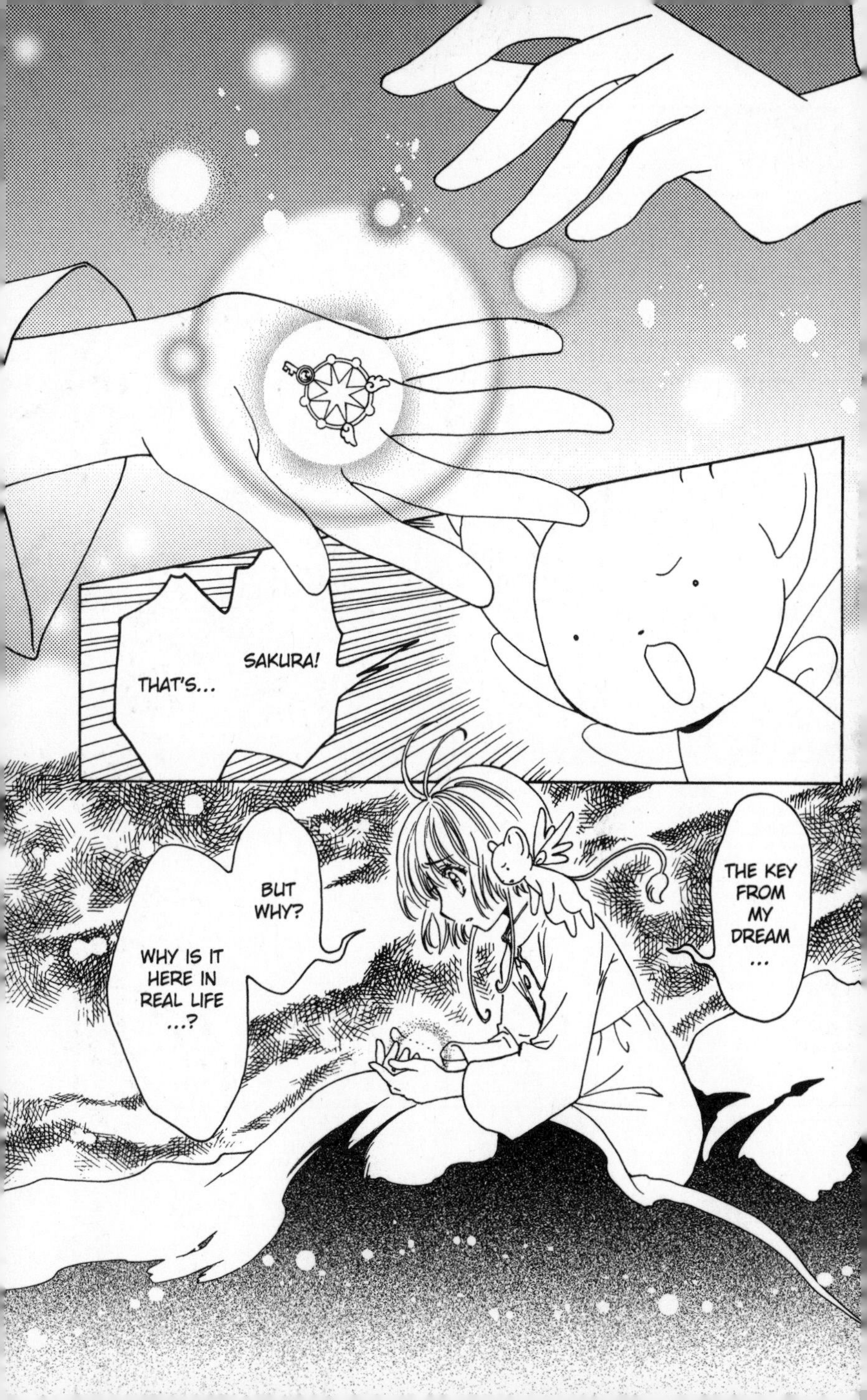
SAKURA!
THAT'S...
THE KEY FROM MY DREAM ...
BUT WHY?
WHY IS IT HERE IN REAL LIFE ...?

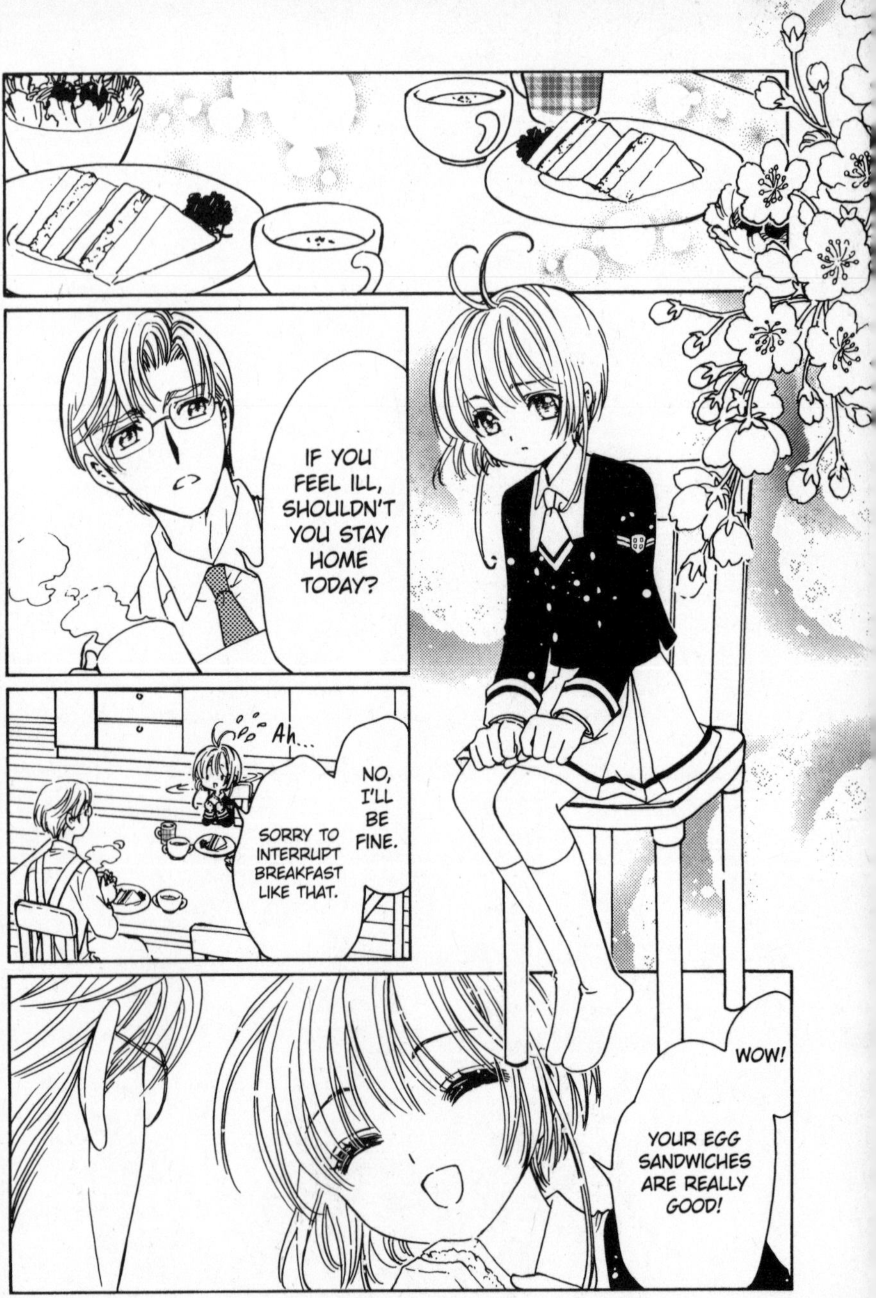
IF YOU FEEL ILL, SHOULDN'T YOU STAY HOME TODAY?
Ah...
NO, I'LL BE FINE.
SORRY TO INTERRUPT BREAKFAST LIKE THAT.
WOW!
YOUR EGG SANDWICHES ARE REALLY GOOD!

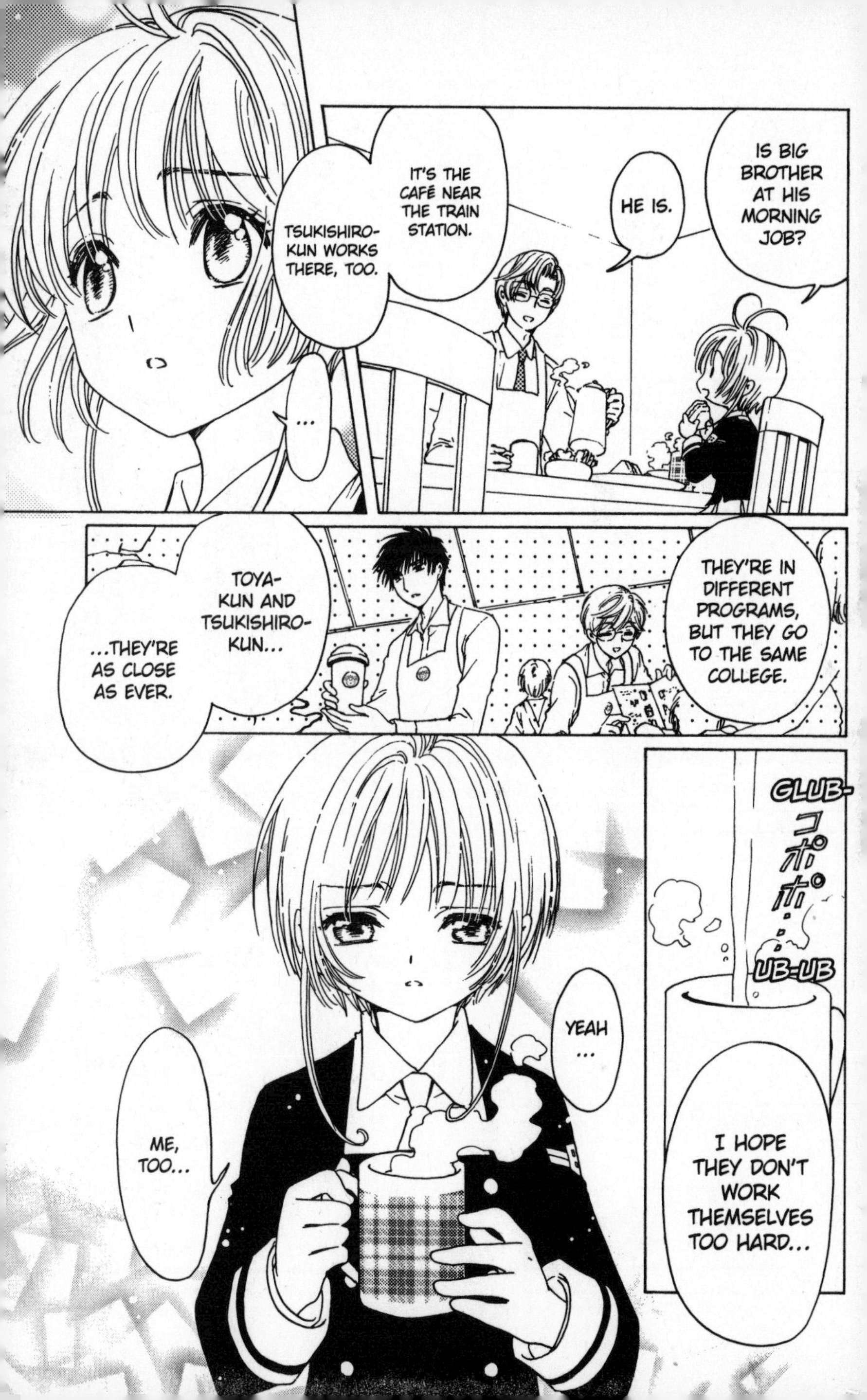
IS BIG BROTHER AT HIS MORNING JOB?
HE IS.
IT'S THE CAFÉ NEAR THE TRAIN STATION.
TSUKISHIRO-KUN WORKS THERE, TOO.
...
THEY'RE IN DIFFERENT PROGRAMS, BUT THEY GO TO THE SAME COLLEGE.
TOYA-KUN AND TSUKISHIRO-KUN...
...THEY'RE AS CLOSE AS EVER.
GLUB-
コポポ
UB-UB
I HOPE THEY DON'T WORK THEMSELVES TOO HARD...
YEAH...
ME, TOO...

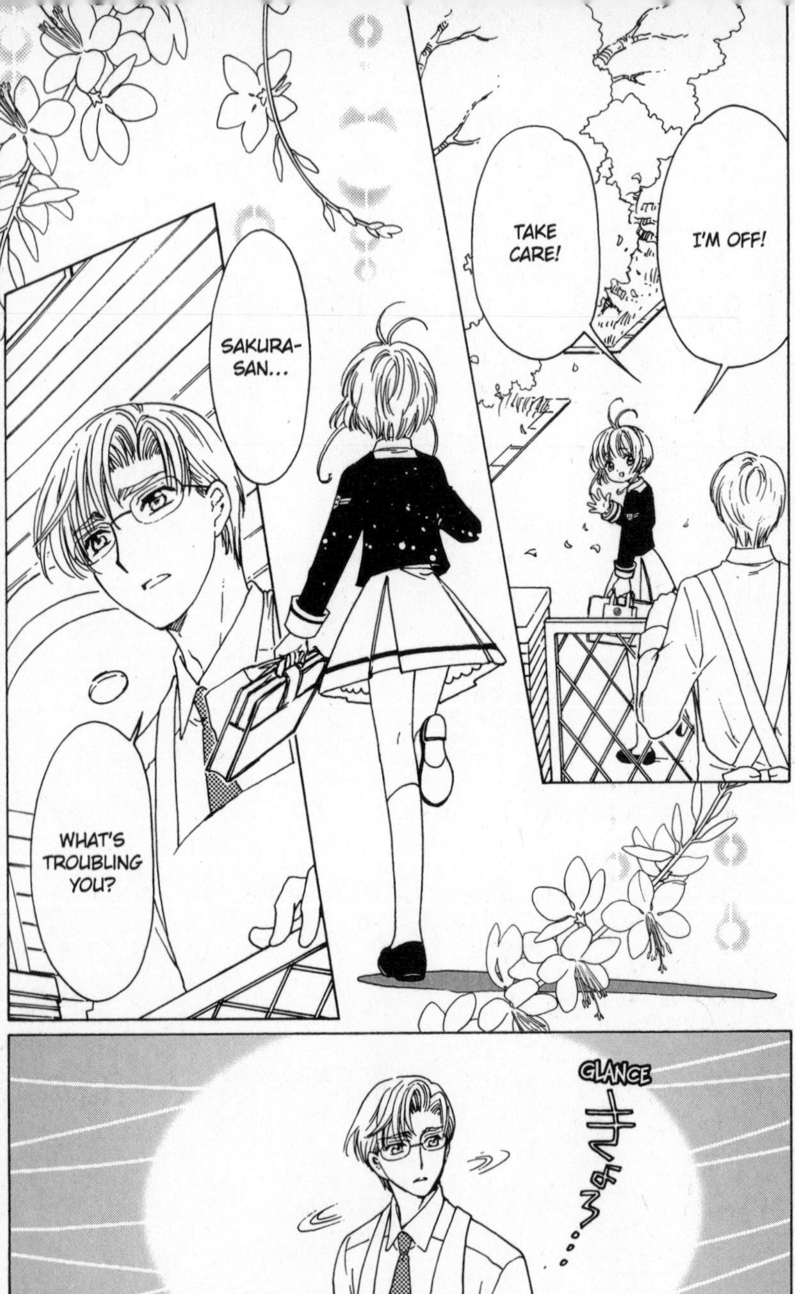
I'M OFF!
TAKE CARE!
SAKURA-SAN...
WHAT'S TROUBLING YOU?
GLANCE

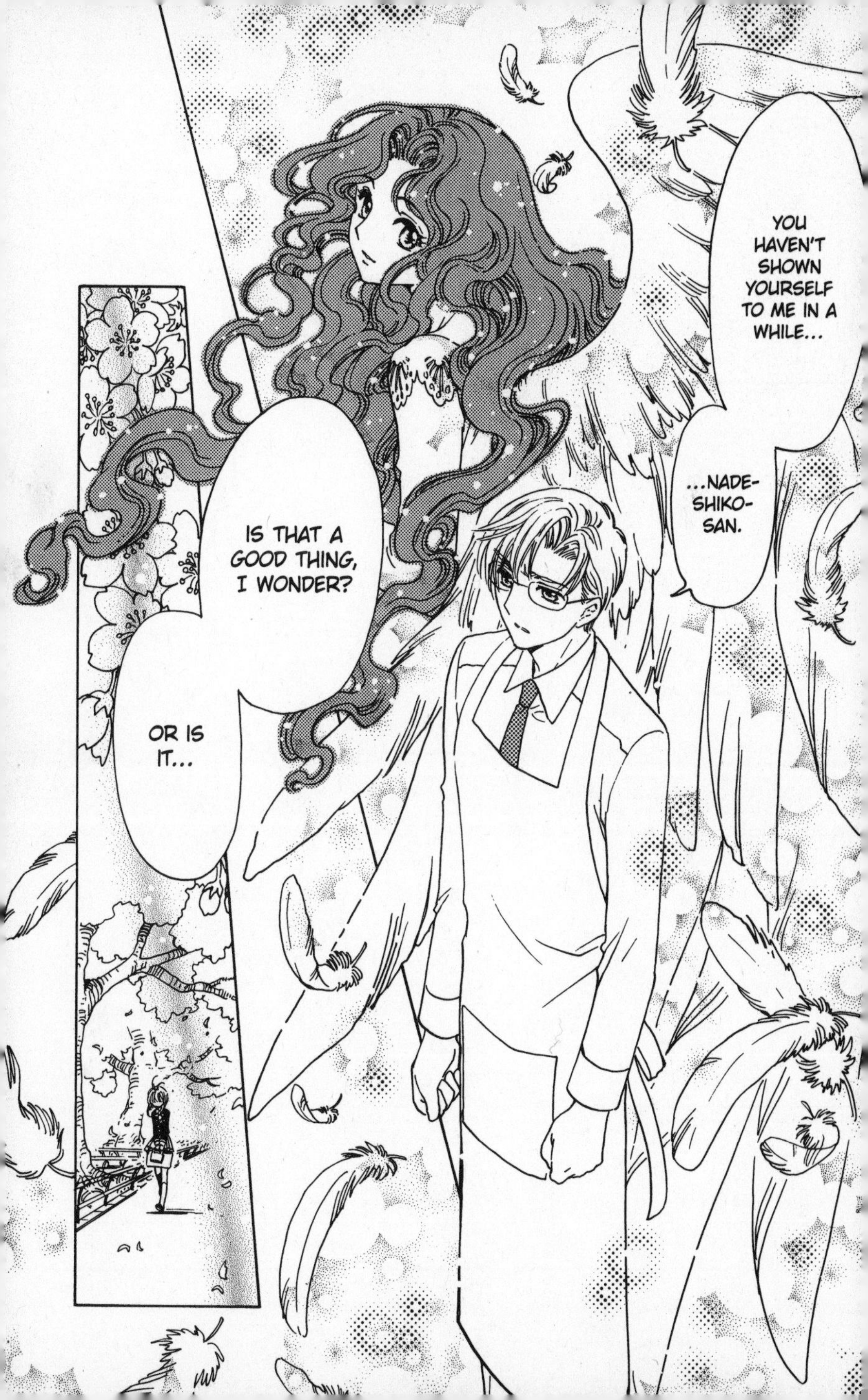
YOU HAVEN'T SHOWN YOURSELF TO ME IN A WHILE...
...NADE-SHIKO-SAN.
IS THAT A GOOD THING, I WONDER?
OR IS IT...

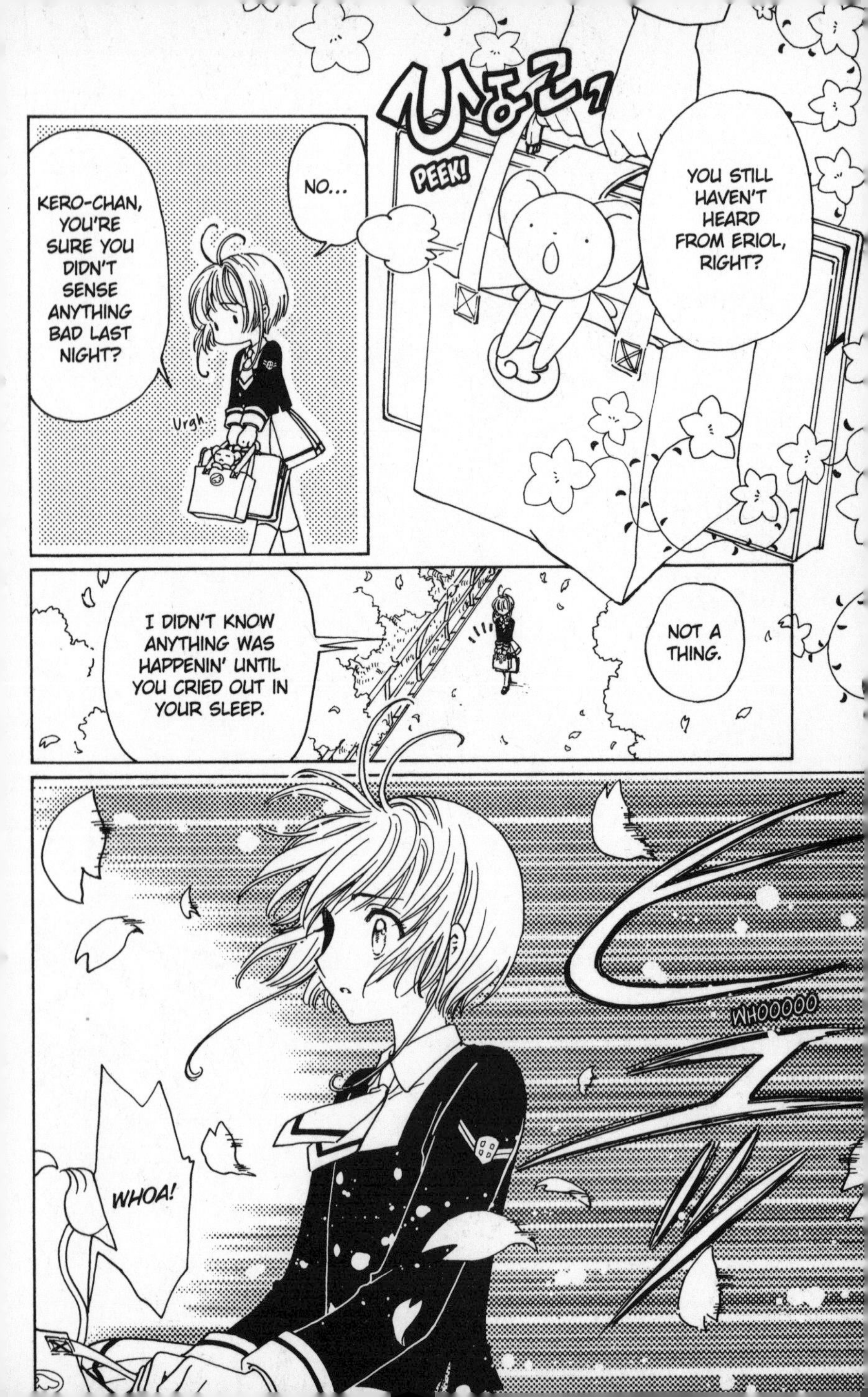
PEEK!
YOU STILL HAVEN'T HEARD FROM ERIOL, RIGHT?
NO...
KERO-CHAN, YOU'RE SURE YOU DIDN'T SENSE ANYTHING BAD LAST NIGHT?
Urgh
NOT A THING.
I DIDN'T KNOW ANYTHING WAS HAPPENIN' UNTIL YOU CRIED OUT IN YOUR SLEEP.
WHOOOOO
WHOA!

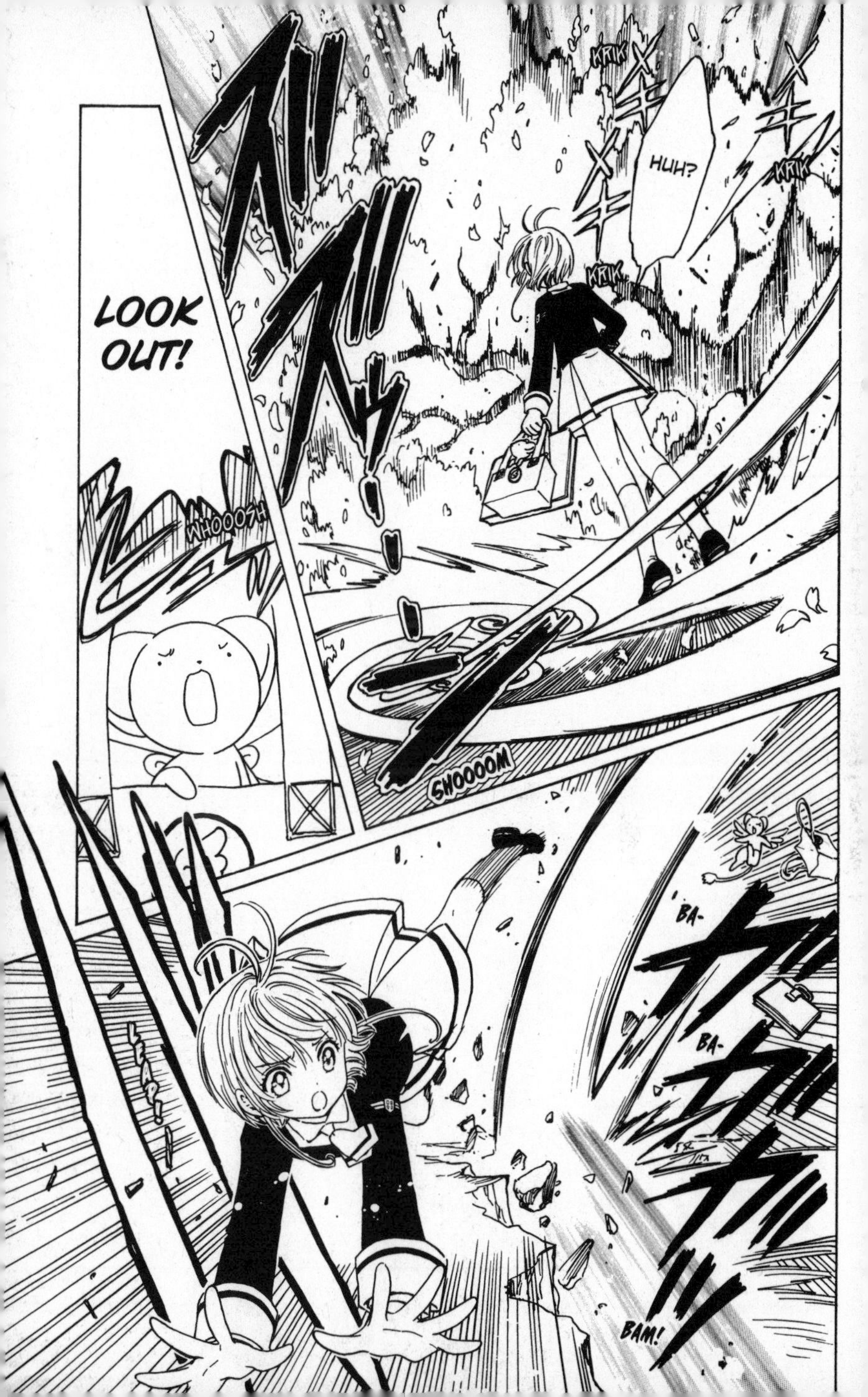
KRIK
KRIK
HUH?
KRIK
LOOK OUT!
WHOOOSH
SHOOOOM
LEAP!!
BA-
BA-
BAM!

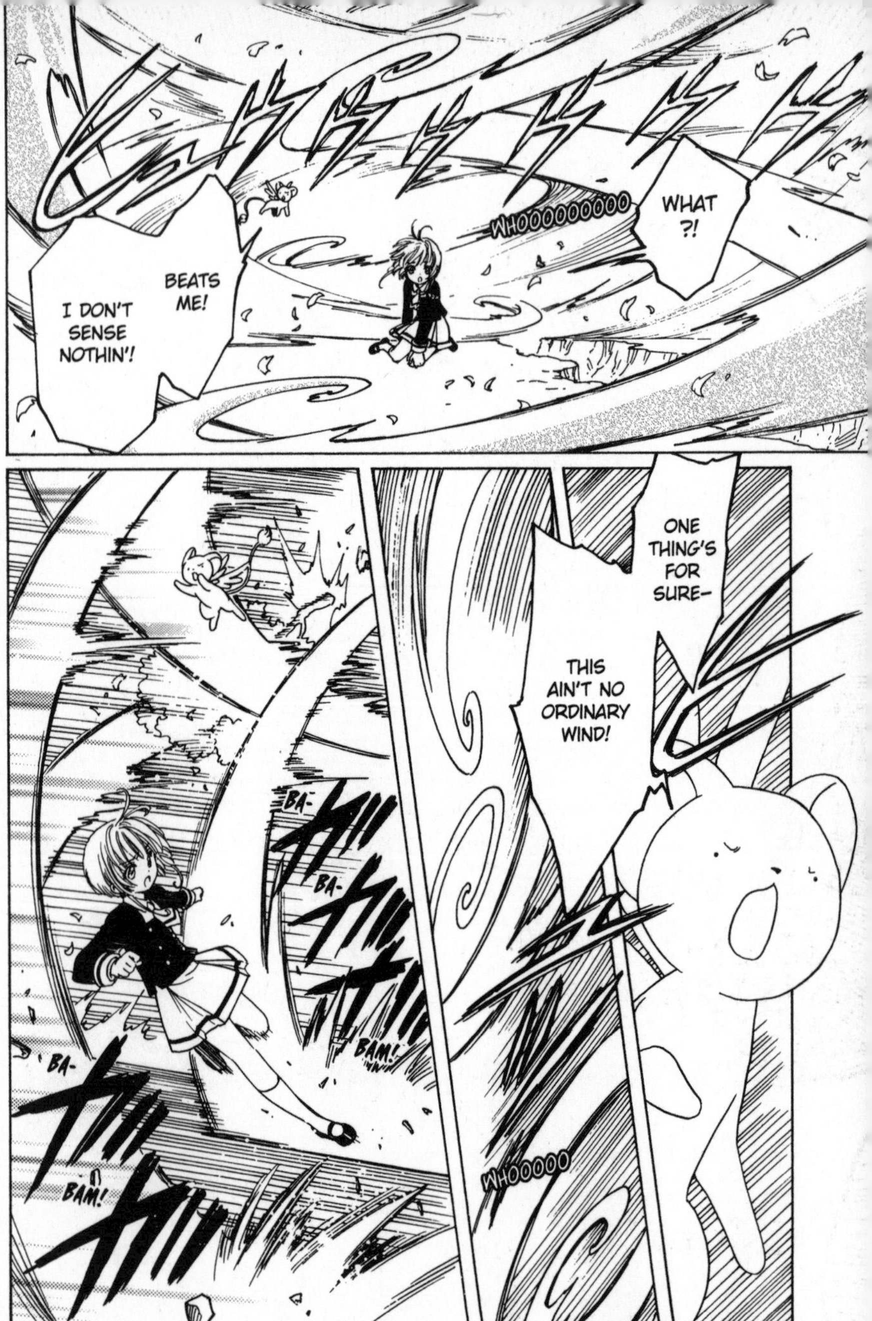
WHAT ?!
WHOOOOOOOOOO
BEATS ME!
I DON'T SENSE NOTHIN'!
ONE THING'S FOR SURE-
THIS AIN'T NO ORDINARY WIND!
WHOOOOO
BA-
BA-
BAM!
BA-
BAM!

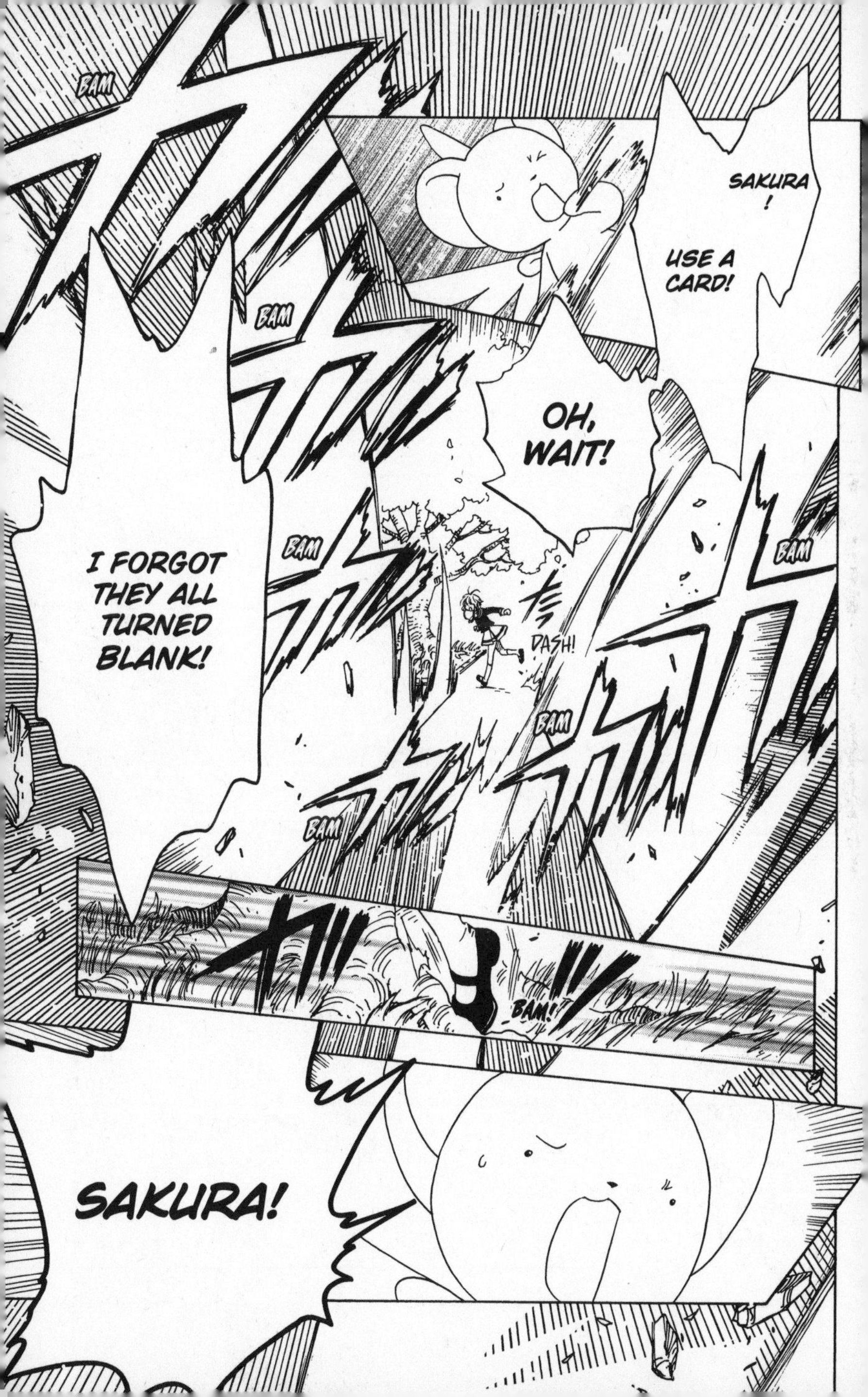
BAM
SAKURA!
USE A CARD!
BAM
OH, WAIT!
I FORGOT THEY ALL TURNED BLANK!
BAM
BAM
DASH!
BAM
BAM
BAM!
SAKURA!

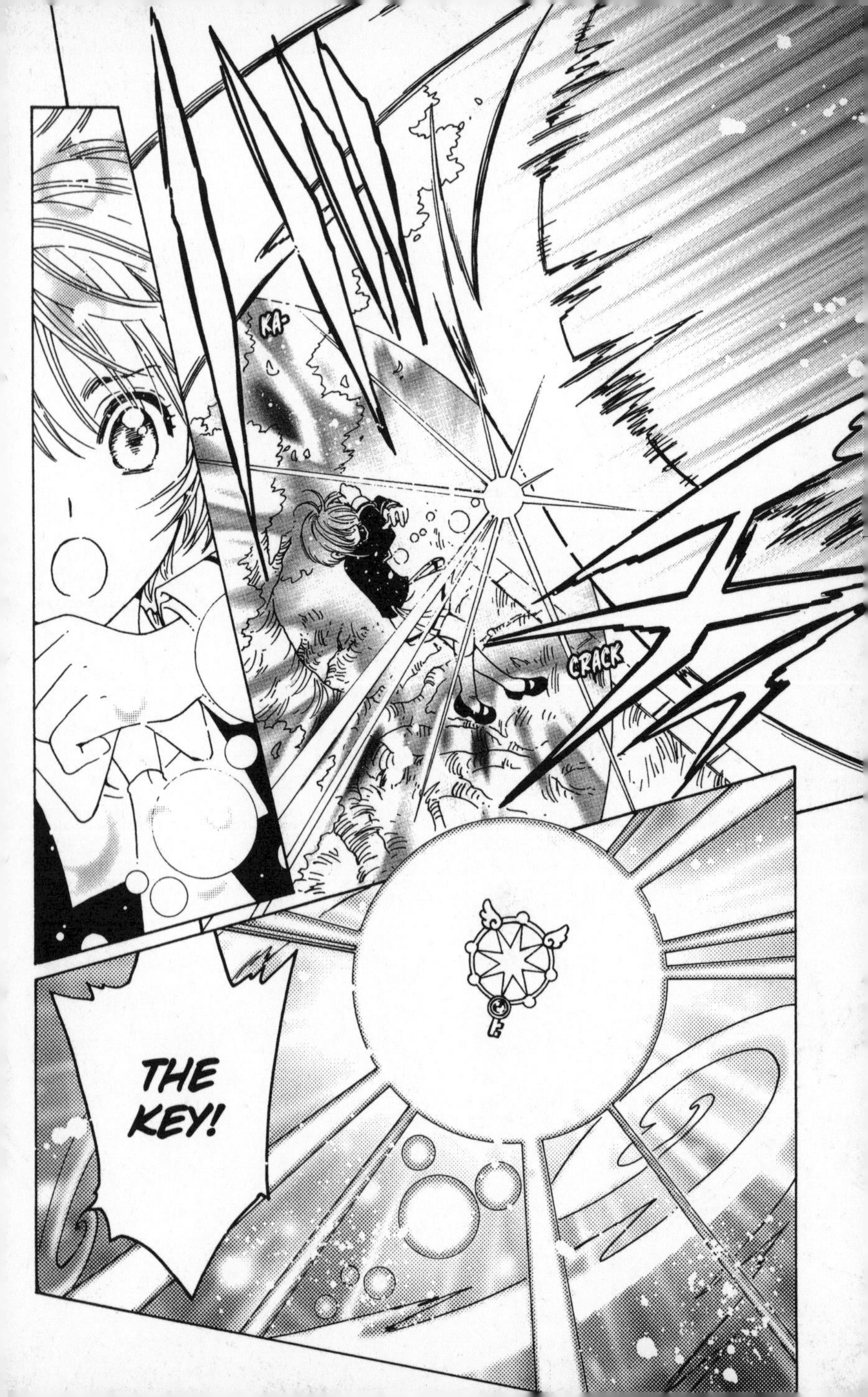
KA-
CRACK
THE KEY!

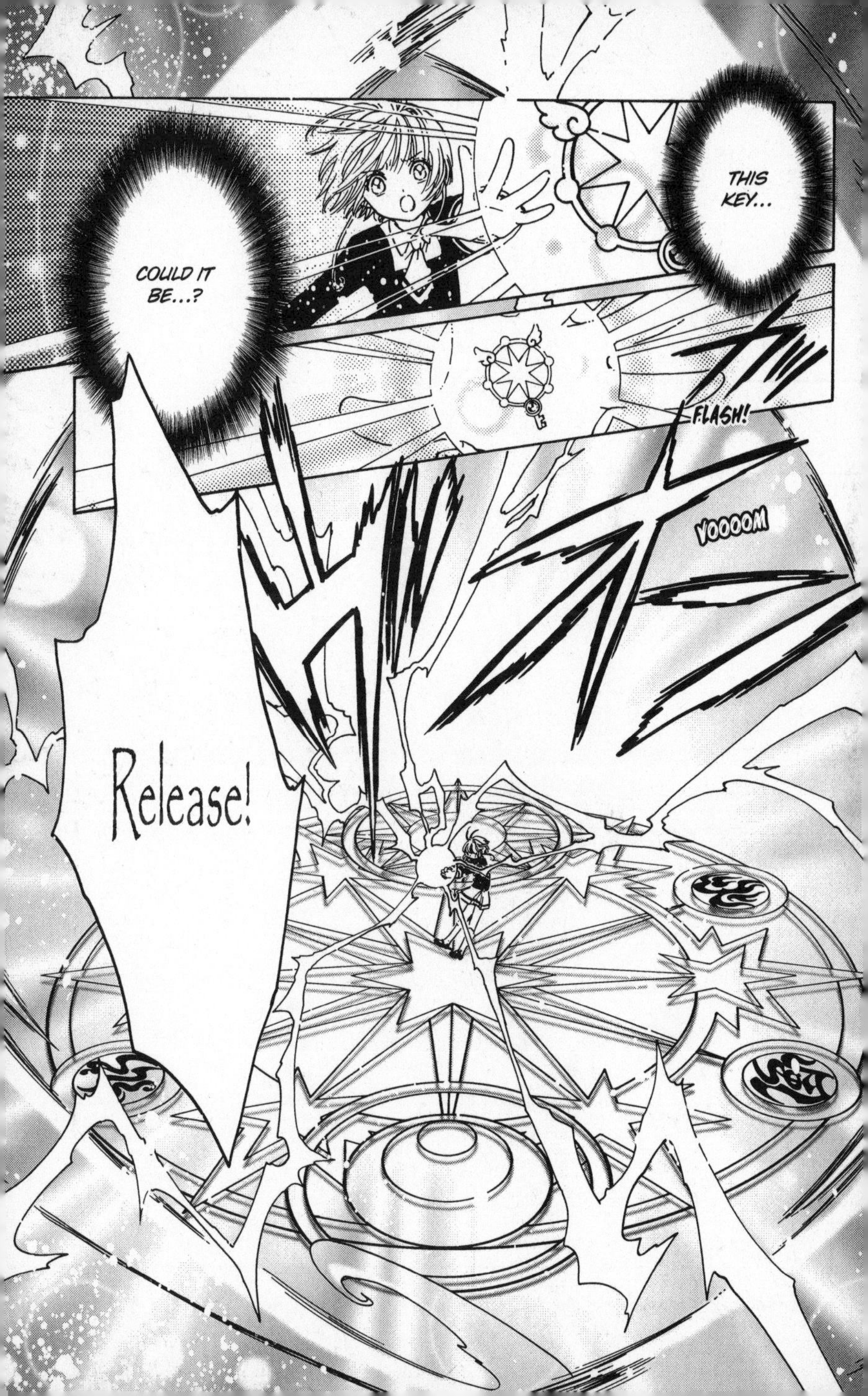
THIS KEY...
COULD IT BE...?
FLASH!
VOOOOM
Release!

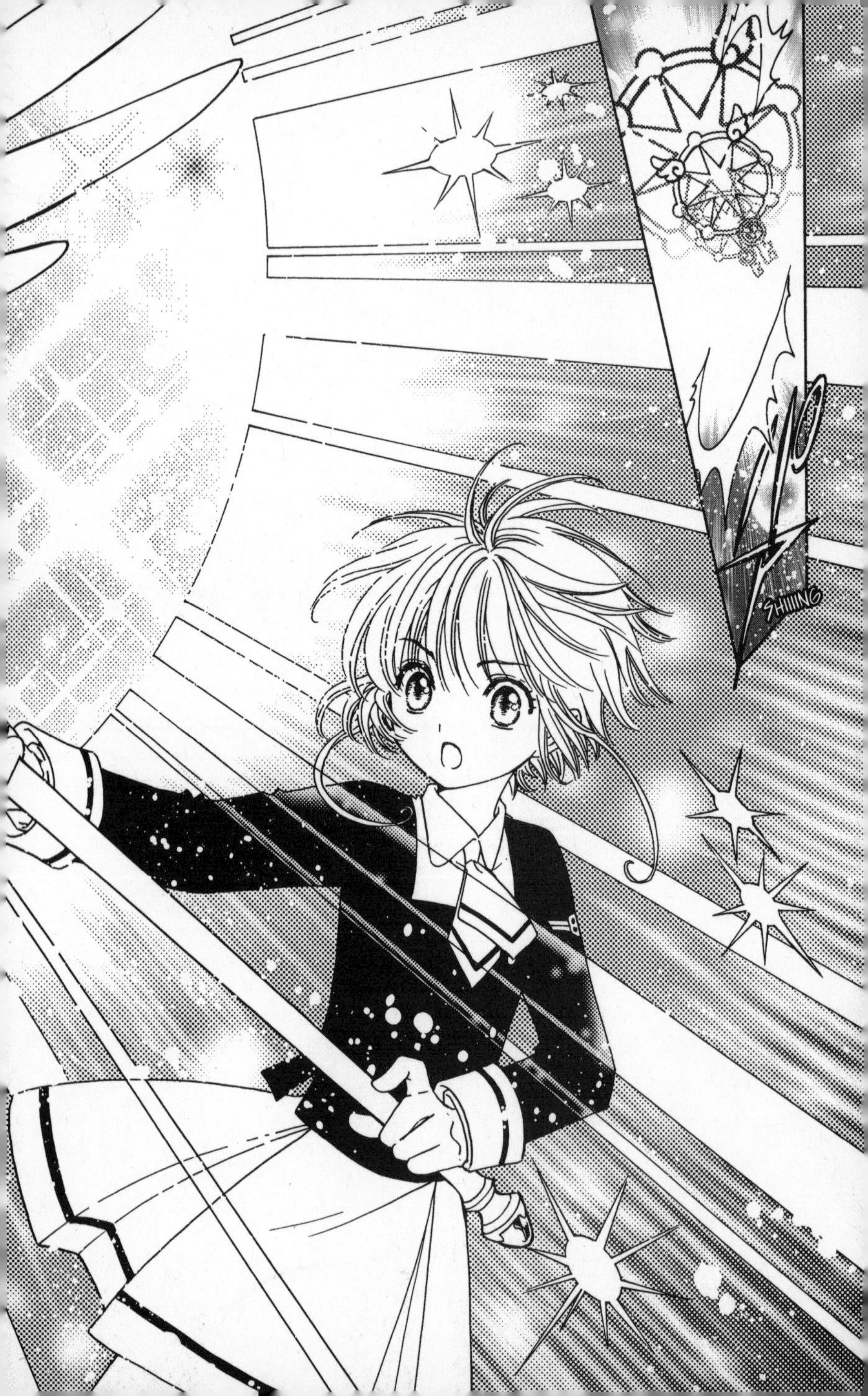
SHIIING

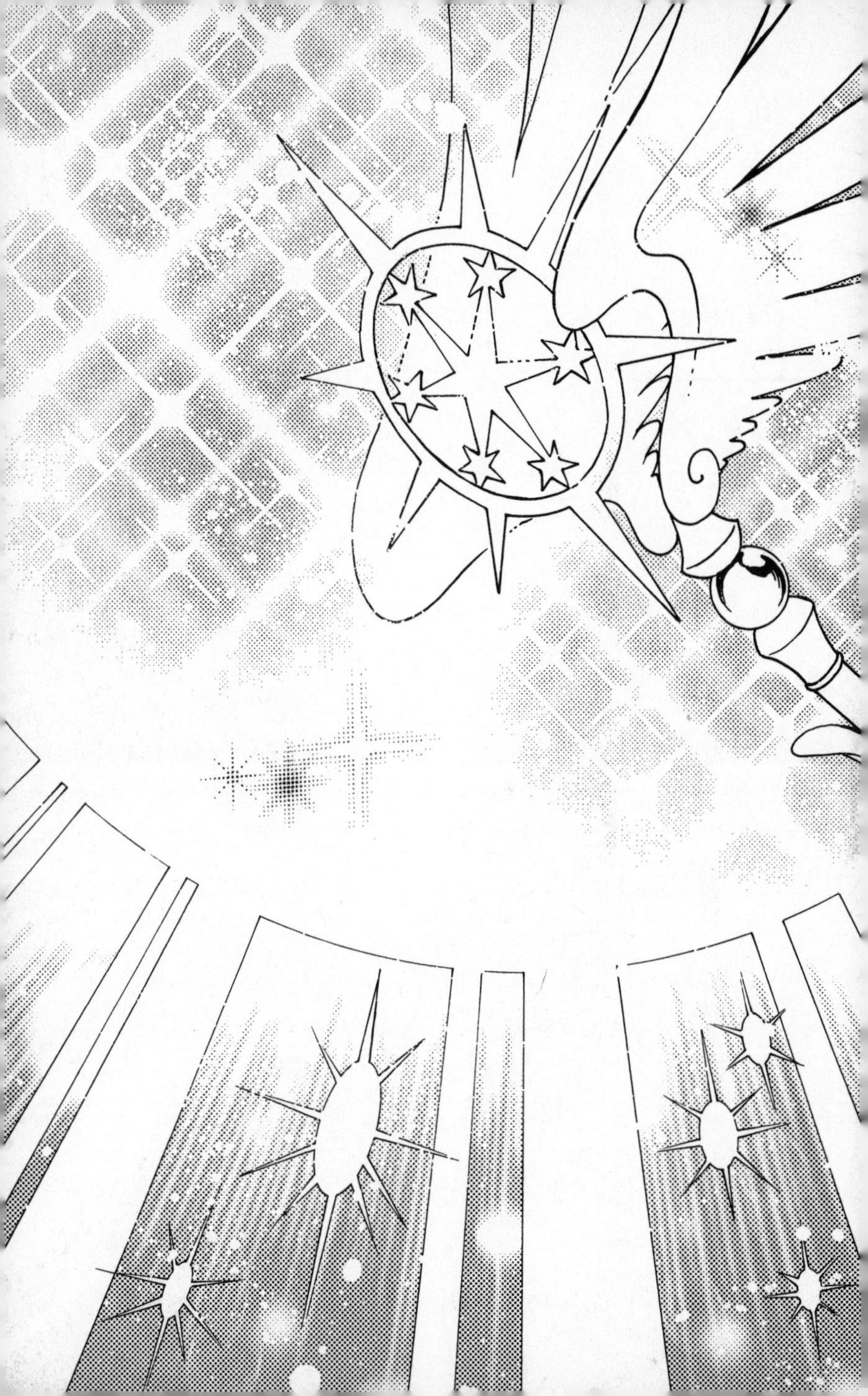

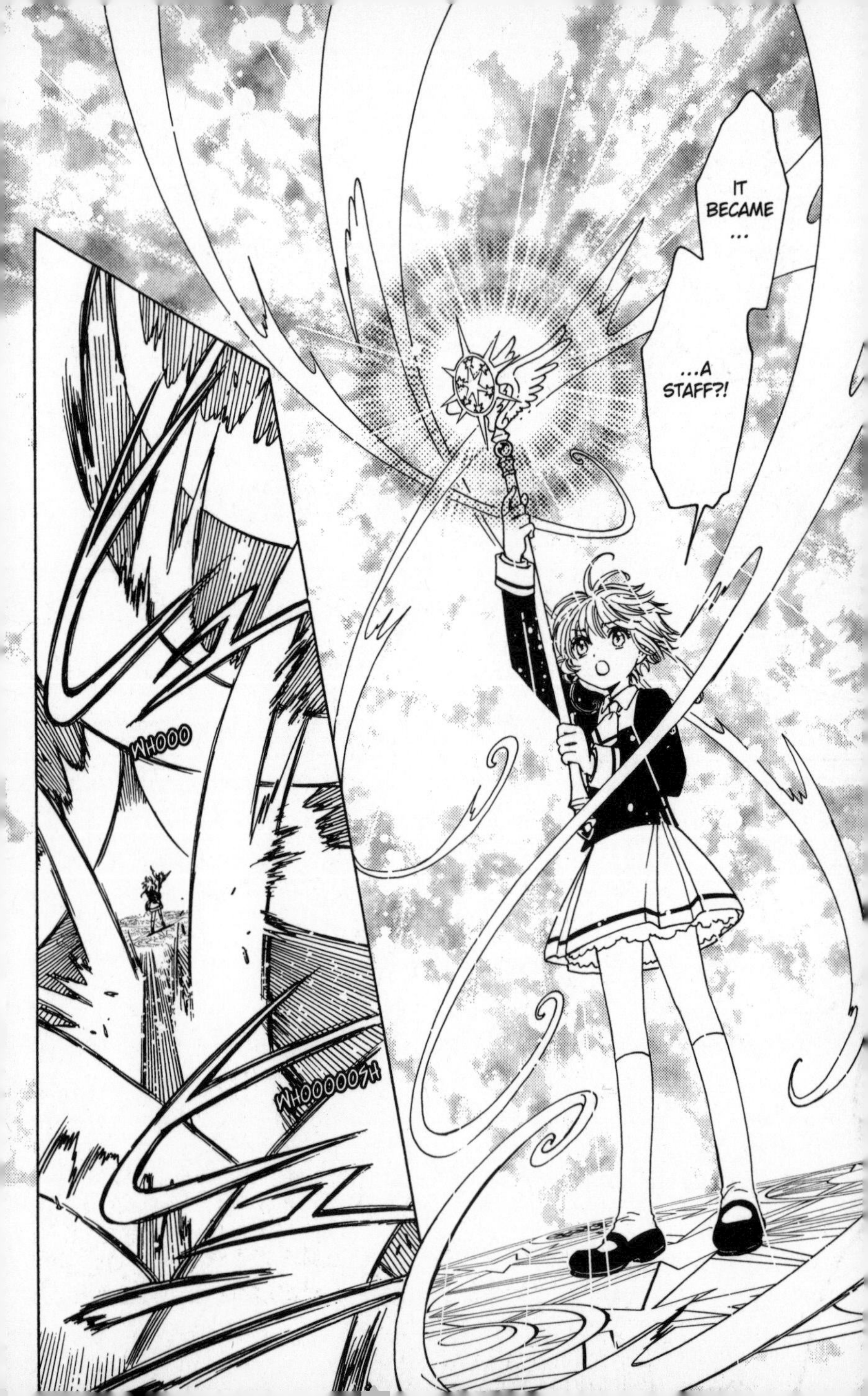
IT BECAME ...
...A STAFF?!
WHOOO
WHOOOOOSH

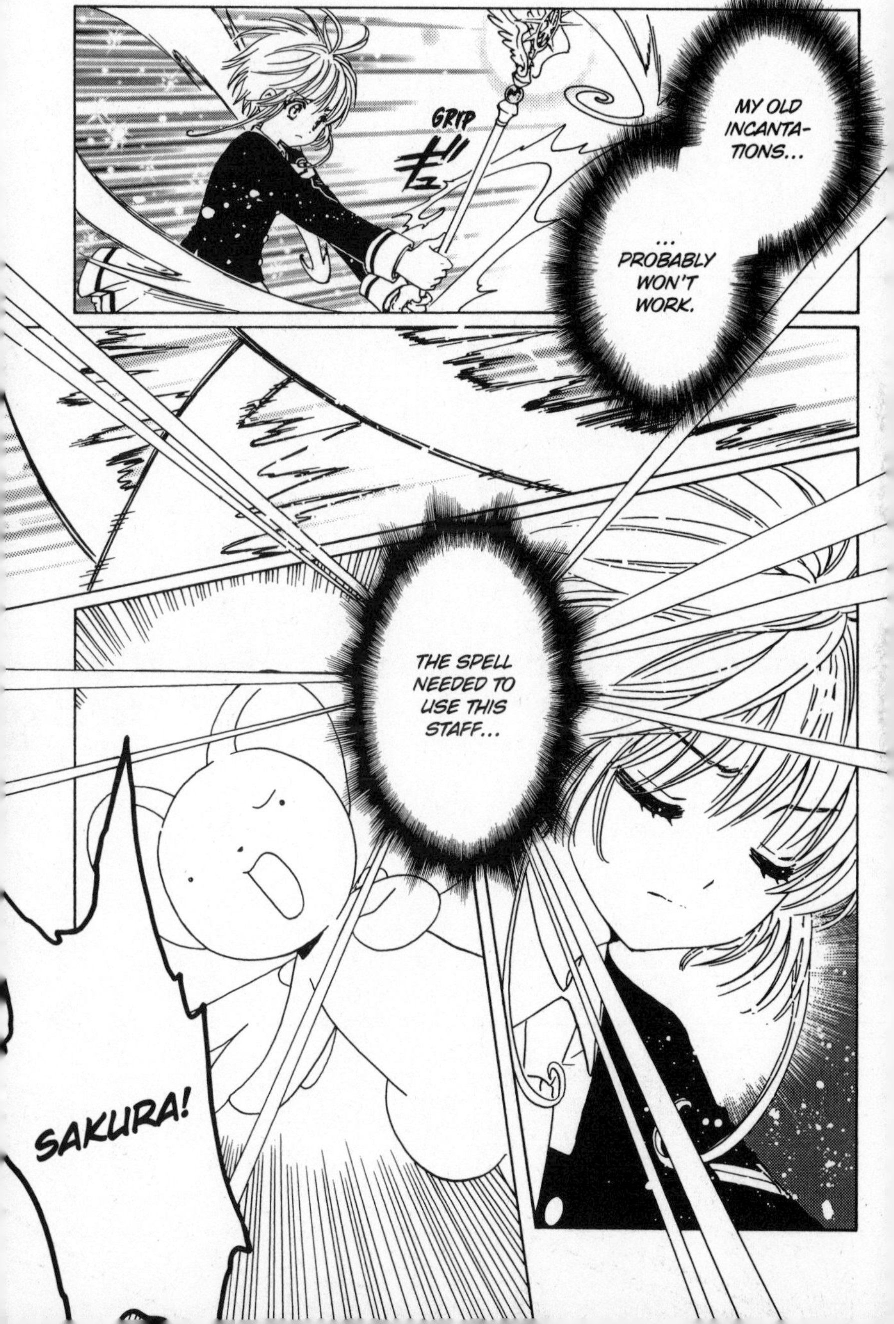
MY OLD INCANTATIONS...
GRIP
...PROBABLY WON'T WORK.
THE SPELL NEEDED TO USE THIS STAFF...
SAKURA!

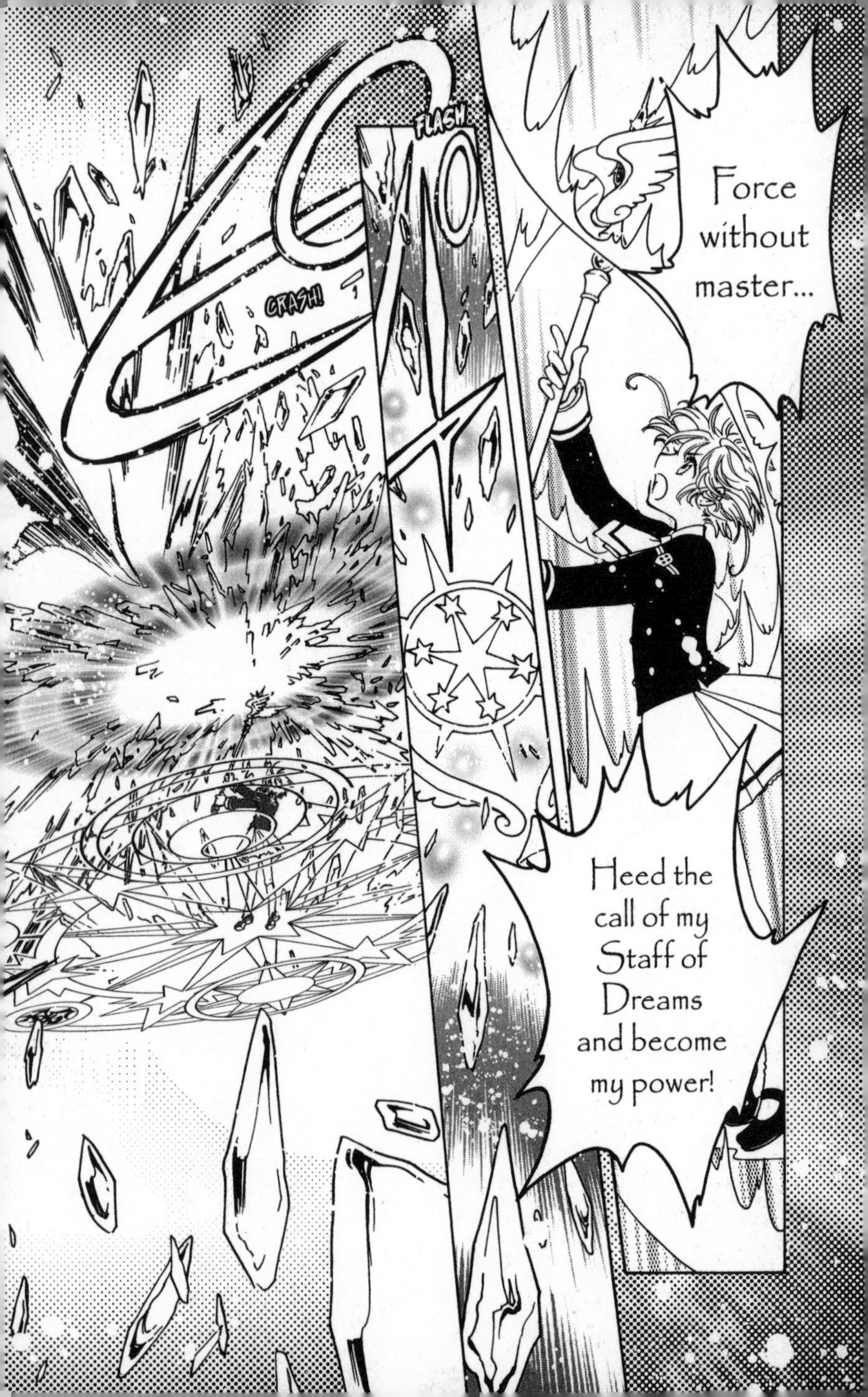
Force without master...
Heed the call of my Staff of Dreams and become my power!
FLASH
CRASH!

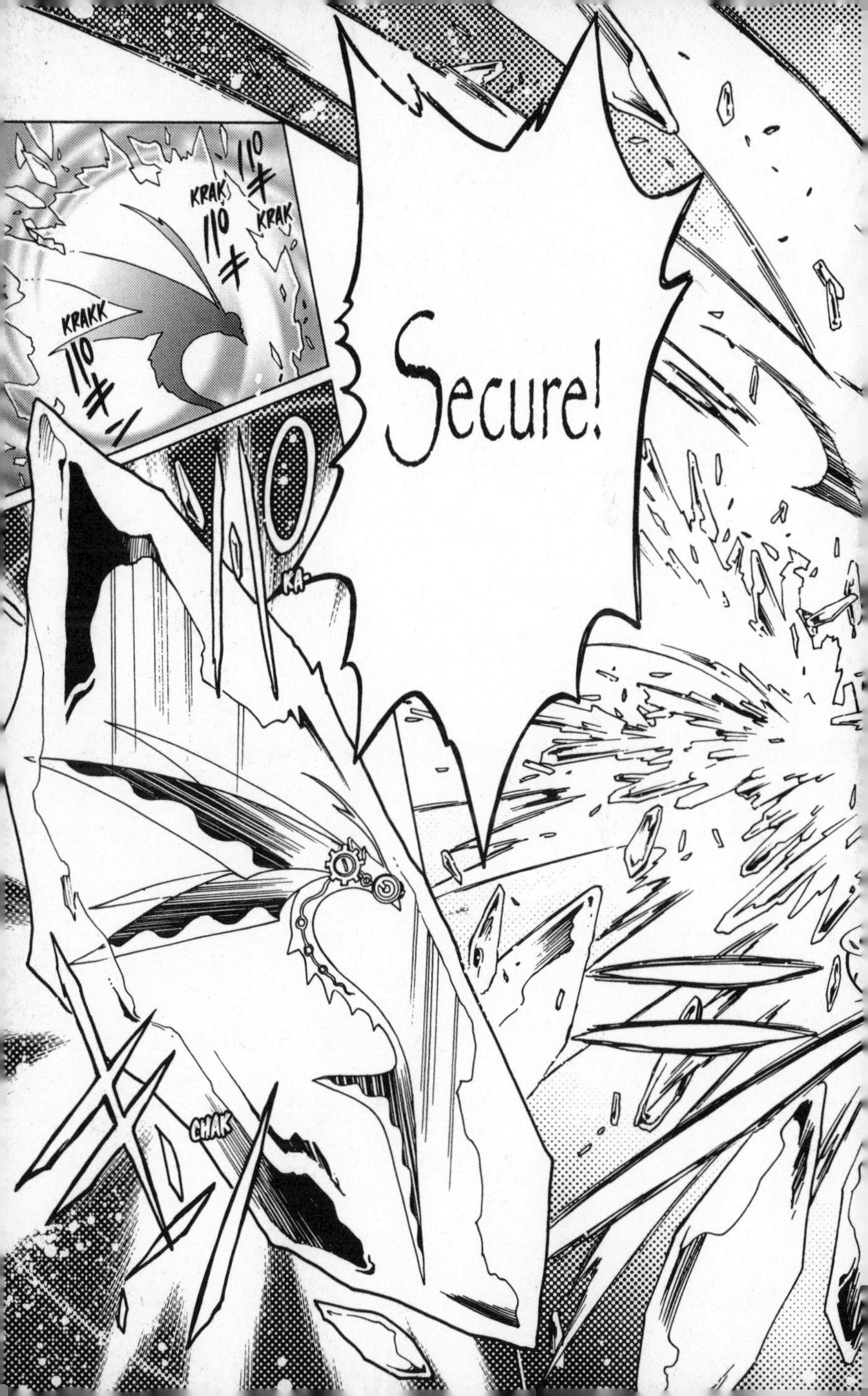

Secure!
KRAK
KRAK
KRAKK
KA-
CHAK

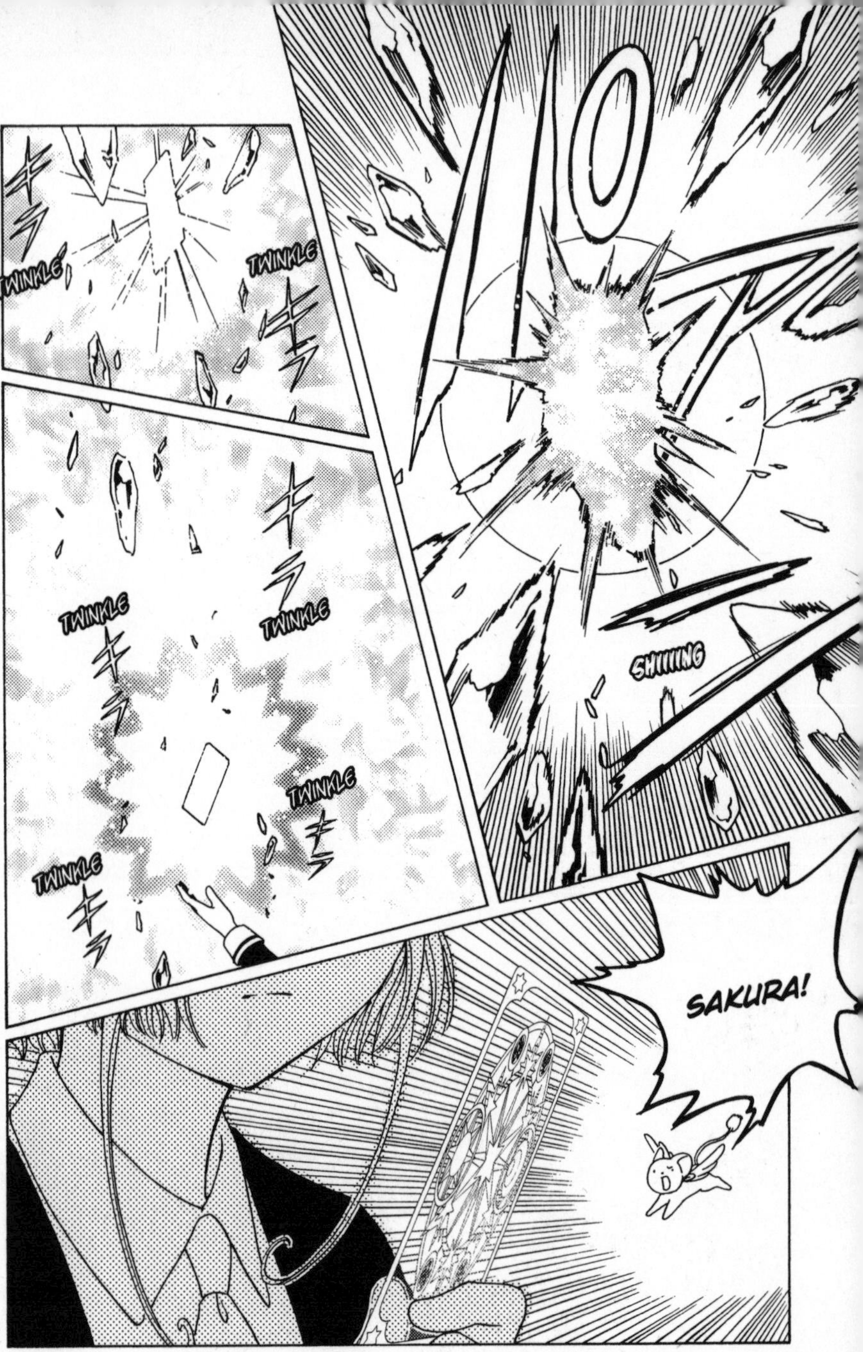
SHIIIING
TWINKLE
TWINKLE
TWINKLE
TWINKLE
TWINKLE
TWINKLE
SAKURA!

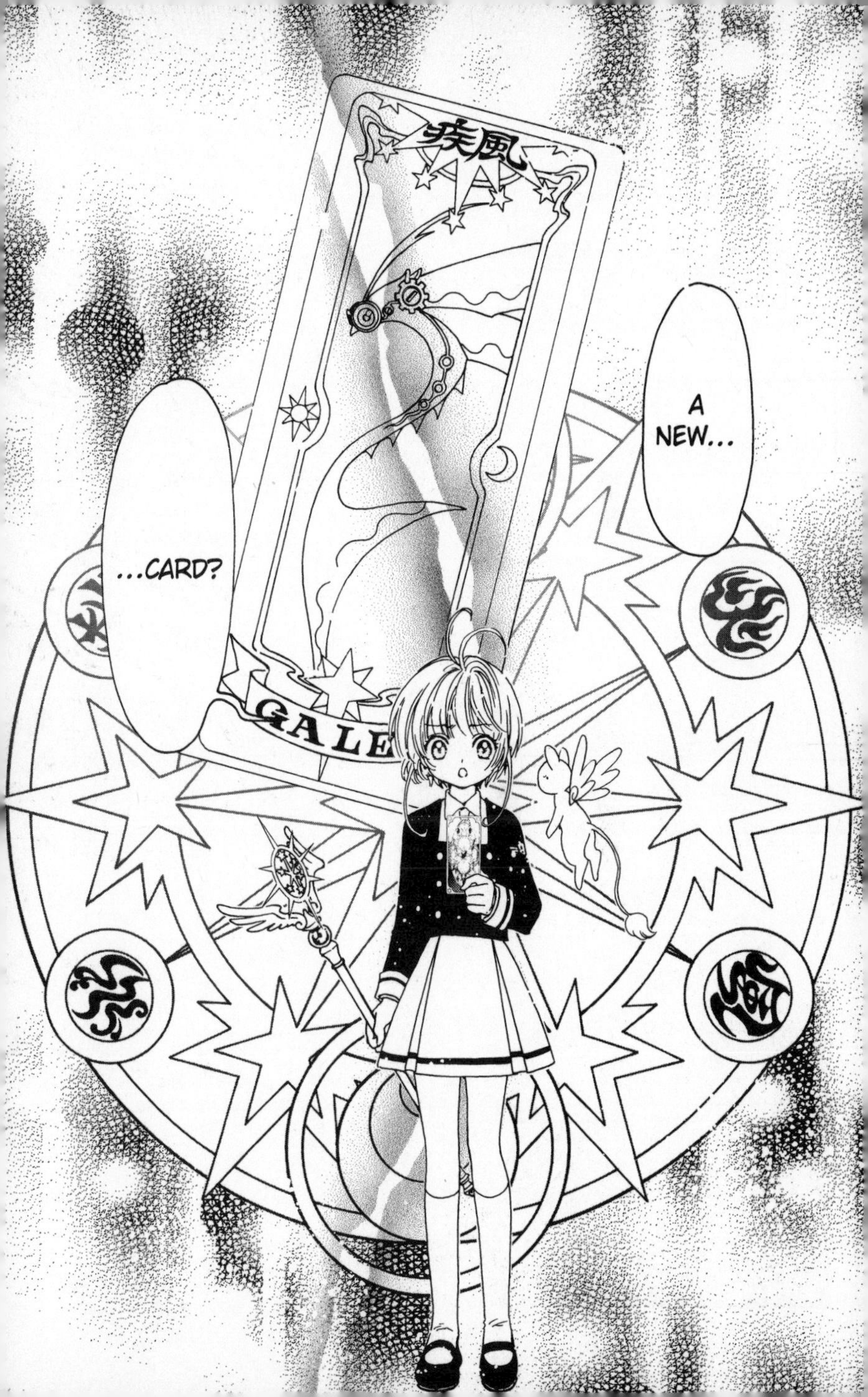
A NEW...
...CARD?
疾風
GALE

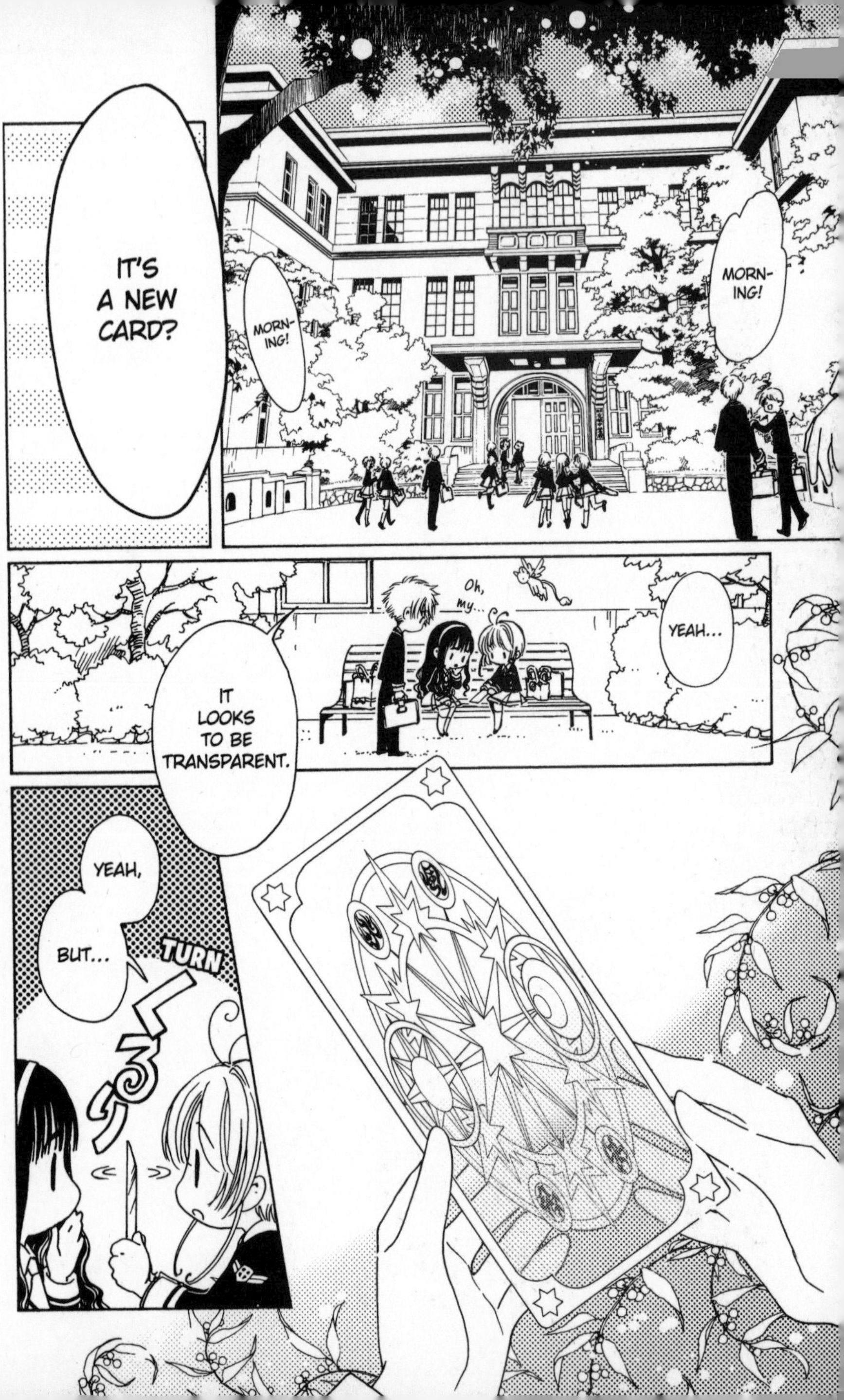
MORN-ING!
MORN-ING!
IT'S A NEW CARD?
YEAH...
Oh, my...
IT LOOKS TO BE TRANSPARENT.
YEAH, BUT...
TURN

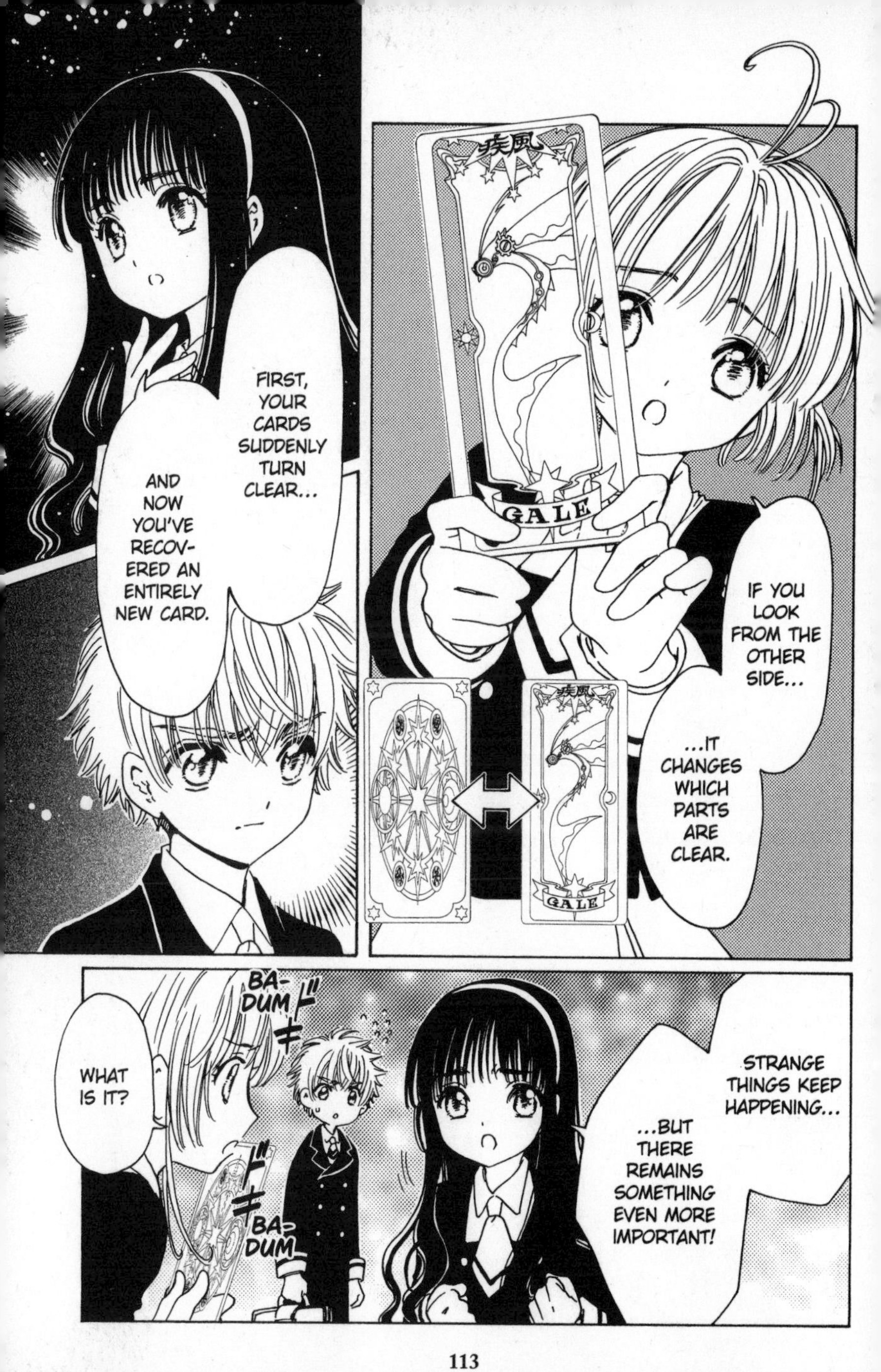
GALE
IF YOU LOOK FROM THE OTHER SIDE...
...IT CHANGES WHICH PARTS ARE CLEAR.
GALE
FIRST, YOUR CARDS SUDDENLY TURN CLEAR...
AND NOW YOU'VE RECOV-ERED AN ENTIRELY NEW CARD.
STRANGE THINGS KEEP HAPPENING...
...BUT THERE REMAINS SOMETHING EVEN MORE IMPORTANT!
BA-DUM
BA-DUM
WHAT IS IT?

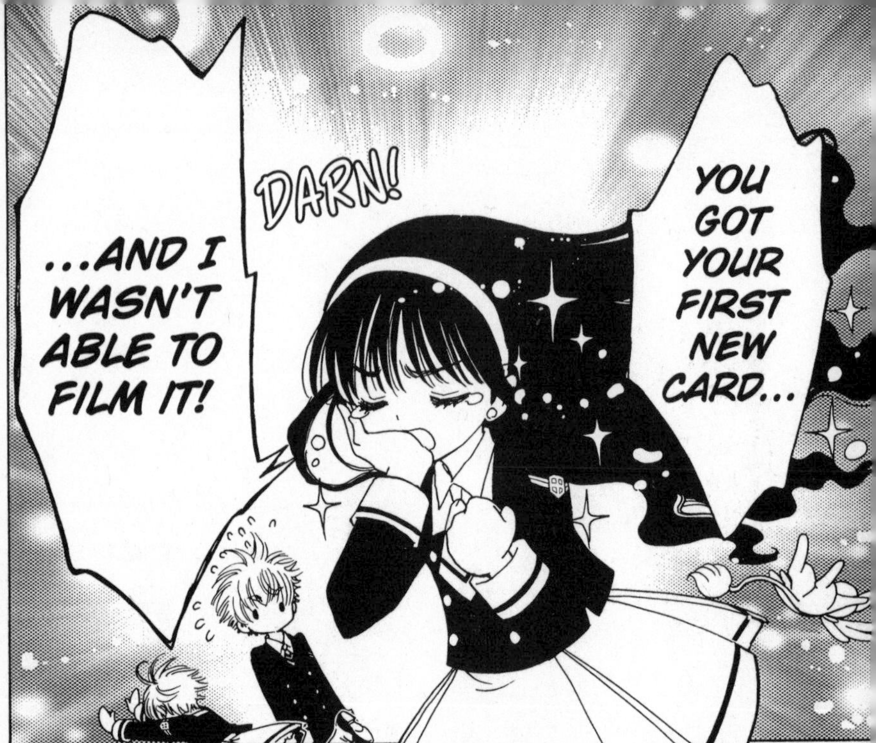
YOU GOT YOUR FIRST NEW CARD...
DARN!
...AND I WASN'T ABLE TO FILM IT!
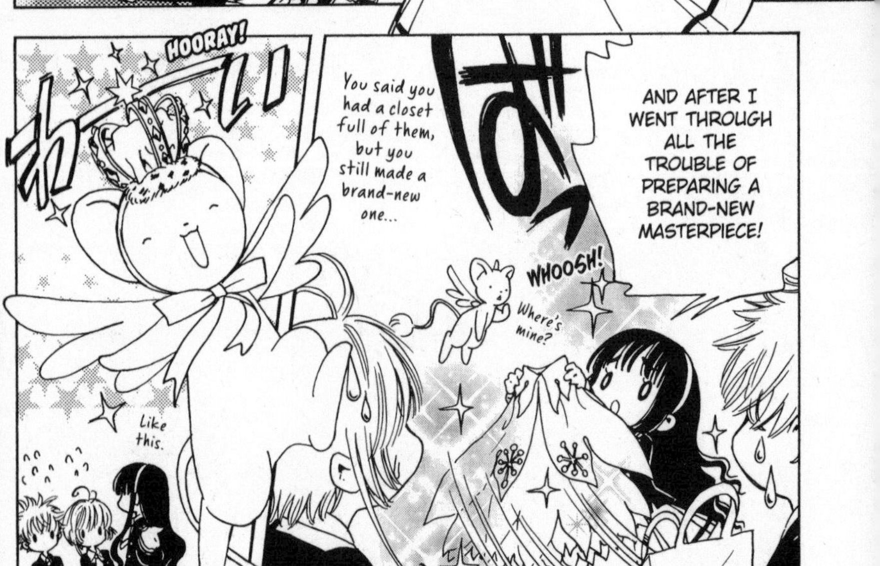
AND AFTER I WENT THROUGH ALL THE TROUBLE OF PREPARING A BRAND-NEW MASTERPIECE!
You said you had a closet full of them, but you still made a brand-new one...
WHOOSH!
Where's mine?
HOORAY!
Like this.

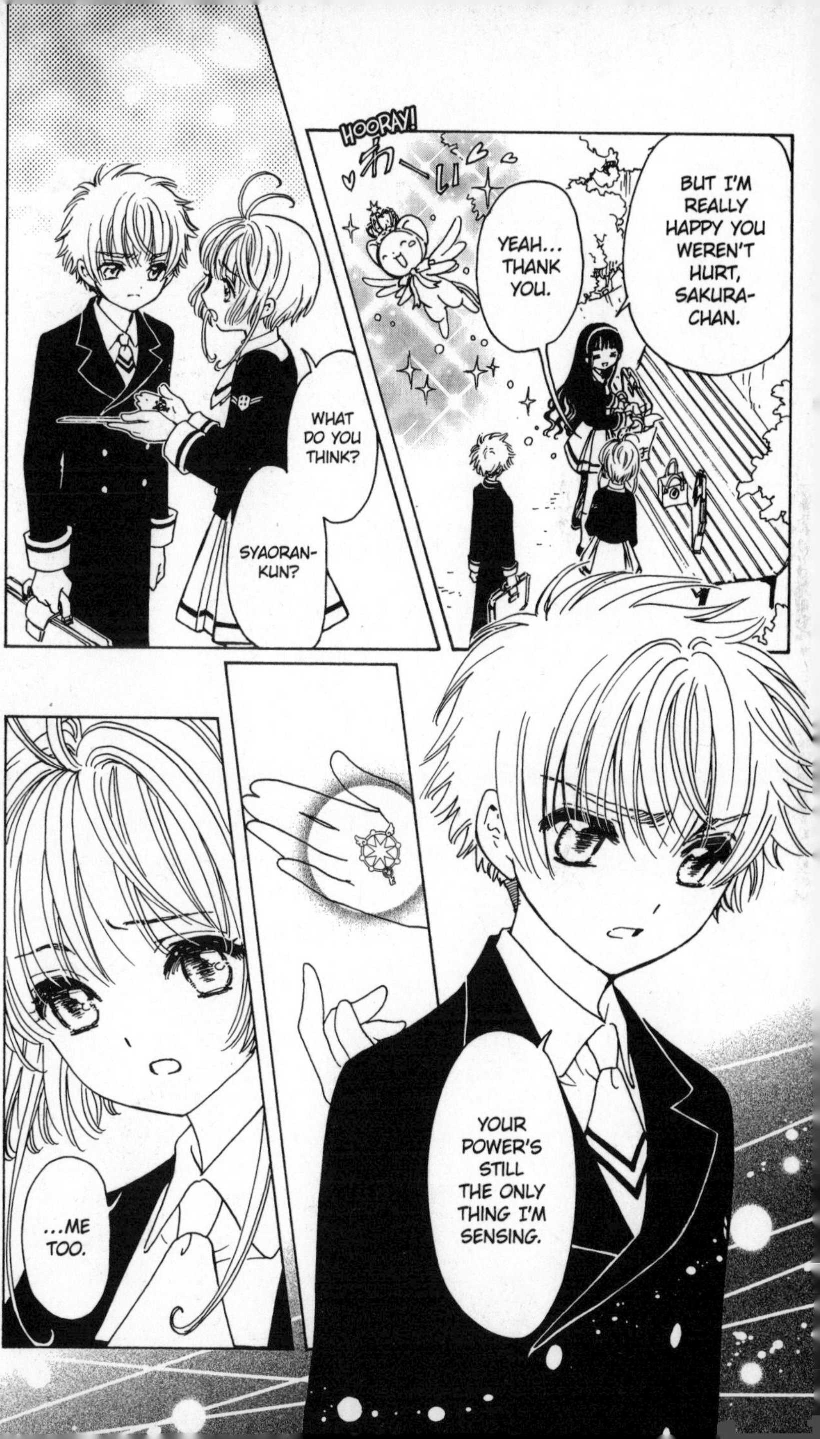
BUT I'M REALLY HAPPY YOU WEREN'T HURT, SAKURA-CHAN.
YEAH... THANK YOU.
HOORAY!
わーい
WHAT DO YOU THINK?
SYAORAN-KUN?
YOUR POWER'S STILL THE ONLY THING I'M SENSING.
...ME TOO.

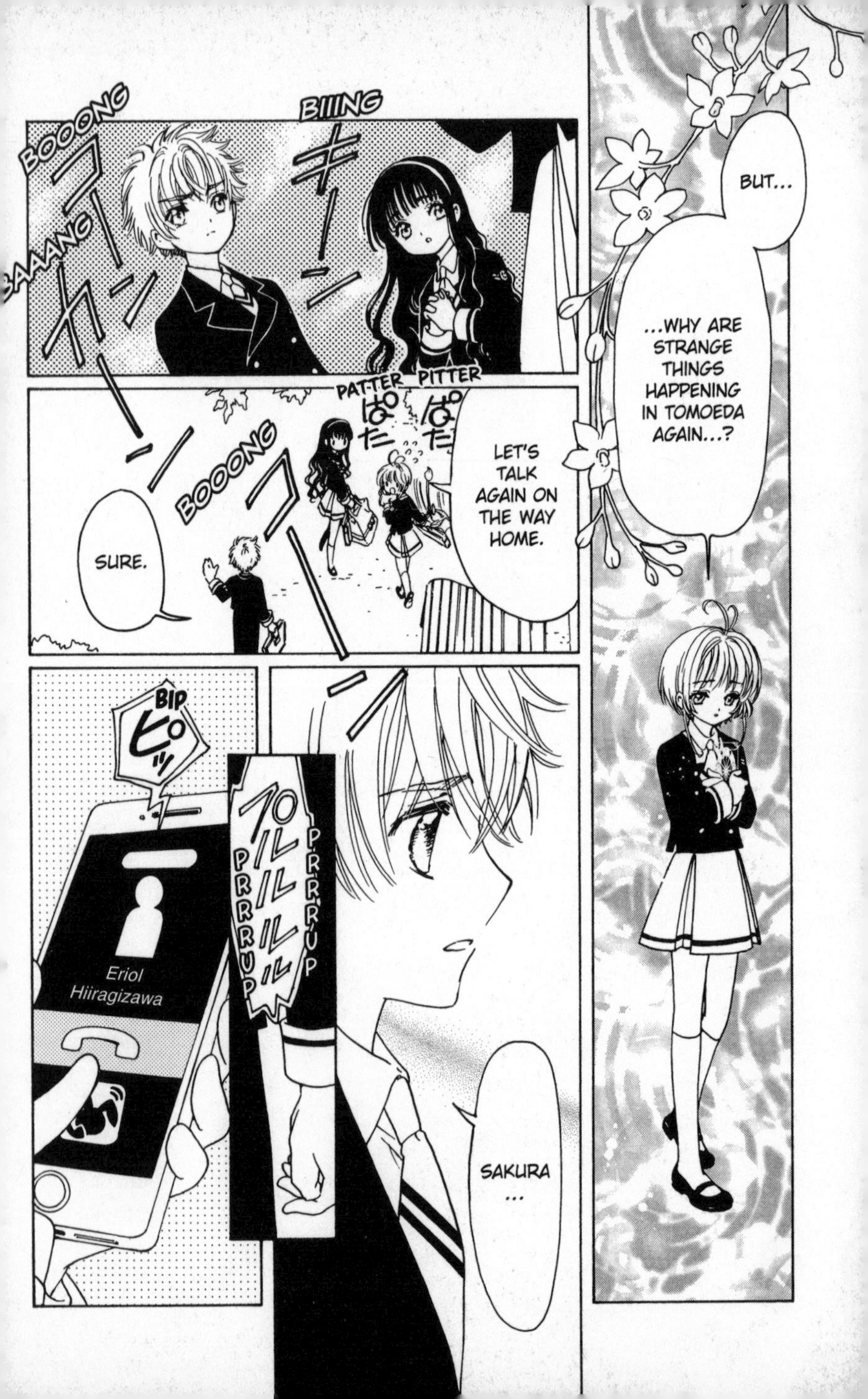
BUT...
...WHY ARE STRANGE THINGS HAPPENING IN TOMOEDA AGAIN...?
BIIING
BOOONG
BAAANG
PITTER
PATTER
LET'S TALK AGAIN ON THE WAY HOME.
BOOONG
SURE.
PRRRRUP
SAKURA ...
PRRRRUP
BIP
Eriol Hiiragizawa

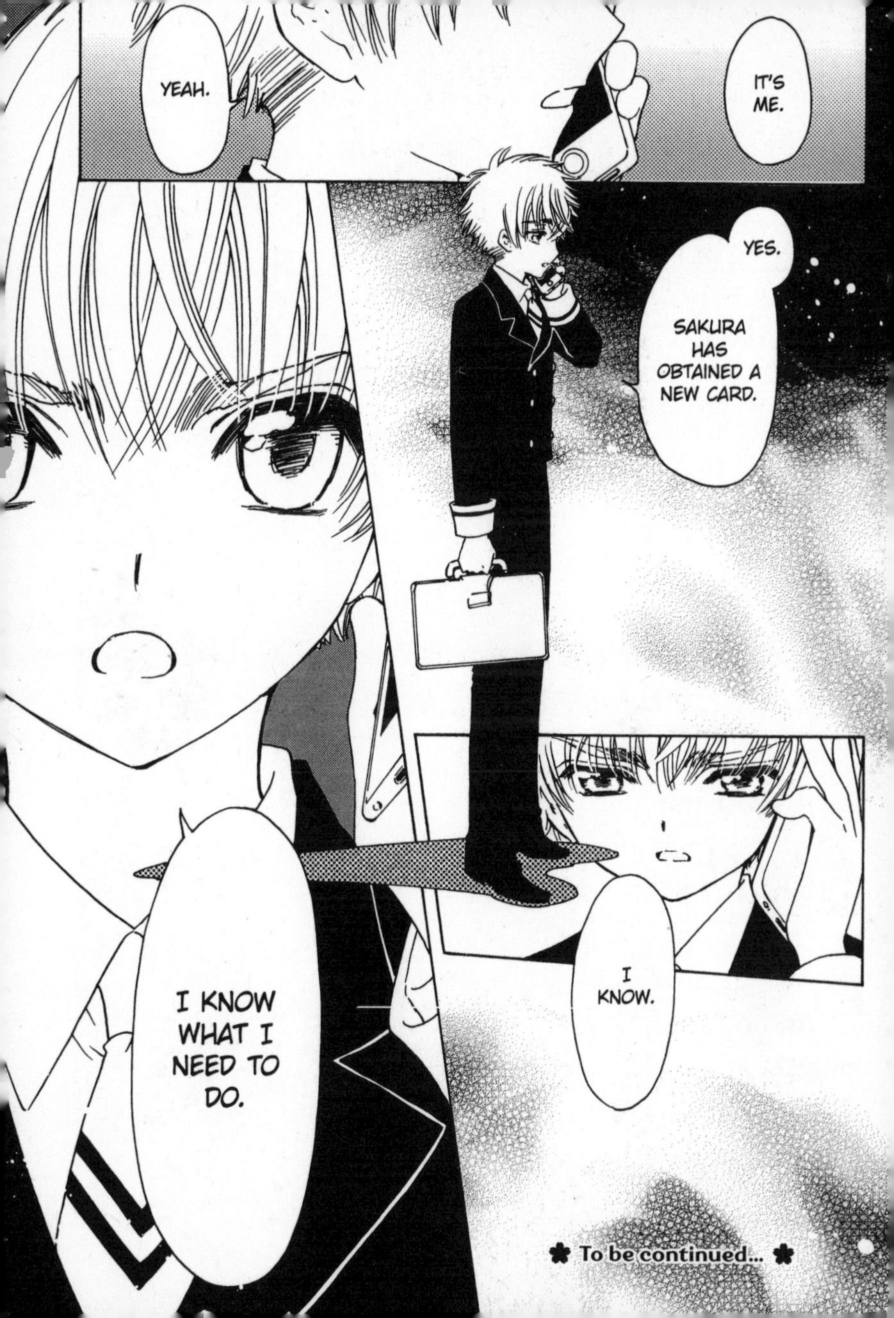
IT'S ME.
YEAH.
YES.
SAKURA HAS OBTAINED A NEW CARD.
I KNOW.
I KNOW WHAT I NEED TO DO.
To be continued...

Cardcaptor Sakura

CLEAR CARD

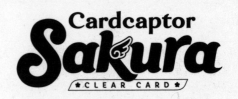

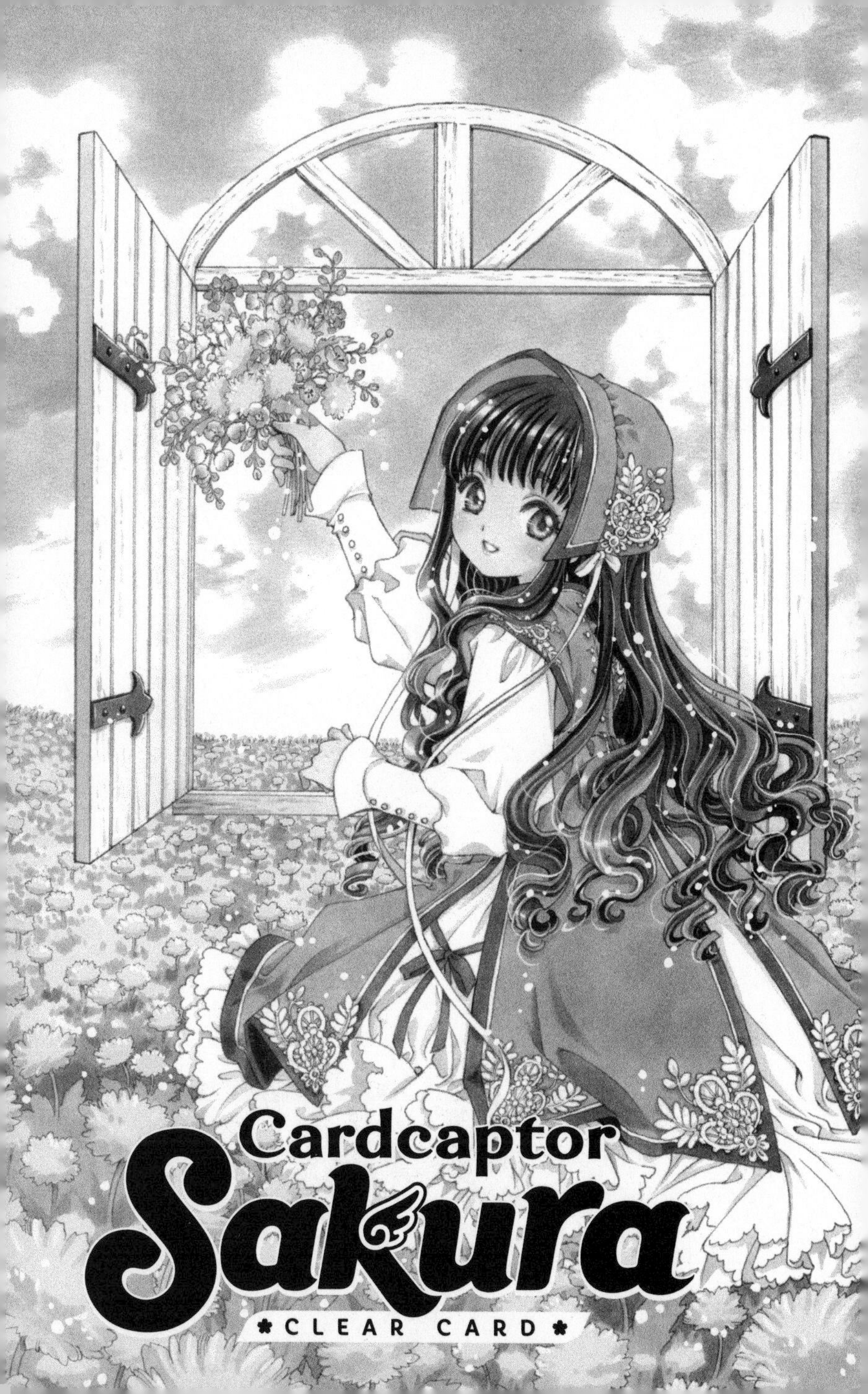
Cardcaptor
Sakura
CLEAR CARD

Cardcaptor Sakura
CLEAR CARD

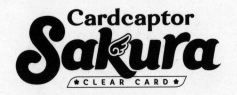

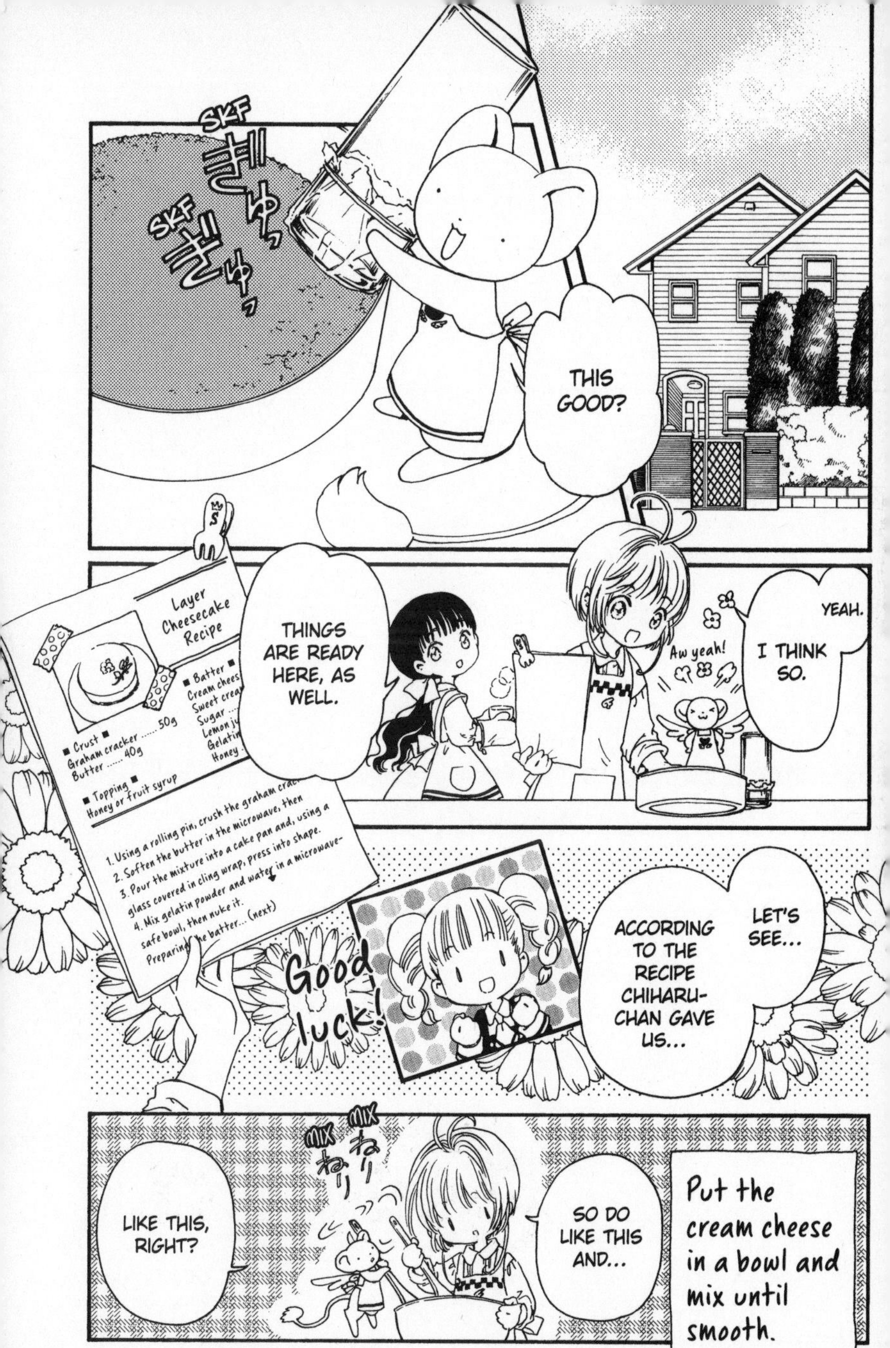
SKF ぎゅっ
SKF ぎゅっ
THIS GOOD?
YEAH.
I THINK SO.
Aw yeah!
THINGS ARE READY HERE, AS WELL.
Layer Cheesecake Recipe
■ Crust ■
Graham cracker 50g
Butter 40g
■ Topping ■
Honey or fruit syrup
■ Batter ■
1. Using a rolling pin, crush the graham crac
2. Soften the butter in the microwave, then
3. Pour the mixture into a cake pan and, using a
glass covered in cling wrap, press into shape.
4. Mix gelatin powder and water in a microwave-
safe bowl, then nuke it.
Preparing the batter... (next)
LET'S SEE...
ACCORDING TO THE RECIPE CHIHARU-CHAN GAVE US...
Good luck!
Put the cream cheese in a bowl and mix until smooth.
SO DO LIKE THIS AND...
MIX ねり
MIX ねり
LIKE THIS, RIGHT?

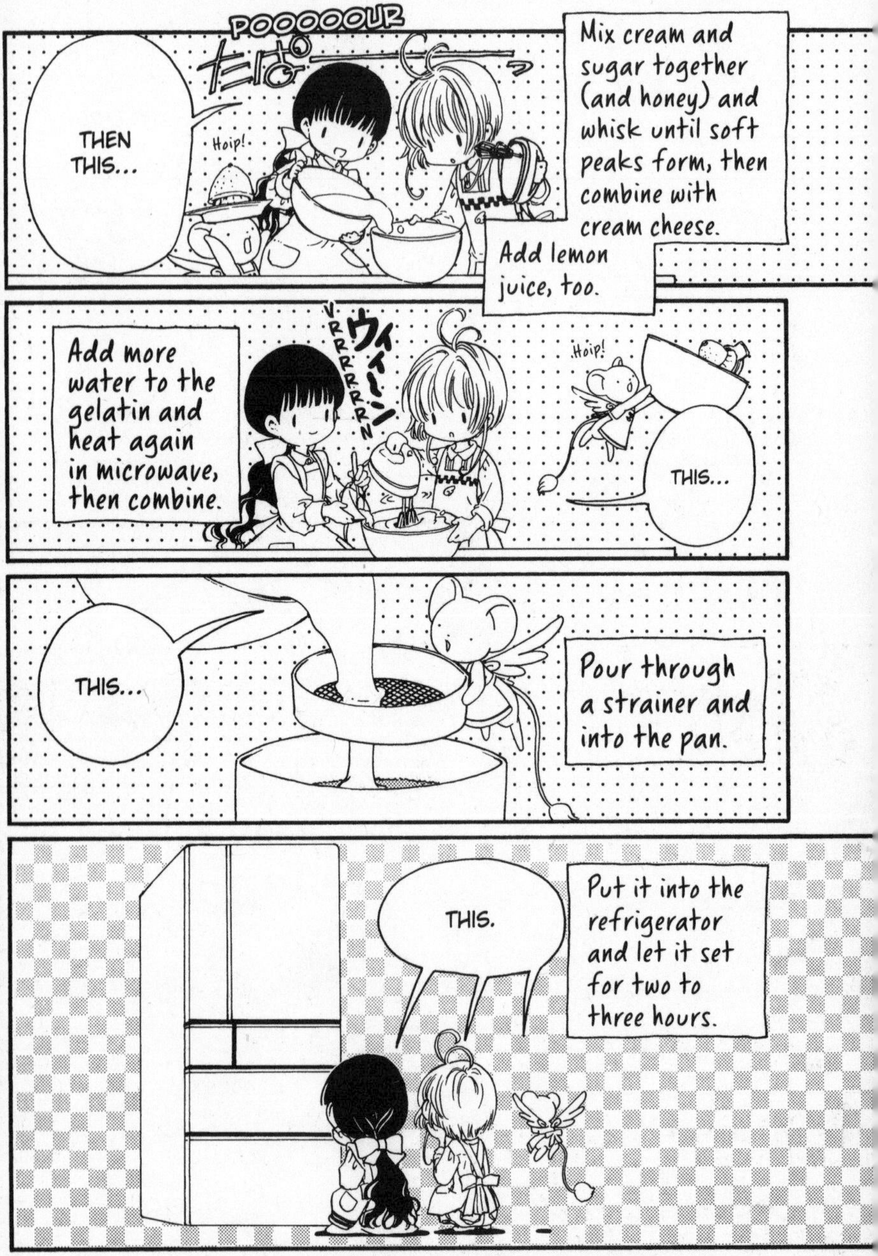
Mix cream and sugar together (and honey) and whisk until soft peaks form, then combine with cream cheese.
Add lemon juice, too.
POOOOOUR
Hoip!
THEN THIS...
Hoip!
THIS...
VRRRRRRRRN
ウィーン
Add more water to the gelatin and heat again in microwave, then combine.
Pour through a strainer and into the pan.
THIS...
Put it into the refrigerator and let it set for two to three hours.
THIS.

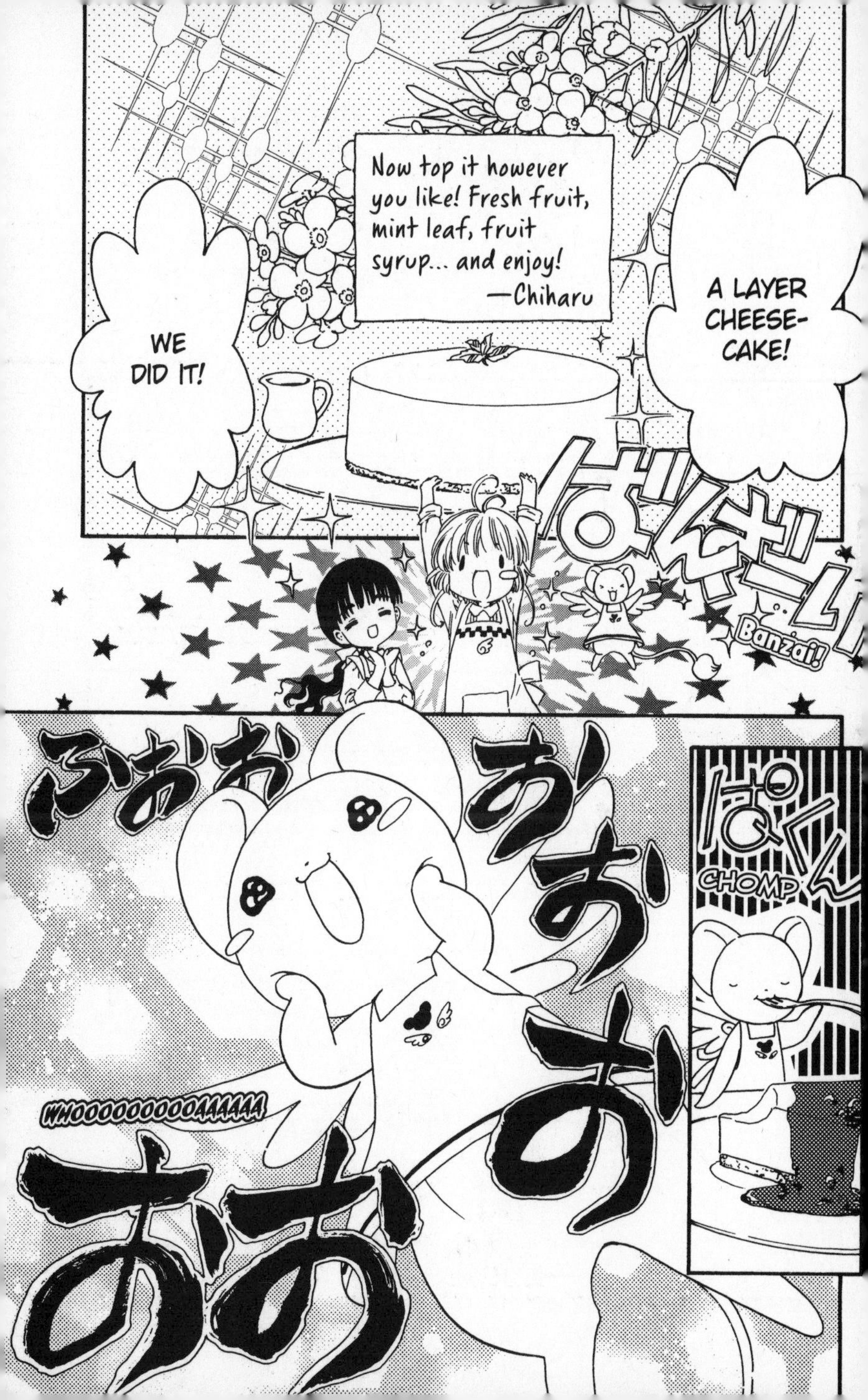
A LAYER CHEESE-CAKE!
Now top it however you like! Fresh fruit, mint leaf, fruit syrup... and enjoy! —Chiharu
WE DID IT!
Banzai!
CHOMP
WHOOOOOOOOOAAAAAA

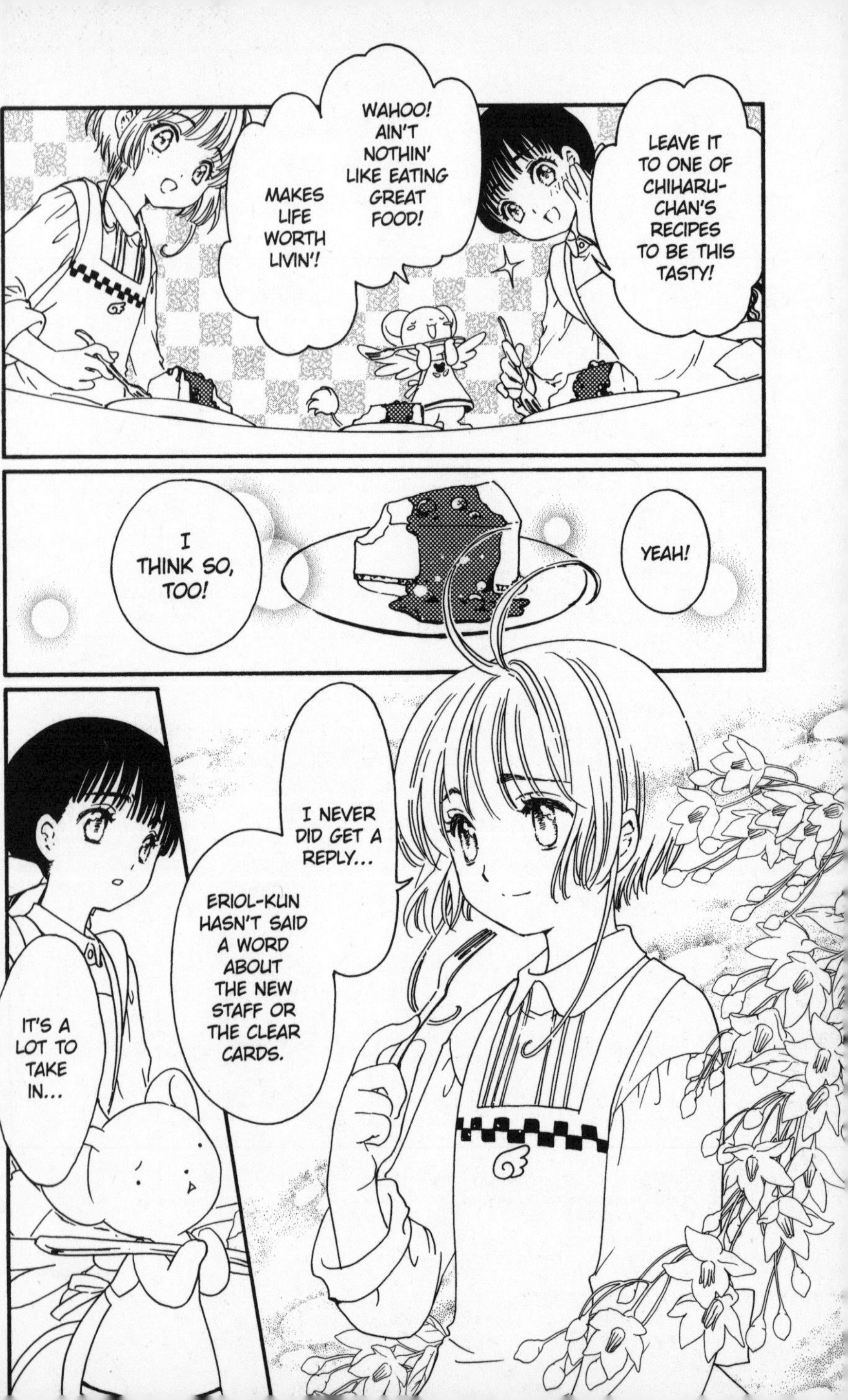
LEAVE IT TO ONE OF CHIHARU-CHAN'S RECIPES TO BE THIS TASTY!
WAHOO! AIN'T NOTHIN' LIKE EATING GREAT FOOD!
MAKES LIFE WORTH LIVIN'!
YEAH!
I THINK SO, TOO!
I NEVER DID GET A REPLY…
ERIOL-KUN HASN'T SAID A WORD ABOUT THE NEW STAFF OR THE CLEAR CARDS.
IT'S A LOT TO TAKE IN…

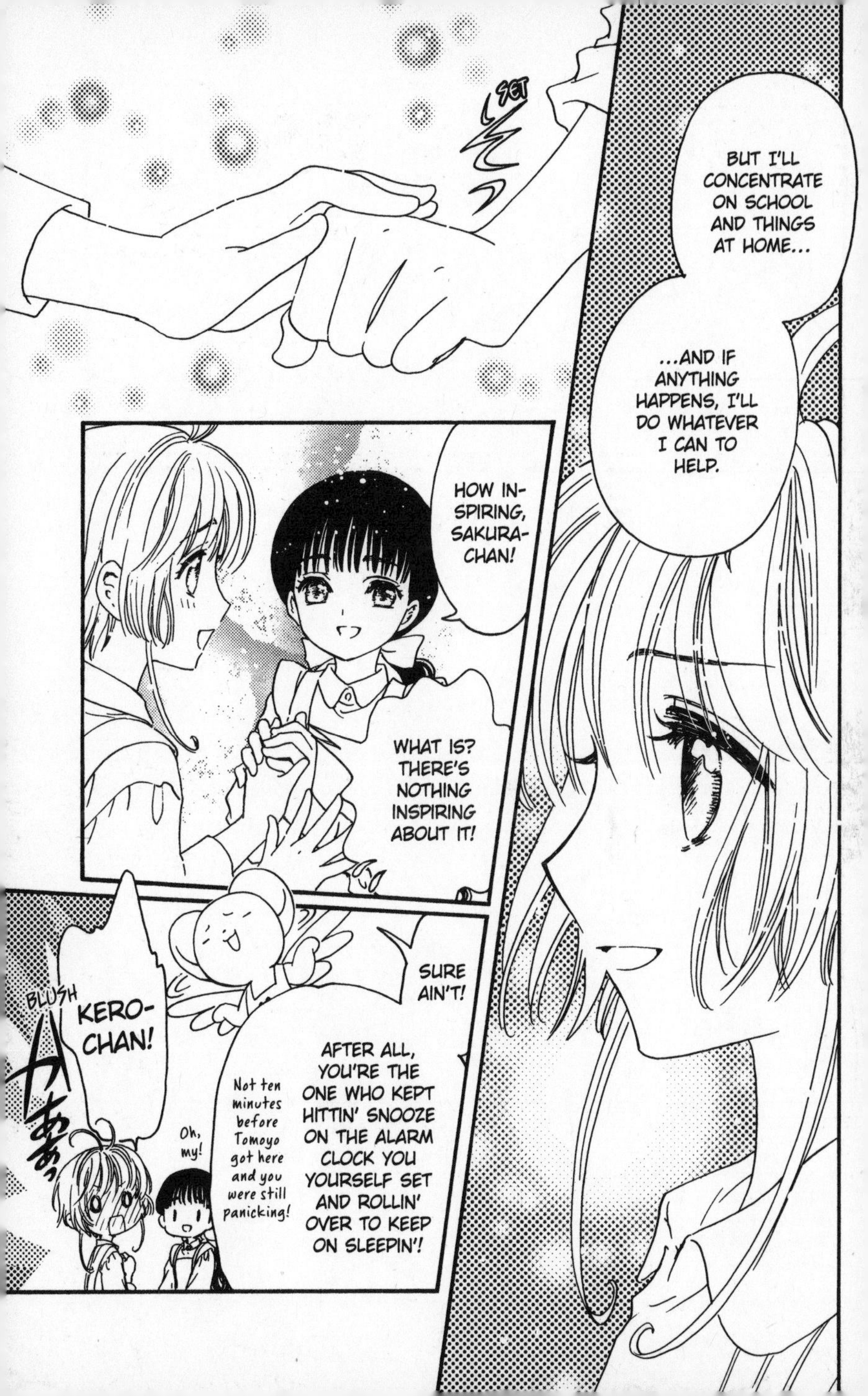
BUT I'LL CONCENTRATE ON SCHOOL AND THINGS AT HOME...
...AND IF ANYTHING HAPPENS, I'LL DO WHATEVER I CAN TO HELP.
SET
HOW IN-SPIRING, SAKURA-CHAN!
WHAT IS? THERE'S NOTHING INSPIRING ABOUT IT!
SURE AIN'T!
AFTER ALL, YOU'RE THE ONE WHO KEPT HITTIN' SNOOZE ON THE ALARM CLOCK YOU YOURSELF SET AND ROLLIN' OVER TO KEEP ON SLEEPIN'!
Not ten minutes before Tomoyo got here and you were still panicking!
Oh, my!
KERO-CHAN!
BLUSH

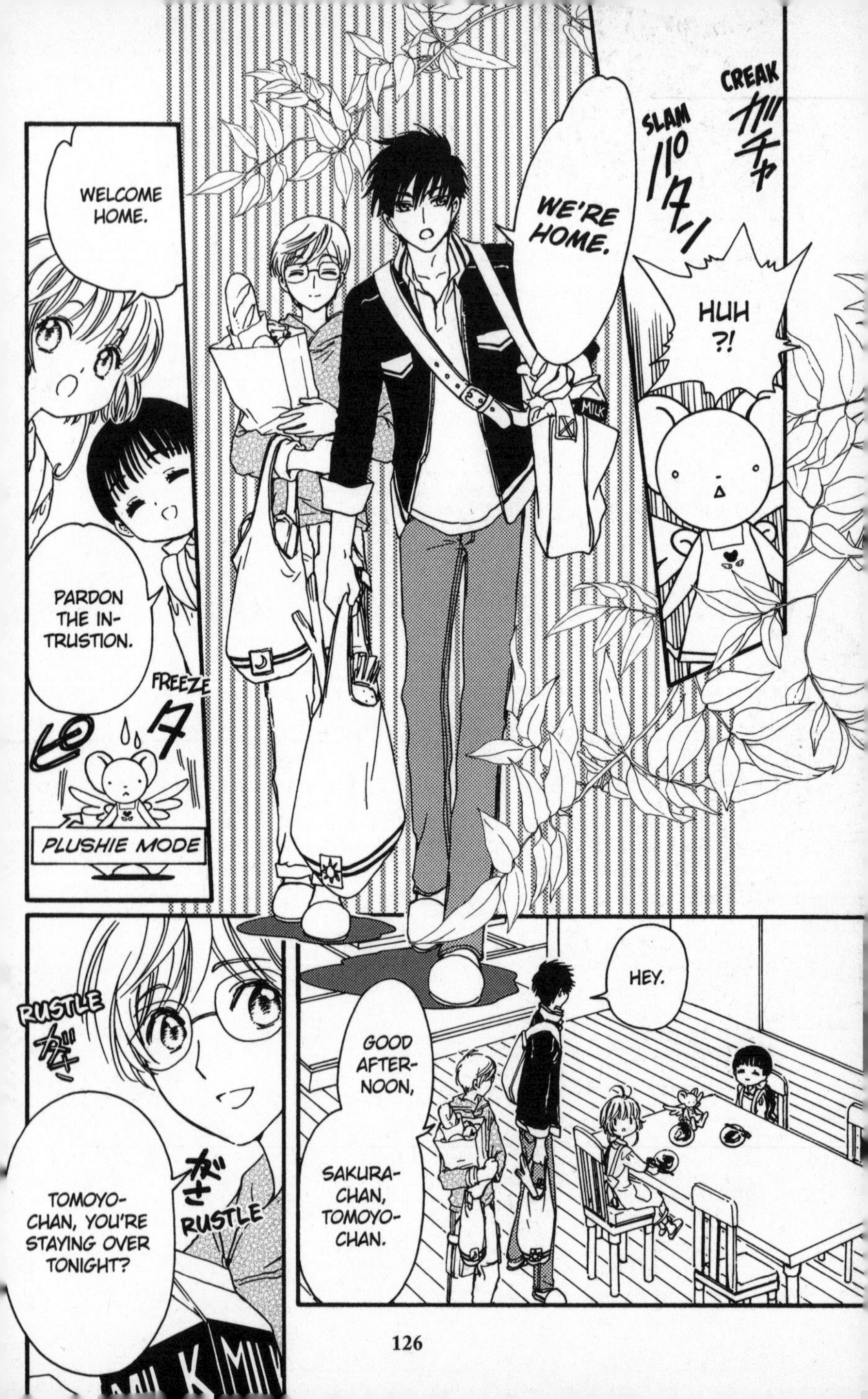
CREAK
ガチャ
SLAM
バタン
WE'RE HOME.
HUH ?!
WELCOME HOME.
PARDON THE IN-TRUSTION.
FREEZE
ピタ
PLUSHIE MODE
HEY.
GOOD AFTER-NOON,
SAKURA-CHAN, TOMOYO-CHAN.
RUSTLE
ガサ
がさ
RUSTLE
TOMOYO-CHAN, YOU'RE STAYING OVER TONIGHT?

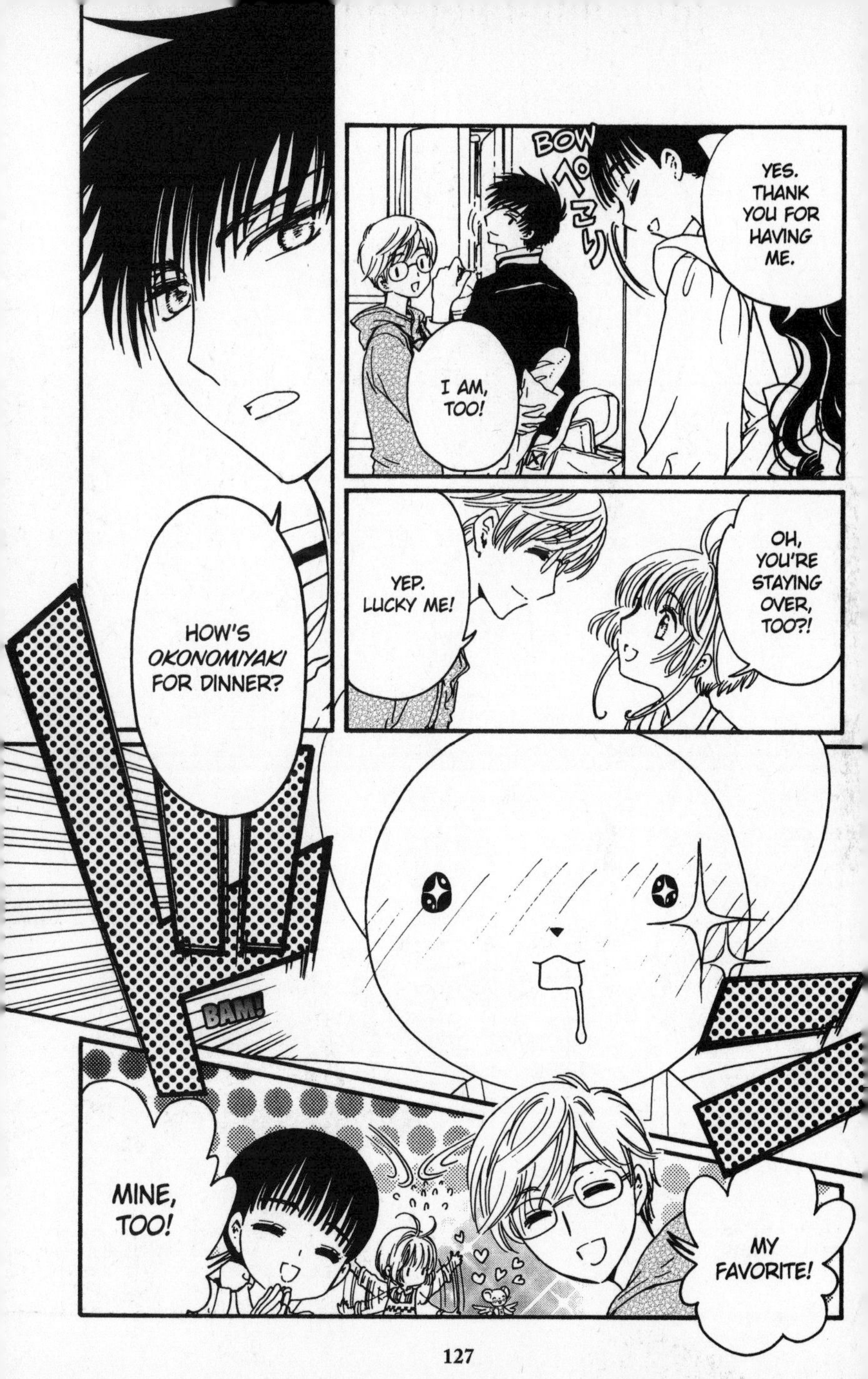

BOW
YES. THANK YOU FOR HAVING ME.
I AM, TOO!
OH, YOU'RE STAYING OVER, TOO?!
YEP. LUCKY ME!
HOW'S *OKONOMIYAKI* FOR DINNER?
BAM!
MY FAVORITE!
MINE, TOO!

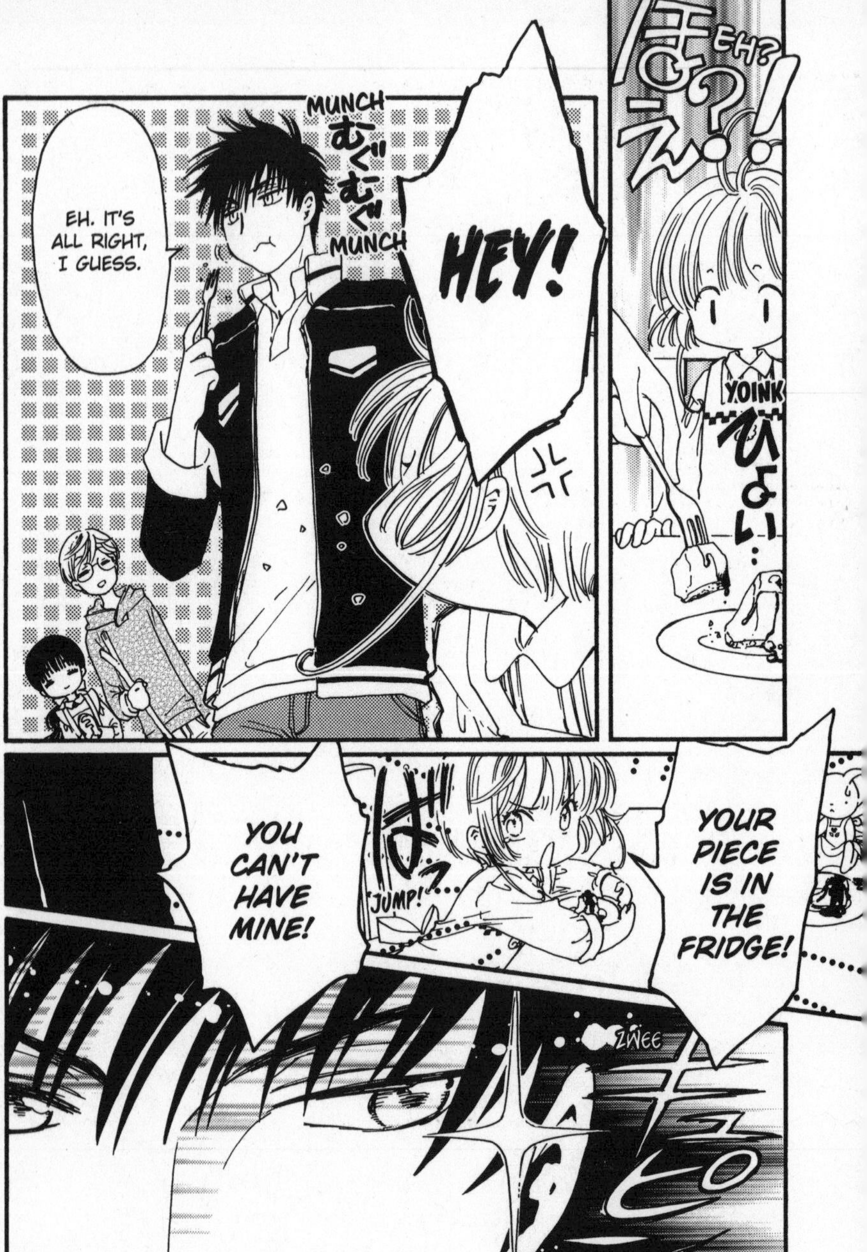
EH?
YOINK
ひょい
HEY!
MUNCH
むぐむぐ
MUNCH
EH. IT'S ALL RIGHT, I GUESS.
YOUR PIECE IS IN THE FRIDGE!
JUMP!
YOU CAN'T HAVE MINE!
ZWEE

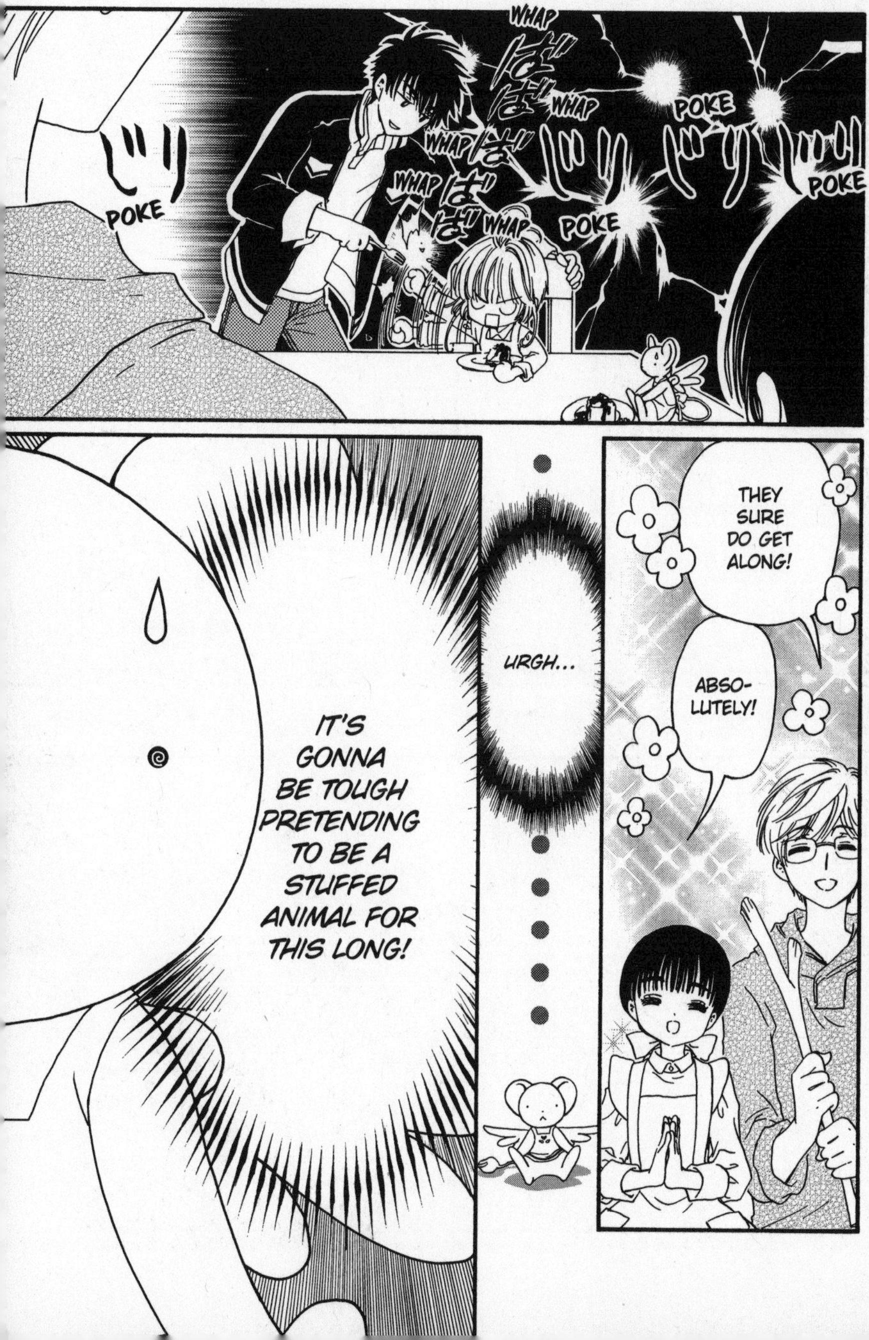
WHAP
ばばばばば
WHAP
WHAP
WHAP
WHAP
POKE
じりじりじりじり
POKE
POKE
POKE
THEY SURE DO GET ALONG!
ABSO-LUTELY!
URGH...
IT'S GONNA BE TOUGH PRETENDING TO BE A STUFFED ANIMAL FOR THIS LONG!

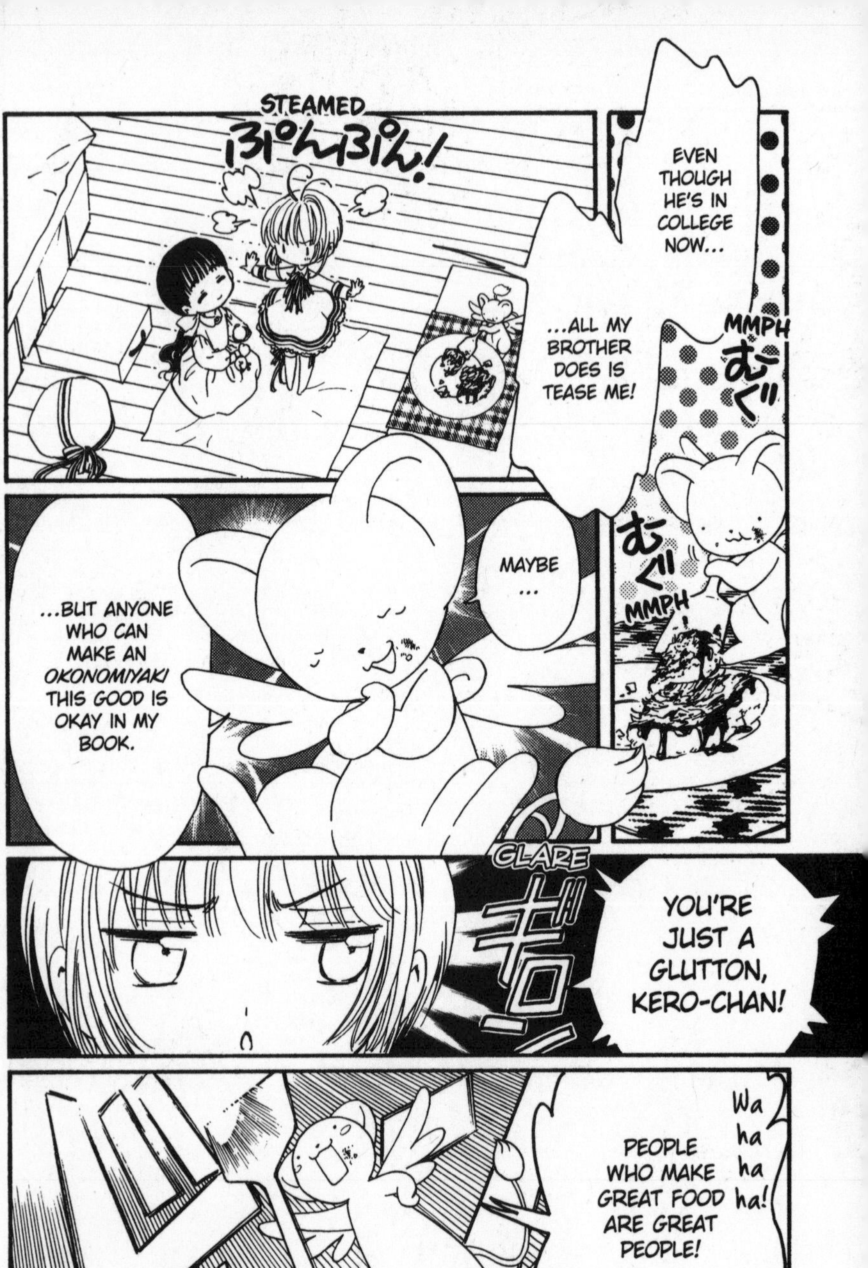
EVEN THOUGH HE'S IN COLLEGE NOW...
...ALL MY BROTHER DOES IS TEASE ME!
MMPH
むぐ
STEAMED
ぷんぷん!
むぐ
MMPH
MAYBE ...
...BUT ANYONE WHO CAN MAKE AN *OKONOMIYAKI* THIS GOOD IS OKAY IN MY BOOK.
GLARE
ギロ
YOU'RE JUST A GLUTTON, KERO-CHAN!
Wa ha ha ha!
PEOPLE WHO MAKE GREAT FOOD ARE GREAT PEOPLE!
BAM!

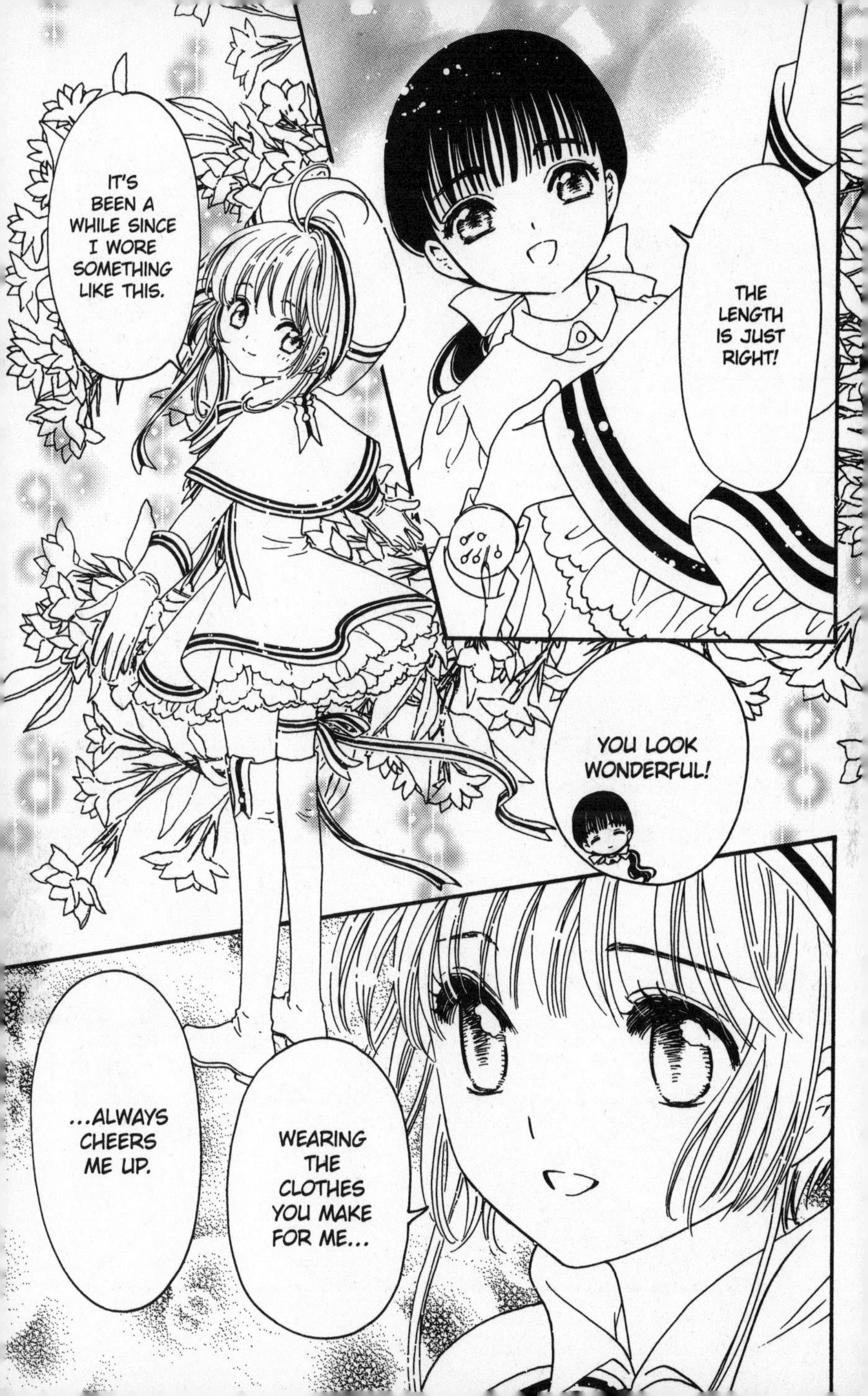
THE LENGTH IS JUST RIGHT!
IT'S BEEN A WHILE SINCE I WORE SOMETHING LIKE THIS.
YOU LOOK WONDERFUL!
WEARING THE CLOTHES YOU MAKE FOR ME...
...ALWAYS CHEERS ME UP.

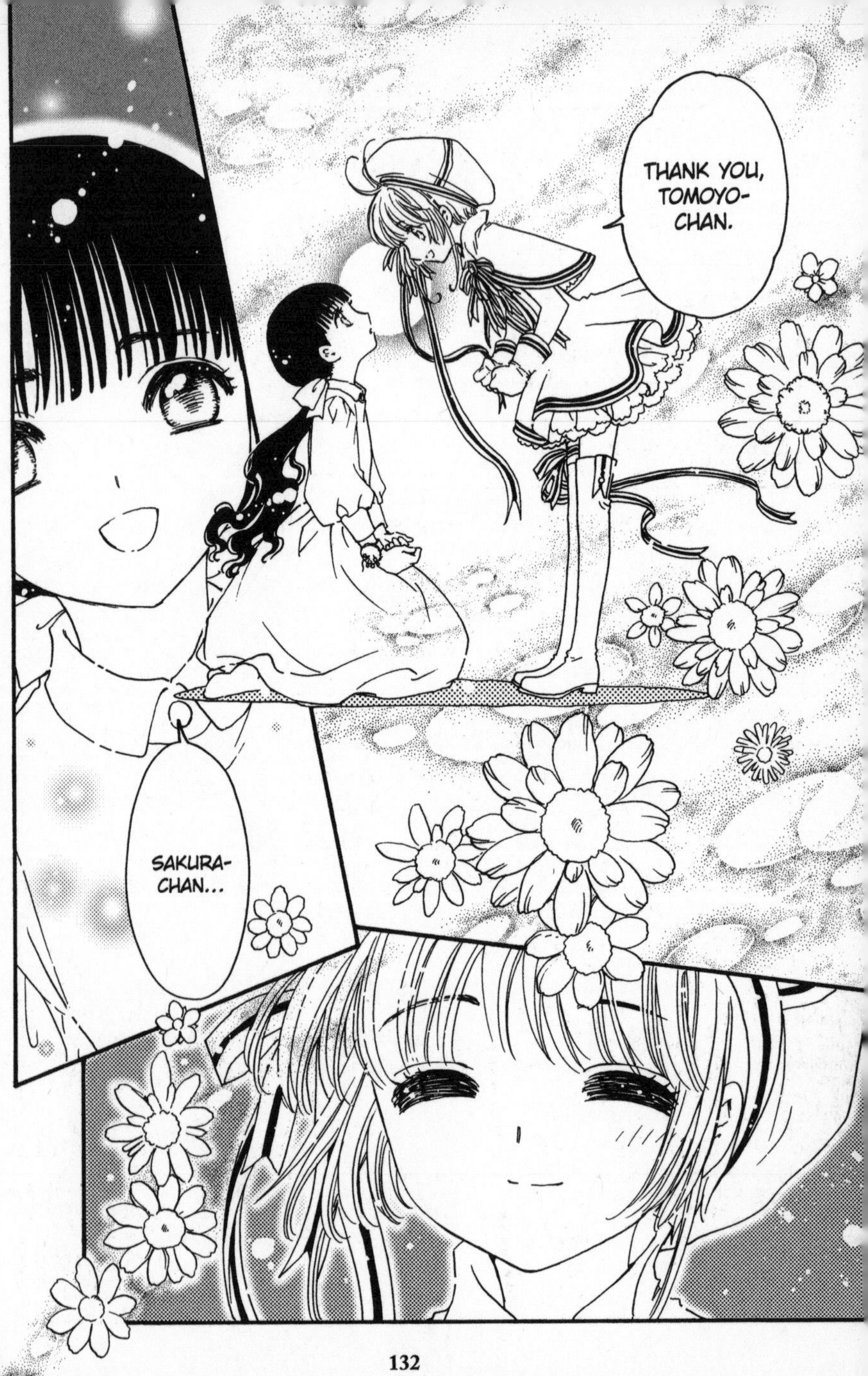
THANK YOU, TOMOYO-CHAN.
SAKURA-CHAN...

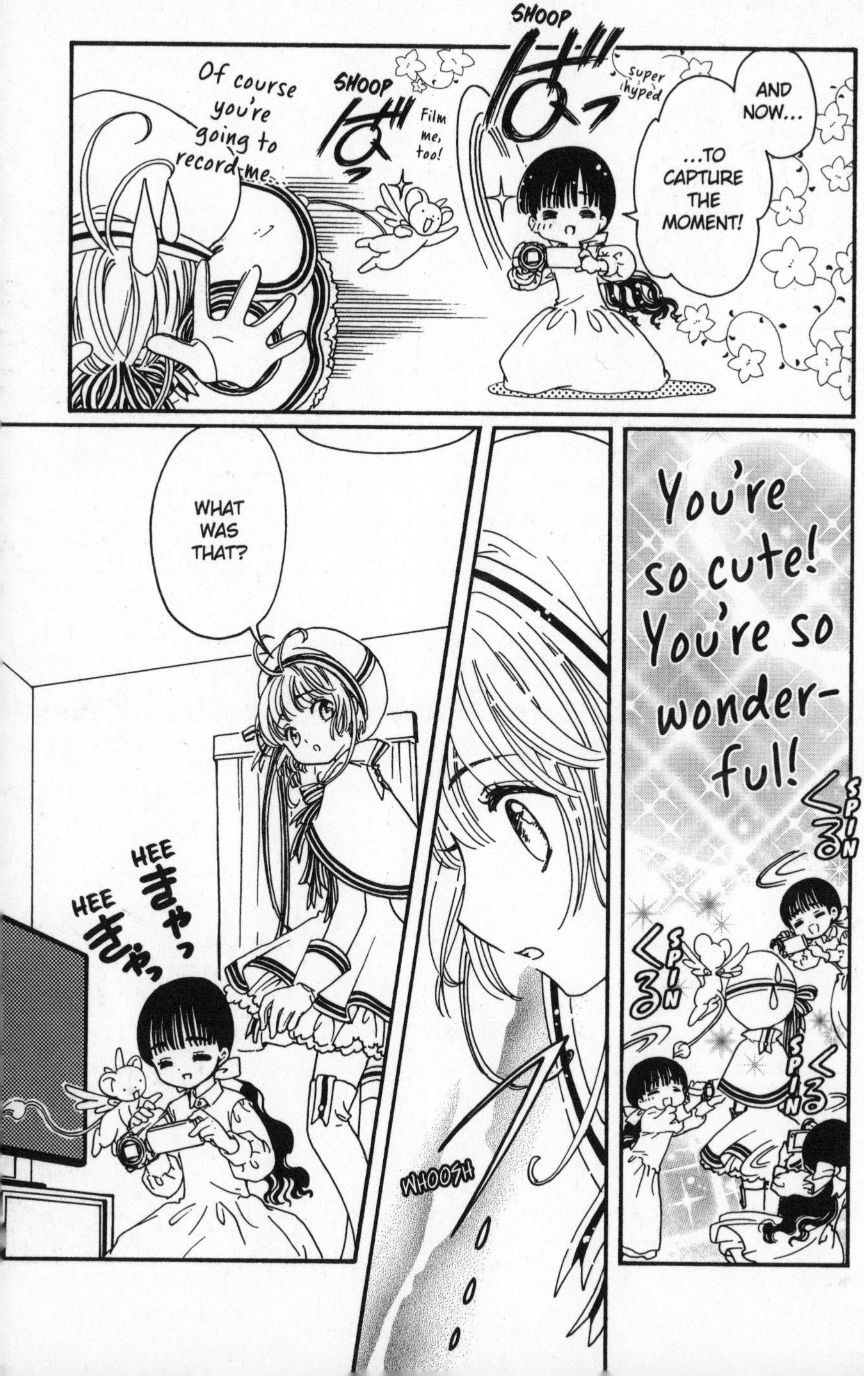
AND NOW...
...TO CAPTURE THE MOMENT!
super hyped
SHOOP
ばっ
Film me, too!
SHOOP
ばっ
Of course you're going to record me...
You're so cute! You're so wonderful!
SPIN
くる
SPIN
くる
SPIN
くる
WHOOSH
WHAT WAS THAT?
HEE
きゃっ
HEE
きゃっ

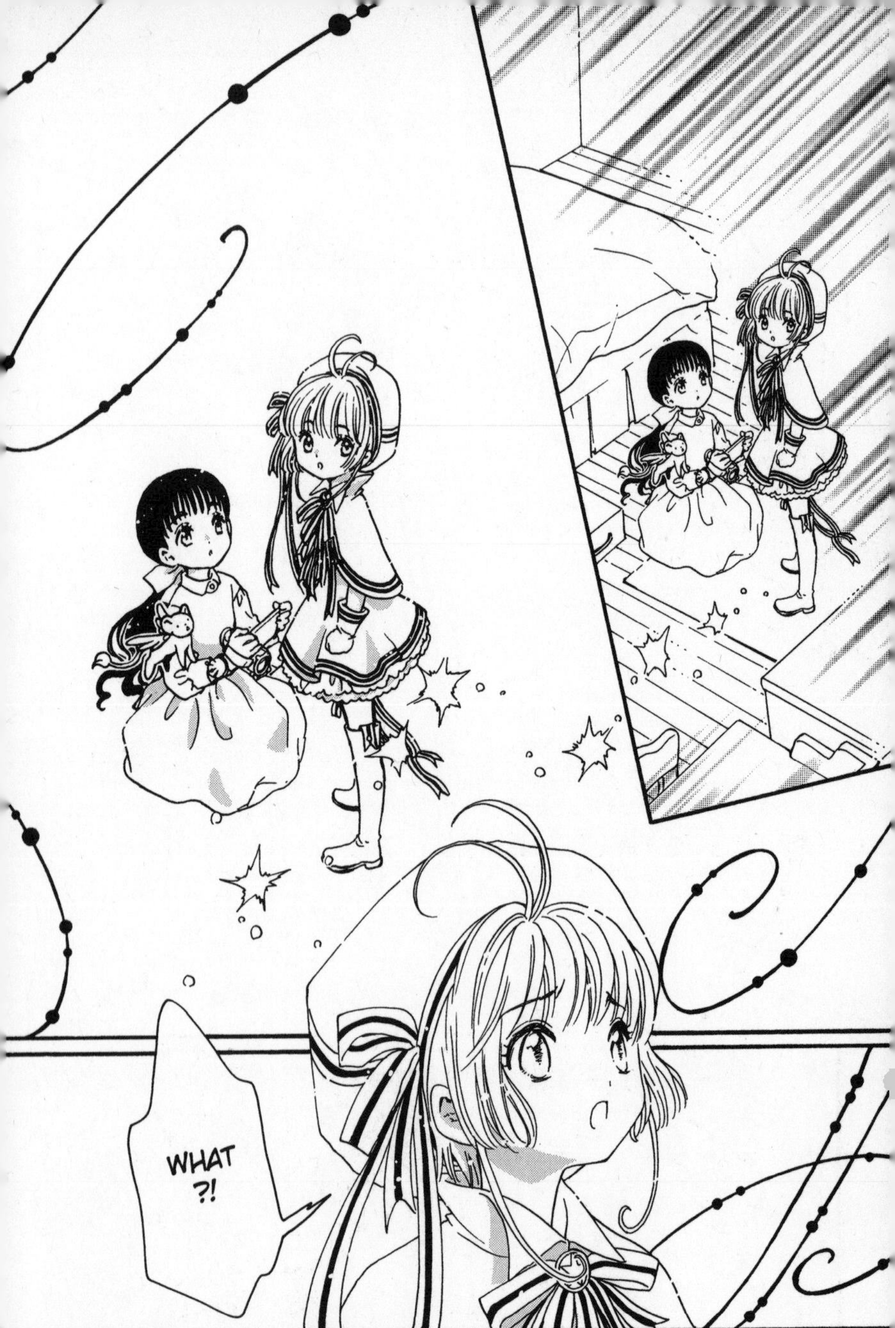
WHAT ?!

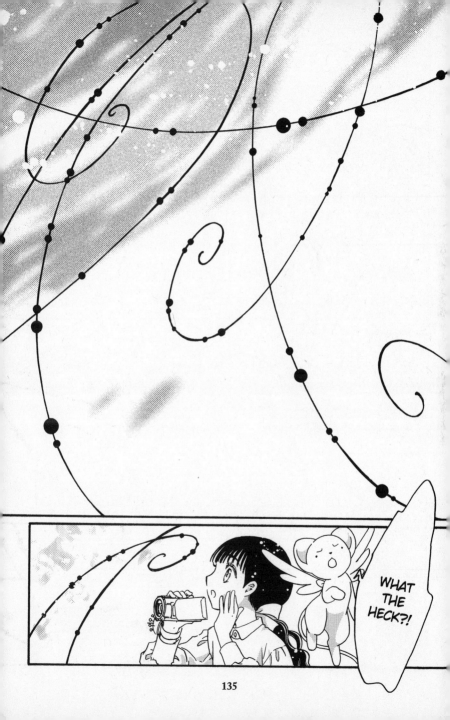

WHAT THE HECK?!

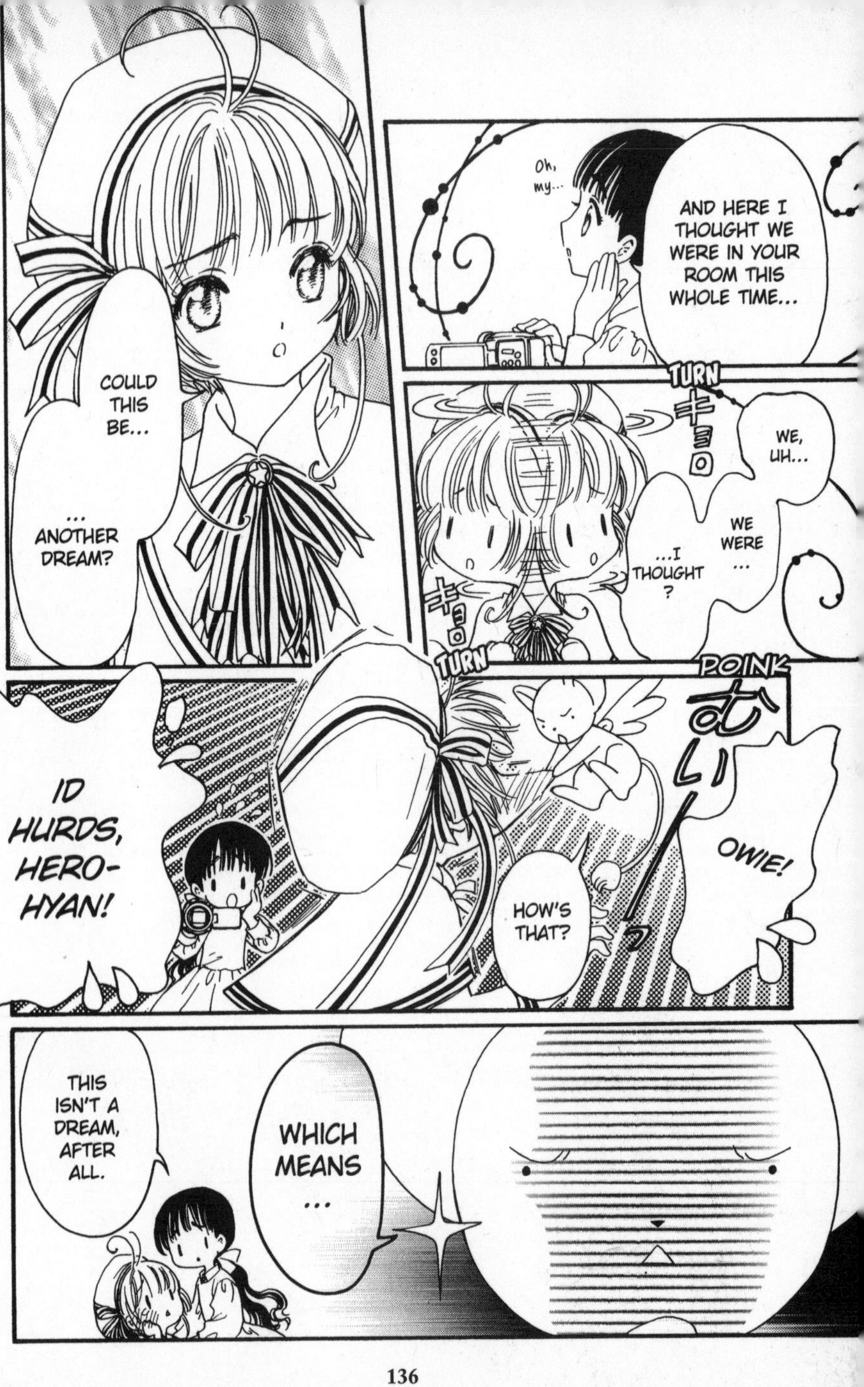
AND HERE I THOUGHT WE WERE IN YOUR ROOM THIS WHOLE TIME...
Oh, my...
TURN
キョロ
WE, UH...
WE WERE ...
...I THOUGHT ?
キョロ
TURN
COULD THIS BE...
... ANOTHER DREAM?
POINK
むい
OWIE!
HOW'S THAT?
ID HURDS, HERO-HYAN!
WHICH MEANS ...
THIS ISN'T A DREAM, AFTER ALL.

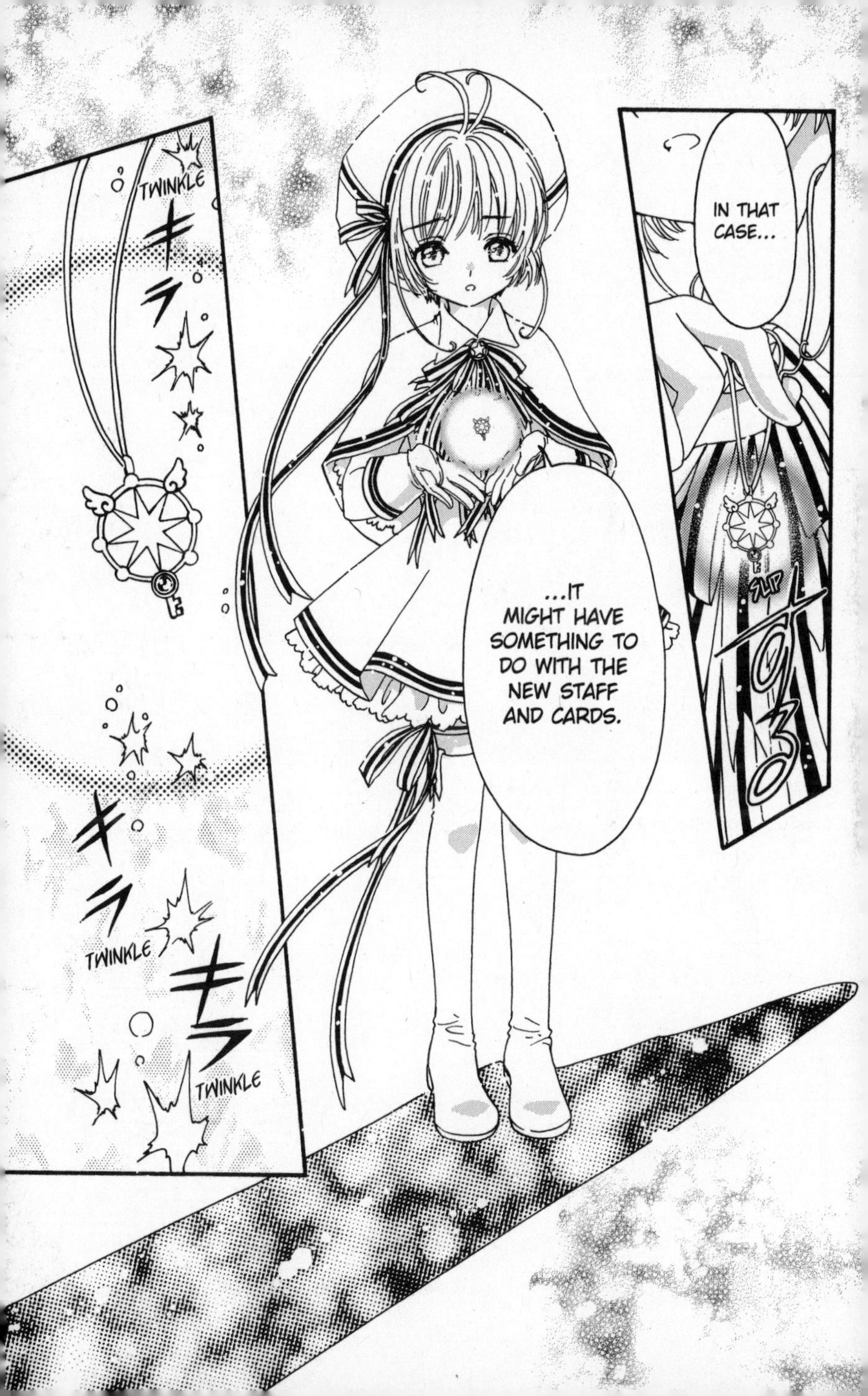
IN THAT CASE...
SLIP
...IT MIGHT HAVE SOMETHING TO DO WITH THE NEW STAFF AND CARDS.
TWINKLE
TWINKLE
TWINKLE

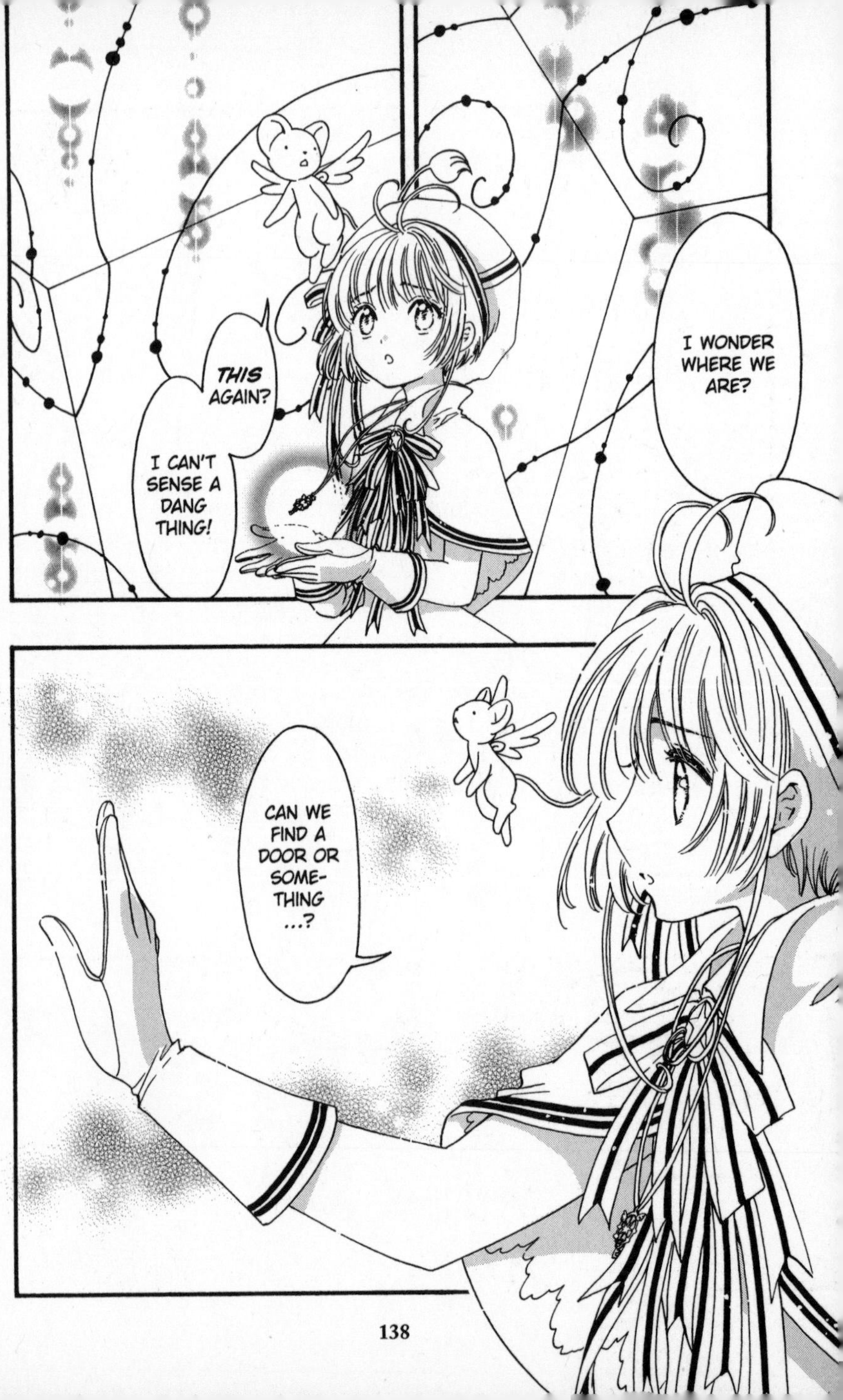
I WONDER WHERE WE ARE?
THIS AGAIN?
I CAN'T SENSE A DANG THING!
CAN WE FIND A DOOR OR SOME-THING ...?

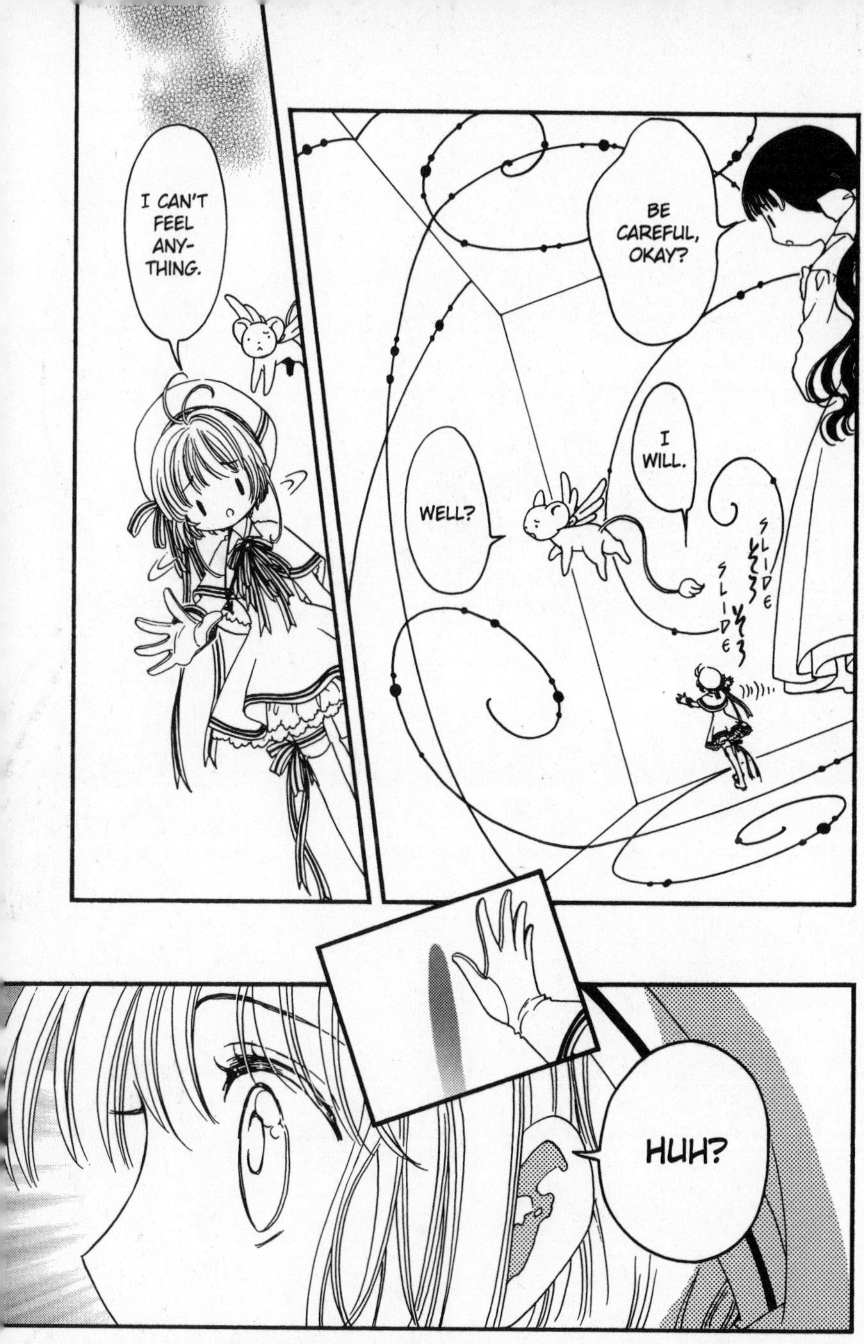
BE CAREFUL, OKAY?
I WILL.
WELL?
SLIDE
SLIDE
I CAN'T FEEL ANY-THING.
HUH?

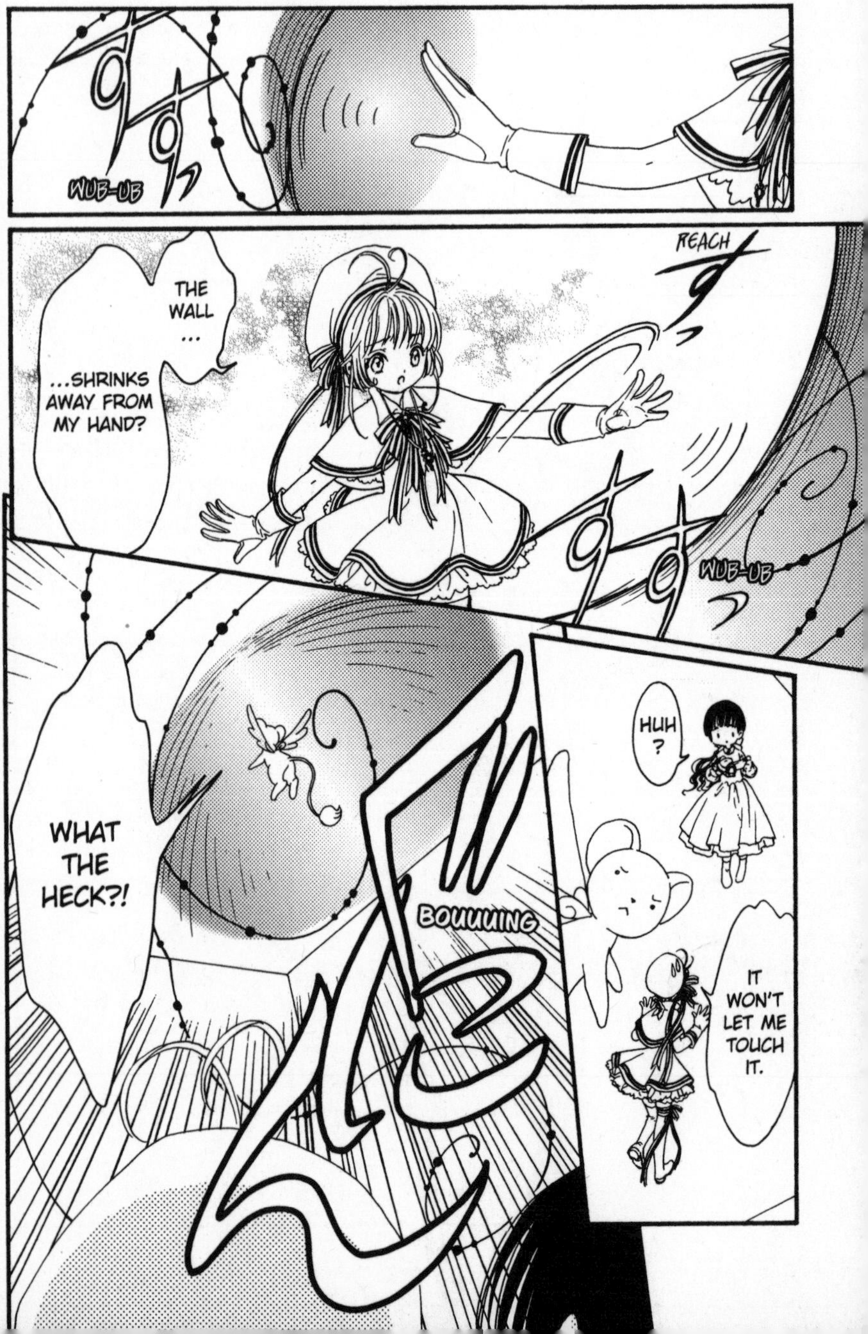
WUB-UB
REACH
THE WALL ...
...SHRINKS AWAY FROM MY HAND?
WUB-UB
HUH?
IT WON'T LET ME TOUCH IT.
BOUUUING
WHAT THE HECK?!

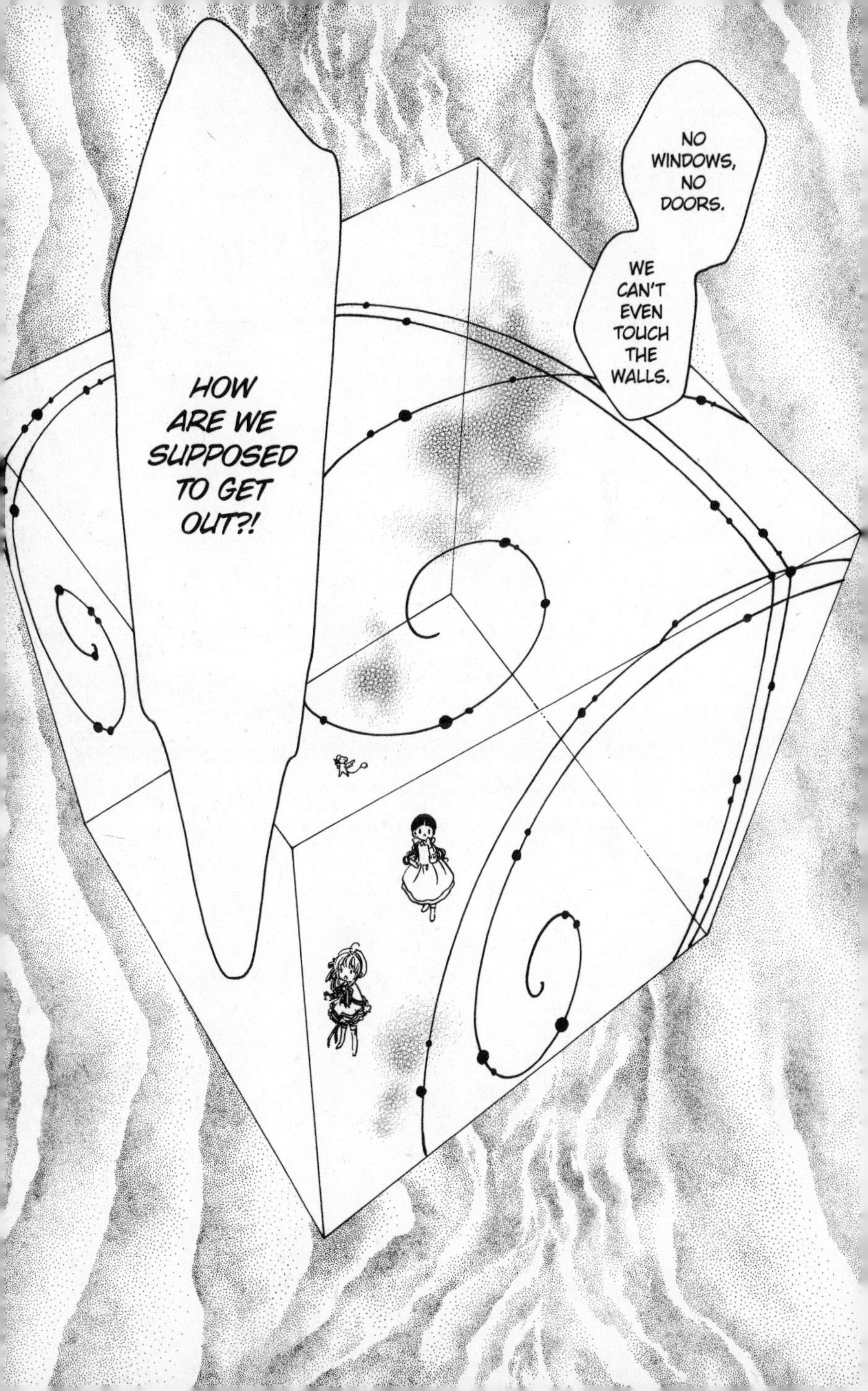
NO WINDOWS, NO DOORS.
WE CAN'T EVEN TOUCH THE WALLS.
HOW ARE WE SUPPOSED TO GET OUT?!

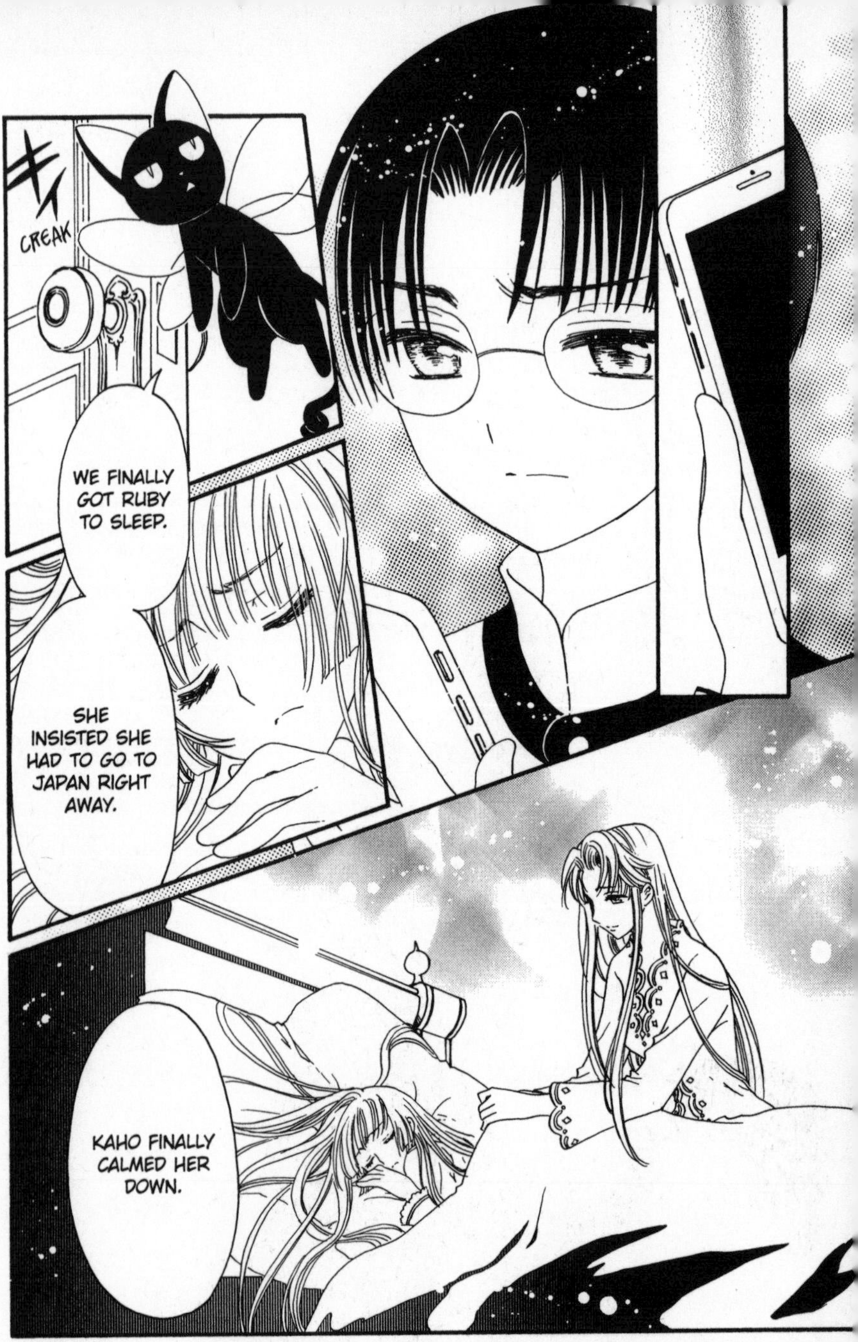
キィ
CREAK
WE FINALLY GOT RUBY TO SLEEP.
SHE INSISTED SHE HAD TO GO TO JAPAN RIGHT AWAY.
KAHO FINALLY CALMED HER DOWN.

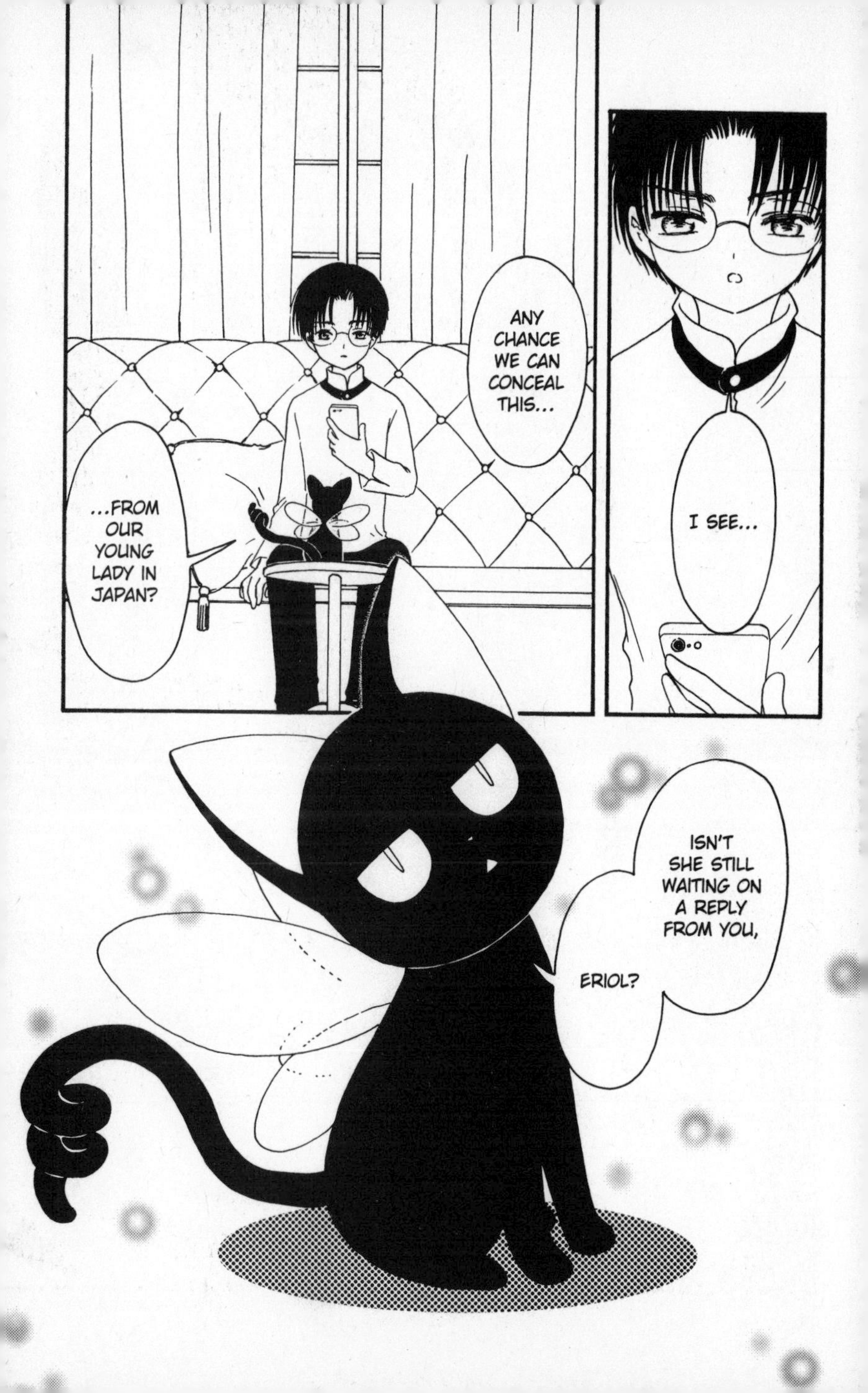
I SEE...
ANY CHANCE WE CAN CONCEAL THIS...
...FROM OUR YOUNG LADY IN JAPAN?
ISN'T SHE STILL WAITING ON A REPLY FROM YOU, ERIOL?

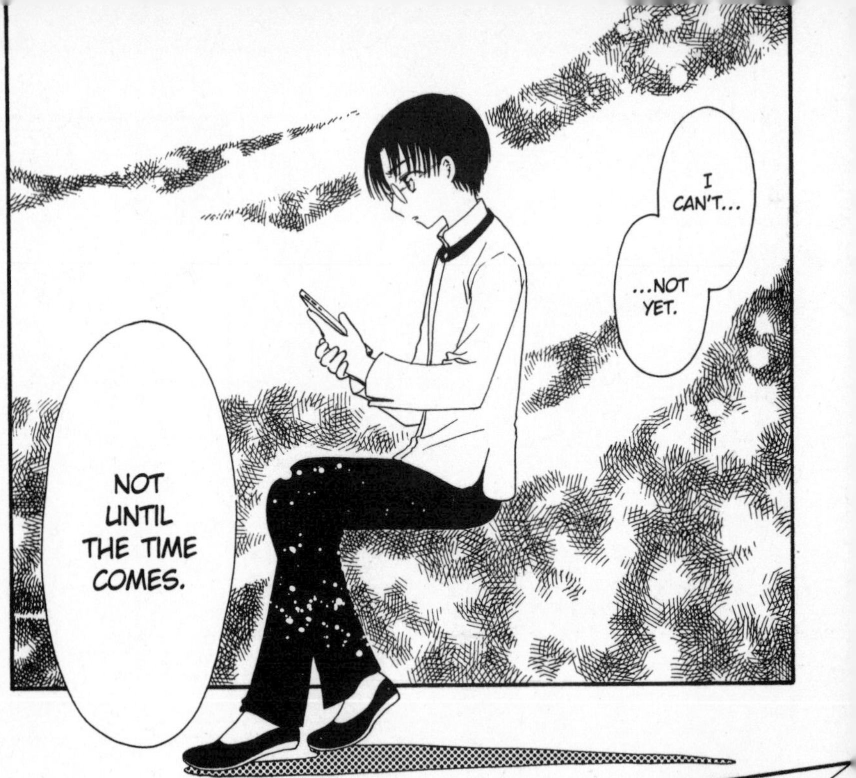
I CAN'T...
...NOT YET.
NOT UNTIL THE TIME COMES.
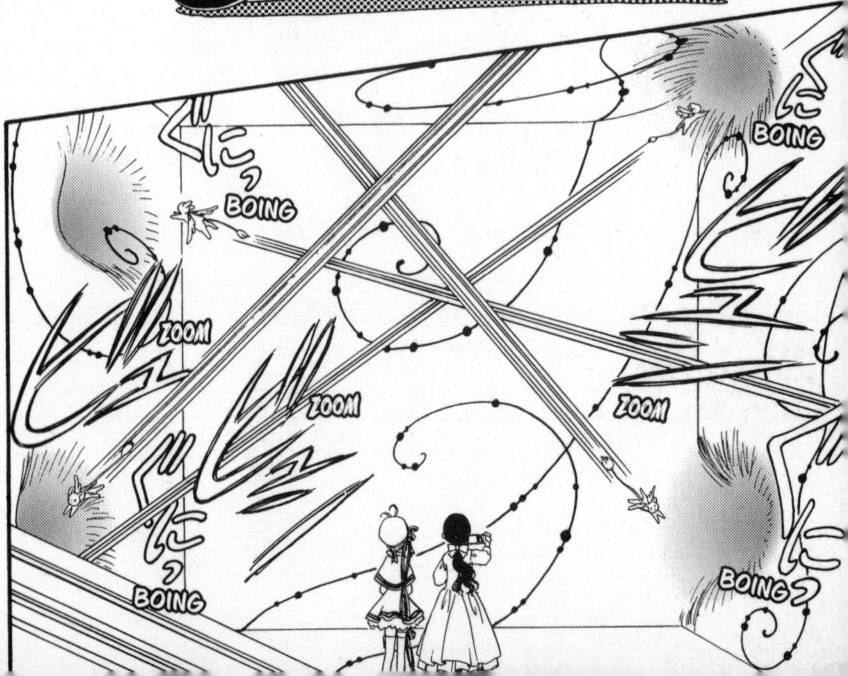
BOING
BOING
ZOOM
ZOOM
ZOOM
BOING
BOING

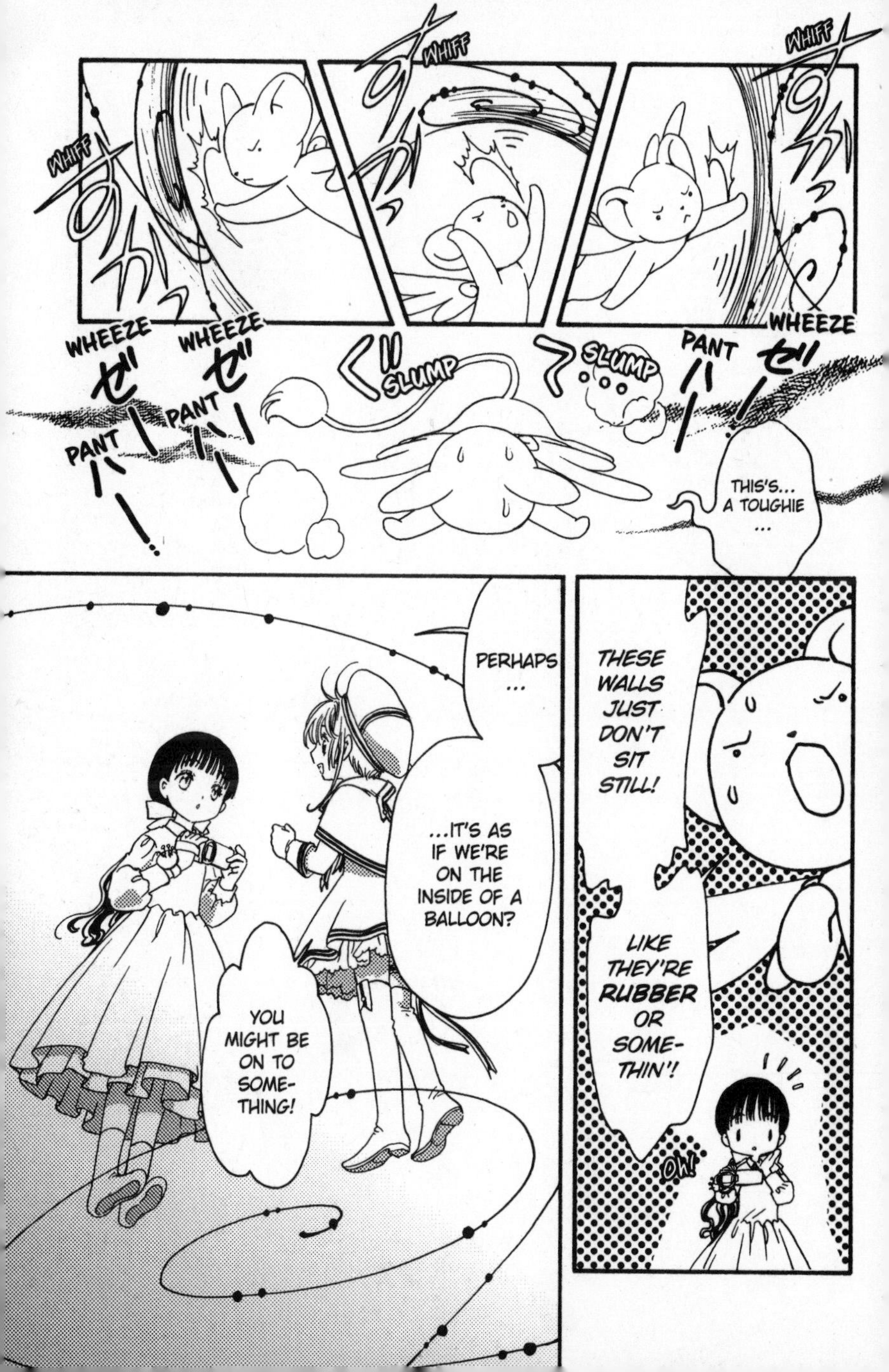
WHIFF
WHIFF
WHIFF
WHEEZE
PANT
THIS'S... A TOUGHIE ...
SLUMP
SLUMP
WHEEZE
PANT
WHEEZE
PANT
THESE WALLS JUST DON'T SIT STILL!
LIKE THEY'RE RUBBER OR SOME-THIN'!!
OH!
PERHAPS ...
...IT'S AS IF WE'RE ON THE INSIDE OF A BALLOON?
YOU MIGHT BE ON TO SOME-THING!

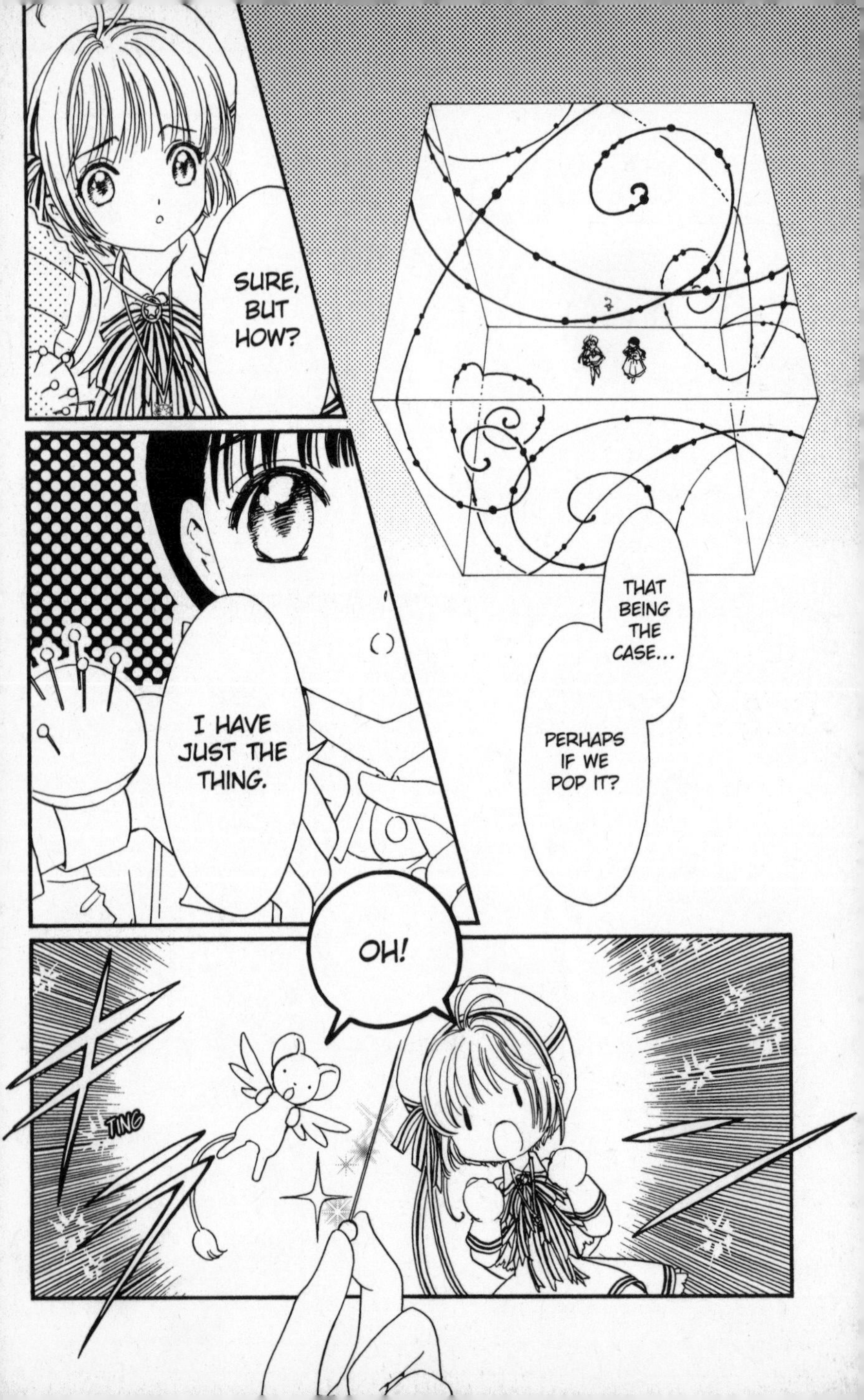
THAT BEING THE CASE...
PERHAPS IF WE POP IT?
SURE, BUT HOW?
I HAVE JUST THE THING.
OH!
TING

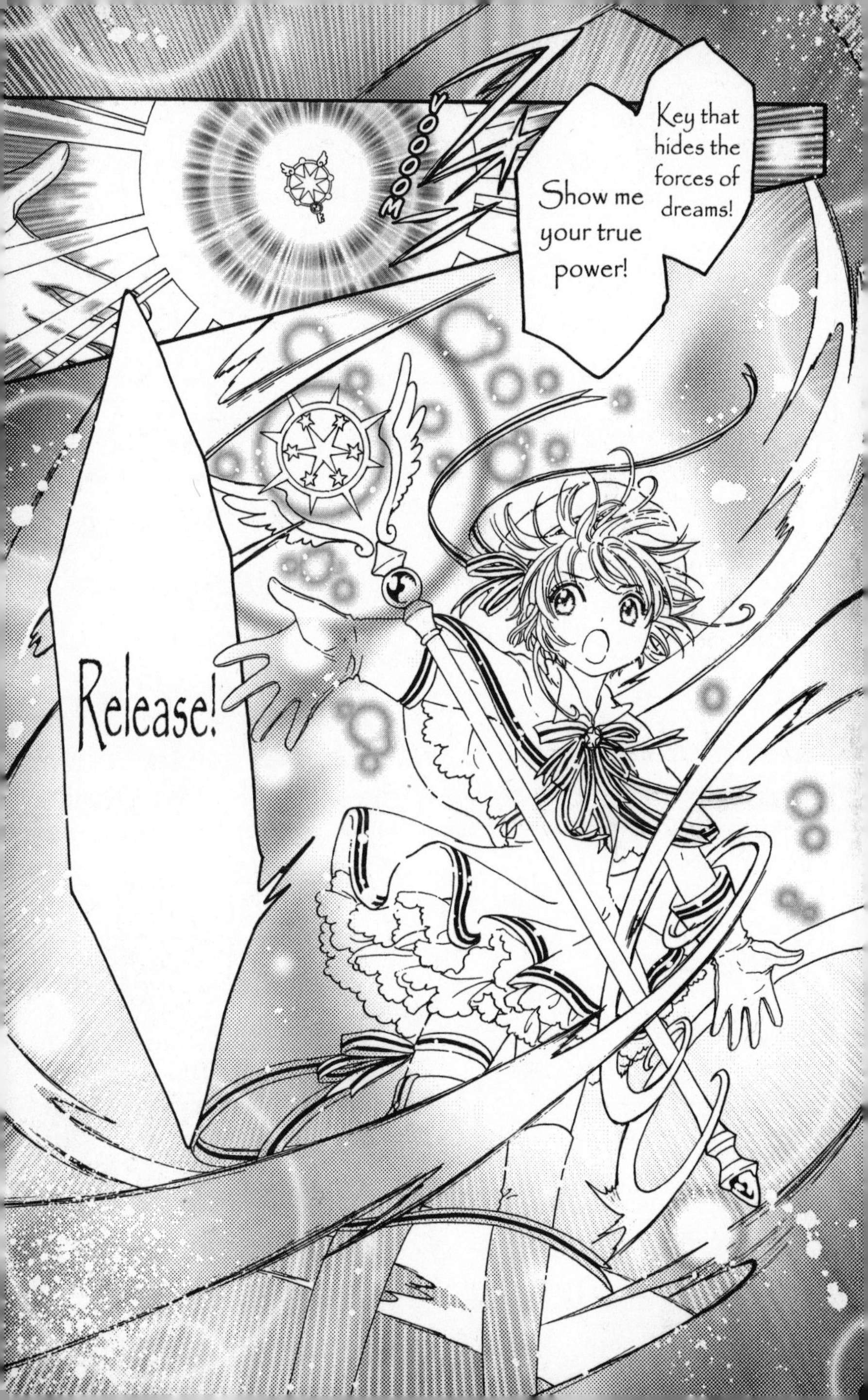
Key that hides the forces of dreams!
Show me your true power!
VOOOOM
Release!

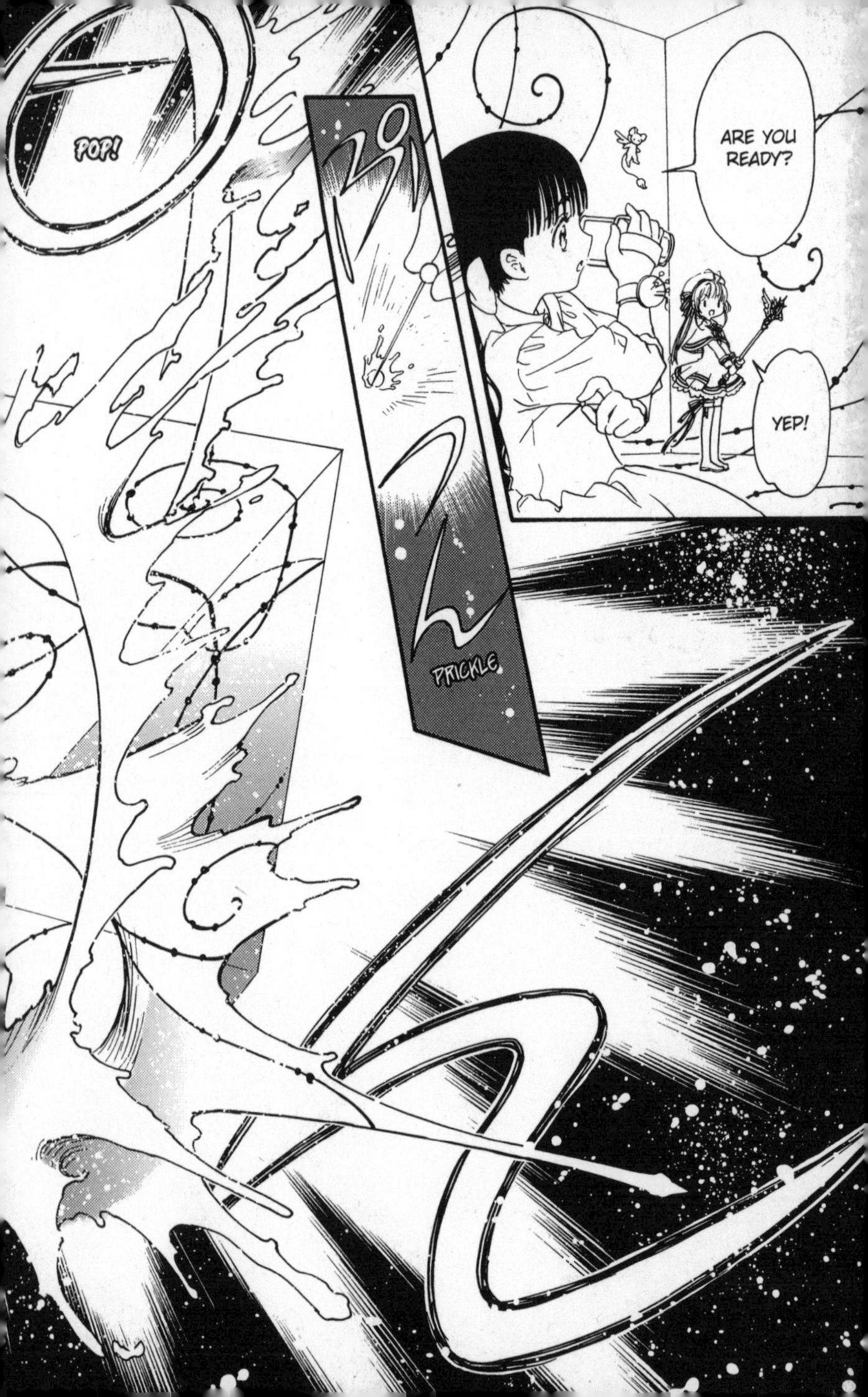
ARE YOU READY?
YEP!
POP!
PRICKLE

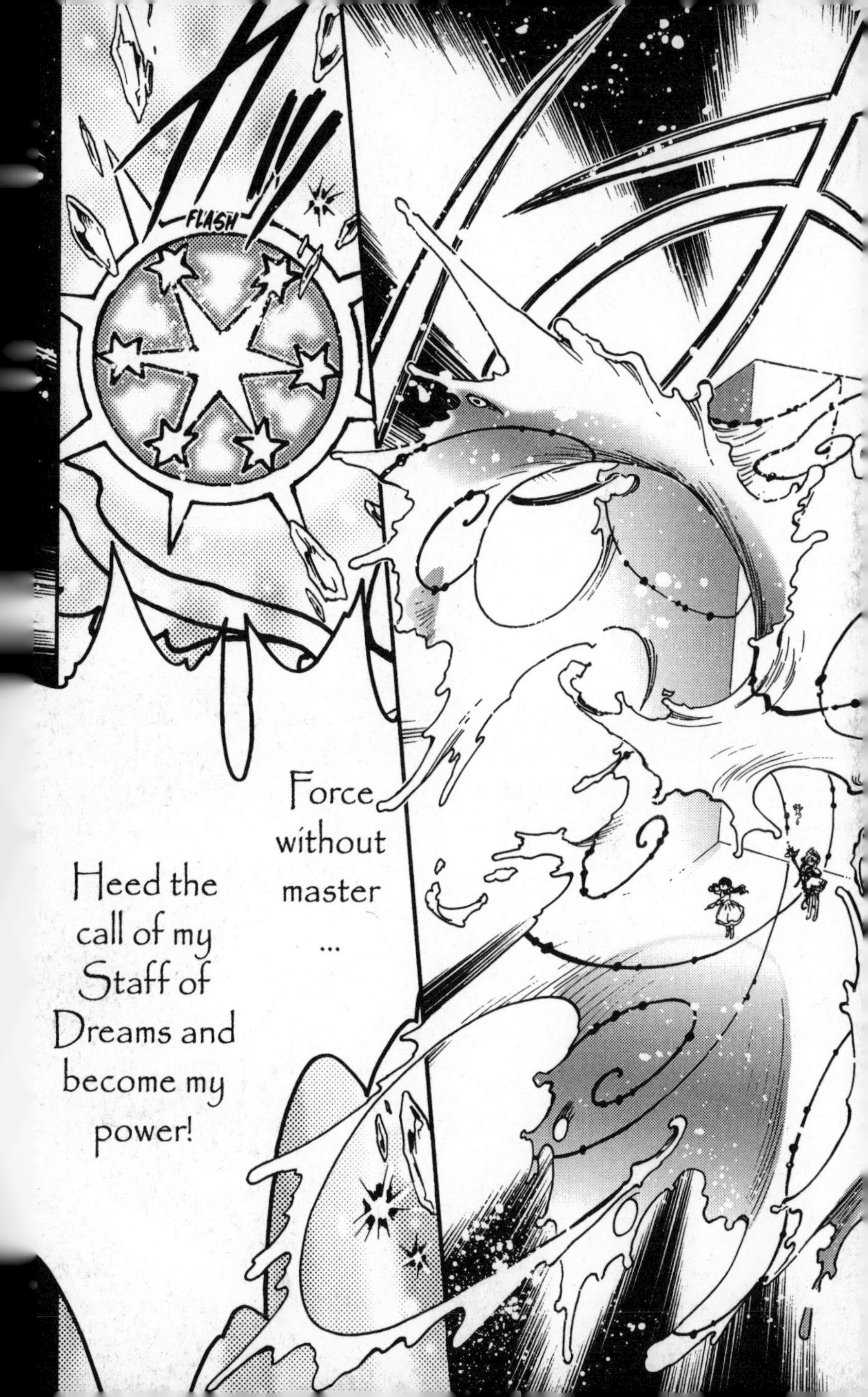
Force without master ...
FLASH
Heed the call of my Staff of Dreams and become my power!

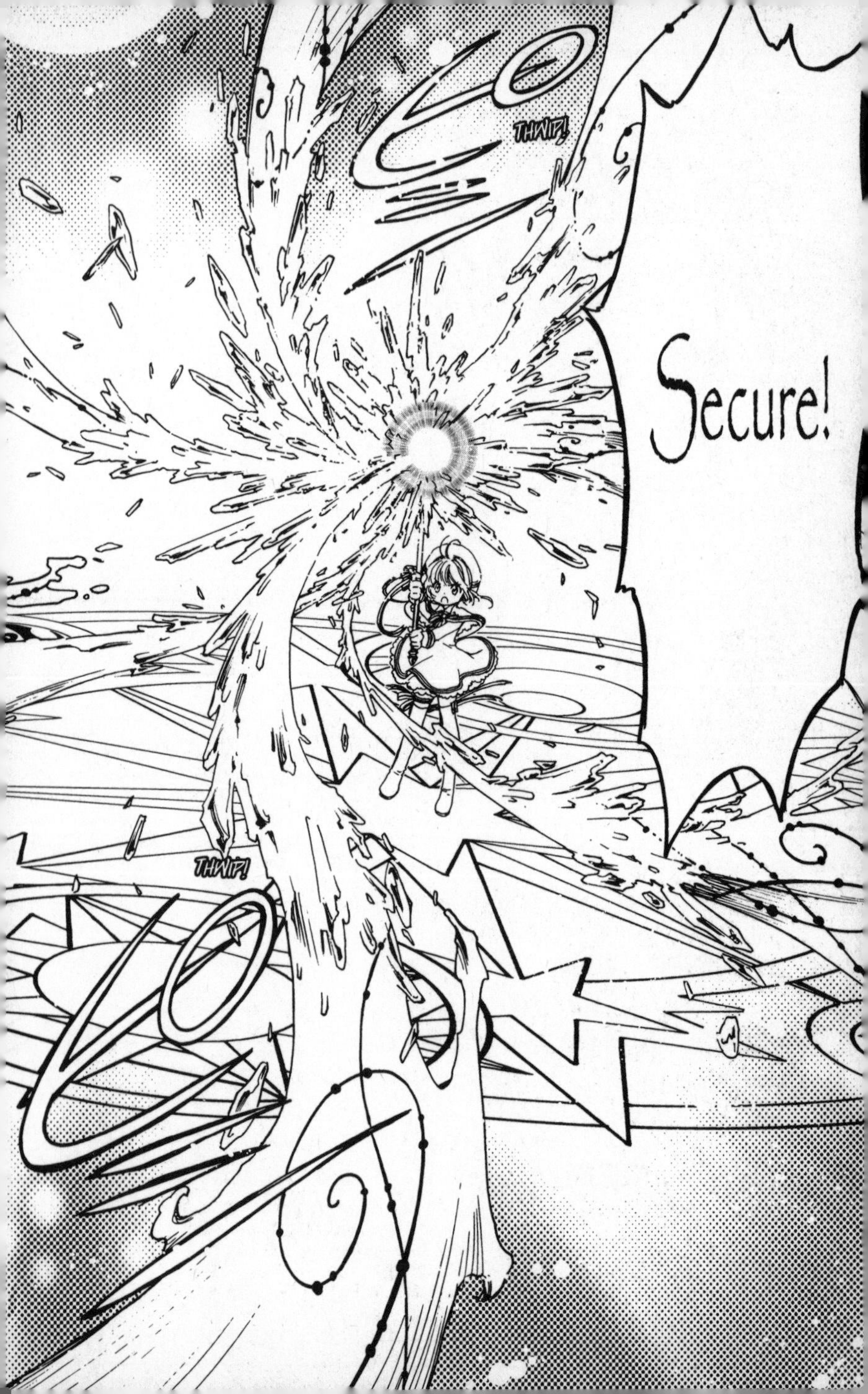
Secure!
THWIP!
THWIP!

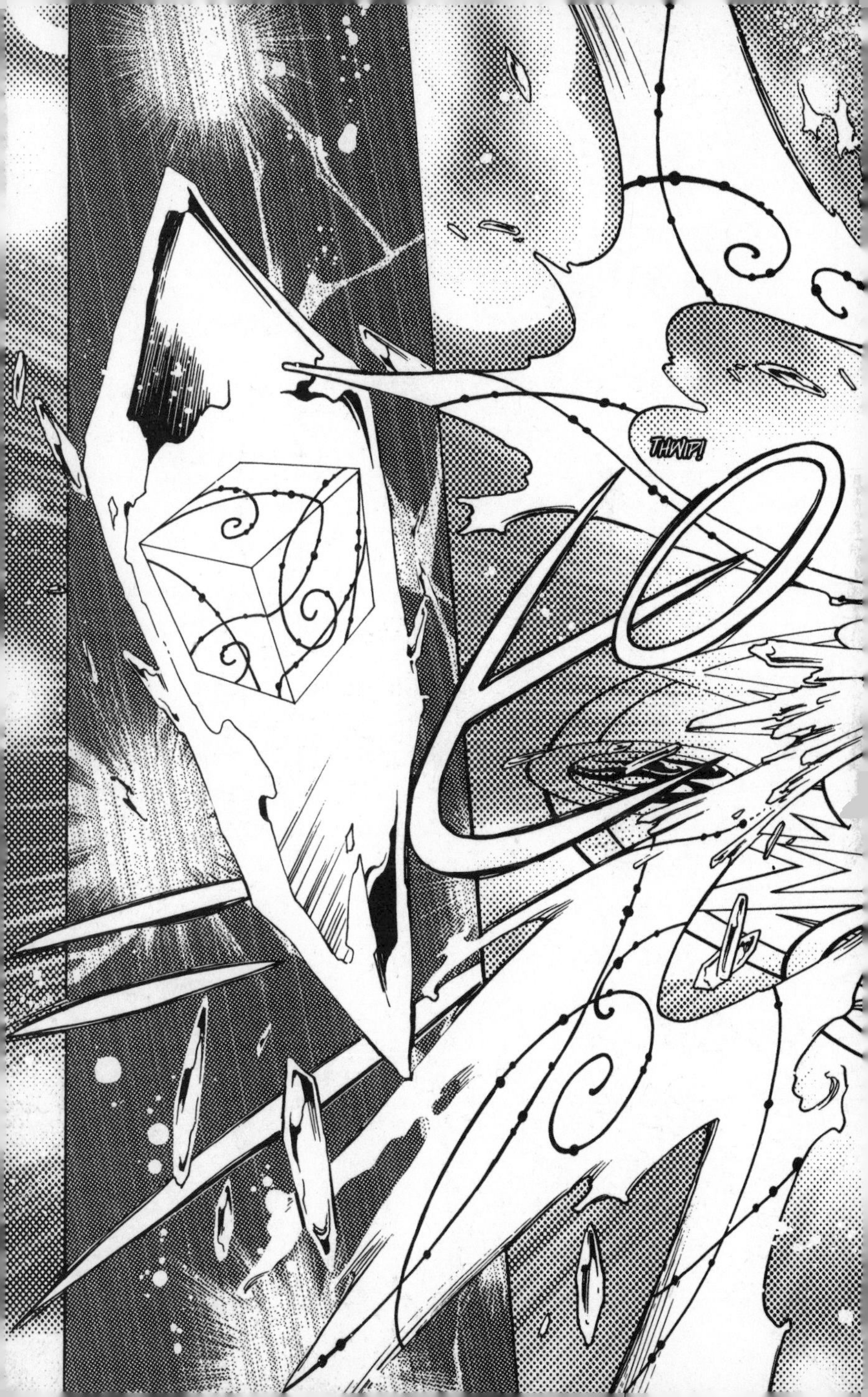
THWIP!

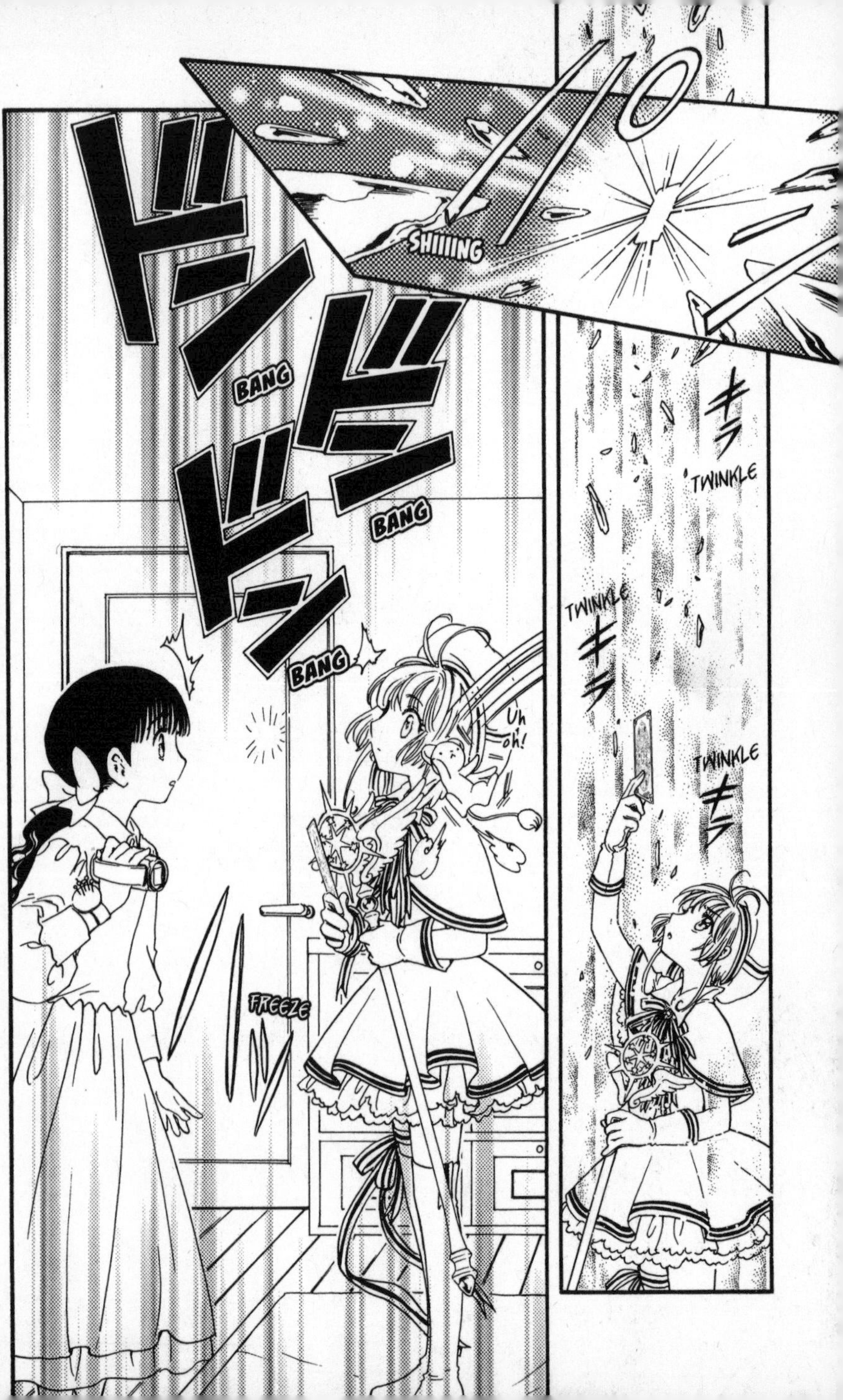
SHIIING
キラ
TWINKLE
TWINKLE
キラ
TWINKLE
キラ
BANG
BANG
BANG
Uh oh!
FREEZE

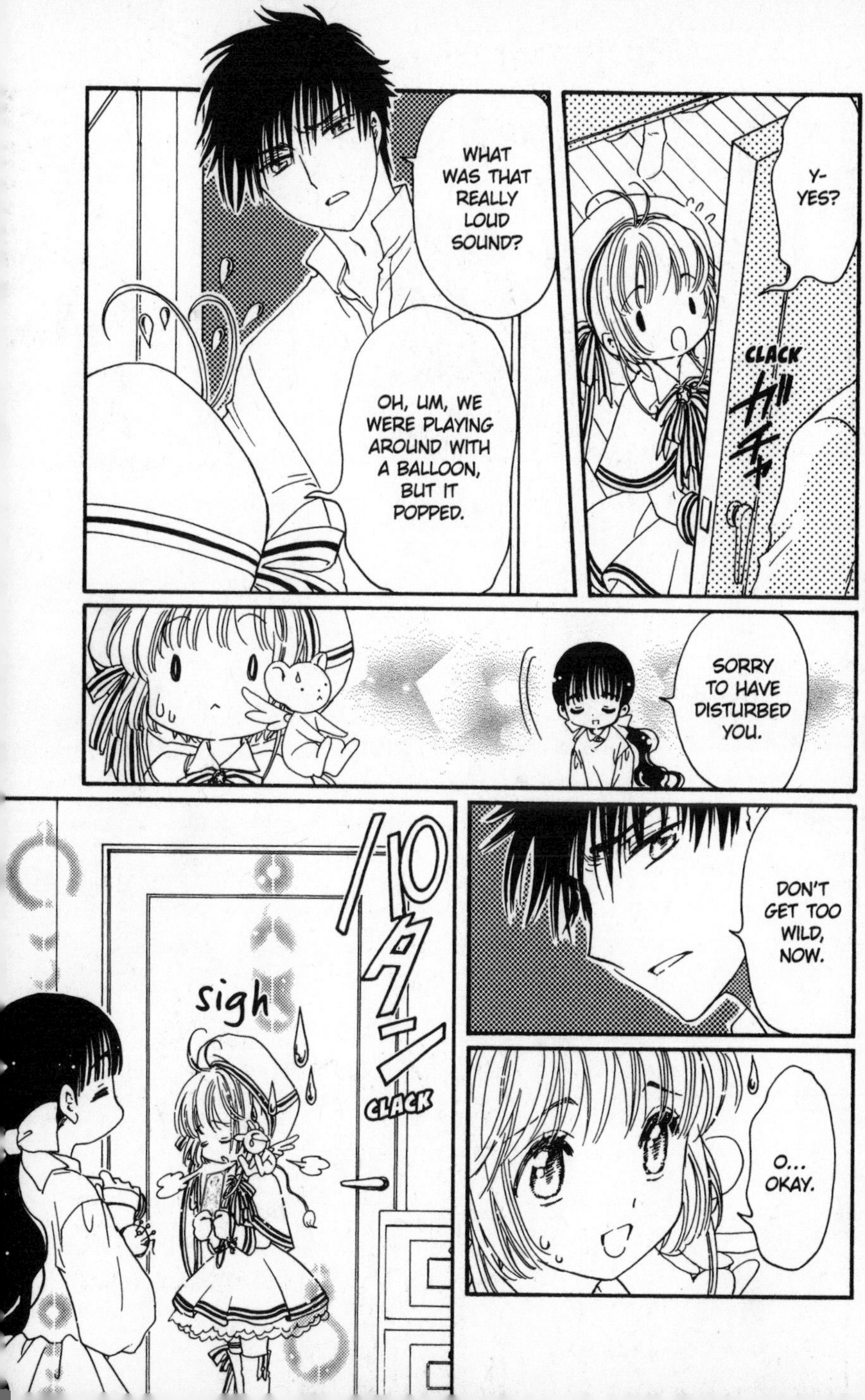
Y-YES?
CLACK
WHAT WAS THAT REALLY LOUD SOUND?
OH, UM, WE WERE PLAYING AROUND WITH A BALLOON, BUT IT POPPED.
SORRY TO HAVE DISTURBED YOU.
DON'T GET TOO WILD, NOW.
O... OKAY.
CLACK
sigh

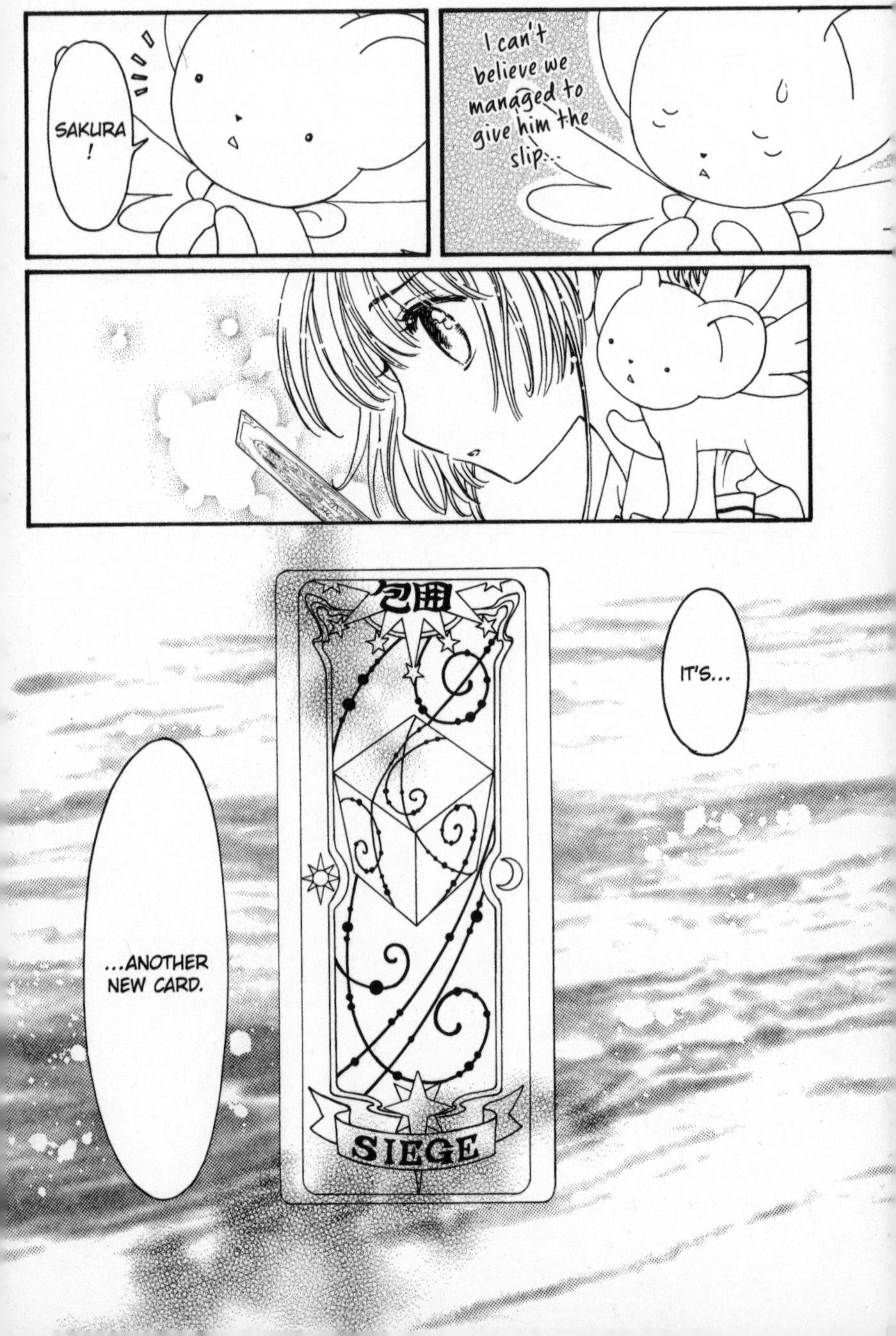
I can't believe we managed to give him the slip...
SAKURA!
IT'S...
包囲
SIEGE
...ANOTHER NEW CARD.

❀ Continued in Volume 2 ❀

Japan's most powerful spirit medium delves into the ghost world's greatest mysteries!

Story by Kyo Shirodaira, famed author of mystery fiction and creator of *Spiral*, *Blast of Tempest*, and *The Record of a Fallen Vampire*.

Both touched by spirits called yôkai, Kotoko and Kurô have gained unique superhuman powers. But to gain her powers Kotoko has given up an eye and a leg, and Kurô's personal life is in shambles. So when Kotoko suggests they team up to deal with renegades from the spirit world, Kurô doesn't have many other choices, but Kotoko might just have a few ulterior motives...

IN/SPECTRE

STORY BY KYO SHIRODAIRA
ART BY CHASHIBA KATASE

The award-winning manga about what happens inside you!

"Far more entertaining than it ought to be... what kid doesn't want to think that every time they sneeze a torpedo shoots out their nose?"
—Anime News Network

Strep throat! Hay fever! Influenza! The world is a dangerous place for a red blood cell just trying to get her deliveries finished. Fortunately, she's not alone...she's got a whole human body's worth of cells ready to help out! The mysterious white blood cells, the buff and brash killer T cells, even the cute little platelets— everyone's got to come together if they want to keep you healthy!

Cells at Work!

はたらく細胞

By Akane Shimizu

Having lost his wife, high school teacher Kōhei Inuzuka is doing his best to raise his young daughter Tsumugi as a single father. He's pretty bad at cooking and doesn't have a huge appetite to begin with, but chance brings his little family together with one of his students, the lonely Kotori. The three of them are anything but comfortable in the kitchen, but the healing power of home cooking might just work on their grieving hearts.

"This season's number-one feel-good anime!" —Anime News Network

"A beautifully-drawn story about comfort food and family and grief. Recommended." —Otaku USA Magazine

sweetness & lightning

By Gido Amagakure

KC
KODANSHA
COMICS

New action series from Hiroyuki Takei, creator of the classic shonen franchise Shaman King!

In medieval Japan, a bell hanging on the collar is a sign that a cat has a master. Norachiyo's bell hangs from his katana sheath, but he is nonetheless a stray — a ronin. This one-eyed cat samurai travels across a dishonest world, cutting through pretense and deception with his blade.

By

Hiroyuki Takei

CardCaptor Sakura Clearcard volume 1 is a work of fiction. Names, characters, places, and incidents are the products of the author's imagination or are used fictitiously. Any resemblance to actual events, locales, or persons, living or dead, is entirely coincidental.

A Kodansha Comics Trade Paperback Original.

Published in the United States by Kodansha Comics, an imprint of Kodansha USA Publishing, LLC, New York.

Publication rights for this English edition arranged through Kodansha Ltd., Tokyo.

First published in Japan in 2016 by Kodansha Ltd., Tokyo, as *Kaadokyaputaa Sakura Kuriakaado Hen* volume 1.

ISBN 978-1-63236-537-8

Printed in the United States of America.

www.kodanshacomics.com

9 8 7 6 5 4 3 2 1

Translation: Devon Corwin
Lettering: Erika Terriquez
Editing: Alexandra Swanson and Paul Starr
Kodansha Comics edition cover design: Phil Balsman